most similar, different outcomes

"The _nature_ of the credit crisis
determining each state's trajec[tory]

Paths toward the
Modern Fiscal State

Paths toward the Modern Fiscal State

ENGLAND, JAPAN, AND CHINA

Wenkai He

HARVARD UNIVERSITY PRESS

Cambridge, Massachusetts

London, England

2013

Library of Congress Cataloging-in-Publication Data

He, Wenkai, 1969–
Paths toward the modern fiscal state : England,
Japan, and China / Wenkai He.
p.   cm.
Includes bibliographical references and index.
ISBN 978-0-674-07278-7 (alk. paper)
1. Finance, Public—England—History.   2. Finance, Public—Japan—History.
3. Finance, Public—China—History.   4. Fiscal policy—England—History.
5. Fiscal policy—Japan—History.   6. Fiscal policy—China—History.   I. Title.
HJ235.H43   2013
336.09—dc23   2012033302

CONTENTS

ACKNOWLEDGMENTS

This book is the result of a long intellectual journey. When I entered the Program in Science, Technology, and Society at the Massachusetts Institute of Technology (MIT) in September 1996, I was interested in the role of technological innovations in modern economic growth. In 1999, I switched into the Department of Political Science at MIT with a strong motivation to explore the role of the state in technological development in late industrializing countries, such as Japan, South Korea, and China. Over the course of my study, however, two areas of scholarship fundamentally changed my mind.

One was the literature in the economic history of Japan and China, which demonstrated the development of vibrant market economies in these two East Asian countries well before they were forced to open by the West. This scholarship decisively challenged the picture of "economic backwardness" assumed by many state-centered political economists of late industrialization. The other was the neo-institutionalists' rediscovery of the crucial role of the state in English economic development before the First Industrial Revolution in the 1740s, particularly the English state's remarkable centralization in tax collection and its amazing ability to raise long-term credits from the market.

What would have happened to nineteenth-century China had it possessed similar institutions of public finance? Was it even possible for similar institutions to appear in China at the time? These questions drove me to take a research direction that was vastly different from my original interest: How did the state manage to create institutions of public finance that not only enhanced its capacity but also enabled it to affect the economy with various fiscal, monetary, and financial policies? In this book, I show that the creation of new institutions is indeed neither a mechanical product of social or political needs nor a result of rational design of agents. Instead, they emerge from an interactive political process rife with uncertainties, unintended consequences, and power struggles. How to explain the creation of new institutions is the central issue of this study.

I owe my greatest intellectual debt to Suzanne Berger and Richard Samuels, at MIT, and to Peter Perdue, now at Yale. Suzanne Berger's insightful advice, sharp criticism, and unwavering support gave me invaluable guidance and helped me travel safely through the jungles of historical detail while staying focused on the main argument. Richard Samuels set a model for how to conduct historically oriented social science. Peter Perdue ushered me into the exciting field of the economic history of late imperial China. His wide knowledge stimulated me to put the Chinese experience in a broader comparative perspective. Without their help and support, it would have been impossible for me to write this book.

I am deeply grateful to Patrick O'Brien at the London School of Economics, who read my very rough draft chapter on England and gave me detailed comments and suggestions. David Woodruff, also now at the London School of Economics, was of tremendous help in the formative stage of this project. A class with Philip Kuhn was instrumental in confirming my interest in the state and economy of late imperial China. Kuhn himself set a paradigm for how to investigate state institutional developments against the background of significant socioeconomic changes. I have profited greatly from ongoing discussions with friends at MIT and Harvard: Amos Zehavi, David Art, Danny Breznitz, Boaz Aztili, Dana Brown, Pat Boyd, Brett Kubicek, Doug Fuller, Rachel Gisselquist, He Yinan, Gabriel Rubin, Matthew Mosca, and Li Cho-ying. Conversations with Ch'iu Peng-sheng from the Academia Sinica in Taiwan were always fruitful and exciting.

I thank the Social Science Research Council for providing me a fellowship (SSRC-IDRF), which funded the archival research in the No. 1 Historical Archives in Beijing in 2005. This support was vital to completing my project. I am grateful for the input of the participants of the SSRC-IDRF Workshop in Charleston, South Carolina, on 9–14 March 2006, particularly Hussein Fancy, Jee Young Kim, James Weir, Moustafa Bayoumi, and Ethan Michelson.

When I was doing archival research in Beijing, Luo Xin and Niu Dayong of the History Department at Beijing University offered me institutional and intellectual fellowship. Mao Haijian and Guo Runtao helped me understand the complicated operation of administrative institutions in the Qing dynasty. I greatly enjoyed doing archival research in the No. 1 Historical Archives together with Ren Zhiyong, who generously shared with me his experience of searching for materials. Nor would my research have been possible without the knowledgeable assistance of the archives staff, especially Yang Xinxin and Liu Ruofang.

When I was an An Wang postdoctoral fellow at the Fairbank Center for Chinese Studies at Harvard University in 2007–2008, Mark Elliott, Henrietta Harrison, and Peter Bol helped me improve the manuscript. I thank the Fairbank Center for providing funds to organize a postdoctoral workshop. I benefited tremendously from the feedback of workshop participants Patrick O'Brien, R. Bin Wong, Ho Hon-wai, Peter Perdue, and Jack A. Goldstone. I am particularly grateful to Ho Hon-wai for his thorough reading and helpful suggestions. It was a privilege to have these exceptional scholars comment on my work.

My colleagues at the Division of Social Science at the Hong Kong University of Science and Technology give me a great intellectual environment to continue this project. I benefited especially from discussions with James Kung, James Lee, Li Bozhong, David Zweig, and Cai Yongshun. I am deeply indebted to Ken Pomeranz for the thorough reading and incisive comments he provided when he visited Hong Kong in February of 2011. Feedback from David Faure, Cheung Sui Wai, Puk Wing Kin, and Wang Shaoguang were very helpful. Detailed critiques by Thomas Rawski, Hans Ulrich Vogel, and an anonymous reviewer for *Modern China* were important to revise the chapters on China. I thank the Research Grant Council of Hong Kong for funding a research trip to Tokyo in the summer of 2009. In Tokyo, advice and comments from

Mitani Hiroshi and Nakamura Naofumi at the University of Tokyo were critical to revising the chapters on Meiji Japan. Kishimoto Mio, Kuroda Akinobu, and M. William Steele generously shared their expertise and thoughts. I am profoundly grateful for the careful reading and insightful comments from Mark Metzler and Katalin Ferber. Steven Ericson helped me avoid some embarrassing mistakes. At Harvard University Press, Kathleen McDermott and Andrew Kinney have been exemplary in facilitating the publication process. Kathleen's suggestions for revision significantly improved the presentation of the argument. Chinese and Japanese names are written surname first.

The long journey toward finishing this project would have been impossible without the strong support of my family. My parents have always had confidence in me. My brother He Yong's presence in Kunming with my parents has made it easier for me to be away from home for such a long period. My mother, Xu Xiaohua, and my late mother-in-law, Marian McGill, traveled to Boston to look after our first baby, enabling me to do a year's archival research in Beijing. My wife, Ellen McGill, has given me tremendous help in many different ways: discussant, critic, proofreader, and editor. There is no way I could have finished this project on time without her. I also want to thank Carmelita Bola for keeping our household in Hong Kong running so smoothly, allowing me more time and peace of mind to work on the manuscript. It has been a great pleasure to share the joy of finishing with our son, James Yuanping He, and our daughter, Mairead Yuanqing He. It is to my family that I dedicate this book.

Paths toward the
Modern Fiscal State

INTRODUCTION

Great economic and political transformations are often associated with the emergence and consolidation of new institutions. However, social scientists are ill equipped to explain the creation of new institutions. The powerful analytical tools developed by rational-choice institutionalists to understand how institutions influence policy outcomes or shape actors' preference say very little about the dynamic question of their emergence.[1] Moreover, the rise of new institutions often covers a long time span. Thus methods or theories with a short time horizon are ill suited to handle this temporal dimension when seeking a causal explanation.[2]

Institutional development is a highly political process as various institutional arrangements have quite different impacts on interest redistribution.[3] Therefore, the creation of new institutions is a process rife with interactions between socioeconomic structure, in which institutions are deeply embedded, and actors with different ideas, interests, and institutional blueprints.[4] These interactions generate multiple possible outcomes in institutional development.[5] If we take the observed outcome as the only or inevitable end result and neglect alternative outcomes, we implicitly commit the mistake of selection bias in small-N case studies.[6]

How shall we find a temporal causal mechanism that can explain the emergence and consolidation of a new institution out of the multiplicity

of outcomes possible in the uncertain process of institutional development? This book addresses this question by examining the birth of the
modern fiscal state, which is characterized by an institutional innovation
of using centrally collected indirect taxes to mobilize long-term financial
resources from the markets. I selected three episodes of institutional development for a comparative historical analysis: England between 1642
and 1752, Japan between 1868 and 1895, and China between 1851 and
1911. Although these three instances of institutional transformation
happened in different times and places, and under quite different international circumstances, their sequential features of institutional development are surprisingly similar.

First, prior to each episode they shared many important points in
state formation and market development.[7] Second, they all experienced
a period of fiscal difficulties when the existing decentralized institutions
became badly fitted to the greatly changed socioeconomic structures.
The dysfunction of the old institutions was particularly severe in England between the 1600s and 1630s, in Japan between the 1820s and
1860s, and in China between the 1820s and 1840s. As existing institutions became unable to provide the state adequate revenue to maintain
domestic order and handle threats from abroad, big events took place:
the English Civil Wars in 1642, the Meiji Restoration in 1868, and the
Taiping Rebellion in 1851. The choice of starting point for each episode
is thus neither arbitrary nor convenient. Third, financial pressures subsequent to these events forced state actors in each case to search for new
approaches to public finance. They conducted many similar experiments,
such as short-term borrowing, taxing domestic consumption, and issuing
state fiduciary credit instruments such as paper notes. In all three cases,
indirect taxes from domestic consumption and customs eventually became the major pillar of state income.

However, the outcomes of institutional development varied. England
after the 1640s first transformed into a traditional fiscal state resting on
taxation.[8] Starting with excessive dependence on short-term credits, it
became a modern fiscal state in the 1730s when it converted its debts
into perpetual annuities secured by centrally collected indirect taxes,
particularly the excises. In 1752, the dominance of the "3 percent Consol," the stocks of perpetual annuities at 3 percent, indicated the consolidation of the modern fiscal state in England. Japan after the Meiji

Restoration relied heavily on nonconvertible paper notes, which constituted de facto long-term liabilities of the state. A modern fiscal state
emerged in Japan in the late 1880s as the government centralized the
collection of indirect taxes, took on long-term domestic loans, and attained convertibility of government paper notes. China went through a
number of important institutional developments after 1851, such as an
increasing reliance on revenues from indirect taxes collected by salaried
officials and the introduction of bills of exchange into the state's fiscal
operation. Similar institutional changes were vital to building the modern fiscal states in England and Japan. However, fiscal decentralization
persisted in China, and the Qing government was unable either to issue
convertible paper notes or to take on long-term loans.

These three historical cases allow us to investigate the complete process of the emergence of a new institution, an advantage often unavailable in the study of ongoing institutional development in the contemporary world. This research is thus useful to understanding more recent
efforts to build effective institutions to collect taxes and manage state
finance in developing and emerging market economies.[9] A comparison
of two different successes at building a modern fiscal state (England and
Japan) and a "negative case," in which the country failed to make this
transformation (China), helps identify the causal mechanism of the creation of a new institution.[10]

The Modern Fiscal State

Politically, the state is defined as the political organization that monopo-
lizes legitimate coercive force over a delimited territory.[11] But this Weberian definition does not address the institutional character of the state in
public finance. From the economic point of view, Weber defines the modern state by its capacity to achieve a monopoly over the creation of currency.[12] However, this characterization is too strong. Take England, the
undisputed leading country in the development of modern capitalism, for
example. Throughout the entire eighteenth century, the English economy
suffered from a serious shortage of currency of small denominations. This
was mitigated mainly by privately minted copper coins and privately issued and locally circulated "token-money."[13] The English government did
not monopolize the supply of currency until the Coinage Act of 1816.[14]

From the perspective of public finance, the literature on state formation usually makes a distinction between the fiscal state (or *tax state* in
Schumpeter's term), which rests on tax revenue, and the domain state
(or *demesne state*), which draws income primarily from crown-owned
property, such as estates, forests, and mines. The transition from domain
to fiscal state was a significant change in early modern Europe as taxation redefined the state-society relationship.[15] In the twentieth century,
the domain state continued to exist in various forms. The former state-
socialist countries were essentially domain states as the state derived the
majority of its income from direct management of state-owned enterprises. The postsocialist transition is thus a return to a tax state in which
the state depends on tax institutions to collect revenues while letting
private actors deal with risks and opportunities in running enterprises
for profit. In late developing countries, the lack of necessary administrative institutions to collect tax revenue often forces the state to directly
own and manage industrial enterprises as a source of income.[16] This too
is basically a kind of domain state. In practice, it works only for states
that possess rich natural resources, such as petroleum and natural gas.[17]

The fiscal or tax state derives its revenue from taxation. However, this
concept is still too broad, as it includes quite different kinds of economies. For example, a fiscal state may rest on taxation in kind, or in
coins, or in paper money. Yet it is obvious that the relationships between
the state and economy are different in nature among these three kinds of
fiscal state. Moreover, a dependence on taxation tells us nothing about
whether the institution of public finance is centralized or not. For this
reason, I make a distinction between the *modern fiscal state* and the *traditional fiscal state*.

The traditional fiscal state uses its tax revenue mainly as income to
meet its current spending, and the state is not involved permanently with
the financial markets. It can rely on decentralized fiscal institutions to allocate specific items of revenue to meet particular speeding needs. This
is not a static concept; a traditional fiscal state may use some of its tax
revenue to raise short-term loans in emergencies. But once the emergency
has passed, it clears its debts and goes back to its previous condition. In
contrast, the modern fiscal state has two closely connected institutional
features. First, it centralizes tax collection, which allows the state to allocate spending out of a consolidated source of revenue. This greatly

improves efficiency in managing government finance. Second, it can use centrally collected revenue as capital to leverage long-term financial resources from the markets. It thus achieves an economy of scale in mobilizing financial resources.

The emergence of a modern fiscal state is dependent on the level of commercial development in the economy. First, the use of speedy credit instruments such as bills of exchange to remit the collected tax revenue and allocated government expenditure between the center and local governments is indispensable for fiscal centralization; only in this way can tax revenues be conveniently aggregated by the center before allocating spending. In contrast, when taxes are collected in kind or the collected revenue is transported in the bulky form of specie, it makes more sense for the state to have a decentralized fiscal operation that assigns government spending directly from specific sites of tax collection to places of spending.

Second, a commercialized economy allows the state to extract indirect taxes such as customs and duties on domestic consumption. Such a diversified tax base helps safeguard the creditworthiness of the state. Moreover, indirect taxes such as those levied on consumer goods like liquor and tobacco are politically less difficult for the state to collect. This is because they fall not directly on individual consumers but rather on big producers and wholesalers. Producers and wholesalers of major consumer goods can transfer the burden of increasing taxes to ordinary consumers. They thus lack the motivation to oppose the government over heavy consumption taxes. The number of ordinary consumers is quite large, making the cost of monitoring participation in antitaxation campaigns formidably high. Yet the benefit of falling prices is an inclusive "public good," which anyone can enjoy regardless of whether he or she participates in antitaxation movements. It is therefore difficult to organize ordinary consumers to oppose high rates.[18] In contrast, direct taxes such as the land tax and property tax are either inelastic or politically costly as they target powerful social groups.

In this light, the modern fiscal state is unlikely to appear in an agrarian economy that has neither interregional financial networks to transfer money nor a tax base to tap indirect taxes. However, a commercialized economy is a necessary rather than a sufficient condition. This is attested by the histories of England, Japan, and China.

State and Market Development

Economic historians have demonstrated the vibrancy of economic development in China and Japan after the eighteenth century. Important features included increasing commercialization of agricultural production; proto-industrialization in the economic core areas (the Lower Yangzi delta in China and the Kinai region in Japan); the expansion of the urban economy; the growth of interregional long-distance trading of staple goods, such as grain, cotton cloth, silk, and so on, which gave birth to a unified national market and further stimulated regional division of labor; de facto labor mobility; and the rise of merchants whose money-making activities were seen as morally legitimate.[19] Such conditions also characterized the market economy in early modern England before the mid-eighteenth century.[20]

In England, London-based private financial networks had developed by the 1640s.[21] Similarly, the development of market economies in Japan and China by the early nineteenth century was accompanied by the growth of sophisticated financial markets. These private financial networks connected major cities and market towns and were able to transfer money across time and space with speedy credit instruments, such as bills of exchange. In eighteenth-century Japan, these networks centered on Osaka and extended mainly to Kyoto and Edo.[22] In China, in addition to the local native banks (e.g., *qianzhuang*) that developed in the eighteenth century, bankers from Shanxi Province began to link up major cities and market towns from the 1830s onward.[23]

In seventeenth-century England, the expansion of commercialized sectors became an important tax base from which the state could draw indirect taxes. For Japan, nonagricultural sectors (commerce, finance, service, and so on) are estimated to have accounted for about 50 percent of gross domestic product (GDP) in the 1860s.[24] For China, the total value of staple commodities involved in domestic long-distance trade, such as grain, cotton, and tea, is estimated at 387 million tael of silver in the 1840s.[25]

Not every important aspect of economic development in pre–Industrial Revolution Western Europe can be found in China and Japan in the eighteenth and early nineteenth centuries; for example, there appear to be no parallels to the high concentration of skilled craftsmen in urban areas and the thriving engineering culture in English manufacturing appear.[26] Nevertheless, from the perspective of studying the emergence of a modern fiscal state, pre-1642 England, pre-1868 Japan, and pre-1851 China all satisfy the two necessary conditions: expanded commercial sectors for the state to tap indirect taxes and cross-regional private financial networks to remit money.

Meanwhile, England, Japan, and China all have long and continuous histories of state formation.[27] In England, an early modern state had become entrenched in political life by the early seventeenth century. It had the following characteristics: First, the central government was the ultimate source to legitimate the use of political power in localities, and it claimed the sovereign power in coinage and foreign affairs. Second, the execution of political power was centrally coordinated through highly impersonal and formal means, embodied particularly in the procedures for issuing, transmitting, and preserving government documents. Third, the organization of the central government became more institutionalized, and the regular administration of government was handled more by officials than by the king or his personal retainers. As an impersonal sovereign of the state, the monarch was subject to the constraints of both formal institutions of government and informal norms, such as "taking counsel" from Privy Council and Parliament.[28]

This kind of early modern state, characterized by a unitary judicial and administrative conformity imposed by a centrally coordinated network of political power, can also be found in nineteenth-century China and Japan. The bureaucratic state had a long history in China. During the eighteenth century, the Qing government's central coordination of political power in provinces was carried out through a highly institutionalized administrative apparatus consisting of the Six Boards and the Grand Council (Junjichu). Memorials directly transmitted from provincial governors or provincial treasurers to the emperor were confidential under the Grand Council system.[29] However, policy debates based on the memorial system were not secret. When provincial governors were asked by the center to comment on policy suggestions presented in one particular memorial, they all had a chance to read the copied memorial before they reasoned whether the suggested policy change would work under the specific circumstances in each province. After receiving responses from provincial governors, the emperor always asked ministers of the relevant boards and the members of the Grand Council to conduct collective deliberation. Major policies were usually initiated after reasoned debates rather than by the personal will of the emperor. This was particularly the case in the making of highly technical financial and fiscal policies.

Although provincial governors were often permitted to adjust central policies to suit local circumstances *(yindi zhiyi)*, central sanction was crucial. For example, the mintage in provinces of copper coins with various content and fineness so as to better respond to local demands for cash had to be approved by the center.[30] In response to a severe scarcity of copper coins in the markets, an imperial decree dated 5 September 1749 allowed the use of private and even foreign copper coins in Fujian, Zhejiang, and Zhili Provinces as a practical measure *(quanyi kexing)* to mitigate the dearth of cash.[31] However, when the scarcity of copper coins was mitigated after the 1770s, provincial governors were ordered to use government-minted copper cash to exchange for the private copper cash circulating in the market.[32] The Qing government explicitly considered the use of privately made copper cash an offense against the state sovereignty in coinage.[33]

The development of the early modern state in Japan can be traced back to the late sixteenth and early seventeenth centuries. In the eighteenth century, the political authority of the shogunate *(bakufu)* in Edo (today's Tokyo) over domain *(han)* governments grew steadily in both administration and regulation, even though the emperor in Kyoto remained the nominal sovereign. Although domain lords—particularly those in western Japan who were not nominated by the shogunate *(tozama daimyō)*—had a certain degree of autonomy in governing their own territories, their laws could not contradict the laws issued by the shogunate, and the lords were subject to the shogunate's military mobilization.[34] The shogunate not only monopolized foreign affairs but also became the ultimate arbitrator of the legitimacy of the use of political power in localities.[35] As it handled increasingly complicated administrative and legal matters, the shogunate as the public authority above various domain governments became more institutionalized.[36] In the Kyōhō Reform (1716–1736), the use of administrative and legal precedents became more formalized and systematic, and the shogunate's public governance and the shogun's private affairs were separated.[37]

The monetary consolidation achieved in eighteenth-century Japan was particularly impressive. In 1636, the shogunate began to mint official currency and forbade the use of foreign monies (particularly Chinese copper coins) in Japan.[38] Through the recoinage in 1736 *(Genbun kaichū)*, the shogunate stabilized the exchange rates between gold coins and silver and copper coins.[39] In 1772, it began to cast denominated silver coins *(nanryō nishugin)* and circulate them gradually in the economic circles of western Japan centered in Osaka, which had previously been dominated by silver by weight.[40] Issues of paper notes by domain governments in the eighteenth century had to be permitted by the shogunate. These paper notes were denominated in units of currency minted by the shogunate and were used to alleviate the scarcity of small cash in local transactions.[41]

Nonetheless, sources of state income in these three early modern states varied quite significantly. In England, even though there was a discernible trend toward the tax state in the period between 1336 and 1453, when the royal government increasingly turned to direct and indirect taxes, the state that formed in the sixteenth century was essentially a domain state.[42] The crown's ordinary revenue came from royal estates, customs, and the crown's feudal rights, such as wardship and purveyance (the privilege to have the royal household supplied at prices below the current market prices), not from regular domestic taxation.[43] The crown's ordinary revenue supported not only the royal household but also the royal government in providing governance, domestic order, and justice in peaceful times. This lack of institutional distinction between the crown's personal expenses and the costs of civil government remained unchanged in England until 1830, even after the crown's ordinary revenue was replaced by the Civil List in 1697.[44] Only in emergencies such as invasions or foreign wars could the crown ask Parliament for "extraordinary revenues," which were levied on both property and income. These extraordinary supplies were different from annual taxes as they were justified by the special obligation of subjects to aid the crown in emergencies. The phrase "the king should live of his own" captures the basic character of the domain state.[45] The state in eighteenth-century Japan was an incomplete fiscal state. Although the shogunate established a unitary system of currency, it collected taxes only in the territories under its direct governance, even though it had the authority and power to order domain governments to share public expenditures in river works, famine relief, and national defense.[46] The state in eighteenth-century China was a fiscal state that received most of its tax revenue from land and salt taxes.[47]

Although each state rested on different sources of income, the fiscal systems of these three early modern states were decentralized in operation as revenue was assigned for particular purposes without being transferred to the center. In the case of early Stuart England, the royal government often sent specific items of income directly to meet spending in localities rather than receiving all its income to London.[48] Similarly, in eighteenth-century Japan a large proportion of revenue was assigned for particular purposes without being transferred to the shogunate.[49] In eighteenth-century China, after the fiscal reforms of the Yongzheng emperor (1723–1735), the fiscal system was politically highly centralized as the Board of Revenue supervised and audited the annual accounts of both the collections and expenditures of provincial governments.[50] However, the actual fiscal operation was decentralized as the center retained a large proportion of its income in treasuries at the provincial or even prefectural levels in strategic locations and the center often assigned tax revenue from places of collection directly to destinations of spending.[51]

One important condition for the smooth operation of these early modern states with decentralized fiscal systems was a common paternalistic justification of state power cast in terms of taking care of the subjects' welfare.[52] This legitimation of state power was embodied in concrete "social policies," such as famine relief, improvement of transportation, maintenance of water conservancy, and river management.[53] They defined the obligation of the state to protect society, justified the state's revenue extraction, and implanted an element of "public-ness" in government finance. It was on this moral basis that the central government could require local governments to share costs, while local governments in turn could demand funds from the center.[54] However, this vital role of early modern states in providing public goods has often been neglected by scholars who consider warfare the driving force behind state building.[55]

The state in all three cases experienced a profound fiscal crisis when the existing decentralized institutions of public finance became ill adapted to the new socioeconomic circumstances and could no longer sustain the autonomy and capacity of the state. For example, the price revolution in England between the 1450s and 1650s and in Japan between the 1820s and 1860s severely eroded the fiscal bases of their respective governments.[56] China's experience was more complicated. Silver inflows from the New World caused mild but steady inflation in the eighteenth century. Yet between the 1820s and 1850s, China encountered a prolonged deflation due to scarcity of silver in the domestic economy, which in turn led to widespread tax arrears and unemployment.[57] In each country, the already difficult fiscal situation was greatly exacerbated by new challenges from abroad, which required increasing military expenditures. In consequence, the states became quite weak as their institutions could no longer provide the fiscal basis for state autonomy and capacity.[58] It is thus not coincidental that big events occurred when the state was fiscally depleted: the outbreak of the English Civil Wars in 1642, the collapse of the Tokugawa regime in the Meiji Restoration of 1868, and the beginning of the Taiping Rebellion in China in 1851.[59]

Following these major upheavals, state actors in each case started to search for a new institutional basis for state autonomy and capacity. Sources of revenue that had lower administrative and political costs were particularly attractive. All three states became reliant on indirect taxes, such as customs and the duties on domestic consumer goods. Moreover, they all experimented with various means to use tax revenue to mobilize financial resources from the markets. They even made similar mistakes that resulted in huge discounting of state credit instruments in the markets. In each process of institutional development, we also observe intensive interactions between state actors and powerful private financiers. This phenomenon of influential political merchants (*zheng-shang* in Chinese and *seishō* in Japanese) who had close connections with the government is common to the three countries, in spite of their distinctive political histories. However, the end results and sequences of institutional transformation differ.

England first transformed from a domain state into a traditional fiscal state between the late 1640s and the 1650s.[60] Centralized bureaucracies to collect customs and excises on liquor were established in 1672 and 1683, respectively. After the Glorious Revolution in 1688, England entered into consecutive expensive wars with France and its allies. The English state mainly depended on borrowing, though the option of issuing paper notes was brought up in the early 1690s. After 1713, the English government began to convert its unfunded short-term debts into funded long-term debts with lower interest. The modern fiscal state emerged in the 1720s when the perpetual redeemable annuities came to dominate government borrowing. The central collection of customs and excises enabled the English government to secure the creditworthiness of these annuities. By the 1750s, the newly emerged institutions of the modern fiscal state had been consolidated.

In contrast to England's reliance on short-term financing prior to the establishment of a modern fiscal state, the Meiji government formed in 1868 leaned heavily on long-term liabilities in the form of nonconvertible paper notes to meet its fiscal needs. As a result of the unequal treaties imposed by Western powers, which fixed the tariff level at 5 percent, the option to increase revenue by raising customs duties was not available. From the late 1870s onward, the Meiji government intensively extracted revenue from major consumer goods, such as alcohol, tobacco, and soy sauce. By 1880, the collection of duties on alcohol had become centralized. The modern fiscal state emerged in Japan in the mid-1880s when the centralized institutions of public finance enabled the government to not only issue convertible banknotes through the Bank of Japan but also raise long-term domestic bonds. By 1895, the modern fiscal state was firmly established.

The case of China shows that similar experiments in public finance do not necessarily lead to the emergence of the modern fiscal state. The Qing government issued paper notes between 1853 and 1863 to meet military expenditures incurred in suppressing the Taiping Rebellion. However, instead of pushing the Qing government to centralize government finance, as occurred in Japan, this monetary experiment failed disastrously. Nonetheless, important institutional developments happened in public finance after the 1870s. As in England and Japan, the receipts from customs and the domestic consumption tax (the *lijin* duty collected from wholesalers) became the major pillar of government finance. Provincial governments increasingly cooperated with private bankers to remit taxation and official funds by bills of exchange. But the central government's fiscal operation remained decentralized, with a large number of specific sources of revenue being assigned by the center directly for particular purposes without being transmitted to Beijing. Fiscal decentralization and the inability to mobilize long-term financial resources persisted in Qing China.

Ramifications of the Modern Fiscal State

These institutions of the modern fiscal state significantly enhanced state capacity and autonomy. The discovery by recent scholarship of a "strong state" with an efficient tax bureaucracy overthrows the old view of eighteenth-century England as an amateurish laissez-faire state, which had to depend on the gentry for local governance.[61] We now have a better understanding of the pivotal role played by tax institutions in the well-known "financial revolution" in eighteenth-century England, which allowed the government to take on enormous long-term debt for fighting wars.[62]

The creditworthiness of the English government in the financial markets rested on its ability to extract tax revenue, which made eighteenth-century England one of the most heavily taxed countries in Europe.[63] The fiscal system was highly centralized as local taxes accounted for only 10 percent of the levies of the central government before the 1770s.[64] The composition of English tax revenue underwent significant change as it came to rely more and more on indirect taxes. The receipts from customs and excises accounted for 70 to 80 percent of the total government annual income for most of this time. In particular, the proportion of revenues from excises in the total revenue rose from 26 percent in 1696–1700 to 36 percent in 1711–1715 and to 51 percent in 1751–1755.[65]

As Patrick K. O'Brien has pointed out, the vast expansion of indirect revenues was not only a result of economic development but also a consequence of an administrative revolution.[66] John Brewer further demonstrates that the establishment of a highly centralized bureaucracy staffed by salaried officers allowed the English state to collect elastic and reliable revenues from the indirect customs and excises. In particular, the Excise Department, the biggest department in government during this period, approximated the Weberian ideal of rational bureaucracy, which ensured reliability and predictability in administration.[67] Its defining characteristics included recruitment by examination; professional training; meticulous bookkeeping; centralized supervision based on standardized bureaucratic procedures for the assessment and collection of excises; and promotion on the basis of seniority.[68] The collection of excises was extraordinarily centralized, as the accounts and records of excise officers all over England had to be sent to London for regular scrutiny.[69] These centrally collected excises enabled the English government to make regular interest payments to the creditors of the perpetual annuities, an ability that was vital to the success of this market-based system of long-term borrowing. In contrast, the collection of land taxes was firmly controlled by landowners, which led to widespread underestimation, evasion, and mismanagement.[70]

The success of the eighteenth-century English state in extracting customs and excises and its remarkable abilities to mobilize financial resources provided a solid basis for state capacity and autonomy. In possession of a centralized bureaucracy to collect the vast majority of tax revenue, the government enjoyed more autonomy than did those states that had to depend on local powers for revenue collection. From the 1740s on, the English government mainly used the stocks of perpetual annuities to raise long-term loans from the public and thus became less dependent on the few big financiers.[71] These new institutions of public finance also significantly mitigated conflicts of interests between landowners and the government and between landowners and the moneyed class, as landed wealth did not bear the increasing burden of taxation. They also allowed the executive branch to use lucrative sinecures and pensions to build up widespread networks of political patronage and manipulate members of Parliament, which led to a stable and corrupt oligarchic regime in the second half of the eighteenth century.[72]

How shall we characterize the institutions of public finance in eighteenth-century England? The term *fiscal-military state,* coined by John Brewer, nicely captures its close interactions with the expensive wars that England fought from 1689 to 1815. Nevertheless, this concept concentrates mainly on the use of the state's fiscal resources. In regard to the institutional aspects of public finance, Brewer believes that the centralized fiscal system managed by the Treasury distinguished the English state from other European states by its ability to "keep full accounts of total government revenue and expenditure."[73] However, he overestimates the degree of centralization in the management of government spending at the time. For example, the Treasury before the mid-eighteenth century did not have access to itemized information on expenditures of the army and navy, the two biggest spenders, and could only approve the estimated sum of expenditures required by them.[74] Centralization thus does not define government finance in eighteenth-century England.

As O'Brien and Hunt have pointed out, the powerful English state from the 1720s onward greatly benefited from two interrelated developments, that is, the highly centralized bureaucracy to collect indirect excises and the regular interest payments of the market-based system of permanent debt of the state.[75] The institutional linkage between central tax collection and the creditworthiness of the state's long-term liabilities enabled the English government to mobilize financial resources to afford expensive wars, in spite of widespread waste and corruption in government spending, especially in the army and navy.[76]

Clarifying the institutional features of the modern fiscal state makes it easier to put the eighteenth-century English state, which emerged in a very special historical context characterized by successive conflicts and the enormous expansion of the Atlantic trade, into a broader comparative perspective. For example, Japan established a modern fiscal state in the late 1880s by using centrally collected tax revenues to safeguard the value of banknotes, the legal tender in the economy, issued by the Bank of Japan. Japan made this institutional achievement without fighting any large-scale international wars and remained marginal in the world capital market at the time. In contrast to the long-term borrowing of the eighteenth-century English state, the Meiji government's permanent liabilities were in the form of paper notes from the beginning.

Political economists of late development have long considered Meiji Japan a typical example of how a strong state with a group of coherent leaders can use effective intervention to impose Western models on a backward economy.[77] This view, however, overlooks the highly sophisticated market economy that had developed in Japan before the country's opening in 1858. Meanwhile, the Meiji government started with a very weak fiscal and political basis, and there was no "corporate coherence" among the major Meiji leaders, who were deeply divided by conflicting institutional schemes.[78] The Meiji government's initial involvement in industrial enterprises aimed mainly to derive revenue through direct ownership and management of enterprises in textiles, mining, and railway building.[79] However, these state-managed enterprises suffered heavily from mismanagement and inefficiency.[80] The resulting huge deficits forced the Meiji government to sell off the unprofitable businesses while retaining the profitable ones, such as gold mining.[81]

In contrast, the establishment of centralized institutions of public finance in the 1880s greatly contributed to Japan's modernization.[82] In particular, the modern banking system with the Bank of Japan as the central bank channeled idle capital from nonagricultural sectors (commerce, service, finance, etc.) into industrial development; this was the main source for industrial investment in Japan in the late nineteenth and early twentieth centuries.[83] In the period between 1888 and 1892, even though total government expenditures accounted for only 7.9 percent of gross national product (GNP), the Japanese government played an indirect yet effective role in fostering industrial investment.[84] For example, even though the boom in the formation of joint-stock companies in the late 1880s led to a severe financial panic in 1890, the Bank of Japan continued to discount the bills of those banks that accepted the shares of major railway companies as security. This policy greatly encouraged investment and capital formation in railway construction.[85]

In terms of the composition of tax revenue, the shift to indirect taxes levied on alcohol in Meiji Japan was quite impressive. The revenue from taxing the production of sake and liquor *(shuzōzei)* rose from 12.3 percent of the annual total tax revenue in 1878 to 26.4 percent in 1888. In 1899, this percentage reached 38.8 percent (49 million yen), which for the first time exceeded the land tax (35.6 percent, or 45 million yen).[86] As with the excise collection in England, the duties levied on alcohol in Japan were collected by bureaucrats of the Ministry of Finance.[87] The collection of indirect taxes on alcohol had become highly centralized by 1880. After 1882, the Meiji government requested the newly established Bank of Japan to centrally manage government treasuries across the country, which further enhanced the degree of centralization in public finance.[88] The government granted the Bank of Japan a monopoly on note issuing, which was the most important business of the Bank in its early years. Fiscal centralization also greatly improved the Japanese government's ability to take on long-term domestic credit. For example, in order to modernize the navy, the Japanese government in 1886 successfully floated a long-term (fifty years) Navy Bond of ¥17 million with an annual interest of 5 percent in the domestic market.[89] The rise of the modern fiscal state in Japan paved the way for its growth as a major power in Asia.

In a negative way, China also shows the importance of the modern fiscal state. China had long been ruled by traditional fiscal states. In the eighteenth century, the government collected up to 80 percent of its tax revenue in silver. In the second half of the nineteenth century, significant changes happened in public finance, many of which parallel what we see in England and Japan. For example, the average annual tax revenue more than doubled from some 40 million tael in the 1830s to about 90 million tael in the early 1890s. The composition of tax revenue became more diversified as a result of expansion in both domestic and international trade after the 1860s. While the percentage of the receipts from land taxes in government annual income dropped from more than 70 percent in the 1840s to some 40 percent in the 1880s and 1890s, the indirect revenues from customs, the domestic consumption tax (lijin duties), and the salt tax rose to about 50 percent over the same period.[90]

In both England and Japan, the use of speedy credit notes to remit revenue and official funds was vital to centralizing the management of public finance. In China, private bills of exchange also became increasingly involved in transferring government revenue from the 1860s onward. Between 1875 and 1893, about one-third of the tax revenue sent to Beijing from provincial governments was transmitted by private bankers through bills of exchange, particularly revenues from the provinces of Sichuan, Fujian, Guangdong, and Zhejiang and from customs offices in Fujian, Zhejiang, and Guangdong.[91] The interprovincial transfer of official funds also depended on private bankers.

In late nineteenth-century China, customs and the lijin duty were collected by salaried staff. Under the management of Western officials employed by the Qing government, the Imperial Maritime Customs became a highly centralized and efficient bureaucracy.[92] Meanwhile, most of the officials who collected the lijin duty were government commissioners recruited from among expectant officials. The center required every provincial government to report the names of collecting commissioners and their performance regularly. Good performance often gave collecting commissioners priority for promotion in the bureaucratic system.[93] This was similar to the basic principles in the management of the Excise Department in eighteenth-century England. Much as in

England, military needs drove borrowing; some 77 percent of the total 44 million tael in short-term loans that the Qing government took on between the 1860s and 1880s were used for military purposes, all secured by the revenue from customs and lijin duties.[94] These institutional developments enabled the Qing state to build a Western-style navy strong enough to contain Japan's aggression toward Korea in the 1880s;[95] and to afford both the expensive expeditions to reconquer Xinjiang between 1873 and 1883 and the conflicts on land and sea during the Sino-French War in 1884–1885.

Nonetheless, in contrast to England and Japan, reliance on indirect taxes and the use of private bills of exchange to transfer revenue in China did not prompt further centralization in public finance. In financial matters, the central authority was vital in coordinating provincial governments and the Imperial Maritime Customs to ensure punctual returns of foreign loans.[96] However, the center did not try to raise long-term financial resources. The building of railways and a modern navy prior to 1895 were all funded by the state's limited tax revenue rather than by mobilizing financial resources from the markets as the Meiji government did in Japan. The lack of ability to mobilize long-term financial resources significantly contributed to the defeat of the Qing by Japan in 1895 and its final collapse in 1911. In this light, any characterization of the state capacity in late nineteenth-century China needs to explain both the institutional development in collecting indirect taxes and borrowing through short-term loans that the Qing government had already attained and the lack of further development of fiscal centralization and the state's long-term credits.

Explaining the Rise of the Modern Fiscal State

Why did the modern fiscal state emerge in England and Japan but not in China? A comparative perspective helps us exclude some possible explanations at the very beginning. The modern fiscal state is not a product of an industrial economy. For example, it appeared in England in the 1730s, before the First Industrial Revolution (often dated to the 1740s). Likewise, the Japanese economy in the early 1890s was far from industrial. In this light, the lack of industrialization in nineteenth-century China does not account for the absence of the modern fiscal state.

Economic historians in recent decades have rightly emphasized the importance of choosing comparative units of similar geographic size. For example, Ken Pomeranz and Li Bozhong consider it more reasonable to compare the Lower Yangzi delta, the most developed region in late imperial China, with England, one of the leading economies in eighteenth-century Europe. However, such a region-based comparison ignores the important role of state institutions of public finance in economic and political development. As the modern fiscal state is characterized by the institutional linkage between centralized tax collection and the securing of the state's long-term liabilities, the relative size of tax revenue and these liabilities is not important. Instead, what matters is whether the revenue is centrally collected to safeguard the state debt. This greatly simplifies a comparative study of three countries of different sizes.

For example, China is much bigger than England or Japan. Yet by the second half of the nineteenth century, private bankers in China had established financial networks connecting major cities and market towns, which remitted huge sums of tax revenue and official funds across regions. Similar private financial networks in England and Japan were crucial to the centralization of tax collection and the building of their modern fiscal states. The speedy remittance of official funds thus provided the Qing government the technical means to attain fiscal centralization if it had the necessary motivation. Therefore, territorial size did not determine the creation or failure of a creation of a modern fiscal state.

Different sequences are possible in building a modern fiscal state. Early development as a traditional fiscal state does not confer advantage in making the transition to a modern fiscal state, as seen by comparing China and England. Past history of political centralization also has no bearing on the establishment of a centralized fiscal system; Japan attained this goal before 1880, while China did not. England had established a centralized bureaucracy in collecting customs and excises before it converted tremendous debts into perpetual credits after the 1720s. In contrast, the Japanese government had huge amounts of long-term liabilities in the form of nonconvertible paper notes before it centralized tax collection. Fighting international wars is neither a sufficient nor a necessary condition of building a modern fiscal state. For example, Japan fought no large-scale foreign war between 1868 and 1894. Instead, financial difficulties forced the Meiji government to avoid military confrontation with Russia and China.[97] The Qing government launched expensive military campaigns in the northwest between 1866 and 1883 and fought the Sino-French War in 1884–1885. Yet a modern fiscal state emerged in Japan rather than in China.

Institutions of political representation are not a necessary condition for building a modern fiscal state either. While England had Parliament prior to the rise of the modern fiscal state, a modern fiscal state emerged in Japan before the opening of the Japanese Diet in 1890. This forces us to reexamine the relationship between political representation and taxation. Neo-institutionalists often use Parliament to account for the rapid rise of the English government's income in the eighteenth century. In Margaret Levi's view, Parliament ensured a "quasi-voluntary compliance" from taxpayers, reduced transaction costs in collecting taxes, and thus contributed to the rise of tax revenue.[98] However, Parliament at the time was dominated by landowners, while the increased tax revenue came mainly from customs and excises. It is difficult to argue that members of Parliament represented the interest of ordinary consumers, who detested heavy excise rates. The rising excise receipts therefore did not result from the broad consent of the English people.[99]

Because the royal government depended on its own salaried officers to collect customs and excises, local elites were unlikely to control the royal government through taxation as Jean-Laurent Rosenthal has argued.[100] Robert Bates and Da-Hsiang Lien argue that the English propertied class in the seventeenth century had more power to bargain with the crown as they could hide their mobile assets from taxing officials. This increased the transaction costs of government in collecting taxes, which forced it to make political concessions in return for more revenues.[101] However, the large scale of production of major consumption goods at the time could hardly escape the inspection of government taxing officers. Yet big producers and wholesalers could transfer the burden of high taxes onto consumers, who, as noted previously, had to face the collective action problem in organizing antitax campaigns. Representation is thus not a necessary condition of high indirect taxes.

Some institutionalists use the interest calculations of political elites to explain institutional change. For example, Daron Acemoglu and James

A. Robinson argue that politically powerful groups oppose economic growth only when they know that economic changes will weaken their established power base by enriching potential political rivals.[102] Both Bruce Carruthers and David Stasavage indeed argue that the Whig Party represented the interest of creditors to the English state; its political dominance between 1714 and 1746 greatly reduced the risk of default on state debt and thus contributed to the success of the English financial revolution.[103] However, the increasing scale of long-term borrowing was serviced by revenue extracted from ordinary consumers. The landed elites did not shoulder the burden of heavy taxation, the creditors to the state benefited from punctual interest payments, and the state actors enjoyed much enhanced spending capacity. Given these conditions, why should an English government made up of landed elites default on long-term borrowings?

The special asymmetry of political power between the state and ordinary consumers in extracting indirect consumption taxes implies that political elites should have every reason to welcome the institutions of the modern fiscal state, regardless of whether they were landed elites or the moneyed class. For example, the Qing state in the late nineteenth century could have embraced the modern fiscal state as it already depended on salaried officials to collect half of its annual income from indirect taxes and had successfully honored its huge short-term debts. Thus the variation of final results among England, Japan, and China cannot be explained by the interest conflict between the state and landed elites over taxation issues because all three states used salaried officials to raise substantial indirect tax revenues.

Looking back on these three cases, the institutional characteristics of a modern fiscal state shed new light on the study of state capacity. Both eighteenth-century England and nineteenth-century Japan demonstrate that in an economy with large commercial sectors and financial networks, indirect consumption taxes were more important than land taxes. The use of tax revenue to mobilize long-term financial resources even just from domestic sources is far more effective in enhancing state capacity than direct extraction of land taxes, as illustrated by the case of Japan. For nineteenth-century Japan and China, the ability of the state to penetrate into the village or subvillage level to extract land taxes is thus not an appropriate measurement of state capacity.[104]

As the modern fiscal state established the institutional ability to mobilize long-term financial resources, it vastly increased state spending capacities. This was a salient advantage in interstate competition. The substantial contribution of the modern fiscal state to state capacity thus provides a new perspective to view the great divergence between China and England in the late eighteenth century and between the fall of China and the rapid rise of Japan in the late nineteenth century.

Meanwhile, given the scale and regularity of tax revenue, the state's participation had a big impact on the development of the financial markets. Before mass communication, information regarding the creditworthiness of the state could reach much larger segments of society; in contrast, the reputations of even major private financiers were often confined to their specific trading networks. The modern fiscal state thus profoundly stimulated the development of long-term credit instruments such as paper notes and state bonds; it was a crucial stage in the evolution toward the credit-based modern economy. The rise of the modern fiscal state represents a "great transformation" in the relationship between the state and economy.

Given the functions of the modern fiscal state and the special asymmetry of power between the state and ordinary consumers, which allows the state to extract heavy indirect taxes even without the compliance of the people, state actors in the commercialized economy should all embrace these new institutions. Then how shall we explain its emergence in England and Japan but not in China? The high degree of uncertainty and the multiplicity of possible outcomes in the process of creating new institutions suggest that neither the success of England and Japan nor the failure of China in building the modern fiscal state were inevitable at the start of each episode.

To explain the actual trajectories of institutional development, I construct a causal mechanism that results from the conjunction of appropriate socioeconomic circumstances and a credit crisis rooted in the excessive issue of fiduciary credit instruments. Because the crisis threatened the creditworthiness of the state, it thus constituted a pressing problem for any political actors who came to power. As the center bore the full risk of redeeming these credit instruments, state actors—whatever their political agendas or affiliations—had a strong motivation to search for a means to centralize tax collection and safeguard the value of these credit instruments. The ensuing process of experimentation and learning led to continuous accumulation of effective elements and knowledge, which ended up with the creation of the new institution. Other possible alternatives were eliminated because of their inability to solve the crisis. This mechanism integrates socioeconomic structure, contingency, and agency into one coherent path-dependent causal narrative, which explains the different successful stories of England and Japan as well as the failure of China to attain such a transformation.

1

CREDIT CRISES IN THE RISE OF THE MODERN FISCAL STATE

In the study of institutional development, both rational choice and historical institutionalists have attempted to apply theories about the functions and distributional effects of institutions to explain changes in existing institutions when socioeconomic contexts vary.[1] Variations in political power among major actors can also lead to changes in existing institutions.[2] However, this endogenous approach to institutional development is not very helpful to explain the creation of new institutions when their functions and distributional effects are still unknown. The theory of exogenous institutional change, conversely, emphasizes the role of external shocks, such as wars or foreign occupation, in fundamental institutional innovation.[3]

Nonetheless, the initial stage following the collapse of existing institutions is typically characterized by a high degree of uncertainty because actors no longer have a "road map" to guide their search for alternatives.[4] New institutions thus often emerge from an opaque process that has more than one possible outcome. This special kind of institutional development thus differs from that seen in theories of critical junctures, which mainly address how the specific institutional arrangements formed at critical junctures can reproduce over time so as to produce a divergent outcome.[5]

How then shall we explain the rise of specific new institutions against the high degree of uncertainty and multiplicity of outcomes possible in the process of institutional development? The creation of the modern fiscal state involves two closely connected innovations in public finance: an institution to centrally collect indirect taxes and a financial institution that uses the amalgamated tax revenue to mobilize long-term financial resources in the form of either state bonds or paper notes. This is not a case of simply redeploying or recombining various elements from the pool of existing institutions.[6] It thus can be used as a case study to understand how new institutions emerge and consolidate.

Before the start of each episode, state actors had to face severe fiscal difficulties: England between the 1600s and 1630s, Japan between the 1820s and 1860s, and China between the 1820s and 1840s. Nonetheless, in these well-established early modern states, the stickiness of dysfunctional institutions was boosted by a shared concern between the center and localities over the maintenance of sociopolitical order. This political condition allowed the center to transfer to local governments or even communities the burden of spending in state affairs associated with the common good, such as provision of social welfare, infrastructure maintenance, and even defense.

As state actors in each case did not actively search for alternatives even when they were greatly troubled by fiscal difficulties, the collapse of existing institutions in each event—the English Civil Wars in 1642, the Meiji Restoration in 1868, and the Taiping Rebellion in 1851—is a means to resolve the infinite regress problem in historical causation. That is to say, causes of the rise of the modern fiscal state are unlikely to occur prior to these events.[7] The past decentralized institutions simply could not provide actors the information necessary to conceive the modern fiscal state, such as an accurate estimate of the size of the taxable commercial sectors, or the potential credit available to the government. Detailed historical examination highlights the high degree of uncertainty and the specific multiple institutional schemes that historical actors seriously considered in each process, factors that cannot be accommodated satisfactorily by existing theories of institutional development.

Institutional Background of the Fiscal Difficulties

As noted in the Introduction, the financial basis of the three early modern states varied considerably: the domain state in England, the incomplete fiscal state in Japan, and the traditional fiscal state in China. However, they all experienced a period of fiscal difficulties as established institutions of public finance became ill adapted to greatly changed socioeconomic circumstances. These included the increasing presence of state power in society; population growth and mobility; the deepening monetarization of economic life; the expansion of interregional trade and financial networks; and the emergence of urban sectors. In particular, price fluctuations—either inflation or deflation—not only had a widespread impact on society but also profoundly affected state finance.

Traditional pillars of government income, such as the domain revenues in early Stuart England and land taxes in early nineteenth-century Japan and China, had become either depleted or inelastic. Furthermore, none of these states had yet developed the institutional ability to tap new tax bases in the commercial sectors. As it was impractical to reduce the necessary expenditures for defense, maintenance of political order, and the provision of social welfare, such as calamity relief, these three early modern states faced decades of chronic fiscal troubles.

The domain state formed in England by the mid-sixteenth century did not rely on regular domestic taxation but derived its ordinary revenue from royal estates, customs, and the crown's feudal rights. Domestic taxation seemed unnecessary when the Tudor monarchs could plunder the vast wealth of the church, which owned about 20 to 25 percent of the land in England in the 1530s.[8] Of the total income of the royal government between 1534 and 1547, the revenue from traditional sources and newly seized monastic lands amounted to about 60 percent while the revenues derived from lay taxation and ecclesiastic taxes contributed only 30 percent.[9] Nonetheless, expensive wars with France forced the royal government to sell many ex-monastic and chantry lands between 1540 and 1552; these provided up to 32 percent of the total war expenditures of some £3.5 million.[10] This was not, of course, a sustainable fiscal strategy. From 1588 to 1603, sales of royal lands could only cover some 13 percent of the military expenditures incurred in the Anglo-Spanish war and the colonial wars in Ireland, while 71 percent were funded by lay and clerical subsidies.[11]

Government spending, however, continued to grow. In addition to the rising war expenditures because of a "military revolution" in Western Europe after the mid-sixteenth century,[12] the period from 1450 to 1649 also witnessed a "price revolution." In England, the average price of grain increased about 700 percent, that of industrial products about 210 percent.[13] Prices did not become stable until the 1650s. This price revolution was closely related to changes in socioeconomic circumstances, such as population growth, the expansion of the urban economy, and increasing monetarization.[14] However, the nominal value of the crown's total ordinary revenue rose only from £170,000 in 1547 to £300,000 by 1603, which represented a 40 percent fall in real terms.[15] As a result, the early Stuart government started with constant deficits even in ordinary accounts.[16] As Conrad Russell has emphasized, the increasing discrepancy between expenses necessary to maintain the state and the shrinking ordinary revenue was the primary cause for the "functional breakdown" of the royal government during these years.[17]

Political actors in early Stuart England were aware of two options for fiscal reform. One was to rescue the domain state by cutting government expenditures while raising ordinary revenue. The other was to transform into a tax state by turning the parliamentary supplies from irregular extraordinary revenue granted only in emergencies into regular taxation to fund the government in both peace and war. The latter option seemed quite realistic given that royal estates had been irreversibly shrinking and feudal revenues such as wardship and purveyance were becoming obsolete.[18] As early as 1593, there had been a proposal to create an annual land tax of £100,000 to fund wars.[19] However, in the negotiations of the Great Contract in the 1610s, the royal government failed to reach an agreement with Parliament over how to use a national land tax to replace the crown's major feudal revenues.[20] Many members of Parliament considered such a tax unacceptable. The landed class was particularly hostile to the national survey of land that such a levy would require.[21] As local gentry firmly controlled the assessment and collection of parliamentary supplies, the royal government could do little to overcome severe underassessment and widespread evasion.[22]

Nonetheless, the failure of the Great Contract did not imply a fundamental conflict between the crown and Parliament. Both sides accepted the fiscal principle of a domain state that formally separated the crown's ordinary revenue from the extraordinary revenue granted by Parliament in emergency. Both looked back at the consolidation of the domain state in the late fifteenth and early sixteenth centuries for inspiration to overcome the current financial difficulties.[23] The royal government hoped to derive more income from better management of its own ordinary revenue. In order to press more revenue from the royal estates, royal financial officials tried hard to uncover "concealed" rents and lands that belonged to the crown, to disforest and sell timber, to drain the fens, and even to encroach on commons.[24] The crown also revived some medieval feudal rights, such as knighthood and forest fines, and sold general pardons and titles of baron and peer for more revenue.[25] Moreover, royal officials implemented "mercantilist policies," such as granting monopolies to commercial projects with an aim to share the expected business profit.[26] However, these efforts to rescue the obsolete domain state were fiscally unproductive and politically unpopular.

As Conrad Russell has reminded us, the conflicts between the royal government and Parliament in this period should be viewed against the institutional framework that both sides accepted.[27] For example, critics of the granting of monopoly were concerned about the disturbances caused by the abuse of monopolies, and they pointed out that the monarch and his councilors had a duty to preserve the social order.[28] In response, the royal government was prepared to repeal many unprofitable measures, such as patents of inns, alehouses, and gold and silver thread, while preserving a few fiscally productive ones, such as the monopoly of tobacco.[29] Likewise, the disputes between the crown and Parliament over customs duties in the 1620s occurred in the shared recognition of the king's prerogative to raise the outdated rates of customs duties.[30]

One major constitutional debate between Parliament and the crown was over the annual collection of ship money. Ship money was a non-parliamentary levy, and in 1635 it was extended to the whole country to sponsor the newly established professional royal navy. As its collection was based on the directly assessed individual wealth in each county and major town, ship money became a de facto nationwide direct tax.[31]

However, according to the fiscal constitution of the domain state, ship money did not belong to the crown's "ordinary revenue," and therefore its levy could be justified only by emergencies and implemented only by vote of Parliament. Yet in the peaceful years of 1634–1635, there was no imminent threat to England. In making its case, the royal government appealed to the crown's duty to protect the realm under the new circumstances of naval warfare, which made it urgent for England to build a professional navy.[32] The continued collection of ship money, in spite of its unsettled legal status, illustrated the tension between the obsolete institutions of the domain state and the new reality.

Several factors contributed to the stickiness of the institutions of the domain state in early Stuart England. The severe fiscal difficulties in the 1610s forced the royal government to reduce the expenditures of the royal household, wardrobe, pensions, navy, ordnance, and garrison. This retrenchment continued into the reign of Charles I (1625–1642).[33] Although the English government could not afford costly offensive strategies, it could retreat from the power struggles in Continental Europe because of the English Channel. The less costly defensive strategy allowed the royal government to stop the nonparliamentary means to raise military expenditures, such as the benevolence and the forced loans of 1626–1628.[34]

More important, the royal government transferred to localities much of the costs of national defense, the implementation of the poor law, the maintenance of order and infrastructure.[35] Local gentry collected various "rates" to disburse these state affairs in their regions.[36] The major role of the center in this fiscal decentralization was to provide coordination and guidance.[37] Only when local governments were reluctant to strictly implement measures such as isolation and confinement in preventing plagues did the central government take more intervening initiatives.[38] Fiscal decentralization and local gentry control over the assessment and collection of both parliamentary supplies and nonparliamentary levies, such as ship money, to a large extent contained the tension between the center and localities. Any intention on the part of the royal government to excessively extract revenues could be effectively blocked by the noncooperation of local elites.[39] The shared goals between the center and local elites to maintain social order were thus crucial to sustain the fiscal decentralization.

In contrast to the domain state in England in the 1600s, the state in early nineteenth-century Japan rested on taxation. Yet it was an incomplete fiscal state because the shogunate, which acted as the central government, collected taxes not across the whole country but only from the territories under its direct administration. This resulted from the previous history of state formation. When the shogunate unified Japan in 1603, one major pillar of government revenue was not taxation but its control of the output of gold and silver in Japan, one of the major producers of precious metals in the world in the early seventeenth century. The profits from gold and silver mines were almost equivalent to the revenue collected from the land tax in the early seventeenth century.[40] With the declining output of gold and silver mines after the mid-seventeenth century, land taxes *(nengu)* became the principal source of shogunal income. In the Kyōhō Reform (1716–1736), the shogunate tried to improve yields by encouraging reclamation of new lands, updating the assessment of agricultural output, and collecting land taxes at a fixed rate that could motivate peasants to produce more.[41]

Over the course of the eighteenth century, the income of the shogunate became inadequate to sustain its role as the central government. However, instead of taxing the whole territory, a move that would have been resisted by domain governments, the shogunate transferred the burden of increasing state affairs, such as public expenditures in river works, calamity relief, and infrastructure maintenance, to domain governments, which acted as local governments. These measures included the imposition of levies, such as construction services *(kuniyaku bushin)* and the handover of river works and flood control projects *(otetsu bushin)*.[42] Tokugawa fiscal institutions after the 1730s were thus characterized by a division of labor in state expenditures between the shogunate and domain governments.

Between 1760 and 1786, the shogunate adopted active mercantilist policies in the Tanuma Reform to tap revenues from nonagricultural sectors, including foreign trade. It imposed new taxes on sake, soy sauce, and water wheels, which were collected through the intermediaries of villages, business guilds *(nakama)*, wholesale agencies *(tonya)*, and government-granted monopolies *(kabunakama)*. To ease the economic distress of domain lords and also to earn profits, the shogunate forced big merchants in Osaka to provide it with low-interest loans *(goyōkin)*;

it then re-lent the money to domain lords. The shogunate also sought to benefit from the commercial development of the colony of Ezo (today's Hokkaido) and from the export of Japanese goods, such as copper and dried sea products, to Chinese and Dutch merchants.

Fiscal productiveness to a large extent determined the fate of these policies. The shogunate was forced to repeal the levies on silk thread, lamp oil, and cloth when the collection by monopoly-holding urban merchants led to large-scale riots by small producers. The loans to domain lords and the commercial development of Ezo became fiscal drains and had to be curtailed.[43] Although financial officials understood the fiscal importance of encouraging exports of Japanese goods, the shogunate in 1787 restricted copper exports so as to meet the domestic demand.[44]

The shogunate's efforts to diversify the tax base coincided with a highly hostile environment. Severe natural calamities, including unusually cold weather, droughts, and volcanic eruptions, caused widespread crop failure and serious famine.[45] Despite falling revenues from land taxes, the shogunate as the central government was obliged to provide famine relief and funds for resuming agricultural production; to prepare reserves of grain and funds against future calamities; and to prevent the fall of rice prices through government procurement.[46] Between 1786 and 1817, rising expenses forced the shogunate to reduce administrative and shogunal household expenditures, dispense its cash reserves, and transfer larger shares of expenditures on river works and other construction projects to domain governments.[47]

With the advent of the nineteenth century, the disputes with Russia over the northern frontiers and the appearance of British warships in Japanese waters made it urgent for the shogunate to increase defense spending in Ezo and the Tokyo Bay area.[48] Parsimony was no longer viable. In 1818, the shogunate began to use currency debasement to raise revenues. By 1832, the total profit to the shogunate from recoinage was as high as 5.5 million ryō, an enormous amount given that its annual income was less than 1 million ryō at the time.[49] Despite criticism of currency debasement, the shogunate's financial officials seem to have expected that the increased monetary input in this form could reverse the decline of rice prices and stimulate economic transactions. They debased the currency with small denominations and increased the mintage of copper coins. They hoped that increasing economic transactions might absorb the monetary input and thus avoid inflation. However, a 75 percent rise in prices from 1818 to 1838 forced the shogunate to stop recoinage in 1844.[50]

The pressure to increase defense spending continued through the 1840s as Japan observed the military superiority of the British over the Chinese in the Opium War (1840–1842). The shogunate tried to extract more revenue from land taxes by uncovering reclaimed land that had remained untaxed and by more accurate assessments of agricultural output, particularly the value of lands used for cultivating cash crops. However, it did not possess the administrative ability for such a formidable task.[51] Moreover, rural commercialization had produced significant social differentiation within villages. The shogunate could not tap directly the landlords or rich farmers on whom it depended to maintain local order and administration.[52]

The stringent fiscal situation of the shogunate did not lead to its immediate collapse, however. As the central government, it could mobilize domain governments to adopt Western-style cannons to strengthen the defense of Japan. The pressure to increase defense expenditures was thus transferred to domain governments because national defense was considered in the "public" interest of Japan rather than the shogunate's "private" matter.[53] Fiscal decentralization continued after the arrival of Matthew Perry's fleets in 1853 as the shogunate permitted domain governments to retain funds that should have been handed over to the center *(jōnōkin)* for strengthening local defenses.[54] Much as in early Stuart England, the shared concern about domestic stability and national defense on the part of both the shogunate and domain governments was vital to support existing fiscal decentralization.

Unlike the domain state in early Stuart England, eighteenth-century China was a fiscal state that derived the vast majority of its income from land and salt taxes. In contrast to the incomplete fiscal state in Tokugawa Japan, the central government in China taxed the whole territory governed directly by its administrative institutions (China proper). After the Qing government lifted the ban on maritime trade in 1685, exports of raw silk, tea, and porcelain attracted huge amounts of silver into China. During the reign of the Qianlong emperor (1736–1796), the government encouraged private investment in domestic trade and mining and reduced taxes levied on commercial transactions.[55]

The greatly expanded domestic economy provided the state with a growing tax base. Although the government fixed the quotas in the collection of land taxes and often granted tax remission or even exemption to regions struck by natural calamities, silver reserves of the central government grew considerably. Despite expensive military campaigns in Central Asia, Tibet, and Burma, the amount of silver deposited in the Board of Revenue was as high as 80 million tael of silver by 1795.[56] When the central government needed extra revenues for fighting wars or constructing river works, it often appealed to sales of nominal titles *(juanna)* and levies of "contributions" *(baoxiao)* on the privileged merchants who were granted monopolies in selling salt and in doing business with Westerners.[57] In response to the slow but steady inflation in the eighteenth century, both the provincial and prefectural governments often collected surcharges besides the official rates to cover government expenditures when the center did not adjust the quotas for both taxation and government expenditures accordingly.[58] These adjustments, however, were inadequate to handle the Qing government's fiscal difficulties, which resulted from the defects of its monetary institutions.

In the Qing monetary system, copper coins were denominated currency minted by the state. But the unit of copper coin is one *wen,* the smallest unit used in market exchanges (like one cent in the American monetary system). The Qing government set 1,000 wen copper coins equal to 1 tael of silver, but it did not cast silver coins, and silver was used as a currency by weight. In addition to the standards of *kuping tael* used for government finance, different regions often had their own standard of silver tael. Silver and copper coins had distinctive roles in market transactions and could not easily substitute for each other in practice. Therefore, the bimetallic monetary system in Qing China was not a parallel standard system. The light and high-value silver was used mainly for wholesale and interregional trade, but it could hardly serve as small change as it was impossible to cut silver into minute pieces. In contrast, the low-value and bulky copper coins provided the small change used for daily transactions, but they were too heavy to be carried in large quantities for long-distance trade. As silver determined the value of commodities and cost of manufacturing, it was the de facto standard currency.[59] Before the 1820s, such use of copper coins as small change was not unique in Qing China but common even in countries in which the state minted silver or gold coins because it was technologically impossible for states to cast small cash by silver or gold.[60]

Overseas silver was thus crucially important for the expansion of interregional trade in a large country like China. Between 1680 and 1830, it is estimated that silver from abroad caused a 280 percent increase in Chinese silver stocks.[61] However, from the 1820s on, the opium trade caused a large volume of silver to flow out of China. Silver drainage in this period was further worsened by China's sluggish exports to Europe, a drop in global silver production, and a sharp reduction of American silver coins entering China.[62] Between the 1820s and 1850s, China's domestic silver stocks are estimated to have fallen some 40 percent.[63] This led to a severe domestic deflation.

Scarcity of silver raised the exchange rate between silver (kuping tael) and copper coins (wen) far above the official rate of 1:1000; it reached 1200–1500 in the 1830s and even went above 2000 in some regions in the 1840s (yingui qianjian).[64] The high value of silver in regard to copper coins had profound economic and social consequences. For example, the actual tax burden on peasants and salt merchants increased significantly as they had to exchange copper coins for silver to pay taxes. There were thus nationwide tax arrears and increasing unemployment, typical features of a deflationary economy.[65]

The Qing government's initial response was to reduce and even stop the mintage of copper coins, hoping that a reduced supply of copper coins would drive up their value and thus resume the official exchange rate with silver in the markets. However, this policy was ineffective.[66] In this situation, government officials and scholars began to debate alternative monetary policies to address the severe scarcity of silver in the economy. One option was to mint denominated silver currency. Provincial governments in Jiangsu, Fujian, and Zhejiang in the 1830s experimented with minting silver coins. However, the center did not use coercion to circulate these silver coins as legal tender in the economy, and these efforts to cast denominated silver currency were abortive.[67]

The other proposal was to abandon the use of silver in public finance, which was equivalent to replacing the silver standard with a copper one. However, the low-value and bulky copper cash was not suitable for interregional trade and public finance in a large country like China. Two supplementary measures to resolve this problem were proposed: to cast new copper coins with bigger nominal values *(daqian)*, such as 5 wen *(dangwu)*, 10 wen *(dangshi)*, and even 1000 wen *(dangqian)*; or to issue paper notes denominated in copper coins *(xingchao)*.[68] Many statecraft scholars and officials considered the issuance of paper notes as an important solution to the current scarcity of silver, though they had different views on whether silver should continue to be used as currency or how to achieve convertibility of paper notes.[69] However, China's historical experience with paper notes was mixed. Whereas advocates were confident of the state's ability to secure the value of the notes and looked to the positive achievements of the Southern Song dynasty, their opponents argued that the state simply could not force people to accept the "empty" notes, referring to the hyperinflation caused by excessive issue of paper notes in the late fourteenth and early fifteenth centuries.[70] The Qing government was reluctant to take the risk.

From an economic point of view, the massive silver outflow from China in the first half of the nineteenth century was equivalent to a chronic deficit in foreign trade. In order to avoid domestic deflation, the country of deficit can choose to devalue its currency. In the age of metal currency, debasement was a means to do that. The state maintained the same face value of its denominated currency while reducing the content or fineness of precious metals such as gold or silver in mintage. However, the Qing government did not mint its own silver currency but used silver as a currency by weight. It thus could not debase silver currency as a devaluation policy to mitigate domestic deflation caused by silver drainage. The monetary cause of the deflation in China between the 1820s and 1850s is similar to the deflation in the interwar period in the twentieth century when a country continued the gold standard even when suffering from chronic deficits in foreign trade.[71]

Stringent fiscal difficulties forced the Qing government to make several adjustments. It tried to reduce administrative expenditures, dispensed the silver reserves of both the Board of Revenue and Imperial Household, and frequently appealed to the sale of nominal official ranks and real offices to raise revenues.[72] In the 1830s, it also attempted to legalize the sale of salt by unlicensed salt merchants in hopes of raising income by taxing "private sales."[73] Facing inadequate funds assigned from the center, provincial governments became more dependent on the collection of surcharges from both agrarian and commercial sources.[74]

In order to ease its burden, the central government encouraged local gentry in both urban and rural areas to participate in the management of local granaries and maintenance of infrastructure, such as river works.[75] However, these fiscal measures did not remove the root cause of the fiscal difficulties, that is, severe deflation caused by the dearth of domestic silver.

Collapse and Uncertainty

State fiscal difficulties prior to the start of each episode had deep institutional roots. They were not caused, nor could they be resolved, simply by the character of the ruler. As James I and Charles I discovered, in the absence of appropriate taxing institutions, their desire to extract more revenue could not necessarily be achieved, at least on a regular basis. Likewise, the well-known parsimony of the Daoguang emperor (1820–1850) in China could not alleviate the domestic deflation. Yet some neo-institutionalists take a surprisingly noninstitutional approach by portraying taxation as a direct conflict between the monarch and society or between the crown and the property owners without considering the effects of tax institutions.[76]

In fact, the maintenance of state power did not require that the center aggregate as much revenue as possible. Instead, a shared concern between the center and localities to preserve the social and political order to a large extent complemented the decentralized fiscal system. This political condition was indispensable for the transference of the financial burden from the center to localities. In each case we observe reasonably successful state efforts to alleviate fiscal pains by mobilizing local governments and even local communities to share the increasing cost of state affairs. Local participation reduced the burden of increasing spending demands on the central government; in the process, it entrenched fiscal decentralization and further decreased the urgency to search for alternative institutions. The mutual reinforcement between fiscal decentralization and local participation in the maintenance of sociopolitical order resulted in a degree of political stability, no matter how precarious it seems in hindsight.

In this situation, we do not observe an active search for alternative institutions by state actors, although they might be imagined. For example, in England, the Privy Council in 1627 proposed a nationwide excise on beer, ale, and cider as a nonparliamentary levy justified by the fighting with France and Spain. Because the war ended in 1628, this proposal was not implemented.[77] In Japan, the shogunate between 1844 and 1853 did not experiment with new taxes but relied mainly on the land tax and "forced loans" from urban merchants. In China, the Shengjing General Xi'en in 1843 suggested that the government levy a tax of 10 percent on the net profit of a wide range of business establishments, including banks, pawnshops, and warehouses. Xi'en pointed out that, in addition to bringing in an estimated annual yield of several million tael, such a levy was equitable as the heavy tax burden on peasants and light tax on businessmen violated the principle of fairness. The center, however, considered it administratively too difficult to check the accounts of each shop.[78]

Nonetheless, the ability of existing institutions to adjust was limited. Intensified fiscal decentralization weakened the capacities of the central government and thus made it more vulnerable. In England in the 1630s, ship money and customs were the two principal means by which the royal government avoided insolvency.[79] As the royal navy consumed ship money and the syndicate of customs farmers controlled the collection of customs, the royal government's ability to borrow remained quite poor.[80] Government financial stability in the 1630s was thus precarious. In spite of a lack of financial resources, Charles I tried to impose religious conformity on the three separate kingdoms of England, Scotland, and Ireland. His religious wars with Scotland in 1637–1640 provided an opportunity for the Irish to rebel in 1640. The war on two fronts seriously weakened his ability to deal with domestic opponents. The mounting mutual mistrust between Charles I and the Long Parliament ultimately led to their armed conflict in 1642.[81] This split within the ruling class was seized on by radicals who advocated parliamentary, and later popular, sovereignty. A traditional rebellion thus evolved into a great republican revolution.[82]

When Japan was forced to open in 1858, the gold standard that had been in effect since 1772 collapsed quickly as the high value of gold in Western countries caused a massive outflow of the resource.[83] In order to avoid deflation, the shogunate in 1860 was forced to debase its gold currencies. Between 1861 and 1868, the shogunate minted only 667,000 ryō of its nominal standard gold currency (Man'en *koban* and *ichibukin*) but

47 million ryō of silver coins (Man'en *nishu-gin*), which made silver the standard currency in practice.[84] Between 1860 and 1867, it relied heavily on the mintage of silver and copper currencies to raise revenues, including using the Mexican silver dollar acquired through foreign trade as raw material for its mintage of silver coins.[85] In 1863, the profit from mintage accounted for 52.6 percent of the shogunate's total annual income.[86] Most domain governments did not have effective means to meet their spiraling spending needs and simply turned to the issuing of paper notes. A few domains, particularly Satsuma (one of the leaders of the Meiji Restoration in 1868), raised income mainly by counterfeiting the shogunate's currency.[87] In consequence, the amount of currency in Japan is estimated to have increased from 53 million ryō to 130 million ryō between 1860 and 1867.[88] The price level rose more than 200 percent in the same period. Severe inflation not only weakened the shogunate's fiscal capacity but also damaged its legitimacy.[89] This is crucial to understanding its fall.

In contrast to the inflation in Japan, the Qing government could not use debasement as devaluation to mitigate the domestic deflation caused by the scarcity of silver. In consequence, it decided in the late 1830s to curb silver drainage by prohibiting the opium trade, which led to the Opium War with the British.[90] Domestic deflation continued after China's defeat. The Qing government turned again to the question of how to convert to a copper standard, yet no consensus emerged from the debates among officials and scholars.[91] The financially exhausted state became vulnerable to mounting unemployment and social disorder. As a result, the Taiping Rebellion, which originated in remote Guangxi Province in 1851, quickly escalated into a great civil war.[92]

The onset of three big events, the Civil Wars in England in 1642, the Meiji Restoration in 1868, and the Taiping Rebellion in China in 1851, initiated institutional reforms in public finance. The ensuing wars provided an opportunity for state actors to put into practice previously unimplemented or genuinely new fiscal measures , such as the levy of taxes on domestic consumption and the massive issuing of state fiduciary instruments of credit, including bills of short-term borrowing and paper notes. However, actors did not know in advance which of their institutional experiments would provide a solid basis for the autonomy and capacity of the state. Under conditions of high uncertainty, centralization was by no means inevitable.

In the collection of indirect taxes, for example there are three different institutional arrangements possible between the center as the "principal" and the collecting agents. The first is a rental contract (tax farming): the government farms out the collection to the agent (usually a big merchant) in return for a prefixed income (rent). The second is a shared contract: the government receives its revenue according to a prefixed ratio with the agent. The third is centralization: the government turns collecting agents into waged labor. As Edgar Kiser points out, there is a severe information-asymmetry problem between the central government as the principal and the collecting officials as the "agents."[93] The collecting agents will not reveal their "private information" about the effective ways of collection to the center as agents stand to benefit from this information asymmetry. In the initial stage of institutional development in each of our cases, the center had little ability to accurately estimate the potential yields of indirect taxes. Where the information cost of centralizing the collection of indirect taxes is too high, the center may instead prefer a rental contract (e.g., tax farming) or a shared contract with collecting agents.

Fiscal decentralization is thus a very likely outcome even after the state comes to rely on indirect taxes. For example, English efforts to centralize public finance first appeared in the early 1650s. However, the early years of the Restoration (1660–1667) witnessed a reversion to a decentralized system that looked quite similar to that of the early Stuart period (1603–1642). The royal government relied on tax farmers for both the collection of its ordinary revenues and for short-term credit. In post-1868 Japan, a decentralized institution of public finance similar to that found in a federal system and fiscal centralization were both likely outcomes. Even when state actors decided to centralize public finance after 1871, they were well aware of two possible tempos: a gradual and stable one or a rapid and risky one.[94] In China, fiscal decentralization persisted from the 1870s to the 1890s, even though the indirect tax revenues on domestic consumption (the lijin duties) and customs accounted for nearly half of the annual government income.

In regard to connections between indirect tax revenue and the state's participation in the financial markets, there are also several possible outcomes. For example, the Qing government between the 1860s and 1890s relied on decentralized fiscal institutions to reliably service the huge amount of short-term foreign loans borrowed in times of emergency. Even where the state had established centralized institutions to collect indirect taxes, the final outcome of a modern fiscal state cannot be taken for granted. For instance, the collection of excises was centralized by 1683 in England. Yet the linkage between central tax collection and the reliable interest payments on the English government's long-term borrowing was not firmly established until 1720. Before England's entry into the War of the Spanish Succession in 1701, the option of clearing all short-term credit and returning to a debt-free state was more influential among political actors than the risky and ambiguous prospect of floating perpetual debt.[95]

Given the uncertainty and multiplicity of possible outcomes, the time interval between the cause and final outcome, which is a typical feature in historical causation, complicates the search for a causal explanation. How can we demonstrate that the final result is not due to factors that arose in this interval?[96] We may avoid this problem of spurious causality by looking for causes from some point close to the observed result. However, to shorten the time horizon of historical causation increases the danger of omitting causally relevant factors.[97] For example, if we try to find the causes of the rise of the modern fiscal state in post-1720 England or post-1880 Japan, we miss vital institutional developments, such as the central collection of indirect taxes on consumption, established in England by 1683 and in Japan by 1880.

The collapse of existing institutions at the beginning of each episode is indeed a critical juncture of great uncertainties and multiple possible outcomes, and the functions or distributional effects of various institutional schemes to be experimented with were not yet known to the actors.[98] There is much room for agency, but actors did not possess the rational capacity to design the modern fiscal state as the optimal result.[99] New political actors who take power can initiate institutional innovations.[100] But the stickiness of existing institutions of public finance restricted both state and social actors in conceiving or implementing new alternatives, so the taking over of the state by new political actors (e.g., a rising merchant class) in and of itself does not suffice to dispel uncertainty.

Ideas may help actors overcome uncertainty.[101] However, when involved actors have quite different or even conflicting ideas, the ideational model of institutional development becomes less powerful to explain the final outcome. Learning from foreign experience is sometimes considered particularly helpful in dispelling uncertainties in building new institutions.[102] However, this approach has its limits. Even where state actors are in agreement over importing foreign approaches, different foreign models may provide conflicting lessons. In Meiji Japan, for example, willingness to learn from the West did not necessarily reduce the degree of uncertainty, as Western experiences were heterogeneous, and not all of them fit Japanese circumstances.[103] In public finance, Britain in the nineteenth century depended on taxation, while the Prussian government still relied heavily on managing industrial enterprises for revenue. The national banking system in the United States was decentralized, but the Bank of England was highly centralized.

The distributional effects of institutions imply that the use of political power is an integral part of institutional development. However, in a highly uncertain process of institutional development, powerful actors do not necessarily know which institutional arrangements would best serve their interests. The use of political power by itself does not guarantee success in various experiments in public finance (e.g., forcing people to accept state fiduciary credit instruments at their face values). Sequence-based mechanisms simply beg the question of why one particular sequence is causally more important than others that yield different outcomes.[104] Feedback effects do not dictate one particular direction of institutional development, as different interpretations by, and reactions of, actors could lead to quite different institutional outcomes.[105]

What kind of mechanism can reduce the degree of uncertainty over time and thus explain the final outcome as against the alternatives possible in the process? Both evolutionary theory and path dependence aim to explain an observed outcome while taking into account uncertainty, contingency, and multiple possible outcomes in the process of change. Evolutionary theories based on actors' trial-and-error experiences are very illuminating to our understanding of technical or organizational changes.[106] In studying institutional innovation, however, we should not assume that a collective process of learning by doing will naturally happen among political actors who are often divided by ideas, institutional preferences, interests, and power struggles. The earlier movers in the process of institutional experimentation may encounter a high probability of failure, rather than the "advantage of first mover." To lose political power is often the price to pay for major policy failures. State actors should thus be risk-averse in dealing with new institutional elements, particularly risky credit instruments such as paper notes or long-term credit. The evolutionary approach is thus inadequate to account for the rise of the modern fiscal state as it cannot tell us how and why state actors had the motivation and opportunity to keep trying various new institutional arrangements, regardless of the political dangers, until they attained the observed outcome.

The theory of path dependence integrates into one unified explanation contingency, multiple possible outcomes at the initial stage, and irreversibility at the later stage toward an eventual outcome that is unpredictable ex ante.[107] Path dependence itself is not an explanatory theory but a description of a nonlinear dynamic process in which the probability distribution of the eventual outcome is dependent on previous events through time. Underlying mechanisms include increasing returns, externalities (positive or negative), complementary effects (or self-reinforcement), and lock-in.[108] As a "branching process" having a multiplicity of equilibria, a path-dependent explanation is tightly coupled with a counterfactual argument of "what might have happened," that is, alternative paths that the process might have taken to other possible outcomes.[109] However, because of the nondeterministic nature of a path-dependent process, no theory can tell us which initial contingent event or agents would set the path-dependent process on its way from the initial multiplicity of equilibrium to that "damned point," after which the path moves irreversibly toward a specific outcome.[110]

Let us take England's transformation into a modern fiscal state as an example. When did this process become inevitable? In a pioneering study of how institutions affect economic performance, North and Weingast suggested that the parliamentary sovereignty established in the Glorious Revolution in 1688 was the key to the success of the English government's long-term debts because Parliament secured the English government's commitment to protect the property rights of creditors.[111] But it is difficult for this theory to explain the dominance of short-term unfunded borrowing in the Nine Years War between 1689 and 1697, which accounted for more than 70 percent of the total government debt.[112] Although North and Weingast took the founding of the Bank of England in 1694 as the institutional basis of government long-term credit, this new financial institution was by no means permanent in its early years. As J. Lawrence Broz and Richard S. Grossman have demonstrated, Parliament could legally withdraw the bank's charter by returning the principal of its loans to the government, and Parliament did in fact use this as a credible threat in negotiating contract renewal with the bank.[113] Parliament in 1688 thus does not explain the rising importance of long-term credit of the English government from 1714 onward.[114]

In order to find a causal linkage spanning the interval between 1688 and 1714, North and Weingast provide a dynamic explanation. In their view, as society became more familiar with the "predictability and commitment" of the new parliamentary monarchy in protecting property rights, the perceived risk of lending to the government was reduced and so long-term borrowing began to grow after 1693.[115] However, as Brewer has noted, England's success at building a market-based system of long-term borrowing was far from self-evident even in 1697, let alone an unavoidable outcome of the country's entry into European power struggles in 1688.[116] According to Larry Neal, the English government did not fully establish the creditworthiness of its perpetual annuities in the markets until the 1720s. From then on, the pressure to serve the ever-increasing debt by punctual semi-annual interest payments forced it to ensure efficient revenue collection from indirect taxes, and the path toward the dominance of stocks of perpetual annuities at 3 percent became ineluctable.[117]

But why did the mutually reinforcing process between the government's punctual interest payments and increasing confidence in its long-term credit not appear earlier? This question of timing is more perplexing when we consider that the centralized bureaucracy to collect customs was formed in 1672 and the Excise Department in 1683, both prior to the Glorious Revolution. The post-1688 Parliament cannot explain these two institutional innovations. Kiser and Kane attribute them to structural changes made before 1688, such as "the development of efficient communication, transportation, and record-keeping." They argue that these changes increased the monitoring capacity of the royal government in centralizing the collection of indirect taxes.[118] However, these socioeconomic conditions by themselves did not provide the motivation for the government to centralize tax collection by finding effective means to supervise collecting officials. They therefore cannot explain the timing of the emergence of central collection of indirect taxes.

In order to account for the evolution of centralized public finance bureaucracy in Europe, Thomas Ertman highlights the importance of timing of participation in the European geographical struggles. In his view, the necessary condition for the rise of bureaucratic management of public finance is that previous development in education and finance had prepared a pool of competent and well-educated persons from which the state could recruit financial officials. Therefore, countries that entered the geographic struggles prior to the availability of such a pool (e.g., before 1450) had to rely on patrimonial practices, such as "propri-etary officeholders, tax-farmers, and officeholder-financiers" to meet state fiscal needs.[119] Yet the causal effects of timing are not salient in the case of England. As Ertman himself acknowledges, England got involved in European geographical struggles from the 1100s to the 1480s. In the end, he mainly appeals to enhanced parliamentary supervision during the two wars with the Dutch (1665–1666 and 1672–1674) to explain the emergence of centralized bureaucracies in the collection of customs and excises.[120] However, in this period, customs and excises were the crown's ordinary revenue, and Parliament had no power to intervene in their collection and use.[121] In this light, timing may constrain choices but by itself does not necessarily account for the observed outcome.

To explain the final result against the initial indeterminacy and mul-tiple possible outcomes, Jeffrey Haydu suggests that reiterated problem solving may provide the needed causal linkage between events in differ-ent time periods when a common problem forces different actors to come up with solutions.[122] But he does not lay out why and how a prob-lem becomes common to actors with different interests, ideas, and po-litical agendas. Moreover, his examples of the "problems to be solved" include employer-union conflict, labor mobility, and poverty. Different approaches to these general social problems often lead to a wide range of outcomes, rather than converging on a single direction of institu-tional development.

In applying the insights of path dependence, the biggest problem is that its explanatory power is not retrospective to the early stage where the process of change is still open to various possible outcomes. In the study of democratic consolidation, for example, the possible sources of path dependence—institutional density, large setup costs, coordination effects, and adaptive expectations—do not suffice to cause an irreversible path toward consolidation at the beginning of democratic transition. At that point, it is still possible for political actors to actively compete to modify the institutional arrangements to advance their respective interests.[123] In particular, it is unlikely for actors in the initial period of institutional development to implement all the reinforcing elements simultaneously.[124] In this case, an institutional innovation may seem ineffective due to the absence of complementary arrangements. Therefore, the complementary effects that consolidate institutions do not necessarily explain their emergence.

Overcoming an Exogenously Produced Credit Crisis as a Mechanism

How shall we explain the rise of a modern fiscal state in England and Japan but not in China in a process characterized by an initial high degree of uncertainty and a multiplicity of possible outcomes in the process? The three episodes of institutional development at hand share crucial features: (1), the stickiness of existing yet dysfunctional institutions; (2), the collapse of these institutions in big events and the beginning of the search for alternatives; and (3) experimentation with various institutional arrangements under conditions of uncertainty. A possible outcome is one that actually appeared in the process yet did not persist, such as decentralized institutions in England and Japan; or one that could have appeared, such as centralization in China; or one that actors carefully deliberated yet did not implement, such as the conversion of government debts into paper notes in England. To avoid imposing information or knowledge unavailable ex ante to historical actors on their "rational" calculations, I conduct a "deep" comparative historical analysis that reconstructs the goals, constraints, and uncertainties that historical actors actually took into account in their policy making.

The mechanism that I develop to explain the rise of the modern fiscal state results from the conjunction of appropriate socioeconomic conditions and a credit crisis caused by the excessive issue of fiduciary credit instruments such as bills of borrowing unfunded by tax revenue or nonconvertible paper notes. Such a credit crisis originates as an unintended consequence of events or policies and is therefore exogenous to subsequent institution building. No state actors floated these credit instruments with an aim to establish their preferred institutions. However, such eventfully produced credit crises significantly affected institutional development; they changed the course of history and produced the final outcome.[125]

The causal leverage of this eventful approach to institutional development derives from the special nature of the credit crisis. First, it threatened the creditworthiness of the state and constituted a common problem that had to be solved, regardless of which group of political actors came to power. As the central government that issued the credit instruments had to bear all the financial risk of redeeming them, it could no longer pass the burden to local governments. It thus fundamentally changed the risk distribution between the center as the principal and local governments and tax collectors as the "agents." The center now had a strong incentive to break the "lock-in" of decentralized fiscal institutions by figuring out how to better monitor the performance of tax-collecting agents. The credit crisis thus provided the necessary motivation to attain fiscal centralization. Second, the magnitude of the issued credit instruments seriously constrained the options for solution. It excluded the writing off of the debt, for example. Nor could state actors simply use coercion to secure the value of the issued credit instruments in the markets. Redemption of the credit instruments imposed a "hard criterion" to evaluate the effectiveness of the institutional arrangements being considered or experimented with, an opportunity not often seen in the complex and opaque political world.[126]

The attempt to overcome such a credit crisis provides the temporal causal chains to account for the emergence of a modern fiscal state. Actors' efforts to find an institutional solution led to a process of experimentation and continuous accumulation of effective elements. The need to resolve this credit crisis created an opportunity for competent financial officials to play dominant roles in the search for effective institutional arrangements. As state actors grappled with the same credit crisis, they could learn from their own successes and mistakes, as well as from those of their rivals. In this situation, useful institutional arrangements and key personnel with demonstrated expertise were more likely to be preserved, even though they might be legacies of political rivals. The struggle to protect the value of the issued credit instruments thus could lead to a de facto collective learning process among competing political actors and a continuous accumulation of effective institutional elements, methods, and personnel.

With the accumulation of effective institutional blocks and personnel, state actors came to realize a mutually reinforcing relationship between state long-term liabilities and central collection of taxation. That is to say, reliable collection of indirect taxes boosted creditors' confidence in the state's long-term credit instruments; and the pressure to safeguard the creditworthiness of the state forced state actors to maintain and improve the efficiency in central collection. This drove institutional development irreversibly toward the final observed outcome of the modern fiscal state, an end result that few could have anticipated.

Appropriate socioeconomic conditions were indispensable to sustain actors' experimentation and learning until they established the mutually reinforcing effects between centralized tax collection and the creditworthiness of state long-term liabilities. For example, the ability of existing private financial networks to float the heavily discounted credit instruments in the market, whether bills of short-term borrowing or nonconvertible paper notes, is vital. If economic actors refused to hold them, then state actors would have little chance to find the appropriate institutions to resume the value of these credit instruments.

Socioeconomic conditions also significantly affected the efforts of state actors to centralize tax collection and the viability of specific forms of state long-term credit. For instance, centralized collection of indirect taxes on domestic consumption is closely connected with the scale and the degree of concentration of the consumption sectors in the economy. The more concentrated the production and sale of major consumer goods, the less costly for the state to collect centrally as it needs to supervise only a limited number of big producers and wholesalers, usually in urban areas. The state may deliberately encourage the formation of monopolistic wholesalers or producers, with an aim to reducing the cost of tax collection. In so doing, the state basically divides the monopolistic profit with these large-scale producers or wholesalers. In contrast, centralized tax collection is much more difficult to achieve

when major consumer goods are in the hands of numerous small producers or retailers.

This causal account of the rise of the modern fiscal state as a dynamic
process to overcome a crisis of fiduciary credit instruments relies on the
accumulation of effective institutional arrangements and competent
officials in public finance over time. This in turn gradually reduces uncertainty and increases the likelihood of one particular institutional
outcome against the multiplicity of alternatives. It therefore has the ge-
neric character of path dependence, that is, an increasing probability of
one particular outcome resulting from the increasing interconnections
between institutional arrangements and actors' behavioral patterns and
cognitive frameworks through time.[127] The socioeconomic conditions
are the "boundary conditions" of the path-dependent institutional development toward the modern fiscal state.[128]

The conjunction of a severe crisis of fiduciary credit instruments
with particular socioeconomic circumstances determined both the direction and tempo of the observed institutional development in England and Japan. For China, the same mechanism both explains the
institutional development that had actually taken place by the late
nineteenth century and demonstrates the rise of the modern fiscal state
as a real possibility.

In the case of England, the tremendous amount of short-term bills
unfunded by any anticipated income that the government issued between 1665 and 1672 constituted the credit crisis that provided strong
incentives for the royal government to centralize the collection of both
customs and excises. In 1689, the Dutch invasion of England brought
the country into two almost consecutive wars with France, the Nine
Years' War (1688–1697) and the War of the Spanish Succession (1702–
1714), which were unexpectedly expensive and prolonged. The enormous debt created by short-term and unfunded long-term borrowings
after 1714 forced the English government to convert them into long-
term debts reliably funded by its current tax revenue. In this process,
socioeconomic conditions, such as the dominance of London in the English economy and the underdevelopment of domestic financial networks outside the London area, significantly affected the path toward
the modern fiscal state. Instead of turning its debts into banknotes float-

ing in the whole economy, an option explicitly considered in the late 1710s, the English government converted them into low-interest stocks of perpetual annuities.

In the case of Japan, the credit crisis originated from the issue of nonconvertible paper notes to fund the military campaigns to overthrow the shogunate in the Meiji Restoration in 1868. As the new Meiji government had to meet huge spending needs before it could establish taxing institutions, it had no option but to continue its reliance on the de facto nonconvertible paper notes. The Japanese government's decision to adopt the gold standard in 1871 had huge unintended consequences as it greatly exacerbated the problem of note redemption as a result of the steadily increasing value of gold in international markets after 1873. The resulting threat to the central government significantly determined the trajectory and fast tempo toward fiscal centralization, particularly the central collection of indirect taxes on alcohol production by 1880. The vibrant domestic economy created a strong demand for currency; this was vital to support the circulation of nonconvertible paper notes in the economy in this period. Although the direction toward creating a central bank to attain convertibility of paper notes became clear in the early 1880s, the confrontation between the Meiji government and the parliamentary movement made the modern fiscal state emerge in a highly deflationary economy between 1883 and 1886.

The case of China illustrates the consequence of the disjunction of the necessary socioeconomic conditions and the credit crisis. The Qing government issued paper notes in 1853 to meet its military spending in suppressing the Taiping Rebellion, but this destructive and prolonged civil war severely disrupted the domestic economy and interregional financial networks and made government finance more decentralized. These conditions caused the notes to fail. After the civil war in the mid-1860s, the center became unwilling to reintroduce credit instruments in government finance, though the domestic economy and interregional financial networks had recovered and even expanded in the 1870s and 1880s. The absence of a credit crisis involving the center led to the persistence of fiscal decentralization. Nonetheless, the pressure on provincial governments to meet urgent spending orders from the center forced them to search for institutional arrangements, methods, and personnel so as to improve supervision in the collection of lijin duties in the provinces. Could the Qing government have utilized these resources to centralize the collection of lijin had a credit crisis threatened the center? By taking the indemnity to Japan in 1895 as a proxy to such a credit crisis, I use the Qing government's payment as a natural experiment to test the counterfactual argument of the modern fiscal state as a possible outcome in China in the late nineteenth century.

2

ENGLAND'S PATH,
1642–1752

In England's transformation into a modern fiscal state between 1642 and 1752, we can discern a clear sequence in which previous institutional achievements provided a basis for subsequent institutional development. A fiscal state that rested on customs, the monthly assessment (the predecessor of the land tax in 1692), and excises became firmly established after the English Civil Wars. In the Restoration period (1660–1688), the management of the royal government's ordinary revenue became more centralized; the royal government centrally collected customs in 1672 and excises on liquors in 1683. In fighting the Nine Years War and the War of the Spanish Succession, the English government came to depend on long-term borrowing. From the 1720s on, the reliable and elastic receipts from indirect taxes such as excises and customs enabled the English government to make punctual interest payments on its long-term debts, which led to the dominance of stocks of perpetual annuities at 3 percent, the famous system of "3 percent Consol," in 1752.[1]

But this sequence is clear only in hindsight. If instead we move forward from 1642 with the actors through a historical context full of uncertainties, we face multiple possible outcomes. The proto-centralization in public finance that appeared in the 1650s soon collapsed. When the Stuart monarchy was restored in 1660, the degree of fiscal decentralization and government dependence on tax farmers for secure income and short-term credit seemed quite stable. When centralized institutions to collect customs and excises were established by 1683, the state did not seek long-term loans but tried to clear its liabilities. Even when the English government in 1714 was forced to convert the massive short-term debts accumulated in the Nine Years War and the War of the Spanish Succession into long-term liabilities, there were still two different options. One was to turn them into stocks of perpetual annuities with lower interest rates. The other was to let the Bank of England take over the debts in return for a monopoly right to issue banknotes. Why did England move onto the path toward a modern fiscal state based on perpetual debt rather than one on paper notes?

Neither fiscal centralization nor the market-based system of long-term credit was inevitable. Instead, both resulted from the need to overcome two consecutive credit crises arising out of international wars and involving fiduciary credit instruments. The first happened between 1666 and 1672, when the government depended heavily on the Treasury Orders, a credit bill of short-term borrowing unfunded by tax revenue. The other occurred between 1689 and 1713; it included unfunded debts in the form of tallies, exchequer bills, and bills issued by the army and navy to cover their deficits.

These credit crises were unintended consequences of war and thus exogenous to subsequent institutional development. But they significantly affected the direction of institutional development in a context of multiple possibilities and uncertainties. The credit crisis between 1666 and 1672 motivated the crown's financial officials to centralize the management and collection of the crown's ordinary revenue from customs and from excises on alcohol. The efforts to resolve the credit crisis after 1713 forged the institutional linkage between the central collection of indirect taxes and the state's perpetual debts. Socioeconomic conditions, such as the increasing scale of beer production and the geographic distribution of financial networks in England, are important to understand both the efficiency in central collection of excises and why the path toward the modern fiscal state based on paper notes was not taken.

The Path toward Fiscal Centralization

Military spending in the English Civil Wars forced both the royal government and the Long Parliament to seek new means to raise revenue. In 1643, the Long Parliament imposed two new taxes, the excise and the weekly assessment. Excises fell on a large variety of consumer goods, including beer, tobacco, and cider. The weekly assessment was a direct tax imposed on the property and income of each county and town with fixed quotas. In 1646, it became the monthly assessment.[2] In the 1650s, the Commonwealth regime depended on revenue collected from customs, excises, and the monthly assessment.[3]

Central management of government finance also appeared. In 1654, the Council of State in the Protectorate regime ordered customs, excises, and other sources of revenue to be paid directly to the Exchequer.[4] This trend toward fiscal centralization represented "a step toward a truly modern concept of state finance in which revenue would be consolidated and expenditures paid out of the general revenue fund, rather than out of designated revenues."[5] Meanwhile, the Commonwealth regime in the 1650s adopted a system of deficit financing in anticipation of its future tax revenue to support its army and navy. For example, the navy treasurers issued bills of imprest and warrants to the contractors who provided the navy with goods and services. These short-term credit instruments, which could be assigned or sold in the markets, filled the interval between the expenditures and the arrival of tax revenue, after which they were cleared.[6]

The unique position of London in the English economy facilitated government attempts to centralize the collection of taxes. Some 70 to 80 percent of the customs revenue was collected in London. Moreover, London and its surrounding areas were the richest regions in England. Of the £53,436 monthly assessment that Parliament levied on the area under its control in 1645, over two-thirds came from the eastern and home counties.[7] Of the excise revenue collected from 30 September 1647 to 29 September 1650, London contributed 56.7 percent.[8] Centralized tax collection was thus easier to attain when more than half of government income was collected in London and its environs.

However, the underdevelopment of financial networks and small scale of production in England in the 1650s severely constrained institutional development toward long-term borrowing. There were still no nation-wide financial networks to transmit money. Between 1654 and 1659, the vast majority of tax revenue into and government expenditure out of London were still transported in specie rather than by bills of exchange.[9] Payments to the New Model Army were also made in coins, which were sent out from London once a month to regiments scattered in various locations.[10] Transport of a large quantity of specie was difficult and time-consuming. It was therefore more convenient to assign the revenue from places of collection directly to destinations of spending. For example, parts of the excise were collected and disbursed locally rather than being sent to London.[11] The centralization of the monthly assessment began to decline as Cromwell permitted the receivers-general to send collected revenue directly to garrisons or regiments instead of transmitting all the receipts to London.[12]

Socioeconomic conditions at the time also made it difficult for the central government to extract elastic revenues. The boom in England's foreign trade did not come until the second half of the seventeenth century. The customs directly collected by the Commonwealth and Protectorate governments amounted to only 20 percent of the government's total income.[13] As for excises, the original direct collection by salaried officers aroused many antiexcise riots between 1644 and 1649, which forced the parliamentary government to repeal the excises levied on meat and home-brewed beer.[14] Because of the small scale and dispersed distribution in the production of excisable goods in this period, the administrative cost of direct collection of excises was quite high. In order to reduce the administrative cost, the government farmed out collection to local elites, who were much better informed about local circumstances.[15] But they were also less likely to sacrifice local interests for the central benefit.[16] The receipt of excises was affected too by the Protectorate regime's active suppression of alehouses between 1655 and 1657.[17]

The monthly assessment was the principal source of the Protectorate's income, amounting to almost half of its total revenue in 1654.[18] Yet local gentry firmly controlled both assessment and collection.[19] To extract more monthly assessment often incurred strong resistance from land-owners. In June 1657, mounting opposition to the heavy burden of the monthly assessment forced the Protectorate to greatly reduce the monthly rate from £120,000 to £35,000.[20] This caused an annual loss of more than £1 million, which the government was unable to cover from other sources of revenue.

Inadequate taxing ability reduced the credibility of the Protectorate government. After 1652, the City of London refused to lend to it as its past debts had not yet been cleared.[21] In 1658, the City would not even accept the government's anticipated income as security for lending.[22] In the 1650s, contractors to the army and navy were major creditors to the government. The vast majority of the total new debt incurred by the navy between 1651 and 1660 was owed to its victuallers.[23] However, they lacked the resources to provide long-term loans to the government. When the Protectorate was unable to clear its previous short-term debts on time, the navy victuallers would accept only cash payments.[24] The bankrupt Protectorate government quickly collapsed when it did not profit from the war with Spain in 1656, even though its total debt in 1659 was a mere £2.2 million, which "was equivalent to only one year's average revenue, a level of short-term debt comparable to the average debt of the period 1660–1690, and considerably less than that after 1700."[25]

The Stuart monarchy was restored in 1660, and the traditional separation between the crown's ordinary revenue and the extraordinary revenue granted by Parliament was resumed. Nonetheless, England was now a tax state as the crown's ordinary revenues settled with the Cavalier Parliament came from the customs (£400,000), excises on liquors (£300,000), and the hearth tax (£300,000, added in 1662). Although the annual ordinary revenue was set at the level of £1.2 million, they were in arrears because both the government administration and the economy had not yet recovered from the political upheavals and serious depression of 1659 and 1660.[26] In June 1660, the total cash available to the Exchequer was only £141, while the monthly charge of the inherited army and navy was £100,000.[27]

Desperate need for regular income forced the crown to resort to tax farming. In 1662, the government farmed the collection of customs and excises. As in the Stuart period, tax farmers became important suppliers of short-term credit to the crown.[28] Under this fiscal decentralization, particular items of revenue became more important in securing loans than the government's total nominal income. For example, when the City of London lent to the government, the City received payment not from the Exchequer but directly from the collector of specific items of revenue that had been assigned as security.[29]

In 1667, new financiers, particularly the two most powerful gold-smith bankers, Sir Robert Viner and Edward Backwell, became farmers of the customs. They accepted deposits from merchants, gentry, and professionals in both London and the provinces and were thus able to provide better terms to the royal government. Meanwhile, their credit-worthiness in the markets was enhanced by the regular tax revenue at their disposal interest-free prior to its transfer to the government (rang-ing from a quarter to half a year). Their close personal ties with royal officials made their short-term loans to government departments both profitable and secure, which helped them attract more deposits.[30] Major tax farmers utilized both lending to the government and possession of the collected revenue as a liquid asset to strengthen their power in the financial markets. Other financiers thus could hardly offer better terms of lending to the government. As a result, government reliance on tax farming had a strong self-reinforcing tendency.

In order to meet current spending needs, the royal government in this period issued two kinds of short-term credit instruments on its antici-pated income, the tally of *sol* and the tally of *pro*. The former was guar-anteed by a particular source of revenue, but it had low liquidity, as it could not be sold or assigned. The latter could be sold or assigned, but it was not secured by any specifically assigned item of government income, and its redemption at the Exchequer was highly uncertain if the holders of *pro* did not have the right connections.[31] As the royal government did not centrally manage its ordinary revenue, it had to pass the responsibil-ity of redeeming the tallies to treasurers of various government depart-ments. Upon receiving tallies, the treasurers had to either sell them or use them as security to borrow cash from private financiers. The private networks of treasurers in both the government and the financial markets were more important than government institutions in redeeming the tallies.[32]

In 1665, the English government tried to get better terms in the treaty negotiations with Holland; it was totally unprepared for this aggressive strategy to trigger the Second Anglo-Dutch War.[33] Impending war made the credit market in London quite tight. London financiers who lacked confidence in the government's creditworthiness refused to provide fresh credit to the already indebted royal government.[34] In this situation, the English government was forced to adopt the Order system proposed by Sir George Downing, a teller at the Exchequer.[35] The main goal of this proposal was to raise credit directly from the public by issuing a new government credit instrument, the Treasury Order bearing an interest rate of 6 percent. These Treasury Orders were secured on a parliamentary supply of £1.25 million in two years and could be sold or assigned in the markets. Their semiannual payments through the Exchequer were made according to a strict chronological order determined by the date when the subscribers paid their money into the Exchequer. In less than two years, the Order system raised nearly £200,000 from about 900 subscribers.[36]

As the English government could not mobilize the necessary financial resources to fund the Second Anglo-Dutch War, it suffered a humiliating defeat. The defeat itself did not force the government to overhaul its financial institutions. In December 1666, the Commons formed the Commissions of Public Accounts to audit the accounts of extraordinary supplies, which Parliament had granted for the war effort. However, the highly informal way of using Exchequer tallies and the absence of standard bookkeeping in government departments made it extremely difficult to tell fraudulent activities from the normal financial operations.[37] The Commons audit was ineffective and did not lead to fundamental reforms of government finance.[38]

Although the end of the war removed the pressure to increase military spending, the royal government's financial situation was miserable. The financial markets of London in 1667 had not yet recovered from the disruptions of the war, the Great Plague in 1665, and the fire of London in 1666. The average yield of the crown's ordinary revenue fell to £686,000 a year between 1665 and 1667, while the annual deficit stood at some £600,000.[39] The royal government thus could not receive any fresh credit from the markets. Nor could it seek higher advances from tax farmers as their contracts had not expired yet.[40] As peace was resumed, it could not request extraordinary revenues from Parliament. In desperation, Charles II in June 1667 appointed several young officials who had no aristocratic background but did have practical experience in managing financial affairs to form a new Treasury Commission to rescue government finance. These officials included Sir Thomas Clifford,

Sir William Coventry, and Sir John Duncombe. Sir George Downing was appointed treasury secretary.[41]

These treasury commissioners had no other option but to extend Downing's Order system to meet government spending. In contrast to the Orders issued during the war, which were secured by parliamentary extraordinary supplies, the newly issued Orders were safeguarded by the crown's ordinary revenue. Between 1667 and 1670, the amount of the issued Orders stood at a level of some £1.2 million a year.[42] These Orders were fiduciary credit instruments because no lenders' money was actually paid into the Exchequer in advance; and they resembled paper notes as they were issued in small denominations for ordinary transactions in the economy.[43] But unlike paper notes, these Treasury Orders were interest-bearing short-term credit instruments, which had to be redeemed on their due dates (usually a year) at the Exchequer. The amount of fiduciary Treasury Orders thus constituted an urgent credit crisis, which pressured the royal government to find methods to redeem them.

As the Treasury Orders were secured by the crown's ordinary revenue, the treasury commissioners tried hard to centrally manage the collection and spending of the ordinary revenue and to ensure their rapid transmission into the Exchequer. From 1667 on, the treasury commissioners established a meticulous bookkeeping system in government departments, ordered speedy transfer of the collected tax revenue into the Exchequer, and demanded weekly certificates from spending departments to allow for regular checking of accounts.[44] In the course of these institutional reforms, the Treasury became more specialized in managing the finance of the royal government and thus more independent from the Privy Council and the secretaries of state.[45]

Nonetheless, the effectiveness of these important administrative reforms was limited in practice as the Treasury did not have the political authority to control departmental spending so as to generate more fiscal surplus to redeem the issued Orders.[46] Although ordinary revenue increased from less than £650,000 a year in 1665–1667 to £954,000 in 1669–1670, the total government debt rose to nearly £3 million by 1670.[47] On the eve of the Third Anglo-Dutch War (1672–1674), the value of outstanding Orders was more than £1.1 million, and their repayment would have reduced the government's disposable revenue to less than £400,000.[48] In January 1672, the crown announced it would postpone repayment for one year and would pay 6 percent interest.[49] Instead of an intentional default, this Stop of the Exchequer was mainly caused by the government's inability to use its current income to meet both its current spending and the payment of its outstanding short-term debts.[50] However, it was disastrous to the four goldsmith bankers and tax farmers who had bought Orders in the markets at great discount and thus held up to 80 percent of the total outstanding Orders in 1672.[51]

The traditional separation between the ordinary and extraordinary revenues also constrained the efforts of the treasury commissioners to increase the crown's income. Throughout the Restoration period, the Commons controlled as extraordinary revenue both the monthly assessment and any additional income derived from raising the customs duties or the excise rates.[52] Nonetheless, the Commons had no power to oversee the crown's ordinary revenue.[53] The royal government had full discretion on the methods to collect them. As the royal government could not raise government income by broadening its tax base, it had to maximize the receipts from the already settled ordinary revenue of the customs, excises on liquors, and the hearth tax.

The issue of fiduciary Treasury Orders as short-term borrowing bills to some extent reduced the royal government's reliance on tax farmers for short-term credit. And the pressure to redeem them forced the government to extract more revenue from the tax farmers. When the customs farmers tried to get more concessions from the government during contract renewal negotiations in 1670, the treasury commissioners decided to directly collect customs. A board of six commissioners, which included Sir George Downing, was appointed to manage the new centralized collection. This system inherited the whole framework of local administration and personnel, along with the manuals of instruction that the farmers of customs had established. From 1678 onward, the surveyors-general (later the commissioners themselves) periodically inspected the collection in major ports.[54]

Direct collection of excises on liquors all over England was a formidable task. The excise farm in 1662 was very dispersed, as about 75 percent of the country farms went to local gentry in various regions.[55] In order to reduce the transaction costs of negotiating with tax farmers and to obtain better terms, the treasury commissioners encouraged a few major financiers to farm the collection of excises. Big financiers were also interested in possessing more excise revenue. From 1668 on, the government supported the plan of the goldsmith banker William Bucknall and his associates, who had farmed the London excises, to take over the farm of country excises, which had been previously controlled by local elites. By 1671, the Bucknall group controlled nearly 75 percent of the entire excise in England.[56]

In 1672, the Stop of the Exchequer discredited the issue of fiduciary Treasury Orders. The royal government had to use its real income to secure new sources of credit, particularly under pressure of the Third Anglo-Dutch War. As it was difficult for the royal government to get extraordinary parliamentary supplies when the Commons opposed the foreign policy of Charles II, the idea of a total excise farm became very appealing. For the government, a syndicate of financiers who held the new post of receiver-general of a single excise farm could use the aggregated excise revenue to mobilize more credit for the government. For the financiers, control of the total excise revenue would make them more powerful in the financial markets, especially when collectors were required to send their daily receipts to the receiver-general.[57]

Although private financiers were often associated with different political patrons, they shared the same plan of using total excise revenue to raise credit for the government. Their competition for the position of the receiver-general of the excise farm simply gave the government better terms of rent and advance money in negotiating contracts.[58] Fierce power struggles within the government, including the fall of Clifford as the chief treasury commissioner and the rise of Danby as the lord treasurer in 1673, did not hinder the development toward a single excise farm.

The syndicate managing a single excise farm had to confront a serious information asymmetry problem with employees who served as "agents" in collecting excises. Edgar Kiser has argued that the motivation for profit maximization pushed the tax farmer as the principal to develop effective organizational methods to monitor the performance of their collecting agents.[59] However, the same concern for maximum profit can lead to three contractual relationships between the principal and the agent under different distributions of risks. When the principal is more risk-averse than the agent, he gives a rental contract to the agent, which is equivalent to the subfarming of a single excise farm. When the agent is more risk-averse, a share contract is optimal. When the principal bears all the risk, a pure wage contract prevails. In order to understand the emergence of bureaucratic management of waged collectors in the excise administration, we need to analyze the risk that the syndicate of excise farmers had to bear.

The syndicate of excise farming was an important source of short-term loans to the royal government. The control of regular excise revenue as liquid capital enhanced excise farmers' ability to mobilize financial resources in the markets to lend to the crown. This was the financial risk. Politically, in order to secure the royal government's favor and protection, these farmers had to be able to provide short-term credit whenever the government demanded. Because the syndicate of excise farming as the principal bore the full financial and political risks, it was motivated to adopt a wage contract with its collecting agents and to centrally manage excise collection.[60]

As the syndicate of excise farmers profited from using the total excise revenue to mobilize credit in lending to the government, they did not resist the Treasury's request in 1674 to send deputy comptrollers to check the account books and vouchers in the country areas and to "issue an independent quarterly report of all excise receipts" to the comptroller. This allowed the government for the first time to know the "precise annual value" of the excise in England and inspired the Treasury to replace excise farming with direct collection.[61] When government direct collection of excises began in 1683, the Treasury took over the entire organization that the syndicate of excise farmers had established. Former excise farmers and goldsmith bankers managed the Excise Department and continued to use the excise revenue as security to raise credit for the royal government.[62]

In order to improve the management of collection, the Excise Department between 1683 and 1688 endeavored to standardize methods of gauging, assessing, and bookkeeping in the 886 districts or divisions of excise collection in England.[63] Standardization in excise assessment and collection was an important means to overcome the information asymmetry problem between the principal and agents so that central collection could be more efficient. First, it facilitated the supervision and evaluation of excise officers by their superiors, who regularly circuited to inspect local collection. Second, excise officers could be rotated to different collecting positions on a regular basis, which not only prevented them from colluding with local interests but also effectively disciplined them by mutual checks of collection accounts.

Economic conditions in the 1670s and 1680s were favorable to the institutional development toward central collection of the customs and excises. Yields of directly collected customs grew with the expansion of England's foreign trade. The average annual net yield of the customs rose from the highest rent of £400,000 in the farming contract of 1670 to £570,000 in 1681–1684 and £590,000 in 1685–1687.[64] Meanwhile, rising real wages and declining grain and malt prices resulting from good harvests stimulated domestic consumption, particularly of beer and ale, the main daily beverages at the time. This facilitated the development of large-scale common brewers, especially in economically advanced eastern and southern England.[65] The government also encouraged large-scale brewers by giving them favorable allowances of waste and leakage.[66] Large-scale brewers reduced the government cost in collecting excises as they could not easily evade inspection. They were also more resourceful than small brewers at bearing high excise rates. As a result, the receipts of excises on liquors were as high as £620,000 per year between 1686 and 1688.[67]

When the crown and the Cavalier Parliament reached agreement over the settlement of the crown's ordinary revenue in 1660–1662, no one could have anticipated how productive the central collection of excises on liquor would be twenty years later. When Parliament added the hearth tax into the crown's ordinary revenue, the estimated yields of the hearth tax ranged from £300,000 to £1 million, higher than that of the excises.[68] However, central collection of the hearth tax turned out to be a mission impossible. The political and administrative costs of searching individual households were simply too high. The hearth tax was inelastic even when the economy was growing, and by 1688 its net annual yield had reached only £216,000.[69]

The central collection of customs and excises significantly changed the power relationship between the crown and Parliament. Although the Commons firmly controlled the grant of the monthly assessment and additional excises as parliamentary extraordinary revenue, the crown no longer had to ask for these. Between 1685 and 1688, the average annual income of the crown's ordinary revenue rose to about £1.6 million.[70] It enabled James II to afford to maintain a standing army of some 20,000 soldiers, which was the average size of a standing army in contemporary Europe. Neither Parliament nor domestic opponents could challenge him.[71] As the growing government income mainly came from indirect customs and excises, it did not generate direct conflicts of interest between the crown and landowners.

Nevertheless, there was no indication of development toward an institution of long-term borrowing before 1688. The receivers-general of the customs and excises acted both as the official receivers and cashiers of government tax revenue and as private financiers in the financial markets. They used their respective revenue as security to raise short-term loans from the markets and re-lent to the government. Instead of seeking permanent liabilities, the royal government in this period tried to clear its previous debts.[72] The traditional idea that a good kingship should be free from debt remained intact.

Credit Crisis and the Rise of a Modern Fiscal State

The Dutch invasion of England in November 1688 was crucially important to the Glorious Revolution. As Jonathan Israel has emphasized, it was determined largely by Dutch strategic calculation in fighting with Catholic France rather than by the domestic opponents of James II in England.[73] When the Dutch brought England into its conflict with France in 1689, no Englishman could have anticipated that it was the beginning of two decades of almost continuous and extremely expensive wars, the Nine Years War and the War of the Spanish Succession. The mounting military spending, heavy taxation, and economic recessions during the Nine Years War led to severe confrontation between the royal government and Parliament.

As members of Parliament could not determine the making of foreign policy, which was the prerogative of the crown, they tried hard to control public finance. In order to ensure the regular presence of Parliament in national politics, the Convention Parliament in 1690 deliberately voted William III and Mary an inadequate ordinary revenue and also granted the customs, which had been the crown's permanent income since Henry VI (1421–1471), for only four years.[74] The Commons in

1690 established the Commissions of Public Accounts to check the expenditures of major government departments, such as the army and navy, several times, between 1691 and 1697, 1702 and 1704, and 1711 and 1713. The Triennial Act passed in 1694 for the first time guaranteed regular convention of Parliament.

More important, Parliament in 1698 passed the Civil List Act to abolish the century-old separation between the crown's ordinary revenue and the parliamentary extraordinary revenue, which was the last vestige of the domain state. From now on, the three pillars of government income (the land tax, the customs, and excises) became regular parliamentary supplies, and Parliament allocated a lump sum of Civil List (£700,000 a year) to cover the costs of the royal household and the peacetime operations of the royal government.[75] However, the fact that the parliamentary taxes had become permanent in 1698 did not imply that they would be used to sustain the state's perpetual debt.

In regard to the parliamentary supervision of public finance, the biggest obstacle was an absence of standardized and unitary bookkeeping in government departments, particularly in the army and navy, the two biggest spenders. According to the reports of the committee appointed by the Commons in 1695 to investigate the financial management of the army, the regimental accounts were in "endless confusion," which prevented any kind of reasonable estimate of total accounts. The paymaster of the army between 1688 and 1702, the Earl of Ranelagh, kept his accounts "extremely general and vague," not even listing the dates and itemization of particular warrants.[76] In the case of the navy, the Treasury and the Commons received only a very general estimate of its annual expenditures, and did not have access to information regarding specific items of spending. The navy could issue its own navy bills to cover deficits in its current spending before being approved by the Treasury or Parliament.[77] In this situation, parliamentary inquiries into government accounts soon lost their significance.[78]

Parliament after 1688 did not immediately encourage a longer time horizon among creditors in lending to the English government. The Dutch financial experts who came to England with William III's army did not introduce new financial methods to raise long-term credit. The Bank of Amsterdam at the time was mainly a clearing house for trading merchants, and it did not lend directly to the Dutch government. As in

England, the Dutch government depended on receivers-general of various tax revenue for short-term credits.[79] The English government continued to appeal to short-term loans to meet the needed military expenditures when it entered the war in 1689. It issued Exchequer tallies in anticipation of future tax revenue, which were similar to the Treasury Orders issued in 1665, as they were assignable but could be redeemed only at the Exchequer. However, the mounting war expenditures forced the English government to issue fiduciary tallies in 1690 that were not backed by any received loans or specifically assigned revenue.[80] From 1688 to 1693, the total amount of short-term borrowing bearing interest rates of 7 to 8 percent rose to £15 million; this included many bills issued by the Navy, Ordnance, and Victualling Board, which were not secured by any preassigned tax revenue.[81] These short-term credit instruments were heavily discounted in the markets in 1693–1694.

This urgency forced the English government in 1693 to seek long-term credits. The English government tried three methods to raise long-term credit from the public: the tontine, the lottery, and single-life annuities.[82] Despite high interest rates (ranging from 6 percent to 14 percent) and the security of loans on parliamentary taxes, the government could raise only £1.3 million between 1693 and 1697.[83] In addition to direct borrowing from the public, the English government also arranged long-term loans from corporations that received monopolies in overseas trade or banknote issue. These loans were redeemable as the government could repeal the charter by returning the principal of the loan. In this way, the government raised £2 million from the New East India Company in 1698.[84]

Lending from the newly chartered Bank of England in 1694 represented an important monetary experiment with paper notes. Between 1691 and 1693, the English government received at least three proposals to issue bills as legal tender, including the one from the early promoters of the Bank of England. Yet Parliament found the idea too risky.[85] Now it granted the Bank of England a charter as a note-issuing corporation in return for a long-term loan of £1.2 million at 8 percent, which was made in banknotes issued by the Bank. Four-fifths of the Bank's initial capital stock consisted of the government's outstanding tallies, which were discounted in the markets at over 30 percent at the time. Government short-term tallies were thus converted into banknotes. As the Bank of England was a fractional note-issuing bank, the pressure to maintain the convertibility of issued banknotes was smaller than that to ensure the redemption of all outstanding tallies. Nonetheless, the English government's initial experiment with paper notes was tentative. It did not give the Bank the exclusive right to issue banknotes, let alone make them the legal tender.[86] Meanwhile, the credibility of the banknotes in the early years of the Bank was also poor due to the Bank's low ratio of cash reserves. In 1697, the Bank had to temporarily suspend the convertibility of its banknotes.[87]

The Bank of England's issue of banknotes on the face value of heavily discounted government tallies aroused much suspicion and even hostility in both Parliament and the royal government. In 1696, the "country party" consisting of both moderate Whigs and Tories dominated Parliament. They attempted to charter a national Land Bank to provide long-term loans to the government, with banknotes backed by specie and the tangible wealth of land. But the market was glutted with the heavily discounted tallies, and the recoinage in 1696–1697 caused a severe scarcity of cash in England.[88] Because the proposed Land Bank required cash instead of heavily discounted tallies to subscribe the stocks, this plan could not even get started. The failure of the Land Bank prompted the government to issue its own paper credit, the interest-bearing Exchequer bills. The government sought cooperation from provincial bankers to spread their use in areas outside London. To facilitate their circulation, the Exchequer bills were issued in small denominations (£10 and £5). In order to stabilize their value, the government in 1697 set the limit of outstanding Exchequer bills at no more than £2 million.[89]

The low credibility of the English government's long-term borrowing between 1693 and 1697 was largely due to its inability to extract adequate tax revenue to service its rapidly rising debt. Parliament granted various levies of direct taxes on both real and personal property, such as the monthly assessment, the poll tax, and even duties on marriages, births, burials, houses, and hawkers. Due to the administrative and political difficulties in assessment and collection, Parliament gave up the effort to extract revenue from personal income, and the levy of direct tax in the 1690s fell on the assessed landed property in both country and town.[90] Although Parliament rejected the scheme of general excises, it raised extra rates on existing excises and added new items into the list of excises, including seaborne coals, salt, and spices. Nonetheless, severe economic recessions, disruptions of foreign trade, and the cash scarcity caused by the recoinage in 1696 greatly reduced the receipts from both excises and the customs.[91] Mismanagement by the new excise commissioners that William III put onto the Excise Board and political purges of excise officers further reduced the efficiency of excise collection.[92]

When the Nine Years War ended in 1697, the English government had £12.2 million in unfunded short-term liabilities and £5.1 million in funded long-term borrowings.[93] This was an enormous debt for a government whose annual total income was around £4 to £5 million in the 1700s. Unlike the Protectorate regime, which collapsed under a total debt of about £2.2 million in 1659, the English government in the 1690s could seek help from powerful financiers to settle its debts. The rapid development of the stock market in London between the 1680s and 1690s had created a dense social network in which a large number of investors exchanged information and knowledge on how to benefit from the innovations in private joint-stock companies and the English government's debts.[94] Moreover, religious tolerance after the Glorious Revolution attracted Protestant refugees who brought to England not only their wealth but also financial innovations in long-term borrowing and international financial networks.[95] Dissenters and nonconformists were vital to joint-stock companies, such as the Bank of England and the New East India Company, both as directors and investors.[96] These powerful joint-stock companies replaced the receivers-general of the customs or excises in providing credit to the government.

In this situation, the government was increasingly concerned about how to extract more revenue to service its debt. In the collection of excises, the Treasury after 1697 worked hard to improve efficiency and strengthen the centralized management of the Excise Department.[97] From the 1700s on, it became normal practice for excise officers to remit the collected revenue by secure and speedy bills of exchange to private bankers in London.[98] Nevertheless, the path toward long-term borrowing was by no means irreversible in 1697.

Among the joint-stock companies, the East India Company provided long-term credit to the government in return for a monopoly on trade with the Far East. Once it received the charter, it did not need to accept extra risks by taking over the government's unfunded short-term debt.

Fluctuations in overseas trade also limited its ability to expand long-term lending to the government. In comparison, the Bank of England had more potential to convert government short-term debt into long-term liabilities. In 1697, Parliament renewed the Bank's charter to 1719 and guaranteed it as the only note-issuing bank authorized by Parliament. In return for this privilege, the Bank added £1,001,171 into its capital stock, of which four-fifths came from government tallies at their face value (even though they were discounted at 40 percent in the markets), and the rest came from the Bank's own banknotes.[99] In the same year, Daniel Defoe suggested that the Bank increase its capital to £5 million, issue banknotes worth £10 million, and establish branches in every town in England so as to remit money to and from London.[100] In this scheme, the Bank would become a real Bank of England rather than the "Bank of London," which concentrated all its business in metropolitan London. If Parliament made its banknotes the legal tender, the Bank could greatly increase their issue.

However, the Bank in the late 1690s remained a private "investment trust," which profited mainly from lending to the government. Parliament did not offer the status of legal tender to its banknotes, which had to compete with the banknotes issued by other private financiers and the government's Exchequer bills in the markets. This restricted the ability of the Bank to accept more of the government's outstanding tallies. Although the Bank was well known as a Whig-dominated institution, it refused in 1697 a request by Montagu, the chancellor of Exchequer and a major Whig in the government, to hold another £10 million in government tallies unsecured by government revenue as its capital stock.[101] Business calculation outweighed political alliance.

Meanwhile, politics compounded the issue of government debt. When war halted in 1697, the "country party," which consisted of both the Tories and the "country Whigs," was dismayed at both corruption and mismanagement in the government's war finance.[102] These landowners were also resentful of economic recession, high interest rates, and heavy taxes on landed property. In their eyes, government borrowing was simply a transfer of the landed wealth to a small group of financiers. They were hostile toward permanent government debt, and they preferred it to be cleared.[103] Between 1697 and 1701, the Commons passed a series of acts to cut down the scale of the standing army and expenditures and reduce the influence of government financial officials in parliamentary debates.[104] In 1698, the English government had £12.2 million of unfunded short-term borrowings and £5.1 million funded long-term debts.[105] As both the domestic economy and foreign trade recovered, the net tax revenue of the government rose to more than £4 million while government expenditures were cut to £3 million in 1700. In 1701, the amount of unfunded short-term and funded long-term debt was reduced to £9.4 million and £4.7 million, respectively.[106] The shrinking scale of government debt at the end of the seventeenth century made the clearance of the principal at least possible.

However, the sudden death of Carlos II, the king of Spain, rekindled hostilities and led to the outbreak of the War of the Spanish Succession in 1702.[107] When this war ended in 1713, the situation of government debt was completely changed. The total debt of the English government had risen to £48 million, and annual interest payments consumed more than half of the annual government expenditures.[108] At this juncture, the

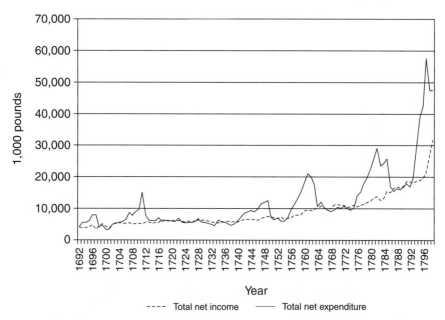

Figure 2.1 Total net income and expenditure of the English government, 1692–1799.
Source: B. R. Mitchell, *Abstract of British Historical Statistics* (Cambridge: Cambridge University Press, 1962), 386–391.

direction of problem solving became clear to the government; it determined to convert the remaining short-term unfunded debt into long-term liabilities with lower interest rates. Despite deep divergence over foreign and religious polices, both the Tory and Whig ministries came to rely more on the indirect customs and excises than on the direct land taxes to raise government income.[109] The pressure to extract reliable indirect revenue to service government long-term debts motivated the English government to improve efficiency in collecting excises, which turned the Excise Department into a neutral administrative department after 1717.[110]

Even though the direction toward perpetual liabilities sustained by indirect taxes became irreversible after 1713, there still remained two distinct paths forward. One was to convert debt into perpetual annuities with lower interest rates, on which the government needed only to make interest payments. The other was to transform the debt into paper notes used in the economy. Prior to 1713, the English government had experimented with both these methods of raising long-term credit.

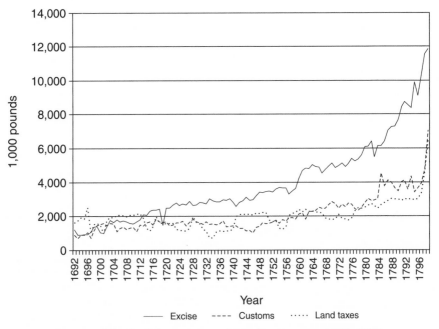

Figure 2.2 Sources of the English government's total net income, 1692–1799.

Source: B. R. Mitchell, *Abstract of British Historical Statistics* (Cambridge: Cambridge University Press, 1962), 386–388.

During the War of the Spanish Succession, the position of the Bank of England in public finance underwent significant changes. It became the major short-term lender to the government by taking government tallies as securities.[111] In return for this, Parliament granted it the privilege to become the only note-issuing corporation with more than six partners.[112] In 1707, the Bank began to underwrite Exchequer bills issued by the Treasury, which not only removed one major rival to its banknotes but also consolidated its importance to the government's short-term finance.[113] As the vast majority of its capital stock came from Exchequer tallies or bills, the government's punctual clearing of these outstanding tallies and bills was vital for the Bank to secure the credibility of its banknotes. Therefore, the Bank had little interest in holding short-term bills that were not secured by preassigned taxes, such as the Navy, Ordnance, and Victualling bills.

In this situation, the Tory government in 1711 chartered the South Sea Company to convert some £9.5 million in outstanding Navy, Ordnance, and Victualling bills at their nominal value into redeemable long-term annuities at 6 percent. The South Sea Company could use the annuities as security to raise capital by issuing stocks that could be freely transferred in the securities market. In return for this, Parliament granted the company a monopoly of trade with the Spanish Empire.[114] As Larry Neal has emphasized, the South Sea Company represented an important method to settle unfunded government debt. Even though the South Sea Company did not have any profitable overseas trade, its stockholders could always benefit from both the annuity payments by the government and the liquidity of company stocks. The poor performance of the South Sea Company after its founding was mainly due to government inability to make punctual annuity payments to stockholders of the Company. As the government's fiscal condition improved after the end of war in 1713, the stock of the South Sea Company gradually reached its par value in 1716.[115]

In 1717, the English government invited the South Sea Company and the Bank of England to bid for the right to take over the remaining £31 million of both irredeemable and redeemable annuities. The South Sea Company would convert these into perpetual annuities. The Bank would incorporate them into its stocks and increase its issue of banknotes accordingly. These two corporations thus represented different paths toward the modern fiscal state, one of perpetual debt and one of paper notes. However, their terms and time span to take over the remaining government debts varied greatly. The Bank could pay the government a maximum of only £5.4 million for this right while the South Sea Company offered £7.6 million. The Bank proposed twenty-five years to assume the government debt by using the nominal value of its stocks in exchange for the assets of government creditors.[116] In contrast, the South Sea Company planned to use the high prices of its stocks in the markets to convert the same amount of government debt within five years.[117] The scheme of the South Sea Company was certainly more attractive. At this time, the English government had demonstrated its ability to reliably collect indirect revenue, so it would be profitable to take over government debts. The Bank perhaps had more favor within the government due to its crucial financial services during wartime. But why did the Bank not offer better terms?

The issue of banknotes was the most important business for the Bank of England at the time, and the amount of its issuance grew from £1.5 million in 1700 to £4 million in 1750. If the Bank of England was to engraft the £31 million of government debt into its capital stock within five years, it would have to enormously increase the issue of its banknotes. In the same period, the amount of coin in the English economy rose from £7 million to £18 million.[118] The monetary stock in England was estimated to be around £14.5 million in 1700 and £30 million in 1750. This means that there was a huge potential for the Bank to increase the issuance of banknotes if they could circulate in the whole English economy instead of only in metropolitan London.

However, the Bank in 1719 had not opened any branches outside London. Major goldsmith bankers did not have large deposits in the Bank of England.[119] As goldsmith banks were not corporations, they could legally issue their own banknotes. Also, the Bank of England had not yet monopolized the transmission of tax revenue and official funds. Even the paymaster general of the Land Forces and the navy treasurer did not put their funds in the Bank of England.[120] Although the Bank had expressed interest in taking over the remittance of tax revenue, it did not succeed due to the resistance of private bankers.[121] As the Bank was not yet a public one that monopolized the remittance of tax revenue and issued banknotes as the legal tender, it could not greatly expand its issuance of banknotes in the short run for the purpose of taking over the remaining government debts.

In contrast, the South Sea Company could simply issue more corporation stocks to exchange the existing irredeemable annuities; the latter had very low liquidity, and the procedures for transferring and cashing them at the Exchequer were slow and cumbersome. When converted into the stocks of the South Sea Company, they could be traded freely in the securities market.[122] Thus the holders of irredeemable annuities had the incentive to voluntarily exchange these assets for stocks even at lower interest rates, for they could benefit from the government's punctual interest payments and the liquidity of the stocks. The South Sea Company could have taken a gradual approach to convert government debt if it was to exchange the irredeemable annuities with the face value of its stocks. However, the company offered to use the market prices of its stocks to do so, which provided the government a method to quickly settle its remaining debts.

In the infamous South Sea Bubble in 1720, the spiraling value of the stocks of the South Sea Company in the markets enticed the holders of irredeemable annuities to exchange their assets for the stocks within months.[123] When the bubble burst in the same year, 80 percent of the irredeemable annuities and 85 percent of the redeemable annuities had been converted into stocks of the South Sea Company. These were turned into perpetual annuities at 3 percent in 1727.[124] For the remaining redeemable annuities with high interest, when the interest rates were low in the markets, the English government could force their holders to accept lower interest rates by a credible threat of repaying the principal of debt.

As the English government had demonstrated its ability to reliably collect indirect revenue from customs and excises and to make punctual interest payments to its annuitants, the stocks of redeemable annuities became a safe investment for small investors. Their low interest rate was compensated for by their remarkable security and liquidity in the markets.[125] From the 1720s on, England moved irreversibly toward the modern fiscal state of perpetual credits. Demonstrated punctual interest payments attracted more subscribers of perpetual annuities, which motivated the government to maintain efficiency in collecting indirect taxes. The modern fiscal state emerged in the 1720s was consolidated by 1752, when the English government shifted its long-term debt into the "3 percent Consol," the redeemable perpetual annuities bearing an annual interest rate of 3 percent.

The distributional effects of these newly emerged institutions of the modern fiscal state significantly contributed to their stability. The reliance on the customs and excises greatly mitigated the tensions between government and the landed class.[126] The Whig ministry could afford to reduce the land tax as a political strategy to appease the Tories. The management of the land tax declined considerably after the 1720s, which led to widespread underassessment and evasion.[127] In comparison, ordinary consumers fell victim to the collective action problem and were unable to resist the rising excises.[128] The low interest rate on the government's long-term borrowing also reduced the conflicts of interest between the moneyed class and landowners. This distributional effect also explains why the efficiency of the Excise Department was an exception rather than the norm in eighteenth-century England. In an oligarchic regime, as long as the government had adequate revenue to securely service its growing debt, neither Parliament nor the royal government had the motivation to clean up corruption so as to further improve overall efficiency in public finance. The collection of the customs, for example, was damaged by patronage politics, sinecures, and the ensuing mismanagement.[129]

Socioeconomic conditions in the first half of the eighteenth century were favorable to the English government's experimentation with various means of long-term credit. In contrast to the economic recession, bad harvests, scarcity of coins, and disruption of foreign trade in the 1690s, the wars of the Spanish and Austrian successions did not disrupt England's foreign trade with the Americas, even though they greatly raised the level of government debt. England's foreign trade expanded steadily after the 1700s. In particular, the reexport of goods from North America and India to European markets via England began to grow rapidly and accounted for 40 percent of total exports by the 1750s. Rising volumes of foreign trade in this period contributed significantly to the rise of the customs revenue, even though the collection of the customs remained inefficient and poorly managed.

The steady expansion of the domestic economy made it able to bear the increasing excise rates on major consumer goods, particularly beer and ale, which contributed a quarter of the total excise revenue in the first half of the eighteenth century. In the collection of excises, the scale of and concentration in the production of excisable goods significantly affected efficiency of collection. The size of common brewers of beer in London had been growing since the late seventeenth century. In the 1720s, technological innovations in beer brewing led to the development of mass production and distribution of beer in London and the larger provincial towns.[130] As small brewers were driven out of the market and the big common brewers increasingly controlled retail outlets, it became much easier to collect the excises on beer.[131] High excise rates and allowances favorable to big producers thus constituted a high barrier of entry into the brewing industry. In other words, the government and big beer brewers divided the monopolistic rent in the production and distribution of beer at the cost of ordinary consumers.

In comparison, excise officers found it hard to collect excises from small and scattered producers. For example, because of the dispersed nature of malting, higher malt duties turned out to be counterproductive as excise officers were unable to overcome the ensuing evasion.[132] For the same reason, the efficiency of excise collection in the provinces was noticeably lower than that in metropolitan London.[133] Likewise, excise officers found it difficult to extract excises from gin consumption as there were millions of distilleries. As a result of widespread evasion and smuggling, duty was paid on only 44 percent of the estimated 14 million gallons of gin consumed in England in 1736.[134]

The dominance of London in England's inland and foreign trade and in the financial markets significantly shaped England's path toward the modern fiscal state. There was a segment of wealthy financiers and investors in London who had enough resources to take enormous amounts of the heavily discounted government short-term bills for future speculative profits between the 1690s and 1710s. These factors provided the necessary time to experiment with various schemes to convert short-term borrowings into long-term debt. As the domestic financial market in the first half of eighteenth-century England was not fully integrated, the tremendous government borrowing in this period did not attract investors from the whole country.[135] Instead, some 90 percent of the

60,000 subscribers to the English government's stock of long-term an-nuities in the 1750s lived in London and the southeast.[136] The financial markets in London had also been integrated with major financial mar-kets in Western Europe (particularly Amsterdam) in the early eighteenth century.[137] As a result, the percentage of foreign holdings of the English government's long-term borrowing rose from 10 percent in 1723–1724 to 20 percent by 1750.[138]

The position of London greatly facilitated the English government's endeavors to achieve central collection of indirect taxes. This was appar-ent in the collection of the customs as more than half of England's for-eign trade went through London in the eighteenth century. In the collec-tion of excises, some 80 percent were collected in either London or its neighboring counties and cities, such as Hertford, Surrey, Bristol, Roches-ter, Suffolk, and Norwich. In contrast, the North, the Midlands, and Wales contributed only 20 percent.[139] London was thus heavily regulated by the Excise Department, and about 18 percent of all excise field offi-cers worked in London in the late eighteenth century.[140]

Historical events and socioeconomic circumstances jointly shaped England's path toward the modern fiscal state between 1642 and 1752. In the 1650s, the dispersed small scale in the production of consumer goods made it hard to attain central collection of excises. The underde-velopment of financial markets made it impossible for the Protectorate government to float long-term credits. But even when socioeconomic conditions were suitable, actors in historical contexts did not automati-cally initiate institutional development toward central tax collection and long-term credits.

Although decentralization and dependence on tax farmers after 1660 appeared mutually reinforcing, events intervened. The Second Anglo-Dutch War forced the financially exhausted royal government to issue massive numbers of fiduciary Treasury Orders to meet its postwar spend-ing needs. Despite its involvement in international power struggles after 1688, the financially shaky English government at the turn of the eigh-teenth century was unwilling to start another major conflict with France. However, the death of the Spanish king meant that England fought two consecutive expensive wars between 1688 and 1713. The astronomical amount of unfunded short-term debt and high-interest long-term loans resulting from these wars meant that their conversion into long-term liabilities so as to reduce government annual interest payments was the only viable option. In both credit crises, the redemption of the issued credit instruments demanded specific institutional arrangements that excluded otherwise possible alternative outcomes, including fiscal decentralization, tax farming, and a dependence on short-term credit. Had such a credit crisis not occurred, the adoption of one of these alternatives might well have "locked-in" historical actors. Finally, as the credit crises threatened the creditworthiness of the state, they constituted a common problem that had to be solved, no matter which political group came to power. The emerging modern fiscal state after 1720 was further consolidated by the mutually reinforcing process between central collection of indirect taxes and the securing of the creditworthiness of the state's perpetual debts.

3

THE RAPID CENTRALIZATION OF
PUBLIC FINANCE IN JAPAN,
1868–1880

By the early 1890s, the Japanese government had built centralized institutions to collect indirect taxes on alcohol and manage government finance. This institutional development helped the Japanese government safeguard the convertibility of the banknotes issued by the Bank of Japan and raise long-term domestic loans. These institutions of a modern fiscal state contrast sharply with the fiscal decentralization and low creditworthiness of paper notes only two decades earlier. How shall we account for this achievement?

The historian Banno Junji characterizes the political development after the Meiji Restoration as a trial-and-error process with multiple possible outcomes.[1] Indeed, the forced opening of Japan in 1858 created a widespread sense of crisis among political actors, and they shared the common aim of protecting the country's sovereignty and independence. In response to Western threats, both the shogunate and major domains such as Satsuma and Chōshū in the 1860s realized the importance of a "rich state and strong army" *(fukoku kyōhei)*.[2] They implemented similar modernization policies, such as introducing Western weapons and technology, reforming military organizations, and sending officials and students to study in Western countries.[3] This has led some historians to claim that a different result in the civil war between the shogunate and Satsuma-Chōshū, which led to the Meiji Restoration, would not have mattered; whoever won would continue to modernize and learn from the West.[4] In this view, uncertainty in institutional development in early Meiji would not be a severe problem because of the consensus among Meiji leaders to learn from the West. Their experimentation with Western models of public finance could gradually reduce the degree of uncertainty and build a modern fiscal state.

However, such characterizations make it hard to understand why Satsuma and Chōshū decided to use force to overthrow the shogunate. Before civil war broke out in 1868, many political actors in Japan were deeply worried about the Western interference that might be incurred by armed conflict between the shogunate and Satsuma-Chōshū. If both sides shared the same modernization program and attitude toward the West, why could they not settle their differences in nonviolent ways? Recent historiography casts new light on these questions by stressing the fundamental divergence in ideas and institutional designs among three major political camps in the 1860s: the Imperial Camp, the shogunate, and the Camp of Public Discussion *(kōgi seitaiha),* consisting of major domains such as Tosa and Echizen. The shogunate and the Camp of Public Discussion came to agree on the importance of building a parliamentary system in Japan, though they had some differences on the design of such a representative institution. In contrast, conservatives at the court and in Satsuma and Chōshū favored restoring an imperial political system. Such fundamental differences forced Satsuma and Chōshū to take up arms to topple shogunate so as to prevent it from forging a political alliance with the Camp of the Public Discussion.

The overthrow of the shogunate by force in 1868, however, did not produce one dominant political group or coalition to determine future institutional development in Meiji Japan. Power struggles continued not only between the Satsuma and Chōshū factions, which dominated the central government after 1868, but also between them and a group that demanded representative institutions to guarantee more "public discussion" *(kōgi)* in policy making. Even among Westernizing officials, severe disagreements over the priorities and speed of transplanting Western models into Japan's different socioeconomic circumstances existed. Thus, the Meiji regime was by no means a coherent political entity that had a consensus over the direction of institutional development.

In public finance, to learn from the West does not entail a single direction of institutional development. As Meiji statesmen were aware, there were quite different models in the West, including the decentralized national banking system in the United States and the centralized Bank of England model in Britain. In addition, major financial officials such as Ōkuma Shigenobu, Inoue Kaoru, Itō Hirobumi, and Shibusawa Eiichi looked to Japan's past for lessons in public finance.[5] Yuri Kimimasa and Ōkuma Shigenobu, who were in charge of financial affairs in early Meiji, had served as "fiscal experts" in their respective domain governments. The mercantilist *(kokueki)* economic policies that various domain governments had implemented to organize business monopolies to control the production and sale of major commodities in the late Tokugawa period provided an important legacy for the early Meiji government, especially in its efforts to float paper notes.[6] However, these policies had resulted in inefficiency and government deficits in some domains; and their critics in the late Tokugawa period had called for bringing more business competition and private initiative into production and commerce.[7] It also remained uncertain whether these policies would work on a national level. Heterogeneous Western experiences and Japan's complex historical legacies thus were not sufficient to dispel the uncertainty in institutional development in public finance.

Opacity in the early Meiji yielded multiple possible outcomes, which included a quasi-federal system; a gradual approach to abolishing the domains and centralization; and a rapid centralization. To legitimize the new Meiji regime by building a Westernized army and navy demanded heavy military expenditures. Yet extraction of taxes could arouse domestic resistance and even riots. As public finance bore the brunt of the conflicts of interests both within government and between the state and society, fierce struggles among political factions complicated institutional development. The probability of policy mistakes was high in the initial stages of institution building. As political rivals were waiting to take advantage of any mishaps, the political cost appeared quite high for those who initiated institutional experimentation. In this situation, even if we characterize the institutional development in public finance in early Meiji as a trial-and-error process, we should not take for granted that experiments would necessarily lead to continuity or accumulation in institution building along one particular path.

Given the multiplicity of outcomes available, how should we explain the rise of the modern fiscal state in Japan? The armed overthrow of the shogunate initiated by the Imperial Camp in January 1868 was a crucial event. Far from being well planned or inevitable, it produced an unintended consequence: the Meiji government's excessive issue of non-convertible paper notes to fund its military campaigns against the pro-shogunate troops in 1868–1869. Dependence on paper notes continued because the new regime did not have adequate revenue to meet its normal spending needs. This credit crisis became more serious as a result of the sudden decision to abolish the domains in August 1871. In consequence, the new central government had to use newly printed paper notes to take over both the expenditures and debts of domain governments before it had developed institutions to extract taxes from the whole economy. The Meiji government's adoption of the gold standard in June 1871 made it extremely difficult to redeem paper notes denominated in gold because of the steadily rising price of gold in the international markets after 1874.

Although the issue of nonconvertible paper notes started as an unintended consequence of the Restoration, their redemption exerted long-lasting effects on subsequent institutional development in public finance. The credit crisis threatened the survival and creditworthiness of the Meiji regime. Regardless of which political faction came to power, it had to face the same problem of how to make the paper notes convertible. The conundrum provided an opportunity for young and capable officials, as well as former shogunate officials, to play crucial roles. They experimented with many different methods, ranging from direct engagement in industry and commerce to building effective tax institutions. Their policy mistakes incurred mounting criticisms from political conservatives within the government and from the political opponents of the Meiji government. However, the question of note redemption determined the direction toward centralization in public finance in a context of multiple possible outcomes. The deepening crisis after 1874 had a great impact on the tempo of fiscal centralization by excluding the more gradual approach.

Origin of the Credit Crisis

The early modern state formed in eighteenth-century Japan was characterized by a unique system of "dual sovereignty." The shogunate acted as the central government, which monopolized state power in foreign affairs and coinage, and had the authority to mobilize domain governments for big public projects, such as water control and defense.[8] Although the shogunate kept the court under firm control, the emperor in theory remained the ultimate source of political authority but delegated the execution of state power to the shogunate *(taisei inin)*, making it the de facto sovereign.

The late eighteenth and early nineteenth centuries witnessed the gradual political ascendance of the court in both domestic and foreign affairs. The inability of the shogunate to handle economic fluctuations and social dislocations made the court an alternative symbol for political appeals. In 1787, for example, in response to the prayers of hundreds of thousands suffering from famine, the court unprecedentedly asked the shogunate to provide relief.[9] The Mito School, the most influential intellectual movement in Japan in the late eighteenth and early nineteenth centuries, emphasized the role of the emperor as the sovereign to unite the Japanese in the face of increasing domestic instability and threats from the West *(sonnōron)*.[10] However, this growing stress on the emperor did not immediately strike a fatal blow to the existing political system. The urgent need to strengthen maritime defense in the 1830s and 1840s could still be accommodated by dual sovereignty. The emperor in theory "delegated" the affairs of national defense to the shogunate, which in turn mobilized domain governments, particularly those located in strategic locations, such as Chōshū, Satsuma, and Mito.

Nonetheless, dual sovereignty came under great strain following the arrival of Perry's fleet in 1853. When the shogunate in 1854 consulted with domain lords about their attitudes toward the opening of Japan, replies varied greatly. The hard-liners, such as the lords of Chōshū, Tosa, Kuwana, and Mito, wanted to use force to expel the foreigners. The majority, including the lord of Satsuma, were concerned about the military superiority of Western powers and thus preferred to avoid immediate conflict. They proposed the opening of some ports as a means of appeasement, which would give Japan time to prepare militarily. The lords of Sakura, Tsuyama, and Nakatsu considered trade with the West unavoidable in the new international circumstances. They advocated enriching Japan through foreign trade.[11] When the court and the shogunate split over opening, the division among domain governments became destabilizing, for lords could ally with the court to turn their dissatisfaction into political action against the shogunate.

In 1857, the shogunal council negotiated the first commercial treaty with the Americans, which had better terms than those in the treaty that Western powers imposed on China after the Opium War.[12] However, its realistic concessions provided ammunition for anti-Western elements in the domains and at the court to attack the shogunate. The draft of the treaty and the agreed opening of Yokohama, Nagasaki, Niigata, and Hyōgo (Kōbe) aroused much opposition among influential political figures, such as Tokugawa Nariaki, the most prominent hard-liner in the shogunate, and the lords of Satsuma and Chōshū. This anti-Western mentality was particularly strong among court nobles and the broader ranks of samurai. Emperor Kōmei in 1858 refused to approve the drafted treaty. Yet under foreign pressure, the shogunate was forced to sign treaties with the Americans, Dutch, British, French, and Russians without imperial sanction. This act, however, clearly violated the "delegation theory of political authority" and made the court a legitimate rallying point for anti-Western radicals.

In 1860, the court, which was dominated by anti-Western nobles, pressured the shogunate to expel foreigners. Mounting calls to "immediately expel the western barbarians" reached a peak in 1863, when Emperor Kōmei ordered the repeal of the treaties and the expulsion of foreigners by force *(hayaku jōi)*. Radicals in Chōshū, the stronghold of anti-Western *(jōi)* activists, bombarded Western ships. Clashes also broke out between Satsuma and the British. Radicals were prepared to topple the shogunate if it opposed the emperor's *jōi* order.[13] The retaliation by Britain, France, Holland, and the United States forced the realistic domain lords of Satsuma, Aizu, and several other domains to collaborate with the shogunate to purge anti-Western radicals in Chōshū and the court so as to avoid the possibility of more humiliating treaties that would follow upon military defeat.[14]

At this point, both the court and major "outside" domain lords *(tozama)* became involved in the making of foreign policy, which was unprecedented in the Tokugawa period.[15] The shogunate could not even mobilize domain troops if domain lords considered the action to be against the interests of Japan, as illustrated in the second punitive expedition against Chōshū in the summer of 1866. The domain lords of Echizen, Chūgoku, and Kyūshū, including those of Satsuma and Aki, refused to obey the shogunate's order as they believed it would weaken Japan's defenses given the threat from Western powers.[16] This formally marked the end of the shogunate's political dominance.[17]

The fifteenth Shogun, Tokugawa Yoshinobu, carried out modernization programs to revitalize the shogunate. Nonetheless, he realized that support from the court was indispensable to maintaining shogunal authority over domain lords. Major domain lords, including those of Satsuma, Tosa, and Echizen, demanded the end of dual sovereignty so as to be "unified" (kyokoku itchi) against Western pressure. In September 1866, Matsudaira Shungaku from Echizen proposed that the shogunate return its sovereign powers in diplomacy, command of the domain lords, and coinage to the court and that policy decisions be made on the basis of "public discussion" among representatives from major domains and the shogunate. Shungaku's proposal was supported by Satsuma, the most powerful domain at the time.[18]

When the British and French envoys in March 1867 requested the opening of Hyōgo in accordance with the signed treaties, the leaders of Satsuma proposed that the court should be in charge of diplomacy and that the question of Hyōgo should be decided by "public discussion" among the court, the shogunate, and major domain lords.[19] Yet the Western powers insisted that the impending opening of Hyōgo be made public six months before the actual opening date of 1 January 1868, which left the Japanese little time to settle their internal divisions. In June 1867, Yoshinobu managed to receive the emperor's sanction to open Hyōgo before obtaining the agreement of great domain lords. This decision severely alienated the latter and became a turning point for realliance of major political actors.[20] The great domains such as Satsuma, Chōshū, and Tosa now agreed that the Shogun should return the sovereign power to the court (taisei hōkan).

Nonetheless, the political future of Japan remained uncertain at this juncture as there were three major camps that had different ideas, agendas, and blueprints. The first was the Imperial Camp, consisting mainly of the anti-shogunate court nobles, and hard-liners in Satsuma and Chōshū. Their aim was to restore an imperial government in which the emperor governed with the aid of his ministers.[21] Many of these court nobles, including Iwakura Tomomi, had been purged and disciplined for their support of the anti-Western radicals between 1860 and 1864. At the accession of Emperor Mutsuhito (the future Meiji emperor) in February 1867, a general pardon allowed them to return to the court. Although there were proposals to build a representative institution within Satsuma, the hard-liners in Satsuma used the term *kōgi* (public discussion) as a strategy to delegitimize the shogunate and to gain support of other great domain lords.[22] Supported by anti-shogunate court nobles, Satsuma and Chōshū prepared to topple the shogunate by force.

The second was the Camp of Public Discussion *(kōgi seitaiha)*. Its leaders included Yamauchi Yōdō (lord of Tosa) and Matsudaira Shungaku (lord of Echizen). This camp had some prominent Westernizing thinkers, such as Yokoi Shōnan from Echizen, who favored a system resembling "monarchical constitutionalism." In this system, the emperor would be the sovereign, yet important policies were to be made by a bicameral legislature *(gijiin)*. The Upper House would be an "assembly of domain lords" and the Lower House made up of "competent and virtuous" people regardless of their social status.[23] Leaders of the Camp of Public Discussion also wanted to learn more about the institutional structure and operation of legislative institutions in Western countries.[24] The proposed bicameral legislature would allow more domain governments to participate in national politics.

The third camp was the shogunate, which possessed a group of competent administrative officials. Shogunate officials who had returned from studying in Holland, such as Nishi Amane and Tsuda Mamichi, planned to preserve the shogunate as the administrative institution and build a new bicameral legislature. The Upper House was to be an assembly of domain lords and the Lower House composed of samurai representatives from each domain. The shogun was to be the real sovereign, in charge of both administration and the Upper House, while the emperor remained a nominal sovereign with only ritual authority.[25]

In the second half of 1867, the relationships among these three camps were still fluid, and the prospect of their struggles remained uncertain. Both the Imperial Camp and the Camp of Public Discussion were dissatisfied at the treaties and the shogunate's decision to open Hyōgo. They demanded that the shogunate return sovereign power to the court, that thereafter foreign policy should be made on a broader basis of public discussion among court officials and great domain lords *(kōgi yoron)*, and that Japan should seek new, fairer treaties with Western countries.[26] The Camp of Public Discussion nonetheless shared with the shogunate the view that the institution of public discussion should have the real authority in policy making. The Imperial Camp, which was preparing to use force against the shogunate, still needed the support of the Camp of Public Discussion. However, the Camp of Public Discussion hoped to persuade Yoshinobu to peacefully return state power to the court and join with them to build new political institutions of representation. Once Yoshinobu did so, the leaders of the Camp of Public Discussion would oppose the armed overthrow of the shogunate.[27]

On 8 November 1867, Yoshinobu formally declared the return of sovereign power to the court. On 2 January 1868, the imperial government was restored *(ōsei fukko)*, putting an end to the shogunate. On 3 January 1868, under pressure from the Imperial Camp, Yoshinobu further announced that he had resigned his post and would return the shogunate's large territories and gold and silver mines to the newly restored imperial government. Yoshinobu's decisions resulted from constant negotiations with representatives of Tosa and Echizen, two leading domains in the Camp of Public Discussion. Leaders of this camp now worked hard to ensure that Yoshinobu joined the new regime and that a bicameral representative legislature should be established. A peaceful Restoration seemed very likely; the alliance between the Camp of Public Discussion and Yoshinobu would be a formidable opponent to the Imperial Camp.[28]

Nonetheless, the Imperial Camp seized the opportunity of the conflict between Satsuma forces and the pro-shogunate troops from Aizu and Kuwana in Toba-Fushimi on 27 January 1868 to launch a military campaign to overthrow the shogunate *(boshin sensō)*. The Imperial Camp was financially unprepared for the war. It had little tax revenue at the beginning, and its creditworthiness remained low in the financial markets. By June 1868, it had only received 230,000 ryō in Osaka and 17,250 ryō in Kyoto through "forced loans" *(goyōkin)*. Yet the estimated expenditures of the Eastern Expedition against pro-shogunate troops exceeded 3 million ryō.[29] As a result, it had to issue paper notes to meet its military needs. By June 1869 the Meiji government had issued 48 million ryō of nonconvertible paper notes denominated in gold *(dajōkansatsu)*.[30] This exigent fiscal measure was highly controversial even within the Imperial Camp; but there was no plausible alternative.[31]

For the Imperial Camp, the optimal sequence would have been to wait until the imperial government had taken control of the shogunate's vast territories before hostilities began. Or they should at least have asked the shogunate to turn the mint over to the court. The mint was not only a symbol of the sovereign power but also an important source of revenue. If the shogunate refused, this would clearly violate the return of sovereign power to the emperor and justify the use of force. Fear of the alliance between the Camp of Public Discussion and Yoshinobu explains why the Imperial Camp went to war without adequate funds. The origin of the credit crisis of nonconvertible paper notes was thus an unintended consequence of the power struggles in late 1867 and early 1868 and exogenous to subsequent institutional development.

Post-Restoration Uncertainties and the Abolishing of Domains

From the very beginning, the Meiji regime was wracked by power struggles among actors with divergent ideas and institutional blueprints. On the political front, the Imperial Camp resisted the attempt of the Camp of Public Discussion to establish a legislative institution. In the matter of public finance, political conservatives and Westernizing officials often took opposing approaches. Centralization was by no means inevitable.

In June 1868, Fukuoka Takachika (from Tosa) and Soejima Taneomi (from Hizen) drafted the Proposals of Political Foundation *(seitaisho)*, which called for a separation of powers among the administration, legislature, and judiciary as the fundamental political principle. Leaders of the Camp of Public Discussion, such as Yamauchi Yōdō (lord of Tosa) and Akizuki Tanetatsu, not only evaluated various legislative systems in Western countries but also invited former shogunate officials who had studied Western constitutionalism, such as Kanda Takahira, Katō Hiroyuki, and Tsuda Mamichi, to join their cause. On 18 April 1869, they set up a deliberative institution *(kōgisho)* consisting of representatives from various domains.

However, political conservatives in the Imperial Camp, particularly court nobles such as Iwakura Tomomi and Sanjō Sanetomi, disliked the Westernizing elements in the kōgisho.[32] After the pro-shogunate troops were completely defeated in June 1869, court nobles and leaders of Satsuma and Chōshū dominated the central government. They reorganized the kōgisho as a mere consultative organization (renamed *shūgiin*) that had no authority in policy making. Prominent figures from the Camp of Public Discussion, including Yamauchi Yōdō, Akizuki Tanetatsu, Katō Hiroyuki, and Tsuda Mamichi, were expelled from the shūgiin. Anti-Western court nobles such as Ōhara Shigenori turned the shūgiin into a forum to attack Westernizing officials.[33]

The Ministry of Finance was a major bastion of Westernizing officials. It became the most powerful ministry in September 1869 when it incorporated the Ministry of Civil Affairs so as to strengthen its supervision over tax collection in the territories of the former shogunate. Ōkuma Shigenobu, who was in charge of the ministry, gathered many young Westernizing officials, including Inoue Kaoru and Itō Hirobumi, around him. He also invited many former shogunate bureaucrats, including Shibusawa Eiichi, to join the ministry. Among the thirteen members of the Office of Reform, the think tank of the Ministry of Finance, nine were former shogunate bureaucrats.[34]

As the unequal treaties made it impossible for the Meiji government to raise revenue by charging higher customs duties, it had at first to depend on taxes extracted from the former shogunate territories. For this reason, many former shogunate officials were retained to help the new government collect taxes.[35] Under the pressure of fiscal difficulties, Ōkuma Shigenobu did not allow reduction in or exemption from land taxes in spite of poor harvests in 1868 and 1869.[36] These harsh measures caused large-scale peasant riots in Hita, Shinshū, and Fukushima. Local magistrates, who bore the brunt of the protests, demanded lower taxation as a "benevolent policy" to legitimate the new regime.[37]

Under pressure to increase government income, Westernizing officials in the Ministry of Finance also tried to directly earn money by investing in railway building and mining. This policy represented the fiscal principle of the domain state and ran contrary to the trend of increasing private entry into the mining of gold and silver, which had begun in the late Tokugawa period.[38] Inoue Kaoru invested government reserve funds to develop mines of gold, silver, and copper.[39] Nonetheless, railway building generated little profit but instead became a serious financial burden. By 1871, the government had invested more than 10 million yen in railways, which represented a huge expenditure for a government with an annual income of 20 million.[40]

Financial officials thence were under heavy attack from political conservatives, not only for their advocacy of Westernization but also for their policy mistakes. Political conservatives, including Saigō Takamori, attributed the fiscal difficulties of the government to Westernizing projects, such as railway building. Conservatives in 1870 were shocked by a foreign loan of £3 million for railway construction that financial officials had tried to obtain.[41] In order to weaken the power of Westernizing financial officials, Ōkubo Toshimichi in August 1870 separated the Ministry of Civil Affairs from the Ministry of Finance and put it under his supervision.

The newly restored Meiji government did not have the necessary fiscal and military capacities to initiate full-fledged centralization, particularly when it had not yet taken over the tax institutions to extract revenue from the former shogunate territories. Although Itō Hirobumi had proposed that the court should select "competent soldiers" from the troops that had been mobilized in the anti-shogunate campaigns to form a central army, the imperial government did not have the money to do so and had to send these soldiers back to their respective domains.[42] In consequence, the Meiji government had to depend on samurai troops from major domains, including Satsuma, Chōshū, and Tosa, to contain antigovernment elements and repress peasant riots. Although officials Gotō Shōjirō, Kido Takayoshi, and Itō Hirobumi favored political centralization, they had to come to terms with reality.[43] In late 1870, Yamagata Aritomo, a major Meiji official who had just returned from investigating the military system in Europe, had to admit that it was premature to replace samurai troops with a centralized conscript army.[44]

In October 1870, the conference on reforming domain institutions held in Tokyo finally reached an agreement that the level of the military budget of domain governments should not exceed 9 percent of their rice output, half of which was to be sent to the center and half kept to fund their own domain armies.[45] As a result, domain governments were forced to reduce expenditures by cutting the stipends of their vassals and the size of their samurai armies. The governments of Tosa, Hisai, and Wakayama proceeded to replace samurai-based domain troops with peasant recruits.[46] Tosa, Hikone, Chōshū, Fukui, and Yonezawa issued bonds to dissolve their obligations to provide hereditary stipends to samurai vassals.[47]

The political situation in 1870 was thus similar to a federal system, which had been attractive to many Japanese since the late Tokugawa period.[48] Domain governments were not allowed to borrow from foreigners without the approval of the center.[49] They accepted the sovereign power of the center in currency so as to achieve monetary unification and end the monetary chaos in Japan.[50] Yet major domains retained much autonomy in reforming their governance in accordance with their particular circumstances, though domain rulers ceased to be hereditary and had to be nominated by the center. The central government first needed to strengthen its taxing capacities over the territories that it had inherited from the shogunate. As the center did not yet have a large-scale standing army, it was unable to impose centralization on domain governments, particularly those such as Satsuma, Chōshū, and Tosa that still had sizeable troops. The center could not even make the domains hand over on time the money they had agreed to contribute to fund the navy.[51] Instead of using foreign conquests to enhance central authority over the domains and thus speed up centralization, fiscal difficulties forced the Meiji government to reject the major Meiji leader Kido Takayoshi's proposal to invade Korea and to avoid conflict with Russia over the Kurile Islands.[52]

As an idea, political and fiscal centralization were quite appealing to financial officials in the government. As Ōkuma Shigenobu made clear in 1870, it would be more practical to use nationwide tax revenues to sponsor a military force under the command of the center and to fund the governance of the whole country.[53] However, in early 1871, the Meiji leaders did not consider it urgent to abolish the domains.[54] Even advocates of abolition, such as Hirosawa Saneomi, admitted that it would take considerable time to merge small domains into bigger ones and gradually enhance central power over domain governments.[55] Yet this gradual path toward political centralization was disrupted by the anti-Western radicals who had been mobilized to overthrow the shogunate in the Restoration of 1868.

The new Meiji regime originally used the signing of unequal treaties to delegitimize the shogunate. In the first state letter to the ambassadors of Western countries on 8 February 1868, the Meiji government suggested it would revise these treaties. Yet in order to make Western powers remain neutral in its campaigns against the pro-shogunate troops, it quickly declared its acceptance of all the signed treaties.[56] On 4 February 1868, samurai soldiers from Bizen attacked foreigners in Kōbe. On 8 March, samurai soldiers from Tosa attacked French soldiers in Sakai. In May, the Meiji government arrested more than one hundred Christians in Nagasaki. From November onward, the persecution of Christians spread to eighteen domains, including Saga and Satsuma, and by February 1870 more than 3,400 Christians had been put into prison.[57] However, the strong reaction from Western powers forced the Meiji leaders to resume the shogunate's appeasement policies. This greatly alienated anti-Western radicals, who then targeted Westernizing officials in the Meiji government. Yokoi Shōnan, a famous Westernizing thinker, was assassinated on 15 February 1869. Ōmura Masujirō, a proponent of a Western-style conscript army, was killed in the same year. Many high-ranking officials in the Meiji government, such as Sanjō Sanetomi, Soejima Taneomi, and Ōhara Shigenori, were openly sympathetic to the anti-Western radicals.[58]

The problem of disbanded samurai became more severe when financially exhausted domain governments, particularly Chōshū and Tosa, began to cut the numbers of their domain troops in 1869. Thousands of samurai soldiers who were dissatisfied with the terms of their demobilization fled to Kurume, Kumamoto, and Akita, whose domain lords were well known for their endorsement of the "immediate expulsion of foreigners." In October 1870, these domains actively colluded with anti-Western court nobles such as Toyama Mitsutsune and Otagi Michiteru and planned to launch a so-called Second Restoration to reverse the appeasement policy and purge the "wicked" Westernizing officials from the central government. In February 1871, anti-Western radicals killed Hirosawa Saneomi, an important Meiji leader and prominent advocate of a Western-style conscript army and domain abolition. His assassination precipitated a political crisis for the Meiji regime.[59] The central government, which had only a small-scale army, had to request the domain lords of Satsuma, Chōshū, and Tosa to contribute their samurai troops to contain the attacks by anti-Western radicals. On 30 March 1871, more than 8,000 samurai soldiers from the three domains arrived in Tokyo. A new round of institutional reform began.

Saigō Takamori and Ōkubo Toshimichi, both of whom led Satsuma troops to Tokyo, were powerful figures in the central government. In addition to protecting the authority of the central government, they had their own political agendas. Saigō considered the Westernizing projects, such as railway building, wasteful and "mindless imitations" of the West.[60] He particularly disliked Westernizing officials in the Ministry of Finance. In his view, these "vulgar officials" did not understand the importance of "virtue" but knew only how to calculate profit.[61] According to Saigō and Ōkubo, the correct way to overcome fiscal problems was to reduce government expenditures by "stopping the projects of railway and steam power" and eliminating "redundant officials."[62] In response, Kido Takayoshi, the leader of the Chōshū faction, tried to protect Westernizing financial officials so as to consolidate his power base in the center. Itagaki Taisuke from Tosa and officials from the domains Higo, Tokushima, and Yonezawa called for the establishment of a national institution that could ensure "fairness and impartiality" in policy making; they aimed to break the control of the central government by the Satsuma and Chōshū factions.[63]

Power struggles in the center lasted a few months and ended up with the decision to abolish the domain system *(haihan chiken)* on 29 August 1871. This fundamental political change was not well planned in advance. Even major financial officials did not have this in mind just three months earlier. For instance, on 19 May 1871, Ōkuma Shigenobu and Inoue Kaoru urged Itō Hirobumi to immediately return from the United States to Japan to participate in the institutional reform of the central government. In regard to the relationship with domain governments, their major goal was to build an institution capable of ensuring that the domains would, as already agreed, share their revenue with the center *(kōnōsei)*.[64]

The immediate result of abolishing the domains was that the new central government took responsibility for the debts of domain governments and the stipends of their samurai. In addition to the total 24 million yen domain debt that it had inherited, the center had to issue another 25 million yen in paper notes to exchange for all the domain-issued paper notes that were still in use.[65] The total amount of paper notes reached about 95 million yen. Thus, before the new central government had established institutions to generate revenue from the whole country, it had shouldered a huge burden of financial liabilities.

In particular, the need to redeem paper notes, to which both the legitimacy and creditworthiness of the new Meiji regime were closely tied, constrained power struggles after 1871. To a large extent, it protected Westernizing officials from political conservatives. Traditional fiscal measures, such as reducing government expenditure, did not directly address the problem of redemption. The financial officials whom Saigō brought to the center, such as Tani Tetsuomi and Tsuda Izuru, had not had much experience in managing paper notes in Satsuma.[66] Iwakura, who was a political ally of Saigō and Ōkubo in the Council of State, had to admit that Ōkuma should be kept in the Ministry of Finance in light of the urgent issue of paper notes.[67] Although Ōkubo became minister of finance after the domains were eliminated, he was not familiar with financial issues, and Westernizing officials such as Ōkuma, Inoue, and Shibusawa continued to manage government finance.[68]

The Impact of the Credit Crisis on Institutional Development

Because the Meiji government had to meet spending needs before it was able to take over tax collection in the former shogunate territories, it had no option but to rely on paper notes to cover its spending needs between 1868 and 1871. The proportion of paper notes in government total income was as high as 72.6 percent between January 1868 and January 1869 and 69.5 percent between February 1869 and October 1869. Although it declined to about 10 percent between November 1870 and October 1871, abolishing the domains in August 1871 and the resulting issue of more paper notes brought it back to 35.3 percent between November 1871 and December 1872.[69] The formidable problem of how to stabilize the value of the paper notes and meet government spending needs provided an opportunity for officials who had previously demonstrated ability in managing finance and paper notes in domain governments to rise to the center.

In addition to building tax institutions, financial officials experimented with various institutional arrangements that were based on their previous experience of "mercantilist" economic policies in the domains. Under these policies, a domain government issued paper notes and lent them as capital to privileged merchants, who formed business monopolies (*shōhō kaisho* or *kokusan kaisho*) to organize the production of local commodities and then sell them to the central markets in Osaka, Kyoto, and Tokyo for specie so as to redeem the value of the domain paper notes. The socioeconomic conditions of Japan to a large extent determined whether similar programs would be effective at the national level.

Yuri Kimimasa, who was responsible for the original issue of paper notes in the Meiji regime, was recommended to the central government for his prior success in managing paper notes for the domain government of Echizen.[70] Yuri established the Bureau of Commerce *(shōhōshi)*, which was staffed by government officials and managers from big merchant houses, such as Ono, Mitsui, and Shimada. These privileged merchants took out loans from the government in government paper notes and were granted monopoly rights to organize the production and export of major Japanese export goods, such as raw silk and tea. The profit that these merchants made in species would help the government stabilize the value of paper notes.[71] However, these merchants could not compete with the traditional commercial guilds *(kabunakama)*, which had already built dense commercial networks with local traders, producers, and farmers.[72] Moreover, they could not monopolize exports due to the opposition of foreign merchants.[73] Their inability to obtain hard cash to pass on to the government left the paper notes unsupported. The notes were discounted at some 60 percent in Tokyo, Osaka, and Kyoto and could not even circulate in the provinces.[74] Yuri was forced to resign in March 1869.

Ōkuma Shigenobu, Yuri's successor, had also been successful in managing paper notes and rescuing the finances of the domain government in Saga.[75] Ōkuma requested privileged merchants in major treaty ports and commercial centers to form "finance companies" *(kawase kaisha)*. The government lent paper notes to these companies, which in turn issued commercial bills and lent these bills to the business monopolies that had been established by domain governments (*shōhō kaisho* or *kokusan kaisho*).[76] Ōkuma attempted to utilize these business monopolies to circulate the paper notes of the Meiji government. However, these business monopolies could not compete with private businessmen, particularly in the most profitable businesses of tea and raw silk.[77]

Nor could the Meiji government manipulate the domestic market as it wished. For example, the government's order on 28 June 1868 forbidding the use of private banknotes and commercial bills issued by private bankers caused a huge panic in Osaka. Although the government was forced to repeal this order within the month, several well-established banking houses in Osaka went bankrupt, including the famous Konoike House, and the Osaka-centered financial networks were greatly damaged.[78]

Nonetheless, the Meiji government asserted the sovereign power over domain governments in monetary issues. For example, it made Satsuma and Tosa stop counterfeiting shogunate coins and forbade domain governments from issuing their own paper notes.[79] In order to facilitate the circulation of government paper notes, Ōkuma appealed to the coercive power of the state. In September 1869, he prohibited the use of specie in domestic transactions and ordered that the paper notes issued and coins minted by previous domain governments be exchanged for government paper notes.[80] In this manner, he excluded "competing forms of money" and established a monopoly for the paper notes issued by the center. To facilitate the circulation of government paper notes in the markets, Ōkuma ordered the printing of paper notes with small denominations for the convenience of ordinary transactions.[81]

The economic conditions in early Meiji were beneficial to Ōkuma's effort to impose nonconvertible paper notes on Japanese society. The civil war in 1868–1869 did not significantly disrupt the domestic economy. Moreover, expanding exports greatly stimulated the domestic economy and the development of interregional trade. As the Japanese had been greatly troubled by the monetary chaos of the 1860s, unified government paper notes provided them a standard medium of exchange in the markets. By mid-1870, paper notes began to be used according to their face value.[82] However, the ratio of government specie reserves to the amount of issued paper notes was close to zero, which was far from sufficient to sustain convertibility.[83] To consolidate trust in government paper notes, Ōkuma publicly promised that the government would use its newly minted currencies to redeem paper notes by 1872.

After the unexpectedly rapid abolition of the domains in August 1871, the new central government was saddled with the much increased liabilities of ex-samurai hereditary stipends. As political centralization was attained before the center was able to tax the entire economy, even conservatives such as Saigō Takamori agreed that foreign loans were the only practical way to meet urgent current needs, particularly the settlement of liabilities with former samurai and peers. At the suggestion of Inoue Kaoru, the Meiji government planned to raise a loan of 3 million pounds (equivalent to 30 million yen) at 7 percent from the United States. The government intended to use 10 million yen to buy back the stipend bonds that it was to issue to ex-samurai and peers, 10 million yen for railway construction and mining, and the rest for government spending. However, this attempt failed as the United States was not yet a major capital-exporting country and the Meiji regime had little creditworthiness in the international capital markets. As a result, the Meiji government managed to borrow only 10 million yen at 7 percent in 1873 from the British Oriental Bank, the major foreign bank in East Asia at the time.[84]

On 23 December 1871 the Iwakura Mission left Japan. Its major purpose was to negotiate with Western powers for a revision of the unequal treaties and particularly for a resumption of sovereignty in deciding tariff rates.[85] The new central government hoped to use this strategy to distinguish itself from both the appeasement policy of the former shogunate and the immediate expulsion of Westerners espoused by the radicals. For the Ministry of Finance, the ability to raise customs revenue was vital because the central government had not yet established institutions to collect domestic taxes.[86] However, the attempt to revise treaties was totally unrealistic because of the resistance of Western powers. As Banno Junji has argued, there were three ways in 1873 for the Meiji government to legitimate itself: foreign aggression, economic development, and creation of a parliamentary system.[87]

Foreign aggression would demand tremendous financial resources at a time when the government was in severe financial difficulties. In 1873, dire fiscal conditions forced Ōkubo Toshimichi, Iwakura Tomomi, and Kido Takayoshi to join together to reject the hard-liners' attempt to invade Korea. This decision split the Meiji government. Saigō Takamori, Etō Shinpei, and Itagaki Taisuke resigned from the government. Itagaki, Etō, Gotō Shōjirō, and others in January 1874 called for the establishment of a parliamentary system so as to ensure that major policies were based on wider consensus. Their demand was supported by the legislative branch of the Council of State *(sa'in)*.[88] In response, Emperor Meiji had to issue a decree in April 1874 promising a constitutional monarchy. The Meiji government then decided to base its claims for legitimacy on its handling of economic issues.[89]

However, financial officials in the center were divided over how to handle the fiscal deficits. As the Ministry of Finance did not have the authority to control government spending, Inoue Kaoru and Shibusawa Eiichi, who were in charge of public finance while the Iwakura Mission was abroad, resigned on May 1873. They published a protest letter that revealed the dire situation of the Meiji government: in addition to the 10 million yen fiscal deficit in 1873, the total government liabilities, including domestic and foreign borrowing and paper notes, amounted to 120 million yen.[90] Mutsu Munemitsu, the head of taxation, also resigned to protest the fiscal difficulties caused by the government's ambitious plans to "implement Westernizing projects in jurisdiction, education, military, and industry simultaneously, without paying heed to the appropriate sequence."[91] Matsukata Masayoshi, who replaced Mutsu as the head of taxation, was also critical of the government's heavy investment in railway building. In his view, the government would go bankrupt before realizing "the big profit that these grand projects might promise in future."[92]

The other urgent issue was how to resolve the stipends of ex-samurais and peers. Although these had been greatly cut in previous reforms, they still cost the government 18.94 million yen in 1873, accounting for some 30 percent of annual government spending. There was little dispute within the Meiji government over the plan to issue stipend bonds to dissolve this obligation. In 1874 and 1875, a total of 142,858 ex-samurai received 16.56 million yen in stipend bonds (bearing an annual interest rate of 8 percent) and 20 million yen in cash to abandon their "entitlement" permanently.[93] However, most of the recipients of stipend bonds sold them in the markets and quickly fell into poverty. As the livelihoods of some 2 million ex-samurai and their family members were threatened, the Meiji government was forced to suspend this policy in March 1875 and search for gradual and stable solutions.[94] The time to clear this liability was extended from the original six years to thirty years. In 1875, officials in the Bureau of Taxation even planned to use a decentralized method to deal with this problem, that is, to entrust prefecture and county governments with solving the stipend problem of the ex-samurai living under their administration.[95]

At this moment, willingness to learn from the West did not necessarily entail rapid industrialization. Kido Takayoshi and Ōkubo Toshimichi both visited Western countries with the Iwakura Mission. Kido concluded that Japan should proceed with "Westernization" gradually as Western countries did not become "rich and strong" overnight.[96] Ōkubo was deeply impressed by the railways and steam-powered industries, but he considered it more feasible for Japan to focus on improving canal and river navigation as seen in countries such as Holland. When Ōkubo was in charge of the Ministry of Civil Affairs, he opposed the heavy investment in railway building undertaken by the Ministry of Industry. Instead, he gave priority to less expensive projects, such as canal and harbor construction and river and seaborne navigation, and he hoped these programs could also provide more job opportunities for unemployed ex-samurai.[97]

It would thus not have been unreasonable for the Meiji government in 1874 to slow down the tempo of centralization and reduce government spending. A gradual centralization could reduce local resistance and give more time for the Meiji government to develop effective tax institutions. Slower fiscal centralization could still support the kind of limited industrialization advocated by Kido and Ōkubo. However, these measures could not help the Meiji government in 1874 solve its biggest credit crisis, the convertibility of the issued paper notes denominated in gold.

The Meiji government originally decided to adopt the silver standard in December 1870. This was based on a realistic recognition of the scarcity of gold and abundance of silver in East Asia.[98] Yet when Itō Hirobumi returned from investigating the American monetary and financial system in 1871, he persuaded the government to adopt the gold standard so as to follow the "general trend" in the West, and the Meiji government set the value of one Japanese yen as equivalent to 1.5 grams of gold.[99] As the mint could not prepare a sufficient amount of coins to redeem the issued paper notes, the government in January 1872 exchanged all the old paper notes with new, good-quality ones printed in Germany.

However, the convertibility of these paper notes was greatly affected by the steady rise of gold prices in the international markets after 1873. Germany became the second country after Britain to switch to the gold standard in 1871, and the United States followed suit in 1873.[100] The price of silver relative to gold fell further after 1875, when the output of silver increased significantly in the United States. As the official price of gold in Japan remained almost unchanged between 1871 and 1883, gold flew out of Japan.[101] In 1874, gold had disappeared from the Japanese market, and the government could mint only silver currency.[102] When Japanese officials opted for the gold standard in 1871, they had not anticipated that the gap between silver and gold prices in the international markets would grow so drastically in such a short time.

Officials of the Ministry of Finance did understand very well that massive gold drainage would make it extremely difficult to redeem the paper notes denominated in gold.[103] By August 1874, the value of paper notes accounted for 71 percent of the total state debt. How to redeem paper notes became the single most pressing problem for the Meiji government,[104] and significantly restricted policy options. Fiscal measures proposed by political conservatives, such as reduction of government expenditures, could do little to address this credit crisis.[105]

Financial officials seriously considered two choices. The first was to return to the silver standard. Seki Yoshiomi, an official in the Ministry of Finance, explicitly suggested that in response to the outflow of gold, Japan should switch from the gold to the silver standard.[106] An 1875 Ministry of Finance document acknowledged that "the most important thing for Japan is to mint more silver coins for foreign trade" and argued that "the casting of gold coins is not urgent at this point."[107]

The other option was to preserve the gold standard. Kawaji Kandō, another Ministry of Finance official, noted that the rising price of gold in the international markets might be the main cause of gold outflow from Japan. He proposed raising the gold price in Japan so as to curb drainage. Yet he did not address the resulting deflationary pressure, nor did he discuss the impact of this policy on the convertibility of paper notes denominated in gold.[108] Another challenge to maintaining the gold standard in Japan was the need to increase Japan's stocks of gold. For this purpose, Matsukata Masayoshi in September 1875 proposed collecting customs in gold rather than in silver currency.[109] However, the Meiji government could not force foreign merchants to cooperate. Ōkuma Shigenobu hoped to use the surplus of foreign trade to improve the gold reserves in Japan.[110]

If the Meiji government had used coins as its currency, it would have been able to return to the silver standard by casting silver coins only. However, the massive amount of paper notes denominated in gold that were already circulating made it extremely difficult to abandon the gold standard at this moment. Politically the government was under pressure from the opposition movement organized by Itagaki Taisuke and Gotō Shōjirō for a parliamentary system. They had long criticized the government's "arbitrary policy making."[111] A switch from the gold to silver standard within three years would have provided them new ammunition. Meanwhile, given the falling value of silver in regard to gold, the adoption of the silver standard would greatly increase the already heavy burden of government liabilities when it had to redeem the gold-denominated paper notes in silver currency.

As a result, Ōkuma Shigenobu and Ōkubo Toshimichi decided to retain the gold standard. They turned their attention to how to increase Japan's exports to the European and American markets so as to earn gold while reducing imports. Under Ōkubo's leadership, the Meiji government in 1875 implemented an ambitious program of "fostering industry and promoting enterprise" *(shokusan kōgyō)* to meet these goals.[112] This program operated on the national and international levels but drew on earlier mercantilist policies by means of which domain governments had aimed to earn coins from the major markets in Osaka, Kyoto, and Tokyo in order to stabilize the value of their issued paper notes.

This aim to increase gold stocks determined the very substance of the shokusan kōgyō program and distinguished it from a general policy of export promotion. For example, the government gave special priority to "direct exports" *(chokuyushutsu)* rather than exports in general terms. In the scheme of "direct exports," government officials and political merchants organized the transportation and marketing of the exported goods to the European and American markets in order to hold on to the gold earned through their sale.[113] The government also encouraged import substitution in the cotton textile, woolen textile, and sugar refining industries by choosing technologies that utilized only domestic rather than imported raw materials.[114] To increase the investment capital at the disposal of the central government, Ōkuma turned the stipends of ex-samurai into compulsory commutation bonds *(kinroku kōsai)*, of which up to 172 million yen were issued between 1875 and 1877. The Meiji government invested these bonds as capital in various projects of import substitution in agriculture and woolen and cotton weaving.

The adoption of the gold standard also significantly affected the Meiji government's efforts to build a banking system. Right after abolishing the domains, financial officials in the Ministry of Finance tried to seek cooperation from private financiers to ensure the convertibility of government paper notes by building a new banking system. They were aware of two different models in Western countries: the decentralized national banking system in the United States and the centralized model of the Bank of England, which monopolized the issue of banknotes. Itō Hirobumi preferred the American approach while Shibusawa Eiichi and Maejima Hisoka wanted to follow the British example.[115] In 1870, Yoshida Kiyonari, who had spent seven years in England studying its financial system, returned to work for the Ministry of Finance; he also recommended the Bank of England model.[116]

On 20 February 1871, Ōkuma and Inoue decided to establish the Bank of Japan along British lines. In August, Inoue and Shibusawa urged the Mitsui and Ono Houses to jointly form a "bank of gold notes," 60 percent of whose capital would be in specie and 40 percent in government paper notes.[117] This effort failed as the two banks could hardly prepare the necessary specie reserves to guarantee the convertibility of some 80 million ryō of paper notes denominated in gold. In this situation, the Ministry of Finance switched to Itō's recommendation of the decentralized American national banking system with the aim of dividing the burden of redeeming paper notes among many national banks located in different regions. On 15 December 1872, the government issued the National Bank Act, which required a national bank to use paper notes to lend to the government at 6 percent in return for the privilege to issue an equivalent amount of convertible banknotes.[118]

Yet the scarcity of gold led to poor performance by the national banks. By 1876, only four national banks had been established, and the total amount of their banknotes fell from 1.36 million yen on 30 June 1874 to 62,456 yen on 30 June 1876.[119] The major difficulty was that

they too could not maintain the convertibility of their banknotes denominated in gold. As Shibusawa Eiichi recalled, the rising price of gold
made holders of banknotes come to national banks to exchange their
notes for gold. Under this pressure, he had to petition the Ministry of
Finance to allow national banks to redeem their banknotes with government paper notes.[120] In August 1876, Ōkuma revised the National
Banking Act, which reduced the required ratio of specie in the capital
of a national bank from 40 percent to 20 percent and allowed national
banks to convert their banknotes using government paper notes instead of specie; and the government set 34 million yen as the upper
limit to the issue of banknotes by national banks.[121] Between 1876 and
1879, the number of national banks increased from 4 to 153, and the
amount of issued banknotes jumped from 1.74 million yen to 33.93
million yen.[122]

Although the Meiji government tried hard to maintain the gold standard, the ambitious shokusan kōgyō programs failed to attain their goal
and instead caused severe fiscal deficits.[123] In July 1877, Ōkuma realized
that it made little sense for Japan to stick to the gold standard given the
low price of silver.[124] On 27 May 1878, the government permitted the
Japanese silver yen, which was previously minted for international
trade only, to be used in domestic transactions and payment of taxation.[125] Japan thus returned to a de facto silver standard. Kawase
Hideji, the head of the Office of Enterprise Promotion in the Ministry
of Finance, admitted in July 1879 that at this stage Japan should not try
to substitute imported goods, which Westerners were more skillful in
making, but ought rather to increase the exports "appropriate to Japan's circumstances."[126]

The failure of shokusan kōgyō programs had serious political consequences. The market values of commutation bonds for ex-samurai fell
sharply as the government-guided investments failed to generate the
anticipated profit. In 1877, the largest ex-samurai rebellion in the Meiji
era (seinan sensō) broke out. In order to repress it, the government had
to issue 27 million yen in paper notes and borrow 15 million yen in
banknotes from the Dai-Ichi National Bank (or First National Bank).[127]
Unemployment among ex-samurai continued to be a significant social
issue even after the rebellion was put down. That same year, of the 12.7
million yen in "enterprise-promotion" bonds that Ōkuma prepared to

invest in infrastructure, transportation, cotton textiles, and agriculture, 3 million yen were aimed directly at solving this problem and relieving ex-samurai poverty.[128] Its political aim was, in Iwakura's words, to "gain the loyalty of ex-samurai for the state" and to prevent them from being "contaminated by European radical thoughts of freedom."[129] However, the inflationary effects of the massive issue of paper notes became obvious in 1879. Even though Japan was now on a de facto silver standard, it became difficult for the Meiji government to redeem its paper notes by silver coins.

The process of political change after the opening of Japan in 1853 was thus full of uncertainties. Even in 1867, when the prospect of ending the shogunate and returning the sovereign power to the court became clear, the relationship among the three major political camps, the Imperial Camp, the Camp of Public Discussion, and the shogunate, remained unsettled. The two possible outcomes at this juncture, a peaceful Restoration or an armed overthrow of the shogunate, held quite different implications for future institutional development. The contingency of political change is especially illustrated by the Meiji government's issuance of, and its continued reliance on, nonconvertible paper notes in the early years after the Restoration.

As an event, the Meiji Restoration in 1868 did not produce a single political group that dominated future institutional development in Japan. With its weak fiscal and military capacities, the newly established Meiji government hardly constituted a "strong state" that could impose central institutions on society. Institutional development in early Meiji had a high degree of malleability as some failed experiments were repealed and major institutional reshufflings also occurred in the central government. Contemporary actors perceived several possible outcomes, such as decentralization similar to that in a federal system or a gradual transition to financial centralization. Even after the sudden abolishing of the domains in August 1871, there were still two tempos toward centralization in public finance: gradual and fast.

Within this context of multiplicity, the special credit crisis caused by the massive issuance of nonconvertible paper notes denominated in gold significantly affected both the direction and tempo of institutional development toward centralization. Traditional fiscal measures, such as retrenchment, were excluded as they could do little to resolve this credit crisis. Competent Westernizing financial officials could continue their institutional experimentation in public finance despite pressure from political conservatives who had ousted the advocates of Western bicameralism from the center of power. The need to redeem the paper notes denominated in gold determined the substance of export-encouraging and import-substitution programs between 1874 and 1878. The observed trajectory and tempo toward fiscal centralization are unlikely to have occurred if there had been no such credit crisis.

4

THE EMERGENCE OF THE MODERN FISCAL
STATE IN JAPAN, 1880–1895

The credit crisis of nonconvertible paper notes significantly affected both the direction and tempo toward centralization in public finance in early Meiji. As the center had to bear full responsibility for redeeming the notes circulating in the economy, the credit crisis changed the risk distribution between the center and local governments. This motivated the central government to actively search for the means to speed up centralization in tax collection and the management of government spending. Peasant resistance to heavy land taxes made the extraction of more revenue from consumer goods appealing. By 1880, the Japanese government had a centralized bureaucracy for assessing and collecting indirect taxes on alcohol. Yields from sake duties turned out to be the primary source of elastic revenue. This fiscal centralization laid a solid ground for the creation of a modern fiscal state.

However, the emergence of the modern fiscal state in Japan in the 1880s remained a highly political process because institution building in public finance affected the distribution of interests in society as well as power struggles within the government. Inflation caused by excessive issue of paper notes after 1877 damaged the Meiji government's legitimacy and greatly stimulated the Freedom and People's Rights Movement *(jiyū minken undō)*. This opposition movement continued to demand the

establishment of a parliamentary system. Although ex-samurai dominated the original movement, in the late 1870s rich farmers and merchants began to participate in significant numbers. They demanded not
only a national parliamentary system but also more autonomy and participation in local governance. These political pressures had a great impact on the Meiji government's efforts to stabilize the value of paper
notes and build a central bank in the 1880s.

In order to curb inflation, the Meiji government had several policy options between 1879 and 1881. These included abandoning the issue of
government paper notes and going back to silver currency; gradually reducing the amount of paper notes in circulation; or sharply cutting down
the issuance of paper notes. Contemporary actors understood that it was
economically more appropriate to gradually reduce the amount of paper

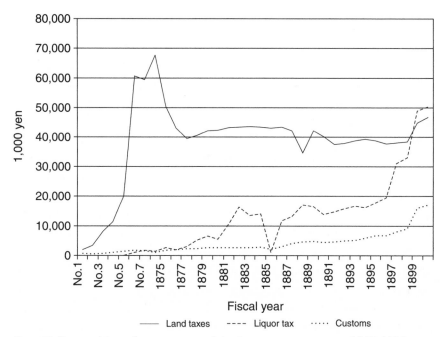

Figure 4.1 Composition of tax revenues of the Japanese government, 1868–1900.
Notes: No. 1: January 1868 to January 1869; No. 2: February 1869 to October 1869; No. 3:
November 1869 to October 1870; No. 4: November 1870 to October 1871; No. 5: November
1871 to December 1872; No. 6: January 1873 to December 1873; No. 7: January 1874 to
December 1874; No. 8: January 1875 to June 1875.
Source: *Hundred-Year Statistics of the Japanese Economy,* ed. Nihon Ginkō Tōkeikyoku (Tokyo:
Nihon Ginkō, 1966), 136.

notes so as to keep inflation under control while avoiding the danger of deflation. Against this background, the profound deflation between 1882 and 1884 caused by Finance Minister Matsukata Masayoshi's policy of rapidly reducing the amount of paper notes was by no means an unavoidable price to pay in order to redeem the paper notes.[1] The gradual approach to redeem paper notes so as to avoid deflation was, however, politically difficult to implement given the complicated conflicts of interest between the Meiji regime and society and within the government itself.

Once the deflation began, however, economic recession and increasing rural poverty severely damaged the political legitimacy of the Meiji regime. It is only against this backdrop that we can properly understand Matsukata's unorthodox financial policies, such as allowing banks to use stocks of railway companies in their cash reserves deposited in the Bank of Japan. Meanwhile, the lack of investment opportunities in a deflationary economy also made it easier for the Japanese government to issue long-term domestic bonds for railway construction and military expansion. Japan's final step toward the modern fiscal state thus illustrates that institutional development in public finance is a highly political process even when its direction is clear.

Credit Crisis and Fiscal Centralization

As discussed earlier, the Meiji government had experimented with various ways to generate revenue. These included state-owned enterprises in modern industries; the organization of direct exports to Western markets; and taxing the economy. The efforts to build a tax state became ever more important when other direct means to create revenue failed. After abolishing domains, there was a division of labor in taxation between the center and local governments. National taxes *(kokuzei)* belonged to the central government and included land taxes, customs, and indirect taxes on major consumer goods, such as alcohol. Local taxes *(chihōzei)* were at the disposal of municipal and prefectural governments; they constituted a prefixed ratio of land taxes and some indirect taxes difficult for the center to collect, such as retail taxes *(eigyōzei)*. The credit crisis of paper notes forced the officials in the Ministry of Finance not only to centralize the collection of national taxes but also to ensure their speedy transmission to the center.

In order to quickly receive its revenue, the Meiji government in January 1869 ordered fifty traditional bankers *(ryōgaeshō),* including the Ono, Mitsui, and Shimada houses, to transmit tax revenue. After abolishing the domains in 1871, these private bankers served as the government's money transmitters *(kawasekata)* and extended their networks to the whole country.[2] Private financiers facilitated the government's efforts to convert the land tax collected in rice into money as their branches received the rice from peasants and sent bills to their headquarters in Tokyo. Although the Ministry of Finance ordered them to send the collected taxes on the fifteenth and last days of each month to Tokyo by bills of exchange, they still benefited from possessing government funds and revenue without paying interest for these brief periods.[3] The relatively stable flows of government revenue and funds enhanced the reputation of these private banks in the markets, and the government avoided the time-consuming transportation of revenue in rice or in specie.

However, the reliance on private bankers to transmit government revenue and spending contained some inherent risks, as the official monies were often lent out for profit. For example, when the government needed large amounts of money to fund its expedition to Taiwan in the autumn of 1874, major private banks that remitted government funds were totally unprepared. Unable to call back all the government deposits that they had lent out in mining, real estate, manufacturing of raw silk, and so forth, the Ono and Shimada houses went bankrupt.[4] The Mitsui house barely escaped by getting an emergency loan from the British Oriental Bank.[5] Although the Ministry of Finance considered returning to the transportation of specie, the high cost and slow delivery time forced it to continue to allow major private banks such as Mitsui and Yasuda, as well as the newly established national banks, to transmit tax revenue.[6] But the government now demanded that these banks provide collateral for the deposited official funds. By 1880, the national banks and major private banks handled up to 85 percent of government tax revenue and expenditures.[7]

As the central government bore the risk for redeeming the paper notes, it had a strong motivation to centralize the management of spending by local governments and government ministries. In 1873, Inoue

Kaoru and Shibusawa Eiichi introduced double-entry bookkeeping into government finance and ordered all government offices and prefectural governments to regularly submit their account books and their budgets for the next year to the Ministry of Finance for inspection.[8] Nonetheless, prefectural governments still had a large degree of autonomy in financial operations. They deducted their expenditures from the collected revenue and sent the residual funds to the center; the reserve funds were also at their disposal.[9]

To put government spending under firmer control, Ōkuma in February 1876 ordered government offices and prefectural governments to return any surplus to the Ministry of Finance for a centralized allocation.[10] As government ministries did not send their accounting records to the center on time, the Ministry of Finance in 1877 had not yet finished auditing government spending dating from two years before. In response, Ōkuma decided to dispatch inspecting officials to check the accounting records of government ministries so as to ensure that future budgets were based on accurate auditing of actual ministry spending.[11] Likewise, to supervise local government delivery of collected tax revenue to the center, the Bureau of Taxation in 1878 sent out taxation commissioners to localities.[12] The management of government finance thus became highly centralized.

In regard to revenue collection, the Ministry of Finance tried various means to raise revenue while reducing social resistance. Customs, which should have been the most important source of income for the new government, could not be effectively exploited as the unequal treaties fixed Japan's tariff level. The extraction of land taxes encountered not only fierce opposition from peasants but also formidable information problems in evaluating the market value of taxable land in various regions.[13]

In regard to domestic indirect taxes, financial officials in the Meiji government considered the commercial sectors important sources of revenue. As early as March 1869, the Guidance for the Administration of Cities and Prefectures issued by the central government clearly stated that "as commerce prospers, the commercial taxes should be gradually collected [and] we can expect a great success when the methods of taxing commercial sectors are ultimately formulated."[14] After the domains were eliminated in August 1871, financial officials put much effort into finding ways to raise indirect tax revenue, particularly from major consumer goods, such as alcohol and soy sauce.[15] In September 1876, Yoshiwara Shigetoshi, the head of the Bureau of Taxation, proposed that the government should reduce land taxes so as to increase peasants' purchasing power. In his view, when peasants' consumption stimulated the development of manufacturing and commerce, the government would be able to extract more revenue from commercial sectors.[16]

In the case of alcohol production, the Meiji government in 1868 decided to break the monopoly held by privileged merchants, which had been set up in the late Tokugawa period. It requested that those who were interested in brewing apply for new licenses. Each brewer would pay a license fee and an annual duty according to the quantity of brewing stated in the license. This policy greatly stimulated the development of local sake brewing, and small producers mushroomed in the countryside.[17] However, their small scale made it difficult for the Ministry of Finance to collect taxes on sake. In the territory administered directly by the Meiji government (the territory of the former shogunate), the ministry had to rely on local magistrates and village headmen to supervise the collection of brewing duties. As a result, a large volume of alcohol remained either untaxed (because of unlicensed brewing) or undertaxed (because of brewing above the quantity reported in the license).[18]

The Ministry of Finance also tried to learn the methods of collecting indirect taxes employed in Western countries. For example, in 1870 it translated into Japanese the regulations and management of the Excise Department *(kokusanzeikyoku)* in Britain and its methods of collecting excises on beer.[19] But financial officials did not consider this model immediately applicable to Japan because the level of economic development in Western countries was vastly different from that in Japan.[20] For example, in early Meiji more than half of brewing houses were of small scale, having an annual output of less than 100 koku.[21] This contrasted sharply with the mass production of beer in nineteenth-century Britain, which greatly reduced the cost of central collection of excises on beer.

After abolishing the domains in 1871, the Meiji government began to set up regulations for taxing alcohol production across the whole country. The duties on alcohol were imposed both on production and sales. Both were collected according to local average prices self-reported by businessmen. Not surprisingly, this led to widespread undertaxation.[22] In 1872, the central government began to conduct surveys and field investigations to compile statistical data on the national economy, such as total population, volume of foreign trade, and total yield of taxation.[23] This information helped the Meiji government better estimate the potential of indirect taxation. On 12 December 1874, taxation officials in the Ministry of Finance proposed the repeal of unproductive indirect taxes, such as the duties on the production of vegetable oil, and an increase of the duties on alcohol production, as sake brewing alone had consumed some 4 million koku of rice in 1873.[24]

In 1877, the central government sent out officials to supervise the collection of duties on alcohol in localities. However, the normal assessment of taxation and supervision of collection were still entrusted to local magistrates. According to one field investigation conducted in March 1878 in two prefectures and twelve counties, most local magistrates were not zealous in implementing the regulations on alcohol production taxes imposed by the center. They either accepted the prices reported by sake brewers as the basis for assessing taxes, or they did not strictly check the real scale of sake brewing in localities.[25] After reexamining the market prices for sake, the government received extra revenue of more than 400,000 yen.[26] Encouraged by this result, the Ministry of Finance decided to set up more centralized institutions to directly assess the output of sake and collect sake duties.

In October 1879, the Ministry of Finance divided Japan into six districts for collecting sake duties. Supervisors sent from the Bureau of Taxation worked with local inspectors to monitor the scale of brewing houses. They not only carefully measured the volume of sake containers but also checked all relevant account records. The supervisors directly reported their findings of the monthly output of sake brewing houses to the Bureau of Taxation. In 1880, all the salaries and traveling expenses of sake inspectors were paid by the Ministry of Finance. To simplify collection, the Ministry of Finance in September 1880 decided to levy one single duty on the output of sake and repealed previous duties imposed on retailers.[27] Inspectors had the power to examine the procedures in sake brewing, which even gave them access to the technical secrets of brewers.[28]

By 1880, the Ministry of Finance had excluded local clerks and magistrates from both assessment and collection and depended on its own officials to collect sake duties. At that time, alcohol production was the biggest manufacturing sector in the Japanese economy; in 1882 it accounted for 44 percent of the total output value of the six major manufactured goods (sake, cotton weaving, raw silk, tea, dyes, and paper).[29] The elasticity in the yields of alcohol taxes was illustrated by a sharp rise from 1.26 million yen in 1874 to 6.46 million yen in 1879.[30] The creation of a centralized institution to collect elastic revenue from sake production enabled the Meiji government to avoid overreliance on land taxes, which were politically sensitive and administratively difficult to collect.

While the Meiji government was centralizing government finance and the collection of sake taxes, its paper notes remained nonconvertible. In 1873, Yoshikawa Akimasa, who was in charge of printing paper notes in the Ministry of Finance, warned that if the government continued to issue paper notes to cover its deficits, it would destroy government finance and cause great suffering to the people.[31] Nevertheless, in order to repress the samurai rebellion led by Saigō Takamori in 1877, the Meiji government again turned to paper notes to meet military expenses. As a result, the total amount of paper notes, including both government paper notes and banknotes issued by national banks, increased from 107 million yen before the rebellion to 164 million yen in 1879.[32] Excessive issue of paper notes produced inflation and the consequent hoarding of silver specie; this in turn caused the falling value of paper notes vis-à-vis silver currencies.

Despite serious inflation after 1877, the Japanese economy underwent significant development. According to a market investigation conducted by the Osaka Chamber of Commerce in 1879, peasant purchasing power had increased. The general prosperity in rural areas had attracted many urban migrants, stimulated domestic trade, and increased imports that met the needs of the rural sector even though imports of foreign luxuries had decreased.[33] Annual output of sake jumped from 3 million koku in 1871 to 5 million in 1879, which provided the Meiji government an important source of indirect revenue.

International markets were also favorable to Japan's exports. The adoption of the gold standard throughout the West resulted in silver inflows into East Asia after the mid-1870s. In 1878, Japan was already on a de facto silver standard as silver currencies were used not only for foreign trade but also for domestic transactions. The falling value of silver was not only an alternative to a "protective tariff" for Japan but also beneficial to Japan's exports. In June 1879, the Office of Customs in the Ministry of Finance asked the chambers of commerce in Tokyo and Osaka to investigate the impact of imports on the Japanese economy so that the government could decide an appropriate level for a protective tariff. The two chambers both considered such a tariff unnecessary and believed that the import of cotton yarn, sugar, and iron was beneficial to the Japanese economy, even though they recognized that a higher tariff level would raise revenue for the government.[34]

At the same time, domestic financial networks became more integrated as national banks and major private banks, such as Mitsui and Yasuda, established nationwide correspondence networks to transmit money across time and regions. As an example, the number of correspondence relationships among the 150 national banks and the Mitsui and their respective branches increased from 10 in June 1877 to 1,027 in June 1880.[35] To promote the circulation of banknotes issued by different banks in Japan, Shibusawa Eiichi, the head of the Dai-Ichi Bank, organized a bank association to coordinate the business activities of its member banks. He was particularly interested in introducing the institution of the "clearinghouse" from the United States and Switzerland, which would settle liabilities and discount bills issued by various member banks.[36] A similar Bank Association was formed in Osaka in 1880, consisting of fifteen major national banks and the Mitsui Bank. It played an important role in coordinating bill discounting and exchange of banknotes among member banks.[37] These dense networks among private banks laid the groundwork for a central bank that would allow the government to regulate the domestic financial markets.

Severe inflation after 1877 led to rising waves of opposition movements, which pressured the Meiji government to establish a parliamentary system. Within the government, financial officials split over the issue of paper notes. Should Japan use silver currencies to exchange all circulating paper notes and thus abandon the issue of government paper notes, or should it restore the value of paper notes by reducing their volume while increasing government silver reserves? Power struggles within the government and confrontation between the state and society complicated Japan's next step toward the modern fiscal state: the creation of an institutional linkage between a centralized government finance and the financial markets.

Political Economy of the Matsukata Deflation

Inflation had different distributional effects on urban and rural areas. Rising prices greatly troubled the urban population, particularly those, such as ex-samurai, who depended on fixed incomes. More ex-samurai joined the Freedom and People's Rights Movement. Peasants benefited from a de facto tax reduction as a result of the increasing price of rice. Nonetheless, rich farmers and local merchants in rural areas pushed for participation in local governance, particularly with respect to such issues as local taxes, water control, road construction, and maintenance of local infrastructure. In regard to national politics, they also called for the establishment of a parliament. The political activism of rich farmers and rural merchants from 1878 onward greatly expanded the Freedom and People's Rights Movement. The number of petitions and proposals for a parliamentary institution jumped from seven in 1879 to eighty-five in 1880.[38] In March 1880, 114 representatives of the Association of Patriots, which counted 87,000 members, gathered in Osaka and presented the Meiji government with a petition for the creation of a parliamentary system.[39] In this influential proposal, the representatives expressed their concern about "massive national debts, overissuing of paper notes, and the rise in prices." They demanded a parliamentary institution be founded to address these severe problems.[40]

In this situation, the stabilization of the value of paper notes was crucial to the Meiji government, not only economically but politically as well. After the assassination of Ōkubo Toshimichi by an ex-samurai on 14 May 1878, Ōkuma Shigenobu had to bear the brunt of the criticism of inflation within the government. In April and May of 1879, he ordered the release of 2.4 million yen in silver coins from the government reserves in an attempt to stabilize the exchange rate between paper notes and silver coins in the market, but to no avail.[41] In April 1880, he ordered the release of another 3 million yen in specie. However, instead of stabilizing the value of the paper notes, this measure caused the ratio of government specie reserves to the total amount of paper notes to drop from 21.5 percent in 1872 to as low as 4.5 percent in 1880.[42] These market reactions indicated that the Meiji government needed to make a credible commitment that it would not issue more paper notes to cover its deficits in future.

Activists of the Freedom and People's Rights Movement pointed out that the ongoing inflation was caused by the government's excessive issue of paper notes.[43] In response, Ōkuma insisted that deficits in foreign trade led to a scarcity of silver specie in Japan, which resulted in the falling value of paper notes and thus inflation. In practice, however, the drop in value of paper notes forced Ōkuma to consider how to reduce the amount of paper notes in circulation by generating a fiscal surplus. On 29 June 1879, he proposed using fiscal surplus to write off 20 million yen of paper notes over seven years. In order to boost public trust in the government's determination to reduce the volume of paper notes, he planned to publish the amounts of the surplus and the resulting reduction in paper notes in newspapers.[44]

At this moment, Ōkuma had not yet given up his plan to stabilize the current amount of government paper notes by increasing government silver reserves. For this purpose, he contended that the government should actively organize direct exports to earn silver from overseas markets.[45] On 28 February 1880, the Ministry of Finance disbursed 3 million yen in silver coins from government reserves as capital to form the Yokohama Specie Bank. Its major mission was to lend government silver coins to privileged merchants to help them organize the production of raw silk and tea and then directly export these products to overseas markets. However, many of the loans from the Yokohama Specie Bank were made through political connections and became nonperforming.[46] Private merchants, especially major raw silk exporters, considered direct export impractical for two reasons. First, they had to compete with foreign merchants who were more familiar with the circumstances of overseas markets. Second, direct exports demanded a lot of capital input before the exported goods were sold in a foreign country.[47]

Inflation and the falling value of government paper notes resulted in serious tensions within the Meiji government. In February 1880, Iwakura Tomomi and Itō Hirobumi orchestrated an institutional reform to strengthen the control of the Council of State over government ministries, particularly the Ministry of Finance. A new Committee of Public Finance, which consisted of Ōkuma Shigenobu, Itō Hirobumi, and

Terashima Munenori, took charge of financial matters. Meanwhile, as the Meiji emperor grew up, he became more actively involved in policy making.[48] The Ministry of Finance could no longer dictate the making of major financial policies.

The disappointing performance of the Yokohama Specie Bank indicated that it was unrealistic for the Meiji government to quickly increase its reserves of silver by promoting direct exports. Therefore, it had to seek ways to restore the value of paper notes by reducing the amount circulating in the economy. At this moment, there were two main options being discussed within the government: to exchange all paper notes with silver currencies or to gradually reduce their amount and thus stabilize their value. Given the pressure from opposition movements and the increasing demands for a parliament, each option had different political implications. Thus the choice was not determined by economic reasoning alone.

In May 1880, Ōkuma put forth a bold plan to achieve the convertibility of paper notes immediately by borrowing from the international markets. In this proposal, entitled "On Changing the Currency System" (also known as the "Specie Exchange Plan"), Ōkuma proposed raising a foreign loan of 10 million pounds (equivalent to 50 million Japanese silver yen) at 7 percent in London. Combined with the 17.5 million in specie available in the Ministry of Finance, the government could exchange 78 million yen in paper notes from the market at a silver–notes exchange rate of 1:1.16. The remaining 27 million yen in paper notes still in the economy would be taken in by the national banks, which used paper notes to exchange for government bonds in return for the privilege to issue the same amount of banknotes. After this exchange, the Meiji government would be able to replace government paper notes with silver currencies, and Ōkuma expected that hoarded specie would reappear in the market. As to the annual interest payment of 3.68 million yen, Ōkuma suggested an increase in tax rates on alcohol, which was expected to generate extra revenue of 6.62 million yen per year.[49]

The major goal of Ōkuma's proposal was to quickly replace the circulating government paper notes with silver currencies. After this exchange, the government would stop issuing paper notes and cast only silver coins. The banknotes issued by national banks were private notes that did not have the status of legal tender. Ōkuma may have been too optimistic about the ability of the Meiji government to borrow from the international markets; and he did not foresee the extra interest that might result in future from a rising pound. But his proposal was hardly a threat to Japan's sovereignty, as his critics charged. The annual interest payments were intended to come mainly from domestic indirect taxes, which the Ministry of Finance already collected centrally.

However, the scheme was quite controversial within the government. Conservatives such as Iwakura Tomomi criticized it as "selling Japan to foreigners." Itō Hirobumi, Inoue Kaoru, and Sano Tsunetami worried that such a large foreign loan would involve a heavy interest burden and incur strong criticism from activists of the Freedom and People's Rights Movement. Representatives from the army and navy, conversely, all supported Ōkuma's plan because it did not cut military expenditures.[50] Matsukata Masayoshi admitted that the plan was "sound from the economic perspective," but he considered it dangerous to take out a foreign loan to exchange paper notes. Instead, he proposed encouraging direct exports so as to increase government silver reserves and gradually reduce the amount of paper notes.[51] As officials could not reach an agreement, Emperor Meiji made the final decision to reject Ōkuma's plan in June 1880.

Although Ōkuma's proposal was not implemented, two important things should be noted. First, even though Ōkuma still held that deficit in international trade rather than excessive issue of paper notes was the major cause of inflation, he now appealed to devaluation of the currency to resolve Japan's deficits in foreign trade. For Ōkuma, import substitution was no longer the main method to resolve Japan's deficit in foreign trade. In his view, outflows of specie caused by this trade deficit would reduce domestic prices while raising those of imports, and thereafter Japan's exports would increase and its imports decrease. Consequently, specie should flow back into Japan through international trade, though the use of paper notes in Japan might delay the proper functioning of this mechanism.[52] Second, and more important, by exchanging silver specie for paper notes, Ōkuma intended to avoid the domestic deflation that would be caused by a sharp drop in the monetary supply. He warned explicitly that although a rapid reduction of the amount of paper notes might help recover their value in regard to silver coins, it would also produce a serious domestic deflation and thus greatly damage domestic commerce and manufacturing.[53]

Ōkuma's concern about the deflationary effects of drastically cutting the amount of paper notes was echoed by leaders in the business community. In November 1880, Godai Tomoatsu petitioned the Ministry of Finance on behalf of the Osaka Chamber of Commerce. He pointed out that an easy method for the government to stop the falling value of paper notes was simply to "intentionally cut down the amount of notes." However, Godai warned that this approach would trigger domestic deflation and thus "block the means of financing and increase the interest rate" and "push the Japanese people into an extremely difficult situation." He urged the government to take the whole economy into consideration in its attempt to restore the value of government paper notes.[54]

After Ōkuma's plan was rejected, the remaining policy option was to gradually reduce the amount of paper notes by generating a fiscal surplus. But how could the Meiji government do this? Growing domestic opposition deterred the Meiji government from raising land taxes. For example, in September 1880, the Meiji government rejected a proposal to collect 25 percent of land taxes in rice rather than in paper notes on the grounds that this would arouse peasant riots and further stimulate the Freedom and People's Rights Movement.[55] It turned to the duties on consumer goods, including alcohol and tobacco, for more revenue. For this purpose, the Ministry of Finance further increased the duty on sake from 1 yen to 2 yen per 100 koku and hoped that heavy tax rates would encourage the development of big brewing houses while driving out small producers.[56] Moreover, to increase the fiscal surplus by up to 10 million yen a year, the Meiji government decided to greatly cut expenditures by accelerating the sale of state enterprises, reducing government purchase of imported goods, and cutting central government subsidies to and spending on local infrastructure, police, and prisons.[57] This represented a fundamental change from the earlier expansionist fiscal policies to a fiscal retrenchment.

There were different opinions on the proposed annual fiscal surplus of 10 million yen. One was to write the surplus off so as to reduce the amount of paper notes. Another, as Inoue Kaoru and Godai Tomoatsu proposed to the government at the end of 1880, was to use it as capital to form a Bank of Japan supported by an insurance company and a trading company. The Bank of Japan would make loans to the trading company to organize the direct export of raw silk and tea so as to earn silver specie from abroad and increase government silver reserves. The insurance company would provide the necessary services.[58] However, this plan ran contrary to the effort to restore the value of paper notes. Also, the disappointing performance of the Yokohama Specie Bank in organizing direct exports made this approach less persuasive.

On 29 July 1881, Ōkuma and Itō jointly drafted a plan to raise 50 million yen by floating government bonds and use this as the capital to establish a central bank. This "big specie bank" was to discount the bills of exchange for Japan's foreign trade, manage government revenue and expenditures, and issue convertible banknotes, "just like the Bank of England in Britain and the Bank of France in France."[59] To quickly obtain the needed capital, Ōkuma and Itō decided to allow foreigners to subscribe. The main goal was to quickly attain the convertibility of paper notes without reducing the monetary level. Compared with the foreign loan of 10 million pounds that Ōkuma had proposed in 1880, this plan appeared politically less controversial. Yet Matsukata Masayoshi strongly opposed it. In a September 1881 report that he sent to Sanjō Sanetomi, the minister of the state, Matsukata warned that "the dependence on foreigners' capital [in the plan of Ōkuma and Itō] . . . might achieve convertibility but would cause future disaster and push Japan into a dire situation similar to that of Egypt, Turkey, or India."[60]

Despite the debates on how to build a central bank, the change to fiscal retrenchment sent an important signal to the markets that the Meiji government would no longer issue paper notes to cover its fiscal deficits. Meanwhile, the government also stopped the risky practice of lending government silver reserves to political merchants and government enterprises.[61] The exchange rate of silver coins to paper notes began to fall after reaching a peak of 1.795 in April 1881, and it stabilized around 1.63 for a few months. In February the Meiji government had shortened the period for peasants to hand over land taxes, which forced them to sell rice even at lower prices. The price of rice began to fall after April 1881.[62]

As part of fiscal retrenchment, the government disbursed less silver specie to purchase goods from abroad. Given the dropping price of silver in the international markets, the Japanese economy on the silver standard would not suffer from chronic deficits in international trade. Even without government-organized direct exports to earn silver from overseas markets, the Meiji government collected customs in silver, which amounted to more than 2.5 million yen of silver specie in the early 1880s. Thus customs revenue was a reliable source to increase government silver reserves for the purpose of attaining the convertibility of paper notes. Under these circumstances, a gradual reduction of paper notes was viable if the government continued fiscal retrenchment. Moreover, when the market became confident in the government's commitment to not issue paper notes to cover its deficits, the hoarded silver coins would gradually come back into the market and help restore the value of paper notes. However, the political situation at the time was hostile to this economically sound gradual approach.

The activists of the Freedom and People's Rights Movement welcomed the policy change to fiscal retrenchment and the stoppage of printing paper notes to cover government deficits. In response to the government's attempt to raise taxes, they argued that the Japanese people had the right to an immediate establishment of a parliament so that their representatives could participate in the making of budgets and tax policies.[63] At the same time, the retrenchment policy greatly stimulated local elites' political participation. As more and more expenditure on road construction, local infrastructure, and civil works came from local rather than national taxes, the new financial burdens pushed rich farmers and merchants to become more involved in local governance.[64] They opposed the attempt to transfer much of the burden of government spending to localities, particularly in the construction of major roads. They wanted a voice in the making of public finance via representative institutions at the national level.[65]

A coalition of ex-samurai, local merchants, and rich farmers in the Freedom and People's Rights Movement was a serious threat to the autocratic Meiji regime. In response, the government adopted repressive measures. The number of newspapers closed ran as high as forty-six in 1881, compared with three in 1879 and twelve in 1880. On 5 April 1880, the government forbade any political association and gathering if it was considered "detrimental to the security of the state," and communications or correspondence among members of prefectural and city assemblies were also prohibited.[66] The political confrontation between the Meiji government and the Freedom and People's Rights activists became explosive.

In March 1881, Ōkuma suggested that the Meiji government hold a national election of representatives at the end of 1882 and establish a British-style bicameral system in 1883. In order for the future government to represent the "will of the people" *(kokunin no yobō)*, Ōkuma argued that the majority party in the parliament should have the right to form a responsible cabinet and that party officials and apolitical civil servants should be strictly separated.[67] His move alienated many members of the government. In the view of Inoue Kowashi, who was drafting a conservative constitution based on the Prussian model, the essence of the British constitutional monarchy was a republican polity of parliamentary sovereignty, in which the monarch was simply a puppet.[68] In October 1881, political conservatives expelled from the government Ōkuma and fifteen other officials who were suspected of being his followers.[69] Matsukata Masayoshi became the minister of finance.

Before the purge, Matsukata Masayoshi had also favored a gradual reduction in the amount of paper notes. In a report on public finance that he submitted to Sanjō Sanetomi, the minister of state, Matsukata had repeated Ōkuma's prognosis of the causes of inflation, that is, inflation was caused not by excessive issue of paper notes but by the lack of sufficient silver reserves, which resulted from deficits in international trade. Matsukata argued that the correct method to stabilize the value of paper notes was to increase government specie reserves by encouraging domestic production and exports.[70] For this purpose, he suggested stopping loans of government cash reserves and instead adopting a new "mechanism of utilizing money" *(kahei unyō no kijiku),* which was a central bank supported by savings banks and investment banks. Savings banks were to channel small deposits into the central bank through the postal networks. The investment bank would then use these aggregated savings to make long-term loans with low interest rates to encourage enterprises in agriculture, manufacturing, and transportation so as to increase exports.[71] This was based on the Belgian model of central banking.[72] However, it was impractical in the short run for the government to channel small savings into state-guided long-term industrial development, so Matsukata's idea remained on paper for the moment.[73]

After Matsukata became minister of finance, he continued fiscal retrenchment by selling state enterprises and tried to raise government
silver reserves by insisting that the Yokohama Specie Bank make loans
for direct exports. To quiet government criticism, he needed to take
measures to curb inflation and prevent the falling value of paper notes.
As it would take longer for the government to increase its holdings of
silver specie, he decided to reduce the volume of paper notes by cutting
the government supplementary paper notes *(yobi shihei)*. These were
originally issued by the Ministry of Finance in 1872 to meet government
spending when the collected tax revenue had not arrived yet within one
fiscal year (from July 1 through the following June 30).[74] After 1876, the
government had increasingly appealed to the printing of supplementary
paper notes to cover fiscal deficits.

In a time of fiscal retrenchment, cutting the supplementary paper
notes was not controversial within the government. Yet despite his
earlier statements, Matsukata now seemed to hold that inflation and
the falling value of paper notes were caused by the excessive numbers
of paper notes issued after 1877 and therefore that the total amount of
paper notes should be quickly reduced to the level of 1877.[75] As a result, he dramatically slashed the amount of supplementary government
paper notes from 13 million yen in 1881 to 4 million yen in 1882 and
further to zero in 1883. In other words, in less than two years, Matsukata reduced the total amount of currency (including banknotes) by
13.7 percent, or the total amount of government paper notes by 17.6
percent. This was the crucial factor that triggered the Matsukata
deflation.[76]

As Matsukata's measure of January 1882 had not even been men-
tioned in the annual budget and government plan for reducing the
amount of paper notes, the market did not anticipate the sudden falloff
in the monetary level. For example, in 1882, Taguchi Ukichi, a prominent critic of the Meiji government financial policies, was wondering
whether the annual cancellation of 3 million yen in paper notes that the
Meiji government had announced could quickly restore the value of
paper notes. Taguchi later admitted that he did not realize the connection between deflation and the cut down of supplementary paper notes
until late 1883.[77] In consequence, rich farmers, landlords, and businessmen who had borrowed from local banks or financial intermediaries

during the prosperous year of 1881 were caught by a rise in the real interest rate and a simultaneous drop in prices in 1882.

The deflation became apparent in early 1883 as peasants' falling purchasing power quickly caused a chain reaction affecting the whole economy. According to a report of the Osaka Chamber of Commerce on 23 February 1883, most of the workshops that used imported cotton yarn to weave coarse cotton cloth to meet the demand of peasants had prospered in 1880 and 1881 but went bankrupt after the spring of 1882.[78] As lower rice prices led to a sharp reduction in the income of farmers, the Dai-Ichi Bank observed that urban merchants found it difficult to sell goods to rural areas.[79] The severity of the deflation greatly damaged the economic basis of the Freedom and People's Rights Movement in the countryside; activists could not easily afford to organize political associations.[80]

Domestic investment plummeted. According to reports of the Dai-Ichi Bank in Tokyo, in 1882 some businessmen, supposing the recession

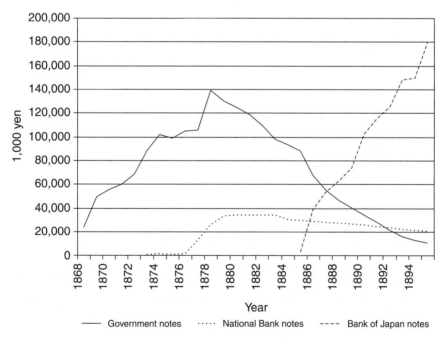

Figure 4.2 Amount of paper notes in Japan, 1868–1895.

Source: *Hundred-Year Statistics of the Japanese Economy,* ed. Nihon Ginkō Tōkeikyoku (Tokyo: Nihon Ginkō, 1966), 166.

would be temporary, still took out loans from banks. However, they ended up in great difficulties as the prices in the markets kept falling. In consequence, after 1882 it became more and more difficult for banks to make loans. The reluctance of the business community to invest led to steady accumulation of idle capital in banks.[81] In late August and early September of 1883, there were few transactions in the markets as most merchants anticipated a further falling of prices.[82]

Matsukata himself did not seem to fully anticipate the deflationary effects when he suddenly cut government supplementary notes. For example, a conflict with China in July 1882 (the *Jingo* Incident) made the Japanese navy and army demand a huge military expansion so as to be able to fight China's newly modernized navy. Matsukata in September planned to raise 7.5 million yen annually by increasing the duties on sake and tobacco. In his view, both the total output and retail prices of alcohol had increased in 1881 in spite of heavy duties, which meant there must be room for higher tax rates. This optimistic estimation shows that Matsukata did not even consider the possible impact of deflation on alcohol production and demand.[83] However, a deflationary economy led to serious tax arrears. In 1883, the total output of sake in Japan fell 35 percent, which further dragged down rice prices.[84] Matsukata was forced to reduce the scale of military expansion with actual expenditure cut by 13 percent and 22 percent from the original plan in 1883 and 1884, respectively.[85]

Although Matsukata made the resumption of the value of paper notes his priority, he could not ignore the nationwide deflation. On 10 December 1883, he admitted that falling prices made merchants hold on to their money and therefore deterred current investment.[86] Yet he insisted that a complete recovery of the value of paper notes would cultivate the virtues of "industry and thrift" among the Japanese, who would then engage in "concrete" rather than "speculative" business activities.[87] However, the shrinking discrepancy between paper notes and silver currency could do little to alleviate the damage that deflation inflicted on the Japanese economy, given that the expectation of further falls in prices discouraged investment and lower investment further pushed prices downward. The market itself would not automatically break this vicious cycle without effective intervention by the state. Matsukata in practice could not afford to wait passively for his "deflation-stimulate-investment" theory to rescue the economy.

In Matsukata's proposal to establish a central bank, he had pointed out that such a "bank of banks" could take such measures as discounting commercial bills or short-term lending to mitigate the seasonal fluctuations of currency so as to regulate the economy.[88] However, the Bank of Japan established in October 1882 was ill prepared to perform such functions. Its initial capital was a mere 2 million yen, and this reached only 5 million in 1883. Yet in the 1880 discussion of central banking, most financial officials had agreed that a capital level of at least 10 million yen was necessary. In contrast, there were 143 national banks and 176 private banks in Japan, which had a total capital of 61.36 million yen in 1883.[89] The number of banks that opened current accounts with the Bank of Japan was one in 1883 and ten in 1884.[90]

The newly established Bank of Japan thus had little ability to regulate the financial markets for the purpose of mitigating the severe deflation in 1883 and 1884. What was worse, the Meiji government first used the Bank of Japan as a political weapon to attack Ōkuma's Constitutional Reform Party. As the funds of this party came mainly from the Mitsubishi Company, the largest shipping company in Japan at the time, the Meiji government on 1 January 1883 established a rival, the Joint Transportation Company (Kyōdō Un'yu Kaisha), to weaken Mitsubishi.[91] The Bank of Japan provided 300,000 yen as a timed loan to the Joint Transportation Company without requiring any collateral. This accounted for 46 percent of its total timed loans in the first half of 1883.[92]

Under the dual pressures of increasing military expenditures and falling tax revenue after 1882, Matsukata first appealed to short-term borrowing from the Bank of Japan and the cash deposited in the Ministry of Finance to meet government spending during the period when the collected revenue had not arrived at the center yet. After 1886, this spending need was met by short-term bonds issued by the Ministry of Finance.[93] Although Matsukata had harshly criticized Ōkuma's plan to take out foreign loans, he himself tried in 1884 and 1885 to borrow from the capital markets in London to acquire necessary specie, but to no avail.[94] Matsukata originally continued the policy to increase government specie reserves by asking the Yokohama Specie Bank to provide loans for organizing direct exports to overseas markets. The poor performance of direct exports, however, forced him to make changes. In July 1884, he permitted the Yokohama Specie Bank to lend to foreign merchants involved in Japan's foreign trade.[95]

Because Matsukata depended on the recovery of the value of paper notes to justify his economic policies, he had to seek measures other than increasing monetary input to stimulate domestic economic transactions. One such measure was to issue long-term state bonds. Severe domestic deflation created an environment favorable to the floating of state bonds as the lack of alternative investment opportunities made government bonds attractive to investors. For example, the stipend and commutation bonds, whose market values had been falling in the inflationary period, now drew a lot of investors, especially as the Meiji government made punctual payments of both interest and principal.[96] Likewise, when Matsukata introduced low-interest long-term bonds in 1884 to raise substantial amounts of capital for railway construction and the modernization of the navy and army, they were oversubscribed.[97] In 1886, Matsukata used new borrowing at 5 percent to convert the state's old debt with higher interest rates (6 or more percent) and thus reduced the annual interest payment by more than 3 million yen.[98]

In addition, Matsukata planned to use discounting of draft bills to encourage commercial transactions. In February 1884, he even urged the Bank of Japan to discount those business bills that had no preassigned collateral. Business leaders such as Shibusawa Eiichi considered this too risky. As a compromise, the Bank of Japan first experimented with discounting bills secured by goods stored in warehouses or by state bonds.[99] Matsukata then lowered the discount rates from 9.49 percent in 1885 to 4.93 percent in 1886. Moreover, he allowed the Bank of Japan to accept not only bonds but also corporation stocks of railway construction, seaborne transportation, mining, and textiles as collateral for low-interest loans.[100] This stimulated an investment boom. The lending of the Bank of Japan rose from 16 million yen in 1885 to 105 million in 1889; and the lending of national banks from 649 million yen to 1,414 million in the same period.[101] The number of corporations in industry, railway, and mining formed between 1886 and 1889 was as many as 1,743, and their total capital came to 1,086 million yen. However, there was a good deal of "bubble" in this boom as many of the corporation stocks were only partially subscribed in cash.[102]

In the received story, Matsukata has often been characterized as an advocate of orthodox economics who rejected government intervention in favor of the market.[103] Yet the risky financial policies of the Ministry of Finance between 1882 and 1890 went against both the model and practice of central banking in Western Europe. Their implementation, despite criticism from the business community, should be viewed against the background of the ongoing deflation, which seriously undermined the legitimacy of the Meiji government. It was politically important to end deflation sooner. Nonetheless, as Matsukata had set the parity of paper notes and silver currency as the supreme goal regardless of the economic consequences, his policy options were quite limited, especially when he could not raise foreign credit. In this situation, he had to rely more on the use of business bills or corporation stocks as a surrogate for monetary input so that he could alleviate the scarcity of currency without increasing the amount of paper notes.

Centralized institutions to collect duties from alcohol production were vital to the Meiji government's ability to service the interest payments on its long-term domestic bonds. As the deflation raised the real burden of land taxes and reduced the purchasing power of rural people, the Meiji government could not extract more revenue from land taxes. Indeed, it had to use force to repress large-scale peasant riots in Gunma, Chichibu, and other regions. Elastic revenues to secure government long-term domestic bonds came mainly from raising the duties on sake production. The social resistance to high sake taxes was very different from that to land taxes.

Before Matsukata became the minister of finance, the Meiji government in September 1880 raised the duty on sake production from 1 yen to 2 yen per koku produced and the license fee from 5 yen to 30 yen. Many small local sake brewers organized petition movements in protest. However, major sake producers in areas such as Hyōgo and Osaka who sold their product to the national market did not participate in these campaigns.[104] In 1882, Matsukata further raised the duty on sake from 2 yen per koku of sake produced to 4 yen and strengthened inspection on unlicensed brewing. Many small-scale sake brewers were driven out of business as a result.[105] Big sake brewers took this opportunity to expand their production. After 1885, the output of sake, which had fallen to 3 million koku, began to revive. The scale of sake production in Japan rose considerably. In 1895, for example, 28 percent of sake houses had an annual production of more than 1,000 koku; another 65 percent produced between 100 and 1,000 koku.[106] The prevalence of larger producers in turn reduced the government's costs in tax collection. The monopoly profit allowed the large sake brewers to bear heavy duties while transferring the burden to consumers.

By the late 1880s, the modern fiscal state had emerged in Japan. The Bank of Japan in April 1883 began to remit government revenue and disburse government spending. This enabled the Meiji government to consolidate the centralized fiscal operation and rid itself of its dependence on private banks to transfer official funds. This achievement put the entire government revenue and funds under the management of the Bank of Japan while simultaneously strengthening the supervision of the Ministry of Finance. Centralized fiscal institutions thus undergirded the operation of the Bank of Japan as a central bank.[107] Central collection of elastic indirect taxes sustained the credibility of the Meiji government's long-term bonds. The Bank of Japan in 1886 monopolized the issue of convertible banknotes, which became the legal tender. As the Bank of Japan established ever more numerous correspondence relationships with private banks, it began to act as the central bank to regulate the domestic financial markets in the early twentieth century.

By the time the Meiji government opened the Japanese Diet in 1890, the institutions of the modern fiscal state had already emerged. In the newly established Diet, debates mainly centered on whether these institutions should be used to fund military expansion or to promote domestic welfare. Representatives from opposition parties demanded lower taxes, increased expenditure on local welfare and infrastructure, and reduced military spending.[108] Meanwhile, officials such as Itō Hirobumi, Inoue Kaoru, and Ōkuma Shigenobu (who rejoined the government as the minister of foreign affairs) planned to make concessions to Western powers in legal affairs in return for a resumption of sovereignty in the customs. They intended to use this means to increase government income by raising tariffs on Japan's expanding foreign trade and thus mitigate the tension between the center and localities in domestic taxation. Yet these concessions were unacceptable to political conservatives.

Notably, the competing agendas in public finance between 1891 and 1894 were all based on the institutions of the modern fiscal state. Even political opponents to the Meiji government did not demand the dismantling of the centralized institutions to collect indirect taxes on alcohol, though they would have preferred lower duties. Nor did they want to abolish the Bank of Japan, which monopolized the issue of convertible banknotes. Instead, they hoped that the Bank of Japan would facilitate lending to rural manufacturing. Likewise, the demand to increase expenditures on local welfare did not challenge the centralized institution for managing government finance. However, this debate was to a large extent short-circuited by the defeat of China in the Sino-Japanese War of 1895. The tremendous indemnities that came with victory allowed the Meiji government to shoulder much of the expenditure on local infrastructure and thus to free itself to some extent from its accountability to opposition representatives.[109]

Overall, the institution building of the Meiji regime was quite malleable, as attested by the splits among major leaders and the changing institutional arrangements. But whoever came to power had to face the formidable problem of how to redeem the massive issue of paper notes. The need to resolve this special credit crisis motivated financial officials to centralize the collection of indirect taxes on major consumer goods and strengthen the central supervision of government finance. This accumulation of institutional arrangements toward fiscal centralization continued uninterrupted in spite of deep political divisions within and outside the government. Dense private financial networks to remit money greatly facilitated centralization of the fiscal system.

Institutional development in public finance was highly political. This is apparent in Japan's last step toward a modern fiscal state in the 1880s. The Matsukata deflation, which was quite severe between 1882 and 1884, might have been avoided had the political situation in 1880 and 1881 been conducive to a "soft-landing" approach to curb inflation. However, the intensifying pressure from opposition movements made it impossible for the Meiji government to gradually reduce the amount of paper notes. Although the direction toward central collection of indirect taxes and a centralized management of government finance was quite clear to actors in 1882, the actual path of institutional development led through a highly deflationary economy that was disastrous to the rural sectors. This environment reduced investment opportunities and made it easier for the Meiji government to issue domestic long-term bonds. The institutions of the modern fiscal state greatly enhanced the Meiji government's ability to mobilize long-term financial resources and allowed the government to use indirect financial policies rather than direct management of enterprises to stimulate industrial development.

5

ECONOMIC DISRUPTION AND THE FAILURE OF PAPER MONEY IN CHINA, 1851–1864

Because the Qing government did not cast its own silver coins, it could not use devaluation to mitigate the severe deflation caused by the dearth of domestic silver stocks between the 1820s and 1840s. When the chronic unemployment and depression of these decades finally triggered the Taiping Rebellion in 1851, pressure mounted to meet the increasing military demands. Between 1851 and 1868, total state expenses in putting down the Taiping Rebellion, the Nian Rebellion, and other smaller uprisings in Guangdong, Fujian, and the southwest ran as high as 300 million tael of silver.[1] This was an enormous amount for a government whose annual income in the 1850s came to some 40 million tael.

In response, the Qing government started to collect indirect taxes on consumption. Moreover, it issued paper money and cast debased copper coins and even iron coins to cover deficits. Receipts from lijin duties quickly became an important source of revenue and helped the Qing government put down the Taiping Rebellion in 1864 and the Nian in the mid-1870s. However, the issuance of paper notes—the first time that the state in China had tried to float government paper notes en masse since the early fifteenth century[2]—was a fiasco. The Qing government repealed paper money in 1864, and its decentralized fiscal system continued.

The existing literature considers the issuance of paper notes as simply one example of desperate "inflationary financing."[3] However, these paper notes and debased copper coins with large face values failed to circulate widely. Contemporaries noted that even as paper notes and debased copper coins were causing severe inflation in Beijing in 1857, prices were low and stable in the suburbs a few dozen *li* outside the capital.[4] Most of the local gazetteers compiled after the 1850s do not mention these paper notes. Their lack of circulation meant that the Qing government did not benefit financially from issuance. This contrasts sharply with the successful circulation of nonconvertible paper notes in early Meiji Japan, even though the government could not redeem them until 1886. State paper notes are fundamentally different from private bank notes. The state can use political power to help confer on its issued fiat paper notes the status of legal tender within its territories.[5] Nonconvertibility thus does not necessarily doom them per se. But why was the Qing government in the 1850s unable even to force its own troops and provincial governors to accept its paper notes?

Some monetary historians still hold that the excessive issue of paper notes demonstrates the hostility of the despotic Qing government to the markets and to the interests of merchants.[6] This view, however, cannot accommodate the Qing government's practical policies toward markets and merchants since the mid-eighteenth century in areas such as the grain trade and coal mining; these policies reflected an increasing recognition among government officials of the importance of the market.[7] In fact, the plan of monetary reform before 1853 was coherent and cautious.[8] The Qing government issued paper notes denominated respectively in the silver and copper coins in the economy. Financial officials at both the central and provincial levels understood that circulation in commercial transactions was vital to the success of government paper notes. To secure the value of paper notes, the government set up money exchange offices *(guanqianju)* in cities and major market towns. These were designed as fractional note-issuing financial intermediaries. The government mobilized private financiers to manage them on the model of contemporary private banks *(qianzhuang)* and tried to use public funds to support their operation. However, this attempt at institution building was abortive.

Why did the issuance of nonconvertible paper notes in China in the 1850s fail disastrously? Why did it not motivate state actors to search for means of fiscal centralization, as happened in Meiji Japan? Socioeconomic conditions matter for institutional development. The market-friendly framework that the Qing government had developed in handling monetary issues since the mid-eighteenth century was vital to its plan to gradually float paper notes. However, this gradual approach was impractical when the brutal wars fought in the economic cores of the middle and lower Yangzi regions disrupted both interregional private financial and trading networks and normal government fiscal operations. Silver notes did not circulate well under such conditions.

Instead of looking for effective methods to float silver notes, Qing officials in 1855 decided to replace silver notes with paper notes denominated in copper coin *(baochao)*. This was the first serious attempt to switch to a copper standard supplemented by paper notes, an idea that had been intensively discussed among statecraft officials and scholars since the 1820s. However, this decision had a huge impact on the institution building to attain convertibility of paper notes. In the war-torn economy of the 1850s, the Qing government could not use grain or salt to back up the value of paper notes and had to use copper coins to redeem them. Moreover, the difficulty of transporting low-value and bulky copper coins in large quantities across regions forced the center to pass the convertibility problem onto provincial governments. Dependence on notes in copper coins thus made redemption efforts highly decentralized. The dynamics of the wartime economy in which the Qing government had to operate were not conducive to building centralized financial institutions to secure the value of state-issued paper notes. This failed experiment with paper notes thus illustrates the necessity of appropriate socioeconomic conditions, such as vibrant interregional trade and nationwide financial networks, for sustaining institution building toward centralization.

Monetary Issues and State Paper Notes

The Qing government's experiences in managing currency and regulating financial markets in the eighteenth century significantly affected the making of monetary policy in the 1850s. To maintain the official exchange rate of 1:1000 between silver tael and copper coins was one major goal. In the early eighteenth century, the Qing government was overwhelmingly concerned about the high value of copper coins in regard to silver.[9] During the reign of the Qianlong emperor (1736–1796), the government formulated a set of market-friendly approaches to manage the currency.

These policies had two important characteristics. First, the government aimed to keep a balance between supply and demand rather than relying on heavy-handed administrative control. For example, in response to market exchange rates of 1 tael of silver to around 700 to 800 wen in copper coins, the Qing government ordered provincial governments to open mints and hoped to use the increasing output of newly minted copper coins to raise the relative value of silver. For the same reason, the center also ordered the regular exchange of copper coins deposited with local governments for silver in the markets.[10] More direct forms of interference, such as prohibition of interregional transporting of copper coins and the limiting of copper coins stocked in private shops and pawnshops, were considered exigent rather than "ever-lasting" policies to mitigate the scarcity of copper coins in the economy.[11]

Second, the government took a realistic attitude toward profit incentives and considered it impractical to force private actors to abide by policies that ran against their economic interests. For example, the government by the mid-eighteenth century was greatly troubled by the counterfeiting of copper coins *(sizhu)* when copper content in official coins was low and by the melting of coins *(sixiao)* when it was high.[12] For example, the Qing financial officials noticed that when the market value of the copper content in the coins was high *(tonggui qianzhong),* people often melted down state-minted coins for copper *(sixing xiao-huai);* yet when it was low compared with the nominal value of coins *(tongjian qianqing),* people often counterfeited government coins for profit *(sizhu sheli).*[13] In a memorial in early 1736, Haiwang, the minister of the Board of Revenue and the Grand Supervisor of the Imperial Household, pointed out that these two activities were closely related to the market prices of copper. In his view, people had a strong incentive to melt down copper coins if both the copper price and the copper content of government coins were high and to counterfeit if copper content was low compared with the face values of the coins. Instead of a state monopoly of copper, Haiwang proposed that the government should lift restrictions on the copper trade and production and adjust the copper content in the minted coins according to market prices.[14] The other minister of the Board of Revenue, Shi Yizhi, further added that prohibiting the copper trade would simply lead to a scarcity of copper in the market, which would further raise the market prices of copper and thus provide even more incentive for people to melt official copper coins. Shi's memorial was highly appreciated by the Qianlong emperor.[15]

As it was impractical to frequently adjust the copper content in minted coins, the question of how to increase the copper supply became the focal issue. For this purpose, the government implemented many measures to encourage private investment, such as opening the state-controlled mining and trade in copper to private merchants. In so doing, it aimed to increase the amount of copper available not only for mintage but also for meeting the demand for copper in the economy. These measures were fundamentally different from the government policies during the preceding reign of the Yongzheng emperor (1723–1735), which declared a state monopoly on copper and forbade its private use or sale *(tongjin)*.

To better respond to different demands for copper coins in various regions, the center granted a certain degree of autonomy to provincial governments in deciding the content and fineness of their minted copper coins.[16] Because of the greatly expanded copper production in Yunnan Province, the dearth of copper and copper coins was relieved after the 1770s, and the market exchange rate between silver and copper coins approached the official rate of 1:1000.[17] Under these circumstances, the Qing government reasserted the state sovereignty in coinage and altered its previous tolerance of privately minted copper coins *(xiaoqian)*, ordering them to be exchanged for government-minted copper coins.[18]

The Qing government was also aware of the increasing use of private credit instruments, such as bills of exchange and promissory notes. In the first half of the nineteenth century, money exchangers, pawnshops, and even sellers of rice and salt in cities often issued private promissory notes denominated in copper coins *(qianpiao)* for daily transactions. In 1836, the center asked for the opinions of provincial governors on this phenomenon. Most replies confirmed the importance of private notes to the economy and considered their prohibition unnecessary or even harmful. Provincial governors proposed to better regulate the issue of private notes so as to ensure their creditworthiness and prevent deliberate fraud.[19] Typical government regulations were to permit only well-established businessmen to issue private notes and to stipulate that the issue had to be jointly secured by other shops *(lianming hubao)*. In handling legal disputes over the redemption of private notes, the government carefully distinguished deliberate fraud from the inability to redeem as a result of low liquidity. For example, if a money exchanger declared bankruptcy when he could not redeem the issued notes, the government usually gave him a certain period of time to return the deposited money to customers. If he could do so, then there was no punishment.[20]

However, in the first half of the nineteenth century, the government found it hard to apply its earlier success in monetary issues to mitigate the severe deflation caused by increasing scarcity of silver. In response, the idea of replacing silver with government-minted copper coins attracted much attention from statecraft officials and scholars. They proposed measures to address the unsuitability of copper coins for interregional trade and wholesaling. One was to issue paper notes denominated in copper coins *(qianchao)*, while the other was to mint copper coins with large nominal values, such as 10 wen, 50 wen, 100 wen, 500 wen, and even 1,000 wen *(zhudaqian)*.[21]

Nonetheless, the Qing government was reluctant to turn to paper notes because of their mixed record in China. Whereas their advocates often looked to the positive experience during the thirteenth century under the Southern Song dynasty (1127–1279), their opponents referred to the hyperinflation caused by excessive issue of paper notes in the late fourteenth and early fifteenth centuries.[22] In response to the suggestion to mint copper coins with large nominal values, officials in the Board of Revenue argued that a big discrepancy between the face value and actual copper content in the minted coins would inspire counterfeiting activities that the government could hardly curb.[23]

Policy discussions did not yield any concrete measures until the breakout of the Taiping Rebellion in 1851. In November of that year, government silver stocks in Beijing had dropped to only 1.87 million tael. Government income could hardly meet the extraordinary expenditures of wars and river works, which amounted to more than 30 million tael of silver between 1851 and 1853.[24] As the sale of nominal official titles *(juanna)* was inadequate to resolve the fiscal difficulties, the government was forced to look for new methods.

The mintage of denominated silver currencies to raise revenue was brought up again. In February 1854, Baoji, a tutor of the Imperial Academy of Learning and a member of the Imperial Clan, suggested minting silver coins *(yinbao)* so as to profit from the difference between the nominal and actual values of silver used in mintage.[25] In 1855, the Fujian governor Lü Quansun made a similar suggestion. He presented to the center two samples of silver coins that he had asked craftsmen in Fujian to make. Nonetheless, the Board of Revenue was afraid that the government could not force the circulation of a new silver currency and rejected this proposal.[26]

One method to cover fiscal deficit was to borrow from merchants. The Qing government had used bills of borrowing in 1850. The money exchange offices established and managed by the Imperial Household in Beijing issued these bills, and the Board of Revenue assigned them, worth 500,000 tael of silver, for the river work in Feng County in Jiangsu Province. The Bureau of River Work sold these notes to businessmen, who then took them to the Board of Revenue to purchase official titles. These bills did not bear interest but rid both the government and businessmen of the burden of transporting silver between Beijing and Jiangsu Province.[27] By 1853, however, tax revenues from the provinces to Beijing had dropped sharply due to the battles with Taiping forces. As officials of the Board of Revenue could not anticipate regular inflows of taxes to Beijing, they showed little interest in the idea of issuing short-term bills of credit *(qipiao)* to raise government income.[28] In the 1850s, the Qing government was unwilling to use high interest rates to attract loans from merchants.[29]

In 1851 and 1853, Board of Revenue officials were mainly concerned about the issuance of paper notes to meet government spending needs. To make the case for feasibility, advocates of paper notes often referred to the use of private notes and bills of exchange. For example, the Fujian governor Wang Yide contended that if paper notes issued by a private money exchanger *(qianpu)* could be accepted in the market, it was reasonable to suppose that paper notes issued by the state could as well.[30] In their view, the state enjoyed two special advantages in issuing paper notes not available to private financiers. First, a private bank might go bankrupt and close, yet the state would not. Second, annual tax collection and government spending constituted a regular loop to circulate government paper notes in large amounts.[31] Moreover, the Jiangsu governor Yang Wending, who consulted merchants in Suzhou over the issuance of paper notes, argued that the government could also use paper notes to mitigate the decades-long deflation caused by scarcity of silver; the recovered economy would provide more tax revenues to the state.[32]

In early 1853, runaway fiscal deficits forced the Qing government to cast copper coins with large face values and print paper notes. In June 1853, the Board of Revenue decided to release a limited amount of copper cash with a nominal value of 10 wen *(dangshi daqian)* in Beijing.[33] Encouraged by its acceptance in the markets, the board requested that all provincial governments adopt similar measures.[34]

In regard to paper notes, in February 1853, the Board of Revenue requested that the censor Wang Maoyin, who was well known for his proposal on paper notes in 1850, serve on the board and formulate relevant policies.[35] The Board of Revenue originally planned to let the Jiangsu government experiment before extending this policy to the rest of the country.[36] Nonetheless, the acting governor-general of Fujian and Zhejiang, Wang Yide, pointed out that this was impractical as the paper notes issued by one province might not be able to circulate in other provinces. Instead, Wang suggested that the experiment should be conducted uniformly in all provinces under central coordination.[37]

On 5 April 1853, the Qing government first printed silver notes *(guanpiao)* to a total amount of 120,000 tael in Beijing. The denominations were 1 tael, 3 tael, 5 tael, 10 tael, and 50 tael; these were designed for the convenience of transactions in the markets.[38] On 7 August 1853, the Qing government ordered provincial governments to issue notes in silver to a total amount of 1.75 million tael.[39] On 17 December 1853, the Board of Revenue further released copper notes *(baochao)* with nominal values of 500 wen, 1,000 wen, 1,500 wen, and 2,000 wen, respectively. The official exchange rate between the two notes was set at 1:2,000 (1 tael silver note equal to 2,000 wen copper notes).[40] On 12 August 1854, the Board of Revenue decided to use paper notes to replace copper coins with large face values, such as 500 wen, 1,000 wen, and 2,000 wen, which had been rejected by the markets.[41] Issuance of paper notes was thus much more important to the Qing government than the debasement of copper coins.

As conceived by the Board of Revenue, the silver notes would substitute for silver in long-distance trade and the copper notes serve for local small transactions.[42] The board also established the Office of Silver Notes *(guanpiaoju)* and the Office of Copper Notes *(baochaoju)* to manage the two kinds of notes. Although counterfeiting of government paper notes was declared a capital crime, the government did not forbid the use of private notes.[43] Although the issue of paper notes started as an exigent fiscal measure to meet government spending, the Qing government hoped that paper notes would continue to be used even after the war was over so as to relieve the scarcity of silver, which had troubled the Chinese economy since the 1820s.[44] Officials of the Board of Revenue understood that it was crucially important for the newly printed paper notes to circulate in the economy. In their words, "even if government paper notes are used in both public spending and collection of taxes, they will not last long if they are inconvenient for the people's daily lives and business transactions."[45]

The board requested provincial governments to set up general money exchange offices *(guanqian zongju)* in provincial capitals and open branches in important market towns and places where large numbers of troops were stationed. These financial institutions would function like fractional private note-issuing banks, and they could rely on government funds as part of their cash reserves to redeem paper notes. The center also asked provincial governments to mobilize well-established merchants to manage these money exchange offices. The plan was to take three years to gradually raise the percentage of paper notes in both government spending and tax collection to 50 percent.[46] The rationale behind the plan to gradually circulate paper notes was that if a certain percentage of taxes had to be paid in government paper notes, then people would have to purchase them from the money exchange offices. Once the creditworthiness of government paper notes was established, people would use them for purposes other than paying taxes. In a memorial on 17 December 1853, officials in the Board of Revenue stressed the vital role of interregional trade to the circulation of paper notes. They concluded that "if the government wants to use paper notes to benefit the people, it should first take care of the interest of merchants."[47]

The use of public funds as cash reserves distinguished the money exchange offices from the private note-issuing banks. In theory, both government and private financiers could benefit from these new institutions. In a premodern economy, the scale of state taxation and expenditures were unrivaled by any private financier. If the money exchange offices began to deposit official funds at the prefectural and provincial level, receive collected taxes, and serve as the cashiers in disbursing government spending, this would greatly enhance the creditworthiness of those private financiers who managed them. Money exchange offices established in different regions could also remit government funds across regions. The government would also benefit if its paper notes came to be circulated in the markets.

Some officials pointed out that the issuance of state silver notes would benefit private merchants in interregional trade. For example, the censor Zhang Siheng argued that both the central and provincial governments should uniformly use silver notes. Zhang based his proposal on the operation of private bills of exchange: merchants would come to Beijing to sell goods and take home silver notes, which could be converted to silver at the prefectural or provincial governments. The government would thus be freed from the burden of transporting the collected tax revenue to Beijing in silver, and merchants would be freed of the burden of taking silver out of Beijing.[48] The Jiangnan director-general of the Grand Canal Yang Yizeng suggested that the Board of Revenue should let provincial governments use silver notes to send tax revenue or other assigned funds to Beijing as the total amount of issued silver notes came to less than 10 percent of the annual tax revenue that the center received each year. In Yang's view, if provincial merchants had confidence in silver notes, they would continue to hold these notes for the sake of convenience rather than convert them into silver, which reduced the pressure on the government to redeem these notes.[49]

The silver notes issued by the Board of Revenue used the *kuping tael* as their unit. Provincial silver notes used local tael or even the foreign silver dollar as their units. In fact, there were more than one thousand standards of tael of silver in use across China at that time. However, this lack of a unified standard tael was not an insurmountable obstacle to the circulation of government silver notes as long as these different units could be easily converted into one common standard. For example, the financial networks established by Shanxi bankers had connected more than twenty major cities and market towns by the 1830s, and they routinely converted various units of silver tael into one common unit *(benping)* in remittance.[50]

The center permitted provincial governments a certain degree of autonomy to try new methods in issuing paper notes, much as it had in the mintage of copper coins in the eighteenth century. For example, the Jiangsu government found that the silver notes received from the Board of Revenue often came in denominations of above 5 tael of silver, which were too big for ordinary market transactions. It asked the Zhonghe Money Exchange Office, which was established in the important market town of Qingjiangpu, to print silver notes in smaller units ranging from 1 tael to 5 tael according to the form of silver notes received from the Board of Revenue. The Jiangsu provincial government justified this measure to the center as an "adjustment in accordance with local circumstances" since it would take months to consult with the center and receive the needed notes from the Board of Revenue. The center immediately approved.[51] The Damei Money Exchange Office in Zhejiang Province and the Yongfeng Money Exchange Office in Fujian Province also received central sanction to issue silver notes denominated not only in the local standard of silver tael but also in foreign silver currency *(yuan)*.[52] In this center-province interaction, if one provincial government found effective methods to float paper notes, they would report it to the center, as illustrated in the collection of lijin duties in 1853.[53] However, both the center and provincial governments encountered great difficulties in floating silver notes.

The Switch to Copper Notes

In Beijing, wars and widespread disorder severely disrupted the shipment of collected revenue from provinces. As a result, silver stocks of the central government were rapidly depleted by civil and military expenditures in Beijing and in Manchuria. On 26 September 1853, the Board of Revenue had only some 100,000 tael of silver on hand, which was not sufficient even to disburse the monthly wages of the banner soldiers stationed in Beijing. Moreover, the anticipated revenues from provincial governments could cover only 20 percent of the 4.6 million tael of silver in expenditure by March 1854.[54]

In March 1853, the Taiping forces occupied Yangzhou and cut off the transportation of tribute grain (caoliang) from Jiangxi, Anhui, Hunan, and Hubei to Beijing via the Grand Canal. The population of some 800,000 in Beijing had to rely on a reduced grain supply from Jiangsu and Zhejiang, which was transported by sea via Tianjin.[55] Trade connections between northern and southern China were also cut off.[56] In October 1853, the news that the Taiping Northern Expedition Forces were approaching Tianjin caused a great panic in Beijing. Within a month, more than one hundred money exchangers were forced to close, while the remaining ones, along with pawnshops, stopped their lending. Many prominent bankers from Shanxi fled Beijing and Tianjin.[57] The transmission of silver through private bills of exchange halted.[58]

Pressured by the dearth of silver in Beijing, the Board of Revenue allowed silver notes to be converted only to copper notes or copper coins but not to silver at the money exchange offices in Beijing.[59] These regulations were obviously unfavorable to establishing the creditworthiness of silver notes in the markets, and they immediately aroused criticism within the government. To boost confidence in silver notes, Wang Mao-yin, the vice-minister of the right of the Board of Revenue, strongly advocated that the government allow merchants to redeem their silver notes at prefectural governments.[60] The board, however, was concerned that convertibility would simply encourage merchants to exchange the notes for specie, which would quickly exhaust the government's already limited silver stocks.[61]

This response illustrates the profound dilemma that the Qing government faced in the initial stages of issuing silver notes. The purpose of these notes was to cover government deficits, and the trust of economic actors was vital to the scheme of using limited silver stocks to mobilize larger financial resources in the form of paper notes. But how could businessmen have confidence in the value of silver notes when they knew quite well that the government was financially depleted?[62] To keep full convertibility in such a situation would likely exhaust government silver stocks in a short time. Yet few people would trust the notes without such a guarantee.

The money exchange offices established in the provinces also had trouble circulating silver notes. In the wartime fiscal operation of the government, provincial governments did not have adequate funds for the money exchange offices to maintain convertibility of silver notes. In the 1850s, the center assigned the vast majority of collected taxes directly to the military supply stations *(liangtai);* much of this would have been transported to Beijing in peaceful years. Provincial governments located in war zones had to send their revenues to the troops. These included the new lijin revenues collected from commercial transactions, which became the most important source for provincial governments to raise income. Funds from other provincial governments were often sent to the military stations instead of going through the provincial treasury as in normal times.[63] As a result, provincial money exchange offices often remained undercapitalized.[64] A guarantee of full convertibility would greatly limit the amount of silver notes that could be issued.

Moreover, silver notes were not easily disbursed through military expenditures and river works, which were the two biggest items of government spending in this period. River works officials needed to convert silver into copper coins so as to purchase construction materials from nearby peasants or small merchants and to pay wages to laborers.[65] Similarly, a large proportion of military spending was on rations for soldiers. Only big grain or salt merchants had sufficient resources to take silver notes for providing goods to the troops, in anticipation of the future redemption of notes. However, the ongoing war and consequent disruption of interregional trade undermined even these powerful merchants.

By 1853, the interregional remittance networks that the Shanxi bankers established had been completely destroyed.[66] After the Taiping forces declared Nanjing the capital in March 1853, they launched a series of campaigns to take control of the grain supply in Jiangxi, Hunan, and Anhui Provinces. The main traffic routes along the Yangzi River now became the major field of combat, blocking the interregional grain trade.[67] On 22 October Wang Maoyin reported that the surplus rice in the Luzhou area of Anhui Province could not be sold to neighboring Jiangsu Province because of the interference of Taiping forces.[68] Prices of grain in Shanxi Province had fallen almost by half as merchants were unable to ship surplus grain to other provinces.[69] Nor could the salt produced in Huainan be shipped out, even though there was a scarcity of salt in the provinces of Jiangxi and Hunan.[70] The production and sale of salt at Changlu, the major salt-producing area in northern China was halted in 1853.[71] Unlike the licensed salt merchants of Southern Song, their Qing counterparts were bankrupted at a crucial moment when the government needed their help to circulate notes.[72]

The suppliers who received silver notes from the troops could thus sell them only to people who wanted to purchase official titles or academic degrees.[73] This was a very limited channel, as those who had already purchased such a title would have no further need for silver notes. The Henan governor Yinggui reported to the center that silver notes were not popular among the people as these notes could be redeemed only after the rebellion had been suppressed, which seemed highly uncertain at the time.[74]

There are numerous reports of the lack of acceptance of silver notes. The Shandong governor Zhang Liangji reported that the military supply stations could use only silver rather than silver notes to purchase from the local markets.[75] When the silver notes worth 200,000 tael of silver that the center had allocated to the Xuzhou military supply station could not be used for local small transactions, the Board of Revenue urged the station to seek help from local gentry and merchants to exchange these notes into either silver or copper coins.[76] Even in some places in Jiangsu Province where soldiers were paid in paper notes, officials emphasized that these notes had to be fully convertible to copper coins at money exchange offices so as to prevent mutiny.[77]

As the troops and river works officials had to use silver to purchase goods from local merchants, they were unwilling to accept silver notes from provincial governments. Officials in local governments or domestic customs who were required to send the collected revenue on to the troops or to sites of major river works found this a good excuse to reject silver notes in tax collection. As the Jiangnan director-general of the Grand Canal Gengchang observed, "Now most of the received revenue in provincial treasuries is transported to military supply stations directly. Because soldiers cannot use the silver notes, the officials then refuse to receive notes in collecting taxes."[78]

As the priority of provincial governors was to send the majority of collected taxes to the troops, they became unwilling to take on the extra burden of redeeming silver notes issued by or received from other provinces. For example, the Guizhou governor Jiang Weiyuan considered the lack of silver in Guizhou Province a legitimate excuse for explicitly refusing to redeem silver notes issued by the military supply stations in Jiangnan or by other provinces.[79] The Jiangsu provincial government could use only its own silver notes locally.[80] The Fujian governor Wang Yide reported that the silver notes issued by the Yongfeng money exchange office barely circulated outside Fujian.[81]

The lack of demand for silver notes contrasted sharply with the need for copper currency in the war zones. Because soldiers had to be paid in copper coins if they were to buy food in the markets, local prices of copper coins often rose rapidly relative to silver wherever the troops went, and soldiers paid in silver could not even buy enough to feed themselves.[82] In response, the Jiangsu government established three money exchange offices in market towns like Shanyang and Qingjiangpu to issue copper notes for the needs of soldiers, small peasants, and retailers.[83]

In economically isolated Beijing, the demand for silver dropped considerably, and the value of silver relative to copper coins plummeted in early 1853.[84] In response to the unemployment among wage laborers due to the closure of private note-issuing intermediaries in the capital, officials urged the government to issue official notes in coins and to lend them to retailers and shopkeepers as substitutes for private notes.[85] In May 1853, the Board of Revenue established four money exchange offices in Beijing, Qianyu, Qianheng, Qingfeng, and Qianyi. They used the copper coins released from the two central mints (*baoquanju* and *baoyuanju*) as cash reserves to issue copper notes. They followed the example of the five note-issuing money exchange offices that the Imperial Household (Neiwu fu) had set up in 1841.[86] In 1854, the Board of Revenue began to use these copper notes to pay the wages of banner soldiers in Beijing.

The lack of circulation of silver notes in both Beijing and the provinces led the Board of Revenue on 28 March 1855 to replace them with copper notes in smaller denominations *(gaipiao yongchao)*.[87] As for the silver notes still held in military supply stations, these were often converted into notes of small denominations issued by specific supply stations *(liangtaipiao)* for use in local transactions.[88] In Beijing, the Board of Revenue entrusted the five money exchange offices managed by private merchants—Yuqian, Yufeng, Yusheng, Yuheng, and Yutai—to handle the issue of copper notes in Beijing. On 22 November 1855, an imperial edict urged every provincial government to set up money exchange offices within three months for the purpose of circulating copper notes.[89] In addition to disbursing government spending, the board also hoped that copper notes would complement the use of coins and take the place of silver in market transactions, thus alleviating the depression caused by the dearth of silver.[90]

Thereafter, only very limited amounts of silver notes were issued for specific purposes. For example, on 15 December 1860, the Shandong governor Wenyi asked the Board of Revenue to issue silver notes worth 174,500 tael of silver for the Jiangbei military supply station to clear debts owed to merchants.[91] This kind of silver note was similar to those that the Qing government would later issue to pay the arrears of wages to officers and soldiers after the Taiping Rebellion had ended. These were debentures rather than a form of general currency in the markets.[92]

However, the switch to copper notes profoundly worsened the convertibility issue. These were obviously easier to transport than copper coins. But their redemption was a different story. War had destroyed the production and transportation of domestic copper in Yunnan Province.[93] The Qing government urged each province to look for copper mines and even tried to obtain an alternative copper supply from Mongolia and Korea.[94] These attempts were stymied by the paucity of natural endowments of copper in these areas.

The severe dearth of copper greatly affected the amount, fineness, and quality of copper coins released from government mints.[95] Copper coins with nominal values such as 5 wen, 10 wen, and 20 wen could not circulate smoothly in the markets as long as the supply of 1 wen coins was inadequate. Yet government mints could not afford to cast 1 wen coins given the lack of copper. Officials of the Board of Revenue were greatly frustrated by this situation. In their words, "the purpose of casting copper coins with large face values is to make a profit to cover deficits; yet they cannot circulate if copper coins of 1 wen are insufficient. However, the current copper stocks are inadequate for minting coins of 1 wen. We see no way out of this dilemma."[96] Mints in Beijing,

Shanxi, Zhili, Henan, and Fujian even went so far as to cast iron and lead coins and even iron coins with big nominal values, which could hardly circulate.[97]

As Beijing could not receive sufficient supplies of either raw copper or copper coins from other regions, the Board of Revenue passed the burden of redeeming the copper notes onto provincial governments. The board divided the issued copper notes into two categories. One was called *jingchao* (also known as *changhao* in the markets); these could be used across provinces but were redeemable only in Beijing. The other was called *shengchao* (also known as *duanhao* in the markets). A provincial government needed to put its stamp on them and was therefore responsible for ensuring their convertibility.[98]

When businessmen carried the copper notes issued for use in the provinces to Beijing, the money exchange offices in the capital refused to redeem them. Officials of the Board of Revenue justified this by the insufficient reserves of copper coins in Beijing and blamed provincial governments for not managing copper notes in their provinces properly.[99] Both the Jiangnan director-general of the Grand Canal Gengchang and the Shandong-Henan director-general of the Grand Canal Li Jun complained to the center that if the copper notes that they received from the Board of Revenue to cover expenditures for river works were not redeemable in Beijing, no businessman would be willing to accept them.[100] In response, the board, unable to transport the amount of copper coins needed to the two Bureaus of River Work in Jiangsu and Shandong, simply requested that they set up their own money exchange offices to redeem their received copper notes.[101] Neighboring provincial governments, however, did not have enough reserves of copper coins to redeem these paper notes issued for river works and thus refused to take them when collecting taxes. In consequence, these notes became worthless in the markets.[102]

In Beijing, the Board of Revenue did not even have enough copper coins to back its own copper notes. It thus required the five money exchange offices to take these notes as capital and asked them to issue promissory notes to pay the wages of banner soldiers. The money exchange offices themselves did not have sufficient copper coins to guarantee convertibility, and they could redeem the promissory notes only with official copper notes.[103] In January 1859, the Board of Revenue had to mobilize fifty private money exchangers in Beijing to circulate government copper notes. The capital's fiscal and economic isolation in these years meant that these private financiers could not turn the copper notes they received into capital for long-distance trade with merchants in other regions. Moreover, the conflicts with Britain and France in 1860 caused a big financial panic in Beijing. People rushed to exchange notes for copper coins, which amounted to more than 10 million *diao* (1 *diao* equals 1,000 wen).[104] By September 1861, copper notes were not accepted in market transactions in Beijing.[105]

The heavily devalued notes provided a chance for local officials to make a profit in tax collection. They forced people to pay taxes in copper coins or silver and then purchased notes from the markets at discounted prices to meet the percentage of notes includable in the revenue submitted to superiors.[106] As long as there was a significant difference between the value of paper notes and metallic money, it would be difficult for the central government to prevent such behavior. One solution would have been to eliminate the chances for profit making among local officials by imposing the paper notes as the only legal currency, as the Meiji government did between 1868 and 1870. And indeed, this idea had arisen. In regard to silver notes, Wang Yide, the governor-general of Fujian and Zhejiang, on 23 April 1854 had proposed that all public spending and tax collection at both the central and local levels should be carried out in paper notes only. This would show the whole realm that government notes were the legal tender and thus create demand for them.[107] However, the Qing government, which was fighting for its survival with the Taiping forces, did not dare to implement such a radical approach.

Not all money exchange offices experienced disaster. There were at least two instances where copper notes succeeded in circulating locally, but in both cases the note issues were not big. Up to 1862 the Tongyuan Money Exchange Office established by the Xuzhou military supply station in Jiangsu Province managed to ensure the convertibility of its issued copper notes by the receipts from the lijin duties collected in copper coins from commercial transactions. These notes were used to pay the wages of soldiers stationed in Xuzhou and could circulate in the adjacent areas. Encouraged by this experience, the director-general of grain transport Wu Tang planned to raise more funds to establish the

Tongyuan General Money Exchange Office in Huai'an, with branches in Shaobo and Qingtao, so as to issue more copper notes to pay the soldiers stationed there.[108] Likewise, copper notes issued by the money exchange office in Xi'an were accepted by local people; the amount of notes in circulation totaled about 300,000 diao.[109]

It is hard to know exactly why these local successes did not inspire the center to find better ways to maintain the creditworthiness of copper notes across the country. The Board of Revenue may have been frustrated by too many failures of copper notes, particularly in Beijing, and thus considered these successes incidental. Moreover, the local experiences did not speak to the crucial issue of how to coordinate interregional transfers of copper coins in large quantities. But this ability was essential to secure convertibility across the country, particularly where local supplies of coins were inadequate to redeem copper notes.

Moreover, a familiar alternative became available in the late 1850s when silver prices began to fall in most regions in China.[110] This change made it possible to go back to silver in public finance rather than continue experimenting. In Fujian, copper notes issued by the Yongfeng Money Exchange Office amounting to 391,600,000 *chuan* (1 *chuan* equals 1,000 wen) became almost worthless in the markets. As a result, the Fujian provincial government decided to stop issuing paper notes and use silver to redeem these copper notes.[111] In Shandong, the falling value of silver allowed the provincial government to substitute it for copper notes in both tax collection and government expenditures.[112] Likewise, the people in Zhili preferred to use silver to pay taxes when silver prices dipped below the official level.[113] Under these conditions, the Qing government formally repealed the issuance of paper notes.

The failure of the Qing government to use issuance of paper notes to overcome its fiscal crisis in the 1850s illustrates the importance of socioeconomic circumstances to state efforts to establish the necessary institutional arrangements to back up its new credit instruments. In England and Japan, the central governments also encountered a lack of trust and devaluation in the markets of their early short-term credit bills or paper notes. Nonetheless, in both those countries we observe a mutually reinforcing process in the transformation toward a modern fiscal state. On the one hand, the state dependence on fiduciary credit instruments forced the state to centralize the collection and management of its tax revenue, and fiscal centralization then raised the state's available income to safeguard the creditworthiness of those instruments in the markets. On the other hand, the ensuing trust motivated the state to strengthen this centralization and secure the reputation of state credit instruments in the financial markets.

However, the fracturing of 1850s China in rebellion and civil war both compromised the domestic economy and necessitated the further decentralization of fiscal operations to maintain military operations. The socioeconomic environment was thus extremely hostile to the un-folding of such a mutually reinforcing institution-building process. Al-though some Qing officials proposed using state coercion to impose government paper notes as the legal tender in the economy, the govern-ment did not dare to implement such a policy at a time when it appeared to be losing to the Taiping forces. Here comparison with the Meiji policy of issuing nonconvertible paper notes between 1868 and 1871 is instruc-tive. The Meiji government, although still shaky, did not have to confront a competing regime. Therefore, using coercion to impose nonconvertible paper notes as the legal tender was more viable. In so doing, the Meiji state removed the possibility for officials who collected taxes to buy dis-counted paper notes and use them at their face value in transferring the collected taxes to the government. Moreover, the expanding domes-tic economy and exports in early Meiji Japan led to a strong demand for currency, which facilitated acceptance of central government notes.

The Meiji government's attempt to circulate paper notes was also sus-tained by the financial networks established by private financiers. Finan-ciers who cooperated with the state could utilize the regular tax reve-nues to enhance their credibility in the financial markets. The government for its part benefited from the speedy transfer of its collected revenue and the financiers' conversion of taxes paid in rice into money in eco-nomically backward regions. Beijing in the 1850s, however, was cut off from both shipments of tax revenue and long-distance trade with the rest of the country. Existing cross-regional financial networks and trans-port infrastructure were shattered by war, which contributed to the lack of circulation of silver notes. The switch to notes in copper coins in 1855 further decentralized fiscal operations; the challenges of copper transport rendered the center unable to effectively coordinate provincial governments to redeem copper notes. Nor could it use commodities such as grain or salt to back up the value of issued copper notes.

The socioeconomic conditions in China in the 1850s also sharply contrasted with those of England at the turn of the eighteenth century. London was the center of England's domestic and foreign trade and yielded some 70–80 percent of customs. Meanwhile, the major wars that the English state fought during its transformation to a modern fiscal state were either at sea or in Continental Europe. It was natural for the central government to centralize its tax revenues in London to supply its troops and navy, and domestic financial and transport networks did not suffer.

Interestingly, while the Qing government repealed paper notes in 1862, a new form of collaboration between private financiers and the government began to emerge in the lower Yangzi delta as the Qing army reasserted control over central China. In 1860, the Zhejiang governor Wang Youling not only entrusted supplies of grain and ammunition to the private banker Hu Guangyong but also deposited official funds in Hu's newly established bank. Like his counterparts in England and Japan, Hu fully utilized his connections with government to establish himself in the financial markets, and by the early 1870s his Fukang Bank had become one of the biggest native banks in China.[114]

With the gradual recovery of the remittance networks, local governments came to send part of the assigned revenues to Beijing through private financiers and particularly Shanxi bankers. For example, in 1859 the Customs of Fuzhou requested a private merchant to remit two items, each worth 50,000 tael of silver, to Beijing within a year.[115] In 1862 and 1863, the Customs of Guangdong, Fujian, and Shanghai and the provincial governments of Guangdong, Sichuan, Zhejiang, Hubei, Hunan, and Jiangxi began to appeal to Shanxi bankers to transfer funds to Beijing. Although the amount of each remittance did not exceed 50,000 tael, the routes of remittance showed that Shanxi bankers had reestablished their financial networks. These connected Beijing not only with coastal cities, such as Shanghai, Guangzhou, Fuzhou, and Ningbo, but also with interior cities, such as Chengdu, Hankou, Nanchang, and Changsha.[116] Moreover, it seems that provincial governments had collaborated with Shanxi bankers in remitting official funds even earlier.[117] This marked the beginning of the private bankers' extensive involvement in the remittance of government funds.

Given these developments, why did Qing China not build a modern fiscal state in the late nineteenth century? An examination of the interactions between the state and economy in China between the 1870s and 1890s demonstrates that a vibrant domestic economy with extensive financial networks and the potential to collect elastic indirect revenues is a necessary, but not sufficient, condition to support the interactive process of building the institutions of a modern fiscal state.

6

THE PERSISTENCE OF FISCAL DECENTRALIZATION IN CHINA, 1864–1911

Public finance in the post-Taiping period exhibited both significant changes and strong inertia, which cannot be accounted for by simple political conservatism on the part of the Qing government.[1] As we have seen, the high value of silver, which had greatly troubled both the Chinese economy and government finance between the 1820s and 1850s, began to fall after 1858. In the mid-1870s, major Western powers went on the gold standard, the price of silver dropped in the international market, and silver poured into East Asia.[2] Inflows of silver stimulated the Chinese economy, and the relative cheapness of silver compared with gold benefited China's exports to the world market. In this situation, the Qing government could continue to use silver as the currency by weight.

The annual tax revenue of the Qing government grew from about 40 million tael of silver in the 1840s to some 80 million tael of silver in the 1880s. Although the Qing government continued to sell official ranks or titles *(juanna)* to raise its income, Qing officials considered this method fiscally unproductive as the actual yield was far below the anticipated amount.[3] What really supported the Qing government when tax revenue was inadequate to meet the expenditures of military campaigns and domestic construction was a new financial policy of taking short-term loans from foreign banks operating in China. Provincial governors also

153

began collaborating with private banks to remit both tax revenues to Beijing and transfer funds between provinces. This extensive participation of private financiers in the operation of public finance was unprecedented in Qing history.

Moreover, the informal provincial finance independent of central supervision that had appeared in the early nineteenth century was formalized after the 1860s.[4] This new institution, known as *waixiao kuanxiang,* allowed provincial governments more autonomy in meeting various spending needs for infrastructure, maintenance of social order, and provision of social welfare.[5] The fact that provincial treasurers in this period did not supervise governors on behalf of the center also enhanced the governors' power in financial issues.[6]

We must keep in mind, however, that the emergence of provincial finance did not represent the rise of political regionalism on the part of governors or a decay of central authority in financial matters. The relationship between provincial governors and provincial treasurers was institutional in nature as the center had the full authority to regularly alternate their posts, which effectively prevented governors from colluding with provincial treasurers to form a power base independent from the center.[7] It is true that the center could not set realistic quotas of spending to accommodate the changing spending needs in provinces, which led to the dysfunction of the quota-based fiscal operation.[8] Nonetheless, this did not imply that the center had lost control of provincial governors in financial matters. First, the center had unambiguous political control over the nomination and tenure of provincial governors and firmly controlled the allocation of military expenditures.[9] Second, it possessed the authority to send assignment orders *(zhibo)* to governors to allocate its funds, which were stored in treasuries in provinces for various spending purposes, and no provincial governor could ignore these orders.[10] Finally, no provincial government could take out foreign loans without central sanction.[11]

In the composition of tax revenue, the biggest change in post-1860s China was that the Qing government leaned more heavily on customs and lijin duties levied on domestic consumption to increase its income. From the late 1860s on, Western officials centrally managed the Imperial Maritime Customs and reliably collected customs for the Qing government.[12] Lijin duties had started as an exigent fiscal measure in 1853, but the Board of Revenue began as early as 1861 to strengthen its supervision over both the collection and spending of these duties. In order to incorporate the lijin revenues in the annual central auditing system *(zouxiao)*, the center required provincial governors to regularly report the amounts collected, the number and location of each lijin collecting station, and the names of collecting officials. By 1874, most provincial governments sent the required accounts to the Board of Revenue, twice a year from provinces in the economic core areas and once a year from those in more remote areas. Only the Board of Revenue had the right to allocate the collected lijin revenues.[13] Because lijin revenues were included in the annual central auditing system just like land taxes and customs and were subject to central allocation, they should be considered central rather than provincial taxes. Even in the case of the 10 to 20 percent of the collected lijin that governors were allowed to retain for spending needs in provinces without being audited by the center, governors explicitly acknowledged that this part of lijin income constituted central rather than provincial revenues.[14]

Despite these significant changes in both the scale and composition of taxation, the Qing government's fiscal operation remained decentralized. Instead of making allocation out of an aggregation of income, the Board of Revenue relied on sending assignment orders to allocate revenue from regions of collection to directly meet purposes of spending in various places. Even for the customs revenue, which was efficiently collected by the Imperial Maritime Customs, the center received only 40 percent into its own coffers while it assigned the rest to be transferred from places of collection to the areas where it would be spent.

Why did the Qing government not use private financial networks to centralize its fiscal operation, as the Japanese government did in the 1870s or the English government did in the 1680s? Why did it not seek long-term credits, given that it had securely honored its short-term foreign debts? The failure to float paper notes in the 1850s had a long-lasting influence on the institutional development of the Qing public finance. This fiasco made the center suspicious and even hostile toward proposals to use credit instruments in its fiscal operation. Considering the time needed to transport silver specie across regions in China, it made much more sense for the center to store a large proportion of its annual income in various treasuries located in the provinces and allocate funds from these to destinations of spending according to the distances involved and transportation facilities available.

The operation of this decentralized fiscal system in practice was far from smooth. Matching discrete items of revenues with various spending needs in different regions entailed a formidable information problem. But as long as the decentralized institutions could accommodate pressing spending needs, the Qing government had little motivation to incorporate the seemingly risky credit instruments into central public finance. In contrast, provincial governors were under intense pressure to meet these urgent central assignment orders for revenues needed for wars, river works, and return of foreign loans. This pushed them to develop methods to supervise the direct collection of lijin duties, the most important source of revenue for governors in the post-Taiping period. These methods were similar to those used in the collection of excises in eighteenth-century England and sake duties in Meiji Japan. The special information and risk distribution in this decentralized fiscal operation helps to account for the development of direct collection of lijin at the provincial but not the central level.

The persistence of a traditional fiscal state in late nineteenth-century China illustrates that where no credit crisis directly threatens the center, state actors are unlikely to search for means of fiscal centralization, even when socioeconomic conditions could support such an institutional development. This implies that had Qing China encountered a credit crisis similar to the ones that occurred in England and Japan, it might well have become a modern fiscal state. A "natural experiment" using the indemnity of 230 million tael of silver imposed by Japan in 1895 as a proxy to a credit crisis borne by the center shows that this counterfactual argument is reasonable. Under this pressure, the center did try to centrally collect lijin duties by using the methods of direct collection developed by provincial governors. Moreover, the Qing government's punctual return of the interest on foreign loans it had taken to pay the indemnity to Japan indicates that it had the administrative ability to build a modern fiscal state through long-term borrowing.

The Persistence of Fiscal Decentralization

With the expansion of both domestic and foreign trade, private financial markets recovered quickly from the 1870s onward. By the 1880s, private financial networks of Shanxi bankers had connected fifty-four big cities and important market towns. Meanwhile, big banks established by merchants from Zhejiang and Shanghai, such as the Fukang Bank and the Yuanfengrun Bank, also created their own webs of interregional remittance.[15] In addition to receiving deposits and providing credit to merchants, these major banks became increasingly involved in public finance. Both Imperial Maritime Customs offices in cities such as Shanghai, Ningbo, Hankou, and Fuzhou and lijin collection stations often designated particular private banks to deposit the collected revenue and remit it to destinations of spending upon receipt of government orders.[16] The total amount of remitted revenue from the provinces to Beijing rose from 19 million tael between 1862 and 1874 to 63 million tael between 1875 and 1893.[17]

The collaboration between private financiers and government funds had great potential to expand. For instance, from the 1860s to the 1880s, the annual revenue designated to Beijing from the provinces rose from 8 million tael to 13 million tael. The tax revenue from the provinces to Beijing and expenditures that the center allocated to provinces represented two opposite directions in the flow of silver. Had the center also used remittance via private financial networks to send funds to provinces, the need to actually transport silver across regions could have been greatly reduced and made government fund transfers much faster and more predictable. Such collaboration between the central government and private bankers might well have been mutually beneficial. As happened in Japan and England, private banks that remitted government funds could have profited from the time interval (ranging from one month to three months) during which they held these monies interest-free before turning them over to the government. The possession of regular government funds would have increased their creditworthiness in the financial markets. The government also could have extended these domestic financial networks by encouraging private banks to take over remittance of revenue to the center in provinces such as Anhui, Shaanxi, and Shandong, which still transported specie to Beijing.

However, this did not happen. The Board of Revenue continued to use the traditional shipment of silver specie to run public finance and was unwilling to incorporate speedy credit instruments into its fiscal operation. In the summer of 1885, two British businessmen from Jardine, Matheson & Co., one of the largest foreign merchant houses in China, proposed to the Qing government the creation of a state bank modeled on the Bank of England. It would receive deposits of the collected customs, issue banknotes that could be used to pay taxes, and manage the receiving of revenue and disbursement of expenditure on behalf of the Board of Revenue.[18] The governor-general of Zhili, Li Hongzhang, supported this proposal and urged that officials learn more about Western state banks that allowed their governments to mitigate the scarcity of money when the financial markets were tight.[19] Yet Board of Revenue officials fiercely objected.[20] Foreign involvement was not the only reason. Even Yan Jingming, who was well known for his competence in managing fiscal matters, showed a deep suspicion of banknotes and remittance of official funds.[21] Officials emphasized the dangers of state issuance of paper notes by referring to their devaluation in the United States and Russia and their failure in China in the 1850s. In their opinion, remittance of official funds by bills of exchange was too risky.[22]

In 1887, Li Hongzhang sent three officials, Sheng Xuanhuai, Zhou Fu, and Ma Jianzhong, to negotiate a bank plan with the American merchant E. S. K. de Mitkiewicz, who represented the Philadelphia Syndicate and the Silver Ring in the United States. The bank under discussion was not designed as a state bank but as one that could raise low-interest loans for the Qing government.[23] Sheng Xuanhuai (1844–1916) came from a family of wealthy native bankers and was an important figure in promoting modern enterprises, including telegraphs, railways, and mining. As early as 1882, he had proposed to Li Hongzhang the creation of a big bank to remit official funds by telegraph.[24] The center rejected this plan but protected its advocates from impeachment by censors.

The Board of Revenue not only refused to incorporate credit instruments in its fiscal operation but even forbade provincial governors from using private remittance to submit taxes when silver prices were high in Beijing.[25] In order to hand over real silver to the Board of Revenue, the Beijing branches of the private banks that remitted tax revenues from the provinces had to convert the received bills of exchange into silver bullion in Beijing. The remittance of tax revenue and official funds was thus constrained by the conditions of private financial markets. When credit was tight, private financiers became reluctant to remit official funds to Beijing, as bankers in Shaanxi and Jiangxi did in 1894 and 1895.[26] The full benefit of remitting government funds between Beijing and the provinces was therefore not realized.

To understand better the persistence of fiscal decentralization, we need to examine more closely how the system ran in the latter half of the nineteenth century. In the newly formed fiscal division of labor between the center and provinces, it was not easy for the center to tap the money that belonged to the provincial finance independent of central supervision. Governors could defend this revenue by emphasizing its contribution to safeguarding the state interest, which included national defense, maintenance of domestic order, and welfare in localities.

For example, the conflict with France forced the Qing government to increase spending on seaborne defense in 1884. The Board of Revenue ordered the provincial government of Shaanxi to hand over to the center the amount of lijin previously retained in the province. Although the Shaanxi governor Bian Baoquan reported to the board the total amount of lijin revenue retained between 1876 and 1881 and the remaining amount stored in Shaanxi, he refused to hand the monies over to the center. Instead, Bian reported that when the expenditures allocated from the center were inadequate or delayed, the Shaanxi provincial government had to turn to the retained lijin revenue for help. Bian further pointed out that the board simply did not have the means to allocate sufficient funds on time to meet all sorts of extraordinary provincial expenditures, including relief for the poor, road maintenance and construction, and funding local academies. As domestic governance was as important as national defense, Bian concluded that even urgent defense matters did not justify the center's attempt to extract revenue needed for provincial governance.[27] The board conceded to Bian.[28]

Although it was difficult for the Board of Revenue to press more money from provincial finances, it still had some 80 million tael in silver at its disposal every year. In the decentralized fiscal operation under the central coordination, only 18 to 28 percent of the center's annual income was sent to Beijing.[29] Between 1880 and 1895, provincial governors managed to send 8 million tael of silver to Beijing *(jingxiang)* on time.[30]

For the rest, some was spent within the province of collection *(liusheng zhiyong)*, some assigned for purposes in other provinces in the form of interprovincial assistance *(xiexiang)*, and some stored in treasuries in provinces for future assignment orders from the center *(cunchu houbo)*. As the Board of Revenue assigned specific revenue items in various places to meet particular spending needs across the huge territory of China, this decentralized fiscal operation was highly complicated.[31]

To run this decentralized fiscal system properly, the Board of Revenue needed accurate information about specific sources of revenue and items of expenditures in localities so as to match them by assignment orders. The annual account reports of expenditures and revenues that provincial governors sent to the Board of Revenue for supervision and audit provided the basis for such information. The fixed quotas for both tax collection and provincial spending to some extent simplified the task for

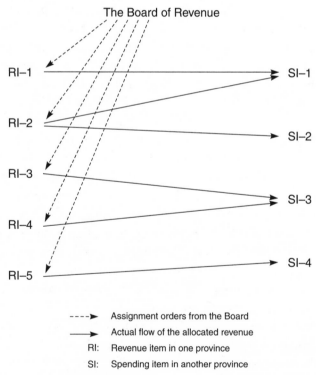

Figure 6.1 Decentralized fiscal operation of the Qing government.

the Board of Revenue to make realistic assignment orders to provincial governors. To give the Board of Revenue a solid grasp of the actual amount of money stored under each item of revenue in treasuries scattered across the country, the Qing government prohibited governors from using the stored money without central sanction.

However, when the quota of expenditures could not meet legitimate spending needs in the provinces, governors often appealed to a method of "informal funding," which was to use the stored money to cover deficits without reporting to the center.[32] These removals differed from embezzlement because the funds were used for public purposes. But if governors did not return all the money to the original account in a timely fashion, the accumulation of removals in provinces over time resulted in severe discrepancies between the actual amounts of silver stored in provincial treasuries and the account numbers available to the Board of Revenue. This practice deprived the Board of Revenue of a reliable information basis to make meaningful assignment orders and further complicated the running of this decentralized fiscal system.

This was not a new phenomenon. For example, in September 1822 the Board of Revenue allocated 500,000 tael out of funds of some 515,700 tael of silver supposedly stored in Zhili Province for calamity relief in the province. However, the Zhili governor Yan Jian reported to the center that there were deficits of 400,000 tael in this fund as a result of removals by previous governors and treasurers to cover deficits in local expenditures, none of which had been reported to the Board of Revenue.[33] The center noted that by the early 1840s millions of tael of silver stored by the center in provinces had been siphoned off by unreported provincial expenditures.[34]

The information asymmetry between the center and provinces worsened in the post-Taiping period when the Board of Revenue could not anticipate variations in local tax collection and spending needs. The amounts allocated by the Board of Revenue to governors were often inadequate or delayed. In response, governors frequently removed money from the stored funds undesignated by the center to cover deficits in local governance. For example, the Board of Revenue ordered provincial governors to preserve certain funds specifically for the seaborne defense in Guangdong Province. Nonetheless, when the center tried to allocate money from this particular item, the general-governor of Jiangnan and

Jiangxi Zeng Guoquan reported that these monies had previously been diverted to cover deficits in meeting the board's other assignment orders, including the revenues sent to Beijing.[35] Likewise, in 1883 the Board of Revenue required each province to take 1,000 tael of silver from the collected lijin revenue every year to set up a special account for disaster relief. In 1890, when the board asked provincial governors to send money from this source to famine-struck areas in Zhili, Guangxi governor Ma Piyao had to admit that the money had been used for other purposes as the expenditures that the center allocated to Guangxi from other provinces either came late or did not arrive at all.[36] This occurred even with the 40 percent of the customs revenues collected by the Imperial Maritime Customs, which were under the direct control of the center. Local customs officers often tapped this fund when they were unable to meet urgent assignment orders from the center.[37]

As the Board of Revenue made assignment orders according to the often fictitious account numbers received from governors, the central allocation gradually lost touch with reality. For example, when the Board of Revenue ordered Zhejiang Province to send 180,000 tael of lijin revenue that was earmarked for the Naval Admiralty to fund the defense in Jiangsu Province in August 1884, the Zhejiang governor Liu Bingzhang informed the Jiangsu government that this fund had already been shipped to Beijing. Jiangsu Province thus had to ask the center to assign the same amount of money from other sources of revenue. In response, the Board of Revenue allocated the money from the salt taxes that the Lianghuai Salt Distribution Commission had owed to the center since 1876. Again Jiangsu Province found out that there was no real money under this item. In desperation, Zeng Guoquan, the general-governor of Jiangnan and Jiangxi, pleaded for the center to allow him to retain 180,000 tael of silver from any fund in Jiangsu that had been designated for submission to Beijing. In his view, this was simply a "transfer of money among items all belonging to the center."[38]

Yet in spite of the messiness of this fiscal operation, the Qing government still managed to fund huge military expenditures, including expensive campaigns to reconquer Xinjiang between 1875 and 1884 (80 million tael of silver) and the Sino-French War between December 1883 and June 1885 (30 million). Moreover, the Qing government repaid the estimated 44 million tael of silver in foreign loans taken between the

1860s and 1880s.[39] The center's political authority over governors to coordinate cross-provincial transfer of revenue was vital to these achievements. In order to meet these urgent assignment orders, governors had no option but to move funds from any undesignated items *(yihuan jiuji)*.[40] This practice was even reflected in the assigning orders from the Board of Revenue when it mandated that governors prepare a certain amount of funds for urgent purposes from "whatever available sources" *(wulun hezhong kuanxiang)*. Urgent domestic needs such as river works or famine relief were also addressed in this fashion.[41] The governors and the offices of the Imperial Maritime Customs in Guangdong and Fujian Provinces sometimes had to borrow short-term credits from domestic banks to meet assignment orders.[42] The infamous extravagance of the empress dowager Cixi was also met by this "informal financing" as governors moved money from ordinary items, such as the maintenance fees of the navy, and sent it to the Imperial Household.

However, governors' success in funding urgent expenditures contrasted sharply with the delays, reductions, and arrears common in meeting regular central assignment orders, which included the interprovincial transfer of revenues to frontier provinces in the southwest and northeast and the maintenance fees of the navy. For the latter, the Board of Revenue in 1880 allocated an annual fund of 4 million tael out of the lijin revenues from Jiangsu, Zhejiang, and Jiangxi and out of customs from Shanghai, Ningbo, Fuzhou, and Guangzhou. However, the amount of money that the navy actually received every year never exceeded 3 million tael.[43]

These examples of dysfunction in allocating ordinary spending in the late nineteenth century were familiar to both contemporaries and historians.[44] Why couldn't the center use its political authority to discipline governors to abide by the central assignment orders in the normal fiscal operation? The key factor was that the Board of Revenue was unable to trace over time the sources of revenues that governors had removed to meet urgent spending needs. It therefore could not tell deliberate neglect from true inability to meet the ordinary assignment orders in provinces.

Success at urgent spending and failure at many regular assignment orders were two sides of the same coin of a decentralized fiscal operation. The difficulties of matching specific items of revenues with particular spending purposes inherent to a decentralized fiscal operation would have been largely mitigated in a centralized system in which the Board of Revenue could allocate spending from an aggregated annual income. A centralized system would have allowed the Board of Revenue to directly manage its treasuries in various regions and thus greatly enhanced the efficiency of the 80 million tael of central annual income. Yet between 1864 and 1894, the central government did not encounter any emergency that it could not handle by this decentralized fiscal system.

Lijin and the Center-Province Relationship

From the 1860s on, lijin duties and customs were two major sources of income for the Qing government. Despite the efficiency and reliability of the Imperial Maritime Customs, the Qing government could not derive more customs by raising tariffs because China's tariff level was fixed by Western powers at 5 percent. Foreign merchants after 1860 were further exempted from paying domestic lijin duties after they paid a supplementary tariff duty of 2.5 percent at treaty ports (zikoushui). But in the collection of lijin duties on domestic consumer goods, including imported opium after it entered China, the Qing government still had full autonomy to decide rates and methods.

As the center let provincial governors determine how to properly collect lijin according to circumstances in their respective provinces, provincial governments had to face the challenge of how to effectively monitor the collection of lijin so as to improve the receipts. If provincial governors could not effectively monitor the performance of lijin commissioners scattered in their provinces, as claimed by the historian Liu Kwang-ching, then the central collection of lijin would have been impossible in late Qing China.[45] If provincial governments had no means to supervise the lijin collection, they would have had a strong incentive to adopt tax farming so as to receive reliable lijin revenues. However, tax farming (baojiao or baoban) was not the dominant method in the collection of lijin in late Qing China before 1894.[46]

Both the central government and provincial governments agreed on the importance of adopting direct collection to replace lijin farming. For example, the Guangdong government in 1861 farmed out lijin collection in ten business sectors to tax farmers. These lijin farmers were not well-established merchants, and their extortionate behavior aroused opposition among local businessmen, who boycotted markets, resisted paying lijin, and even petitioned local governments. As a result, lijin farmers in six business sectors could not fulfill the sum contracted with the government. The situation was even worse in three collecting stations, where lijin was collected by underclerks unsupervised by government officials.[47] In 1862, in order to better control the lijin revenues in Guangdong to fund armies in Jiangsu, Zhejiang, and Anhui Provinces, both the censor Zhu Chao and the general-governor of Jiangnan and Jiangxi Zeng Guofan proposed using government direct collection of lijin to replace farming in Guangdong.[48] As a result, the Guangdong government established a head office of lijin collection in the provincial capital Guangzhou and chose commissioners from among expectant officials to collect lijin in market towns in counties such as Shaozhou, Nanhai, Sanshui, Shunde, and Xinhui. Government direct collection accounted for some three quarters of lijin revenue in Guangdong, while the rest, which came from small items, was farmed out to merchants.[49]

Provincial governments were not controlled by tax farmers either. Even with existing farming contracts for small sources of lijin, provincial governments could terminate the contract and replace it with direct collection upon receiving orders from the center. For example, when the center in 1887 decided to have the Imperial Maritime Customs collect the supplementary lijin duty on imported opium, the Guangdong government ended its contract with merchants who had farmed out the collection of this duty.[50] Likewise, to assist the governor-general of Hubei and Hunan Zhang Zhidong's efforts to resume the sale of salt produced in Guangdong in Fujian, the governor-general of Fujian and Zhejiang Yang Changjun in 1887 did not renew the contract with the salt lijin farmers in Fujian and received the same amount of money from the Guangdong provincial government.[51]

One important motivation behind direct collection of lijin in provinces was that governors, particularly those in rich provinces, were under a great deal of pressure to not only fund local reconstruction and defense but also to meet urgent assignment orders from the center. As lijin was the major source for them to raise revenue, governors had a strong incentive to develop methods to supervise the collection. The collection of lijin in the provinces was typically managed by a hierarchical bureaucracy staffed by salaried commissioners. They were independent from prefectural magistrates but subject to the supervision of governors aided by provincial treasurers.[52] The commissioners mainly came from the pool of expectant officials, men who had already acquired their qualification but were waiting for a post to become vacant.

The historian Luo Yudong argued that the collection of lijin by local gentry merchants in Hunan Province led to more efficiency and less corruption because the gentry came from wealthy families and cared about their local reputation.[53] However, the senior commissioners who managed the lijin collection in Hunan were all officials nominated by provincial governors, and local gentry involved in the collection were selected from a candidate list prepared for the lijin head office in Hunan.[54] These gentry were also salaried staff, and the Hunan governor Bian Baodi considered it important to pay them well so as to avoid abuses.[55] Gentry-merchant collectors' local connections could also lead to undertaxation. For example, when the governor-general of Zhili Li Hongzhang appointed officials to replace the gentry-merchant collection in the city of Tianjin in 1880, annual receipts rose from 20,000 to 60,000 tael in silver.[56]

Instead of targeting small producers or retailers, governors mainly turned to big wholesalers or guilds involved in interregional trade to collect lijin.[57] For example, in Gansu Province, the provincial government in June 1858 ordered tobacco merchants to form three tobacco guilds in Lanzhou and Jingyuan, two major areas of local cultivation, so as to facilitate the collection of lijin on tobacco.[58] Qing officials understood that indirect consumption taxes could be collected either from production sites or from major wholesalers along transportation routes. But there was no large-scale concentrated production of consumer goods in Qing China.

Take the collection of salt taxes as an example. Although the Qing government tried to extract from production sites *(jiuchang zhengke),* the spread of the evaporation method in making salt greatly reduced production costs and encouraged small producers who sold their salt to unlicensed merchants.[59] As the Qing government could not tax the huge amount of salt outside the control of licensed merchants, it in 1831 considered collecting salt taxes at major transportation nodes regardless of whether the salt merchants were licensed.[60] Although this method was not adopted for the salt tax, it was later fully implemented in the collection of lijin duties.

The lijin collecting stations or offices were often established in the following three cases: (1) when a large amount of a given commodity was packaged and ready for transportation; (2) when the package passed certain pivotal nodes in the transportation networks, particularly along key water routes; and (3) when the package arrived in a new market before it was dispatched to small retailers. For the big wholesalers, it was difficult to hide large packages of commodities from government inspection, and the cost of avoiding key transportation routes could be unnecessarily high. As they could pass the burden of lijin duties on to consumers by raising prices, they were less motivated to resist them. This situation resembles the collection of excises in England and duties on sake in Meiji Japan.

Although the center could not set quotas on the indirect lijin as its yields were subject to fluctuations in the markets, it did try hard to supervise lijin collection. In the hierarchical organization of direct collection of lijin in provinces, commissioners of collecting stations or offices were required to send their monthly accounts to their supervising offices *(zhuanju)* each month, along with the collected revenue. After aggregating these accounts, the supervising office sent the accounts to the headquarters of lijin collection *(lijin zongju)* in the following month for inspection.[61] Collecting officials could not stay in their posts more than three years, and their accounts were subject to audit by subsequent commissioners.[62] Regular job alternations and posttransfer audits *(jiaodai)* were similar to the management of excise collection in England and sake duties in Japan.

Regular posttransfer audit was not unique to the collection of lijin but a norm for magistrates in collecting land taxes as well. Nonetheless, a magistrate not only had sources of revenues other than land taxes, such as taxes on land transactions, but also possessed several items of public expenditures. When the allocated official funds were inadequate for the needs of ordinary administration or extraordinary expenses, a magistrate often moved the collected land taxes without the approval of his superiors to cover these shortages. He then could hide the resulting shortfall in the collected land taxes under "arrears from the farmers" in the report to the provincial treasury. This practice was widespread in the eighteenth and nineteenth centuries. For example, the Shandong governor Huiling in 1800 acknowledged to the Board of Revenue that a large proportion of the more than 1 million tael of silver of tax arrears in Shandong in 1799 had been siphoned off to cover deficits in local river works and infrastructure.[63]

The complicated nature of magistrates' account books, compounded by the frequent use of "informal financing," made the posttransfer auditing among magistrates very time-consuming in practice. For example, after the magistrate of Wuchang County Lü Shiqi left his post on 9 February 1812, his successor, Wang Yuchang, found problems in the posttransfer auditing. Wang then asked the superior circuit government to send officials to conduct a third-party audit. The circuit government had to gather the predecessor, who was now in a different post, to go over bookkeeping along with the officials from the circuit government. Almost a year had passed before arrears of 16,124 tael of silver in the collected land taxes were confirmed, and it still remained unclear whether Lü had moved the funds to cover deficits in public expenditures or put the money in his own pocket.[64] Considering the importance of informal financing to county governance, few governors would have the motivation to strictly enforce posttransfer auditing simply to discipline magistrates.

In contrast, the lijin commissioners did not have other administrative obligations. They thus did not have other sources of revenue or official funds to cover arrears in collection. Posttransfer auditing in the collection of lijin had some success. By this method, the Jiangxi provincial government in 1863 found that Wang Yongxu, the commissioner in charge of lijin collection in Jiangxi, had underreported revenue, retained fines, and manipulated the exchange rates between silver and copper cash for personal profit. Wang was deprived of his official title and had to pay back the money.[65] Likewise, the successor to the lijin commissioner in the station of Longjuzhai in Shaanxi Province found that his predecessor, Yu Qi, had underreported the collected revenues. After further investigation, Yu Qi was found not to have handed over some 2,530 tael in lijin revenue.[66] In some cases, the collecting official was held accountable even if the shortage was caused by collusion between his subordinates and merchants. For example, posttransfer audit revealed a shortfall of 2,000 tael in the Houli lijin station in Guangdong Province. The collecting official, Ding Yong, was stripped of his official title and required to return the same amount to the government, even though this deficit was caused by collusion between his inspector and merchants.[67]

In addition to effective posttransfer auditing to monitor lijin commissioners, superior officers could also use the condition of market transactions to evaluate the performance of collection. For example, in a good year for the tea market, the Yunnan governor became suspicious about the falling revenue from the lijin office in Simao and Pu'er, two major tea-producing areas. Inspecting officials examined the records of the collecting official's remittance through the Guangyufeng bank and found that he was not handing over all the remitted money to the lijin headquarters.[68] In cases when the same bundle of commodities went through two lijin stations or checking points, purposeful underassessment by one station could be discovered by the other.[69] In order to motivate commissioners to collect efficiently, governors often recommended to the center those who performed well for either promotion or for priority for tenure in regular offices. For example, Li Youfen, the official in charge of lijin collection in the city of Wuchang, was recommended by the governor-general of Hubei and Hunan Yu Lu and Hubei governor Kui Bin for promotion because Li had doubled the yields by efficient management.[70]

We thus should not assume that governors had few means to discipline and motivate lijin collecting officials. But how, then, do we explain the fact that the annual lijin revenue between 1870 and 1895 stabilized at the level of 14 to 15 million tael of silver and reached only 16 million tael of silver by 1903?[71] Several factors other than embezzlement and mismanagement affected the yields. Government officials at the time were aware that high lijin duties were counterproductive as they simply encouraged evasion.[72] Moreover, Chinese merchants could pay the supplementary customs duties *(zikoushui)* under the names of foreigners so as to avoid paying domestic lijin. As a result, governors often kept lijin duties low to encourage Chinese merchants to pay them.[73] Rivalry for lijin revenue among neighboring provinces through which merchants could choose different routes of trade also contained the rise of lijin in the provinces.[74] Competition from Japanese and Indian tea in the international markets also forced governors in the tea-producing provinces to reduce the lijin on tea.[75] The Qing government's paternalism affected lijin revenue as well, for the center often reduced or even temporarily repealed the lijin duties on rice in years of poor harvests and famine.[76]

To better understand the causes of inelasticity of lijin revenue in late nineteenth-century China, it is important to analyze the methods that both the central and provincial governments adopted to improve lijin collection on major consumer goods, such as tea, opium, and salt. As we know from the collection of beer excises in England and the duties on sake in Japan, an efficient way for the government to extract more indirect taxes is to encourage the formation of large and concentrated producers or wholesalers in major consumer goods. The government can reduce its monitoring cost in tax collection, and these big producers or wholesalers are more capable of bearing heavy taxes as they benefit from the monopolistic profit in the markets. Both the central government and provincial governments in late Qing China well understood this economic calculus.

In the collection of lijin on salt, the governor-general of Sichuan Ding Baozhen in 1877 established an official bureau *(guanyunju)* to transport Sichuanese salt in Sichuan and Guizhou. The official control of salt transportation made it easier for the government to collect salt duties from the licensed merchants who purchased salt from the government, and the government could afford to abolish the transit lijin stations in both Sichuan and Guizhou. To compensate for the loss to the Guizhou government caused by the abolition of its stations to collect transit lijin on the Sichuan salt, the Sichuan government allocated to the Guizhou government a proportion of the collected lijin revenue.[77] The costs incurred by the licensed merchants in selling salt were also reduced. This system simplified government management of the collection of the lijin on Sichuanese salt.[78]

Officials in the Board of Revenue also recognized the importance of collecting lijin at sources of production or from big wholesalers so as to reduce the number of transit lijin stations and thus simplify the management and supervision of collection. For example, in early 1885, the Board of Revenue suggested that tea-producing provinces follow the example of Gansu Province and collect lijin duties on tea from the places of cultivation and cancel all the transit lijin on tea along domestic routes. The underlying rationale was to collect lijin before goods were dispatched so as to reduce monitoring costs in collection.[79] Although governors in major tea-producing provinces considered this impractical given the scattered nature of tea plantation in China, the same approach was extended to the collection of lijin on both domestic and imported opium.

In the collection of a consumption duty of 80 tael on every 100 *jin* of imported opium *(yangyao lijin)* in addition to the normal customs of 30 tael, a number of Guangdong merchants petitioned the center to let them form a company in Hong Kong to monopolize the import of Indian opium into China. The governor-general of Zhili Li Hongzhang supported this plan and reported to the center that this would greatly enhance the efficiency of collecting the lijin duties on imported opium.[80] But this scheme had to be abandoned due to the opposition of foreign opium merchants. Nonetheless, both the center and provincial governors understood that the collection of lijin duties on imported opium would be much more effective when the goods passed customs in large packages before it became dispatched after entering China.[81] Therefore, when the center was not satisfied with the efficiency of provincial governments in collecting this additional lijin duty after imported opium entered their provinces, it shifted the collection to the Imperial Maritime Customs in February of 1887.[82]

Regarding domestic opium, the board in 1890 ordered governors to send separate quarterly accounts of the lijin collected. Those in provinces that collected large amounts of lijin revenue from domestic opium, such as Guangdong, Zhejiang, and Hubei, obeyed the board, even though the reported amount was subject to central assignment orders.[83] In June of that year, the center consulted provincial governors about how to improve the yields from domestic opium in their provinces. Governors in provinces where there was no opium cultivation were not enthusiastic. In their view, a heavy lijin duty on domestic opium was impractical as it would simply be undermined by illegal traffic. Governors of provinces with significant opium cultivation, such as Yunnan and Sichuan, pointed out that it was almost impossible to collect high opium duties from small peasant households.[84]

Nevertheless, several governors did put forward methods for increasing the receipts from domestic opium. For example, the Hubei provincial government established a specialized office in Yichang Prefecture to manage the collection of lijin on Sichuan opium, much of which passed into Hubei through Yichang.[85] The governor-general of Sichuan Liu Bingzhang also proposed converting various transit lijin levied on domestic opium by offices or stations scattered in various regions into one uniform rate levied on major wholesalers in major opium-producing provinces. After paying this single tax, merchants were freed from paying transit lijin in any other province. As Liu suggested explicitly to the center, this method would facilitate the central management of the collection of lijin on domestic opium and extract more revenues.[86]

The center soon ordered the Jiangsu provincial government to experiment with this new method of collection *(tuyao tongjuan)*. In 1891, a general collecting office *(tuyao tongjuanju)* was established in Xuzhou, a major area of opium cultivation in Jiangsu Province. It issued licenses to merchants and levied a uniform opium duty on them. After paying this in Xuzhou, these merchants were not liable for any other transit lijin in Jiangsu Province, including the major lijin offices in Nanjing, Suzhou, and Shanghai. The center even asked the troops stationed in Xuzhou to protect the transportation of opium by the licensed merchants.[87] The center clearly exerted its authority in this matter as it pressured Jiangsu governor Gang Yi to conduct this experiment despite his original reluctance.[88]

A Counterfactual Argument

Is there any way to know whether the attempts to collect a single lijin duty on major transportation nodes or sites of production before 1895 could have led to central collection of indirect taxes? How can we determine whether a modern fiscal state could have been built in late nineteenth-century China had the Qing government encountered a credit crisis of sufficient magnitude? To answer these counterfactual questions, I take the indemnity of 230 million tael of silver imposed in 1895 by Japan as a proxy for a credit crisis where the center bore the full risk. This indemnity was exogenous to subsequent institutional change because the Qing government before 1894 did not anticipate this major conflict with Japan and the limited war did not disrupt the Chinese economy. The magnitude of the indemnity was big enough to force the Qing government to initiate reforms in public finance but did not completely bankrupt it.[89] Therefore, this indemnity can be used as a "natural experiment" to explore the possible institutional changes under a counterfactual situation of a credit crisis on the late nineteenth-century Qing government.[90]

Spiraling military spending after the outbreak of the Sino-Japanese war quickly exhausted the silver reserves of the Qing government. In addition to borrowing 1 million tael of silver from merchants in Beijing, the central government in September 1894 had the Hongkong and Shanghai Banking Corporation (HSBC) issue stocks in London to raise two loans on behalf of the Chinese state *(Zhongguo guojia)*, with customs revenue assigned as security.[91] This was the first time that the central government directly negotiated a foreign loan; previous foreign loans had been taken only by provincial governments under central sanction. After the defeat by Japan, the scale of the indemnity and concomitant military expenditures could not be handled by the existing system. The Board of Revenue was forced to search for alternatives. In June of 1895, it petitioned the court over the urgency of reform under the new circumstances.[92] The aims of reform were explicit in the imperial edict of 19 July 1895, which called for proposals to raise revenue for the military and encourage the development of commerce and industry so as to enlarge the tax base.[93]

The severity of the financial problem demanded that officials come up with concrete solutions. The radical young officials who would later become famous in the Hundred Days of Reform of 1898, such as Kang Youwei, Liang Qichao, and Tan Sitong, could not provide any useful proposals as they had neither practical experience in fiscal matters nor knowledge of public finance in the West or Japan. Instead, the problem provided an opportunity for competent financial officials such as Sheng Xuanhuai, who was recommended to the court in September 1896 by Zhang Zhidong and Wang Wenshao, two powerful governors-general at the time. The efforts to search for new institutions to extract more tax revenue and mobilize more financial resources were not interrupted by the infamous coup of 1898, which aborted the Hundred Days of Reform.[94]

Experiments with new financial policies further exposed the weakness of fiscal decentralization. For example, the Board of Revenue in January 1898 decided to issue state bonds of 100 million tael of silver (named *zhaoxin,* meaning "great trust"). The value of each bond was 100 tael, bearing an annual interest rate of 5 percent; the term was twenty years. However, the Board of Revenue did not entrust the subscription of these bonds to private banks or the newly founded Imperial Bank of China.

Instead of centrally managing the subscription and interest payments, the board distributed these bonds to provincial governments, which were then responsible for the interest payments on the bonds in each province. However, it was difficult for governors in less developed provinces such as Shandong and Hunan to find creditors. Although a sum of 10 million tael of silver was raised through both voluntary and forced subscription, much of it was stored separately in various provincial treasuries, awaiting the Board of Revenue's future assignments. In this decentralized fiscal operation, the center passed the burden of interest payments onto governors but did not have any means to discipline them to pay creditors on time. The delay and even nonpayment of interest severely damaged government creditworthiness.[95]

There were significant institutional changes in collecting indirect lijin duties and salt taxes. The trials to centrally collect lijin duties on domestic opium, which had been implemented in places such as Xuzhou and Hubei before 1894, were now extended to eight provinces by the center. In these efforts to centralize lijin collection, the center drew on a pool of officials who had demonstrated their competence in supervising the collection of lijin in provinces. For instance, the governor-general of Hubei and Hunan Zhang Zhidong recommended to the center the official Chen Yiluo, who had demonstrated his ability in collecting lijin in Jiangning and Xuzhou in Jiangsu Province.[96] In his memorial to extend the central collection of lijin on domestic opium to eight provinces, the vice president of the Board of War Tie Liang particularly recommended Sun Tinglin, who efficiently managed the collection of a uniform lijin duty on opium in Yichang in Hubei Province.[97] Ke Fengshi, who was put in charge of the central collection of lijin on domestic opium, had proved his worth in supervising the collection of lijin in Guangxi Province.

In this new central collection of lijin on domestic opium, officials collected a uniform duty on aggregated opium passing through key transportation nodes. Branch offices submitted their monthly accounts to supervising offices in the province, which then sent account reports to the center every three months. The total revenue collected from domestic opium rose from 2.2 million tael in 1894 to 9.3 million in 1907, of which the center retained 3.7 million tael; the rest was assigned to provincial governments.[98] The Qing government also began to centrally collect the salt tax in 1900 by levying a single duty on the salt shipped through official transportation facilities *(guanyun)* or on the salt fields.[99]

Although the methods used in managing direct collection of lijin in provinces are similar to those found in the collection of excises in eighteenth-century England and late nineteenth-century Japan, the lack of large-scale concentrated production of major consumer goods in China made lijin yields relatively inelastic. Attempts to extract more revenue from domestic opium and salt were often undermined by smuggling. After 1895, the Qing government tried very hard to tax liquor, tobacco, and sugar. However, this effort was constrained by their small scale of production in China. In the case of lijin duties on liquor, for example, the annual lijin yields collected from liquor-producing provinces such as Zhili, Sichuan, Jilin, and Fengtian did not exceed 1 million tael of silver for each province in the first decade of the twentieth century.[100]

In regard to financial reform, the Board of Revenue now considered it important to build a state bank for commercial and industrial development in China. It planned to establish the bank first in Beijing and Shanghai before setting up branches in provincial capitals and major market towns. For this purpose, board officials also wanted to gather more information about the banking systems in Europe, the United States, and Japan and even about the methods used by the native Shanxi bankers.[101] On 27 May 1897, Sheng Xuanhuai established in Shanghai the Imperial Bank of China (Zhongguo Tongshang Yinhang). It was founded as a joint-stock bank with a nominal capital of 5 million tael and a paid-in capital of 2.5 million tael. Among its twelve directors, eight were powerful bankers and merchants, including Yan Xinhou, Zhu Baosan, and Ye Chenzhong. By May of 1898, the bank had opened branches in Beijing, Tianjin, Hankou, Guangzhou, Shantou, Yantai, and Zhenjiang.[102]

Nonetheless, the Qing government remained quite reluctant to use issuance of paper notes to solve the current financial difficulties. Some reformist officials such as Kang Youwei urged the government to learn from Japan's success in transforming public finance. For them, Huang Zunxian's *The History of Japan (Riben guozhi)* was the comprehensive and authoritative guide to the reforms in Meiji Japan. Huang had worked as a diplomat in Japan between 1877 and 1882, and he finished writing this book in the summer of 1887 in China. However, Huang in this book cautioned that the overissuing of paper notes had led to serious inflation in Japan, and he commented that rapid devaluation of paper notes occurred not only in China during the Yuan and Ming dynasties but also in the United States and France. Interestingly, Huang did not mention how Matsukata redeemed paper notes during the 1880s.[103] Officials of the Board of Revenue shared Huang's concerns, and they particularly pointed out that the rapid fall in the value of paper notes was the cause of the biggest samurai rebellion in Japan in 1877.[104] And of course, negative examples were not limited to foreign countries, and Sheng Xuanhuai himself admitted that the government should not ignore its experience with paper notes in the 1850s.[105]

As late as January 1899, officials on the Board of Revenue, who had supported Sheng Xuanhuai's effort to establish a state bank, still considered government paper notes impractical and unlikely to circulate in the economy, as attested by the Xianfeng experiment.[106] Despite the circulation of the banknotes issued by HSBC in many Chinese cities, including Beijing and Tianjin, the Board of Revenue viewed banknotes as purely private credit instruments, with which the state should not get involved.[107] The deep-seated caution of the Board of Revenue on this front significantly restricted the performance of the Imperial Bank of China. Designed as a state bank rather than a commercial bank, it was not allowed to invest its capital in industrial enterprises and real estate. However, the center did not authorize the Imperial Bank of China to hold a monopoly in the remittance of official funds. Nor did it give the status of legal tender to its banknotes. In consequence, the Imperial Bank of China could issue only limited amounts of banknotes, which had to compete with other banknotes issued by foreign and native banks in China.[108] In comparison, note issuing was the most profitable business for the Bank of Japan in its early stages.

In contrast to the distrust of "empty" paper notes, the Qing government was more willing to accept silver coins minted by machine. As early as 1888, it had permitted provincial governments in Guangdong and Hubei to experiment with such coinage. As the minted silver coins smoothly circulated in the markets, the center recommended their adoption in all coastal provinces in July 1894. On 28 March 1896, the Qing government declared the counterfeiting of silver coins a capital crime, ending its long-standing laissez-faire attitude toward denominated silver currency.[109] In February 1900, Zhang Zhidong, the governor-general of

Hubei and Hunan, sent officials of the Hubei Mint to Beijing to help set up the capital mint. As for copper coins, the center also let provincial governments experiment first. When profit from the mintage of copper coins led to excessive mintage in the provinces, the center tried to assert control.[110]

The Qing government in these years was very interested in issuing state bonds to raise domestic loans. Shortly after the establishment of the Imperial Bank of China, the Office of Foreign Affairs *(Zongli yamen)* inquired whether it could provide low-interest loans to the government, as the Bank of England did for the British government.[111] Although the issuance of *zhaoxin* bonds was a failure, the Qing government in paying Japan the indemnity had actually demonstrated the administrative ability to ensure a punctual arrival of revenues from the provinces, which was necessary for floating long-term state bonds.

To pay the huge indemnity to Japan within three years, the Qing government had to borrow from British, French, German, and Russian banks. The annual interest payments amounted to 12 million tael (17 million tael after 1898 because of the rise in the value of the pound). The installments for the French and Russian loans had to arrive in the customs office in Shanghai at the end of the third and ninth month every year and those for the British and German loans at the end of the second, fifth, eighth, and eleventh months. Although these foreign loans took China's customs revenue as collateral, more than half of the actual interest payments came from revenues rather than customs. Among these annual interest payments, 41.2 percent came from the customs revenue collected by fifteen customs offices, 41.5 percent from revenues of lijin and land taxes collected from fifteen provinces, and the remaining 17.3 percent from other funds directly assigned by the center among provincial governments and offices of the Imperial Maritime Customs.[112] In this period, the collection of major lijin and salt revenues was handled by Qing officials, and the money was transferred to Shanghai either through remittance by private Chinese banks or by direct transportation of specie under official supervision.

The Board of Revenue ordered the customs office in Shanghai to report to the board by telegraph as soon as the assigned funds arrived in Shanghai. The board also sent telegrams to press provincial governments if there were arrears in sending the assigned installments.[113] Governors took the central orders seriously. As a result, according to the reports of the customs office in Shanghai, more than 95 percent arrived on time between 1896 and 1899.[114] If the central government did not have sufficient authority over governors, it would have been impossible to attain these punctual interest payments. The evidence thus indicates that the late nineteenth-century Qing government had the administrative ability to ensure punctual arrival of substantial annual interest installments, a necessary condition to secure long-term credits from the markets.

The financial markets in late nineteenth-century China were also ready to help the Qing government raise long-term credit. First, a stock market had emerged in Shanghai between 1862 and 1872, and a specialized stock exchange company (Shanghai Gupiao Pingzhun Gongsi) was founded in October 1882 to facilitate the transactions of stocks.[115] From 1872 to 1883, modern enterprises in transportation and mining raised a total capital of 6.64 million tael by selling stocks in Shanghai.[116] Second, there was a large amount of capital seeking investment opportunities in Shanghai and the coastal regions. By 1894, the estimated total wealth of some 10,000 compradors that was available for investment was as high as 200 million tael.[117] Yet the interest rates on deposits in both native and foreign banks were low; for example, the interest rate of a one-year timed deposit in foreign banks in Shanghai was around 5 percent.

Meanwhile, provincial governors after 1894 experimented with new methods to raise financial resources from the markets. In contrast to the Board of Revenue's use of administrative approaches to raise credit, provincial governments in Zhili, Jiangxi, and Fujian entrusted guilds or wealthy merchants rather than government offices with handling borrowing and interest payments to creditors.[118] Governors understood the importance of securing confidence in the initial stage of domestic borrowing as they were aware that many merchants who had idle capital were observing whether the government could make payments punctually. In the view of the Hubei governor Tan Jixun, if the government demonstrated its ability to assign revenue to return the principal and interest punctually, wealthy merchants would be eager to lend to it in future.[119]

The key institutional components that could have been utilized for building a modern fiscal state of long-term borrowing were therefore available in China. On the one hand, many high-ranking officials understood the importance of entrusting private financial intermediaries with management of the subscription and interest payments of credit bills for state borrowing. On the other hand, the Qing government had the administrative ability to ensure punctual arrivals of the assigned revenues from the provinces to Shanghai.

Although these available institutional elements remained unconnected in reality, it is not far-fetched to suppose that a financial institution similar to the Bank of England could have appeared in late nineteenth-century China. Most likely based in Shanghai, it could have managed the subscriptions and interest payments of low-interest-rate long-term state bonds. Such an institution could have secured political supporters in Beijing by attracting princes and major officials to invest in state bonds, as happened in eighteenth-century England. It could have won the favor of the officials of the Board of Revenue by sending them annual "gifts," as the Bank of England did to the treasury in the eighteenth century.

The Qing government's successful payment of the indemnity to Japan shows that it had the ability to use punctual interest payments to service a long-term credit at the scale of 230 million tael of silver. In this light, a modern fiscal state that used centrally collected indirect revenues to fund a system of long-term state borrowing appears to have been a possible outcome of institutional development in late Qing public finance. Such a development, despite the limits that economic conditions imposed on the rise of indirect taxes in China, would still have enhanced Qing state capacity significantly. However, no historical event did impose a credit crisis on the center to force it to figure out how to put these institutional elements together to achieve the mutually reinforcing effects between punctual interest payments and the increasing confidence of investors in state bonds.

CONCLUSION

History is not just a data generator for social scientists to test hypotheses and build formal models. Instead, history should be an integral part of the causal narrative to explain divergent outcomes in institutional development and political transformation. This comparative historical analysis of three episodes of institutional development in England (1642–1752), Japan (1868–1895), and China (1851–1911) is constructed in and through concrete historical contexts. Its causal narrative attempts to account for a specific "great transformation": the rise of the modern fiscal state. But this approach also holds some general implications for understanding historical causation in complex temporal processes of sociopolitical change. In particular, it seeks to demonstrate how an eventful approach to historical causation can integrate agency, structure, and contingency into one coherent causal story to explain the creation of new institutions through an uncertain and interactive historical process. Where the trajectory of institutional development is determined neither by socioeconomic structure nor by agents with bounded rationalities, a careful analysis of events can help social scientists uncover a causal mechanism without resorting to oversimplification or retreating to a naive form of "history as storytelling."

180

[handwritten margin note: Text seeks to advance both a theory and a method.]

Historical institutionalists in recent years have devoted great effort to conducting detailed analyses of institutional developments or political transformations that occurred in specific historical periods. They have emphasized the importance of uncertainty and contingency and the vital role of agency in institutional change and creation. This comparative account of the emergence of the modern fiscal state in England and Japan but not in China suggests that episode analysis and the study of long-term change in the socioeconomic structure are two distinct yet closely connected components in historical causation.

Prior to each episode examined in this book, similar features in state formation and market development in England, Japan, and China produced several crucially important common preconditions, which facilitate a comparative study. In each case, the existing institutions of public finance became ill fitted to the socioeconomic circumstances: the exhaustion of domain revenue of the royal government in early Stuart England; the inadequacy of shogunal tax revenue, derived from the limited territory under its direct management, to fund the governance of Japan as the central power in the early nineteenth century; the inability of the Qing government to use monetary policy to mitigate the severe deflation caused by the dearth of domestic silver in China between the 1820s and 1840s. Again, in each case state actors were all overwhelmingly concerned with how to overcome the fiscal crisis.

Credit Crises lead to innovation

However, in none of these instances did fiscal crisis lead to a complete breakdown of the state. The common concern to maintain social order shared by the central government, local officials, and elites buttressed all these three well-established early modern states. This political condition was vital for each central government to avoid immediate bankruptcy by making permissible the transfer of state expenditures to local governments and even local communities. The dysfunctional yet sticky existing institutions of public finance thus constrained the ability of actors to conceive alternative institutions. New schemes—taxing the commercial sectors, printing paper notes—were proposed and debated but not implemented before each crisis broke. Thus no one knew whether they would work out in practice. When existing institutions finally fell apart in the English Civil War in 1642, the Meiji Restoration in 1868, and the Taiping Rebellion in 1851, respectively, actors had to grope for new institutions of public finance under conditions of great uncertainty and pressure. To set the collapse of existing institutions in big events as the start of each episode of institutional development allows us to follow Paul Pierson's advice to "go back and look" without falling forever down the bottomless well of history.

But when we do go back to uncertain critical junctures and look forward through the eyes of historical actors, we find ourselves in a context with multiple possible outcomes. Fiscal decentralization seemed to be self-reinforcing in England in the 1660s. Even when the collection of excises and customs had been centralized, state actors in England could have chosen dependence on short-term credit or to clear past debts, instead of searching for institutions of permanent credit. Likewise, fiscal decentralization seemed the more practical option in the eyes of many state actors in early Meiji Japan. Even after abolishing the domains in 1871, powerful politicians preferred a gradual rather than rapid tempo in financial centralization. Although fiscal decentralization persisted in Qing China, the central government showed substantial interest in utilizing the methods of direct collection of lijin duties developed at the provincial level to centrally collect major items of lijin revenues before 1895.

How shall we explain the final outcome against the multiplicity of possible results seen in the process? In hindsight, we can point to several aspects of the modern fiscal state that might appeal to state actors. Its establishment greatly enhances the spending capacity of the state by using centrally collected indirect taxes to mobilize long-term financial resources. The collective action problem makes it difficult for ordinary consumers to organize against heavy extraction of indirect taxes. State actors should thus embrace the modern fiscal state, regardless of whether they are landed or moneyed elites. However, knowledge of these functions and of distributional effects was not available to historical actors in the uncertain process of institutional development. A functionalist explanation therefore cannot tell us why such an effective institution of public finance did not appear in England or Japan earlier. Nor can it explain why the modern fiscal state did not emerge in late Qing China, a polity that also satisfied the necessary conditions for this great transformation.

Enhanced agency at critical junctures does not necessarily dispel uncertainty. Looking more closely at the historical context, we find that powerful political actors were often divided by quite different ideas. In England and Japan, we see widespread suspicion and even hostility toward perpetual state debts or the issuance of nonconvertible paper notes. In late Qing China, where a traditional fiscal operation persisted, important officials did propose establishing a state bank to take on loans for the state. Considering the existence of many institutional schemes among influential state actors in each case, it is difficult to pin down ideas as the "primary cause" in explaining a specific outcome of the interactive and temporal process of institutional development. Learning is an important part of experimentation with various institutional arrangements, yet it does not suffice to set the direction of institutional development for two reasons. First, the range of foreign models known also implies quite different directions of institutional development. Second, to adapt a foreign model to fit domestic circumstances is itself a trial-and-error process, and power struggles often deprived the initiators of institutional change of the opportunity to learn from their mistakes. And we cannot assume that all powerful actors possessed both the motivation and the necessary capacity to learn.

What then of structure? The long-term socioeconomic changes prior to the beginning of each episode of institutional development and the dysfunction of outmoded institutions are the fundamental causes of the uncertainty under which historical actors at each critical juncture search for alternatives. The multiplicity of possible outcomes also resulted from the interactions between the structure and agents who lacked full information about relevant socioeconomic conditions. Even if we grant a large room for agency, actors' bounded rationality does not allow them to foresee which direction leads toward the final outcome of the modern fiscal state in the opaque process of institutional development. The socioeconomic structure provides a stage for the drama of institutional transformation, yet it does not determine the sequence or the end result.

An "eventful approach" based on in-depth historical analysis helps us to resolve this causal indeterminacy that neither agency nor structure alone can handle. We must bear in mind, however, that not all historical events that occur in a given episode of institutional development are causally significant. As I show in this comparative historical analysis of the rise of the modern fiscal state, the causal leverage of events is derived from a special credit crisis produced by events: the state's dependence on fiduciary credit instruments to meet its spending needs, such as the issuance of massive numbers of short-term borrowing bills unfunded by tax revenues in England and the early Meiji government's dependence on nonconvertible paper notes. Instead of being rationally designed or calculated by actors, both were unintended consequences of historical events; desperate actors had no other options. Indeed, to their contemporaries, the opponents of the floating of these fiduciary credit instruments in public finance seemed more reasonable, given the lack of credibility of these bills in the markets.

Once it occurred, however, such a credit crisis had long-lasting effects on the direction and tempo of subsequent institutional development. The fiduciary credit instruments on which the state relied to meet its spending needs constituted a problem that had to be solved by whoever held the reins of power. The use of coercion by itself was inadequate to safeguard the creditworthiness of paper notes or unfunded bills of short-term borrowing. State actors had to experiment with new methods and institutional elements, including risky and unpopular ones. As the center bore the full risk of redeeming these credit instruments, such a crisis helped state actors escape the "lock-in" of fiscal decentralization and motivated them to keep searching for ways to centralize tax collection and the management of public finance. The pressure pushed them to come up with innovative means to effectively monitor the performance of collecting agents in central collection of indirect taxes so as to better secure the creditworthiness of state credit instruments.

The special nature of the credit crisis not only tested the effectiveness of institutional elements being tried out but also provided an opportunity for competent financial officials to play important roles in building a new public finance. Over time, the continuous accumulation of effective institutional elements, competent personnel, and useful experience dispelled uncertainty. The alternative institutions that could have been adopted were eliminated because of their inability to resolve the credit crisis. As actors gradually came to realize the mutually reinforcing effects between the central collection of indirect taxes and state institutions to float long-term credit, the trajectory of institutional development moved irreversibly toward the final outcome of the modern fiscal state. Such a path-dependent process is unlikely to have unfolded had no credit crisis forced state reliance on fiduciary credit instruments.

The socioeconomic structure sets crucial boundary conditions for the trajectory of institutional development without determining its direction. For example, the level of concentration in the production of major consumer goods shaped efforts to centralize the collection of indirect taxes. This is attested by both the relative ease of centralization in the collection of the beer excise in England and sake taxes in Japan and the difficulty of extracting more revenue from duties on domestic opium in late Qing China. Variation in socioeconomic environments provided different possibilities for actors to use tax revenue to secure state long-term liabilities. In England in the late seventeenth and early eighteenth centuries, the underdevelopment of domestic financial networks made it difficult for the English government to float paper notes or the banknotes issued by the Bank of England in the whole economy. Nonetheless, the dominance of London in England's domestic and foreign trade, the concentration of big financiers in London, and the presence of a segment of investors who were looking for secure opportunities greatly facilitated the government's efforts to convert its unfunded short-term credit into low-interest perpetual annuities that could be supported by its tax revenues. Under these circumstances, the institutions of perpetual borrowing prevailed over the option of converting state liabilities into paper notes.

In contrast, the vibrant domestic economy and interregional financial networks in Japan were crucially important for the Meiji government to float its nonconvertible paper notes throughout the whole economy by 1871, before it had established institutions to collect taxes from the entire territory. In the struggle to redeem the value of nonconvertible paper notes already in circulation, the government established centralized institutions to manage public finance and collect indirect taxes. Financial centralization and the founding of the Bank of Japan in 1882 enabled the state not only to attain convertibility of paper money but to raise long-term domestic credit from the markets.

As a negative case in this comparative analysis, China between 1851 and 1911 demonstrates the importance of the conjunction of a credit crisis and proper socioeconomic circumstances to the emergence of the modern fiscal state. The severely disrupted domestic economy in China in the 1850s was simply too hostile an environment for the government's reasonably well-designed plan to build institutions to safeguard the value of its paper notes. The resulting fiasco made state actors reluctant to reintroduce credit instruments into the government fiscal operation. Under new international and domestic circumstances between the 1870s and 1890s, significant changes took place at the provincial level, particularly the creation of institutions to directly collect lijin duties and the collaboration between provincial governments and private financiers in remitting revenue and official funds. However, no event prior to 1895 pushed the central government to extend these methods to centralize the collection of indirect taxes. The center continued to rely on a decentralized fiscal system to meet its emergency needs in fighting foreign wars and returning short-term loans.

Analytically, China's payment of the indemnity to Japan after 1895 is a kind of natural experiment. It illustrates the existence of institutional elements that the Qing government could have utilized to interact with the financial markets in coastal cities for the purpose of building a modern fiscal state based on long-term borrowing in the late nineteenth century. These included the administrative ability to ensure the punctual arrival of revenues for serving the interest payments on long-term credit; the capacity to centralize the collection of domestic indirect taxes; and the willingness to broaden the base of creditors to the state by issuing state bonds with small face values. The failure of China to create a modern fiscal state thus supports my identification of a causal mechanism resulting from the conjunction of a credit crisis and appropriate socioeconomic circumstances.

Once the institutions of the modern fiscal state had emerged, their consolidation was due to their functions to enhance state capacity and their distributional effects, which favored the state vis-à-vis ordinary consumers. The maintenance of the modern fiscal state depends heavily on keeping a balance between the state's tax revenue and its long-term liabilities. Those who manage public finance acquire a strong motivation to try to accurately estimate the taxation potential and elasticity of major sources of revenue. They also have an incentive to encourage the expansion of the economy as it directly means the growth of tax revenue and state ability to mobilize funds. Centralized fiscal institutions played a vital role in making the Bank of England and the Bank of Japan real central banks that not only provided the monetary supply for the entire economy but also served as the lender of last resort in the domestic financial markets. The rise of the modern fiscal state thus laid the foundation for the modern state that is able to regulate the macroeconomy through fiscal and financial policies.

A path-dependent account for the emergence and consolidation of the modern fiscal state does not suggest an end to politics when the path moves irreversibly toward the final outcome. Instead, the newly consolidated institutions of public finance became a primary forum to contest the fairness of taxation and financial policies and the nature of government spending. The regressive nature of extracting heavy excises, for instance, greatly agitated social reformers in England in the late eighteenth and early nineteenth centuries. Likewise, members of the Japanese Diet in the early 1890s heatedly debated the purposes to which the newly established institutions of the modern fiscal state should be put: domestic welfare or foreign aggression? The modern fiscal state therefore provides a new platform for normative and distributional politics. However, the resulting continuous and incremental changes in method and application did not change the core institutional features of the modern fiscal state: the centralized fiscal system that sustained the state's creditworthiness in the financial markets.

NOTES

Introduction

1. On the importance of studying institutional change and development, see Kathleen Thelen and Sven Steinmo, "Historical Institutionalism in Comparative Politics," in *Structuring Politics: Historical Institutionalism in Comparative Politics,* ed. Sven Steinmo, Kathleen Thelen, and Frank Longstreth (Cambridge and New York: Cambridge University Press, 1992), 16–22; Kathleen Thelen, "Historical Institutionalism in Comparative Politics," *Annual Review of Political Science* 2, no. 1 (1999): 369–404; Paul Pierson, *Politics in Time: History, Institutions, and Social Analysis* (Princeton, NJ: Princeton University Press, 2004), 103; and Barry R. Weingast, "Rational Choice Institutionalism," in *Political Science: The State of the Discipline,* ed. Ira Katznelson and Helen V. Milner (New York: W. W. Norton, 2002), 675.

2. Paul Pierson and Theda Skocpol, "Historical Institutionalism," in *Political Science: The State of the Discipline,* ed. Ira Katznelson and Helen Milner (New York: W. W. Norton, 2002); Pierson, *Politics in Time,* chapter 3; and Andrew Abbott, *Time Matters: On Theory and Method* (Chicago: University of Chicago Press, 2001).

3. Jack Knight, *Institutions and Social Conflict* (Cambridge and New York: Cambridge University Press, 1992); Kathleen Thelen, *How Institutions Evolve: The Political Economy of Skills in Germany, Britain, the United States, and Japan* (Cambridge and New York: Cambridge University Press, 2004), 31–33.

4. For the embeddedness of institutions, see Suzanne Berger and Ronald Dore, eds., *National Diversity and Global Capitalism* (Ithaca, NY: Cornell University Press, 1996); and Peter A. Hall and David W. Soskice, eds., *Varieties of Capitalism* (Oxford and New York: Oxford University Press, 2001).

5. Avner Greif, *Institutions and the Path to the Modern Economy: Lessons from Medieval Trade* (Cambridge and New York: Cambridge University Press, 2006), 14–20; Pierson, *Politics in Time,* chapter 5; Ira Katznelson, "Structure and Configuration in Comparative Politics," in *Comparative Politics: Rationality, Culture, and Structure,* ed. Mark Irving Lichbach and Alan S. Zuckerman (Cambridge and New York: Cambridge University Press, 1997), 93–94; Peter A. Hall, "Aligning Ontology and Methodology in Comparative Research," in *Comparative Historical Analysis in the Social Sciences,* ed. James Mahoney and Dietrich Rueschemeyer (Cambridge and New York: Cambridge University Press, 2003), 382–384; Charles Tilly, "Mechanisms in Political Processes," *Annual Review of Political Science* 4, no. 1 (2001): 25.

6. For an excellent discussion of this kind of selection bias in the use of history in the social sciences, see Ian S. Lustick, "History, Historiography, and Political Science: Multiple Historical Records and the Problem of Selection Bias," *American Political Science Review* 90, no. 3 (September 1996): 605–618. For more on selection bias in qualitative studies, see David Collier and James Mahoney, "Insights and Pitfalls: Selection Bias in Qualitative Research," *World Politics* 49, no. 1 (1996): 56–91.

7. Seventeenth-century Britain and eighteenth-century Japan and China were empires that included territories under different administrative and legal institutions: Scotland and Ireland in the case of England; Mongolia, Manchuria, Qinghai, Xinjiang, and Tibet in the Qing dynasty; and Hokkaido in Tokugawa Japan. I therefore use the term "state" in reference only to England (instead of Britain), Japan proper, and China proper. Major institutional changes in public finance happened within the territory of the state.

8. Patrick K. O'Brien and Philip A. Hunt, "England, 1485–1815," in *The Rise of the Fiscal State in Europe, 1200–1815,* ed. Richard Bonney (Oxford and New York: Oxford University Press, 1999).

9. For discussions of the consequences of a lack of effective tax institutions and financial institutions in emerging market economies, see David Woodruff, *Money Unmade: Barter and the Fate of Russian Capitalism* (Ithaca, NY: Cornell University Press, 1999); John L. Campbell, "An Institutional Analysis of Fiscal Reform in Postcommunist Europe," *Theory and Society* 25, no. 1 (February 1996): 45–84.

10. James Mahoney and Gary Goertz, "The Possibility Principle: Choosing Negative Cases in Comparative Research," *American Political Science Review* 98, no. 4 (November 2004): 653–669.

11. Max Weber, "Politics as a Vocation," in *From Max Weber: Essays in Sociology,* ed. H. H. Gerth and C. Wright Mills (Oxford: Oxford University Press, 1958), 78.

12. Max Weber, *Economy and Society: An Outline of Interpretive Sociology* (Berkeley: University of California Press, 1978), 1:166.

13. Peter Mathias, "The People's Money in the Eighteenth Century: The Royal Mint, Trade Tokens and the Economy," in *The Transformation of England: Essays in the Economic and Social History of England in the Eighteenth Century* (London: Methuen, 1979).

14. For the long journey it took for the state to attain a monopoly in the supply of small change, in England and other European countries, see Thomas J. Sargent and François R. Velde, *The Big Problem of Small Change* (Princeton, NJ: Princeton University Press, 2002).

15. On the domain state, see Richard Bonney, "Revenues," in *Economic Systems and State Finance,* ed. Richard Bonney (London: Oxford University Press, 1995), especially 447–463. See also the detailed case study of the transition from domain state to fiscal state in Western Europe in Richard Bonney, ed., *The Rise of the Fiscal State in Europe, 1200–1815* (Oxford and New York: Oxford University Press, 1999). For the domain states in Sweden, Denmark, and some German states, such as Württemberg and Hesse-Cassel in the seventeenth and eighteenth centuries, see Niall Ferguson, *The Cash Nexus: Money and Power in the Modern World, 1700–2000* (New York: Basic Books, 2001), 54–55. For the survival of the domain state in Prussia from the eighteenth century to the early twentieth century, see D. E. Schremmer, "Taxation and Public Finance: Britain, France, and Germany," in *The Cambridge Economic History of Europe,* vol. 8, *The Industrial Economies,* ed. Peter Mathias and Sidney Pollard (Cambridge: Cambridge University Press, 1989), 411–455.

16. Kiren Aziz Chaudhry, "The Myths of the Market and the Common History of Late Developers," *Politics and Society* 21, no. 3 (September 1993): 252.

17. The petro-states are typical domain states in the twentieth century. See Terry Lynn Karl, *The Paradox of Plenty: Oil Booms and Petro-States* (Berkeley: University of California Press, 1997).

18. See the classic discussion in Mancur Olson, *The Logic of Collective Action: Public Goods and the Theory of Groups* (Cambridge, MA: Harvard University Press, 1965).

19. For China, see Kenneth Pomeranz, *The Great Divergence: China, Europe, and the Making of the Modern World Economy* (Princeton, NJ: Princeton University Press, 2000), chapters 1 and 2; R. Bin Wong, *China Transformed: Historical Change and the Limits of European Experience* (Ithaca, NY: Cornell University Press, 1997), 13–14; and Li Bozhong, *Jiangnan de zaoqi gongyehua: 1550–1850 nian* [Early industrialization in the Lower Yangzi delta, 1550–1850]

(Beijing: Shehui kexue wenxian chubanshe, 2000). For Japan, see Edward E. Pratt, *Japan's Protoindustrial Elite: The Economic Foundations of the Gōnō* (Cambridge, MA: Harvard University Asia Center, 1999); David L. Howell, *Capitalism from Within: Economy, Society, and the State in a Japanese Fishery* (Berkeley: University of California Press, 1995); and Hayami Akira and Miyamoto Matao, eds., *Keizai shakai no seiritsu: 17th–18th seiki* [The formation of an economic society: Seventeenth and eighteenth centuries], vol. 1, *Nihon keizaishi* [The economic history of Japan] (Tokyo: Iwanami Shoten, 1988).

20. For the characteristics of a market economy in early modern England, see John Hicks, *A Theory of Economic History* (Oxford: Oxford University Press, 1969).

21. Eric Kerridge, *Trade and Banking in Early Modern England* (Manchester: Manchester University Press, 1988).

22. Shikano Yoshiaki, "Edo-ki Osaka ni okeru ryōgaeshō no kin'yū kinō o megutte" [The economic organization of Osaka's *ryogaesho* money changers in the early modern era of Japan], *Keizaigaku ronsō* 52, no. 2 (December 2000): 237–241.

23. For the roles of *qianzhuang,* see Susan M. Jones, "Finance in Ning-po: The Ch'ien-chuang," in *Economic Organization in Chinese Society,* ed. W. E. Willmott (Stanford, CA: Stanford University Press, 1972), 47–77. For the national financial networks established by Shanxi bankers, see Huang Jianhui, *Shanxi piaohaoshi* [A history of Shanxi bankers], rev. ed. (Taiyuan: Shanxi jingji chubanshe, 2002), 137–145.

24. See Saitō Osamu, "Bakumatsu-Ishin no seiji sanjutsu" [Political arithmetic and Japan in late Tokugawa and early Meiji Restoration], in *Meiji Ishin no kakushin to renzoku* [Innovation and continuity in the Meiji Restoration], ed. Kindai Nihon Kenkyūkai, vol. 14 of *Nenpō kindai Nihon kenkyū* (Tokyo: Yamakawa Shuppansha, 1992), 278.

25. See Wu Chengming, *Zhongguo zibenzhuyi yu guonei shichang* [Capitalism and the domestic market in China] (Beijing: Zhongguo shehui kexue chubanshe, 1985), 251.

26. Jack A. Goldstone, "Efflorescences and Economic Growth in World History: Rethinking the 'Rise of the West' and the British Industrial Revolution," *Journal of World History* 13 (2002): 323–389; Jean-Laurent Rosenthal and R. Bin Wong, *Before and Beyond Divergence: The Politics of Economic Change in China and Europe* (Cambridge, MA: Harvard University Press, 2011).

27. Edward Shils distinguishes these "old states" from many new states that formed only after the end of colonialism in the twentieth century. Edward Shils, *Political Development in the New States* (Paris: Mouton, 1968).

28. Michael J. Braddick, *State Formation in Early Modern England, c. 1550–1700* (Cambridge and New York: Cambridge University Press, 2000), chapter 1.

29. Beatrice S. Bartlett, *Monarchs and Ministers: The Grand Council in Mid-Ch'ing China, 1723–1820* (Berkeley: University of California Press, 1991).

30. Kuroda Akinobu, "Kenryū no senki" [The appreciation of copper cash in the Qianlong era], *Tōyōshi kenkyū* 45, no. 4 (March 1987): 698.

31. *Qianlong chao shangyu dang* [Edicts from the Qianlong reign], ed. Zhongguo diyi lishi dang'anguan, 2nd ed. (Beijing: Dang'an chubanshe, 2000), 2:332.

32. *Palace Memorials* (henceforth *PM*), Box 60, No. 2443–2444.

33. *PM*, Box 61, No. 2482–2484.

34. On the shogunate as the public authority *(kōgi)* above the domain lords, see Fujii Jōji, "Jūshichi seiki no Nihon—Buke no kokka no keisei" [Japan in the seventeenth century: The formation of a military state], in *Iwanami kōza Nihon tsūshi* [The Iwanami general history of Japan], vol. 12, *Kinsei (2)* [The early modern period], ed. Asao Naohiro et al. (Tokyo: Iwanami Shoten, 1994), 3–34.

35. For the emergence of the shogunate as the central power in eighteenth-century Japan, see Mary Elizabeth Berry, "Public Peace and Private Attachment: The Goals and Conduct of Power in Early Modern Japan," *Journal of Japanese Studies* 12, no. 2 (Summer 1986): 237–271; Eiko Ikegami, *The Taming of the Samurai: Honorific Individualism and the Making of Modern Japan* (Cambridge, MA: Harvard University Press, 1995), chapters 7 and 8; James W. White, "State Growth and Popular Protest in Tokugawa Japan," *Journal of Japanese Studies* 14, no. 1 (Winter 1988): 1–25.

36. For a succinct introduction to the bureaucratization of the Tokugawa shogunate and the codification of its legal system in the first half of the seventeenth century, see Tsuji Tatsuya, "Politics in the Eighteenth Century," in *The Cambridge History of Japan,* vol. 4, *Early Modern Japan,* ed. John Whitney Hall (Cambridge and New York: Cambridge University Press, 1991), 432–456.

37. Ōishi Manabu, "Kyōhō kaikaku no rekishiteki ichi" [The historical place of the Kyōhō Reform], in *Bakuhansei kaikaku no tenkai* [The development of the reforms in the shogunate-domain system], ed. Fujita Satoru (Tokyo: Yamakawa Shuppansha, 2001), 31–51.

38. Yasukuni Ryōichi, "Kahei no kinō" [Functions of currency], in *Iwanami kōza Nihon tsūshi* [The Iwanami general history of Japan], vol. 12, *Kinsei (2)* [The early modern period], ed. Asao Naohiro et al. (Tokyo: Iwanami Shoten, 1994), 155–156.

39. Shinbo Hiroshi and Saitō Osamu, "Gaisetsu—19 seiki e" [An overview: Toward the nineteenth century], in *Nihon keizaishi* [An economic history of Japan], vol. 2, *Kindai seichō no taidō* [Gathering momentum for modern growth], ed. Shinbo Hiroshi and Saitō Osamu (Tokyo: Iwanami Shoten, 1989), 27.

40. Mikami Ryūzō, *En no tanjō: Kindai kahei seido no seiritsu* [The birth of the yen: The establishment of the modern monetary system] (Tokyo: Tōyō Keizai Shinpōsha, 1989), 59–63.

41. Shinbo Hiroshi and Saitō Osamu, "Gaisetsu—19 seiki e," 26–31.

42. G. L. Harriss, "Political Society and the Growth of Government in Late Medieval England," *Past and Present* 138 (February 1993): 40; and W. M. Ormrod, "England in the Middle Ages," in *The Rise of the Fiscal State in Europe, 1200–1815,* ed. Richard Bonney (Oxford and New York: Oxford University Press, 1999), particularly 27–33.

43. Customs had an ambivalent status as it belonged to the crown's ordinary revenue yet it was a kind of regular tax. For the importance of domain revenue to the state in the early Tudor period, see B. P. Wolffe, *The Crown Lands, 1461 to 1536: An Aspect of Yorkist and Early Tudor Government* (London: Allen and Unwin, 1970), 25; Wolffe, *The Royal Demesne in English History: The Crown Estate in the Governance of the Realm from the Conquest to 1509* (London: Allen and Unwin, 1971), chapter 1; Penry Williams, *The Tudor Regime* (Oxford: Clarendon, 1979), 58; G. R. Elton, *England under the Tudors,* 3rd ed. (London: Routledge, 1991), 47–57.

44. Basil Chubb, *The Control of Public Expenditure: Financial Committees of the House of Commons* (Oxford: Clarendon Press, 1952), 9–10.

45. See the discussion of the fundamental difference between regular taxation and irregular extraordinary supplies in Richard W. Hoyle, "Crown, Parliament, and Taxation in Sixteenth-Century England," *English Historical Review* 109, no. 434 (November 1994): 1192–1196.

46. For the incompleteness in extracting tax revenue of the shogunate, see Mark Ravina, *Land and Lordship in Early Modern Japan* (Stanford, CA: Stanford University Press, 1999), 24–28. For the political authority of the shogunate to order domain governments to shoulder expenditures of state affairs, see Ōguchi Yūjirō, "Bakufu no zaisei" [The public finance of the shogunate], in *Nihon keizaishi* [The economic history of Japan], vol. 2, *Kindai seichū no taidō* [Gathering momentum for modern growth], ed. Shinbo Hiroshi and Saitō Osamu (Tokyo: Iwanami Shoten, 1989), 152–154.

47. Wang Yeh-chien, *Land Taxation in Imperial China, 1750–1911* (Cambridge, MA: Harvard University Press, 1973), 8–11.

48. Patrick K. O'Brien and Philip A. Hunt, "The Rise of a Fiscal State in England, 1485–1815," *Historical Research* 66, no. 160 (June 1993): 141–142.

49. Ōguchi Yūjirō, "Bakufu no zaisei," 132.

50. Madeleine Zelin, *The Magistrate's Tael: Rationalizing Fiscal Reform in Eighteenth-Century Ch'ing China* (Berkeley: University of California Press, 1992); Chen Feng, "Qingdai qianqi zouxiao zhidu yu zhengce yanbian" [The early Qing memorial system and policy change], *Lishi yanjiu* 2 (2000): 63–74.

51. Wang, *Land Taxation in Imperial China,* 12–18; Peng Yuxin, "Qingdai tianfu qiyun cunliu zhidu de yanjin" [The development of the system of land tax retention and transportation in the Qing dynasty], *Zhongguo jingjishi yanjiu* 4

(1992): 124–133. On fiscal decentralization in China during the Ming dynasty, a state of affairs that the Qing inherited, see Ray Huang, *Taxation and Governmental Finance in Sixteenth-Century Ming China* (London and New York: Cambridge University Press, 1974), particularly 268–279.

52. Quentin Skinner, "The State," in *Political Innovation and Conceptual Change,* ed. Terence Ball, James Farr, and Russell L. Hanson (Cambridge and New York: Cambridge University Press, 1989), 117–118.

53. On the legitimation of state power through government spending to improve societal welfare in early modern England, see Braddick, *State Formation in Early Modern England,* chapter 3; Steve Hindle, *The State and Social Change in Early Modern England, c. 1550–1640* (New York: Palgrave Macmillan, 2000), chapters 2 and 6. For the case of eighteenth-century Japan, see Ōguchi Yūjirō, "Bakufu no zaisei," 153–157. For eighteenth-century China, Zelin emphasizes the role of government expenditure to promote public welfare; see Zelin, *The Magistrate's Tael,* 304. For famine relief in eighteenth-century China, see Pierre-Étienne Will, *Bureaucracy and Famine in Eighteenth-Century China,* trans. Elborg Forster (Stanford, CA: Stanford University Press, 1990); and Pierre-Étienne Will and R. Bin Wong, *Nourish the People: The State Civilian Granary System in China, 1650–1850* (Ann Arbor: Center for Chinese Studies, University of Michigan Press, 1991).

54. For discussion of the roles that early modern states played in providing social welfare, see Michael J. Braddick, "The Early Modern English State and the Question of Differentiation, from 1550 to 1770," *Comparative Studies in Society and History* 38, no. 1 (January 1996): 92–111; and Stephan R. Epstein, "The Rise of the West," in *An Anatomy of Power: The Social Theory of Michael Mann,* ed. John A. Hall and Ralph Schroeder (Cambridge and New York: Cambridge University Press, 2006), 247.

55. For the (over)emphasis on the role of warfare in state building, see Charles Tilly, ed., *The Formation of National States in Western Europe* (Princeton, NJ: Princeton University Press, 1975); Tilly, *Coercion, Capital, and European States, A.D. 990–1992,* rev. ed. (Cambridge, MA: Blackwell, 1992); and Brian Downing, *The Military Revolution and Political Change* (Princeton, NJ: Princeton University Press, 1992).

56. See the overall review of the price revolution in England in C. G. A. Clay, *Economic Expansion and Social Change: England 1500–1700,* vol. 1, *People, Land, and Towns* (Cambridge: Cambridge University Press, 1984), chapter 2. For the upward trend in prices in Japan after the 1820s, see Shinbo Hiroshi, *Kinsei no bukka to keizai hatten: Zenkōgyō shakai e no sūryōteki no sekkin* [Prices in the early modern period and economic development: A quantitative approach toward a preindustrial society] (Tokyo: Tōyō Keizai Shinpōsha, 1978).

57. Wang Yeh-chien, "Secular Trends of Rice Prices in the Yangzi Delta, 1638–1935," in *Chinese History in Economic Perspective,* ed. Thomas G. Rawski and Lillian M. Li (Berkeley: University of California Press, 1992), 35–68; Lin Man-houng, *China Upside Down: Currency, Society, and Ideologies, 1801–1856* (Cambridge, MA: Harvard University Asia Center, 2006), chapters 2 and 3.

58. For the importance of institutions of public finance to the autonomy and capacity of the state, see Theda Skocpol, "Bringing the State Back In: Strategies of Analysis in Current Research," in *Bringing the State Back In,* ed. Peter B. Evans, Dietrich Rueschemeyer, and Theda Skocpol (Cambridge and New York: Cambridge University Press, 1985); Michael Mann, *The Sources of Social Power* (Cambridge and New York: Cambridge University Press, 1986).

59. For an emphasis on financial bankruptcy as the necessary condition for the collapse of the state, see Theda Skocpol, *States and Social Revolutions: A Comparative Analysis of France, Russia, and China* (Cambridge and New York: Cambridge University Press, 1979); and Jack A. Goldstone, *Revolution and Rebellion in the Early Modern World* (Berkeley: University of California Press, 1991).

60. On the importance of the English Civil Wars to the rise of the fiscal state in England, see Patrick K. O'Brien, "Fiscal Exceptionalism: Great Britain and Its European rivals from Civil War to Triumph at Trafalgar and Waterloo," in *The Political Economy of British Historical Experience, 1688–1914,* ed. Donald Winch and Patrick K. O'Brien (Oxford: Published for the British Academy by Oxford University Press, 2002), 246; and Michael J. Braddick, *The Nerves of State: Taxation and the Financing of the English State, 1558–1714* (Manchester: Manchester University Press, 1996), 16.

61. See such examples in Weber, *Economy and Society,* 2:1061–1064. For more recent examples, see Gabriel Ardant, "Financial Policy and Economic Infrastructure of Modern States and Nations," in *The Formation of National States in Western Europe,* ed. Charles Tilly (Princeton, NJ: Princeton University Press, 1975), 196; Tilly, *Coercion, Capital, and European States,* 159; and Bruce G. Carruthers, *City of Capital: Politics and Markets in the English Financial Revolution* (Princeton, NJ: Princeton University Press, 1996), 22.

62. The level of debt of the English government rose from almost nothing in 1688 to £16.7 million by 1697, £76 million by 1748, and £245 million by 1783. See John Brewer, *The Sinews of Power: War, Money and the English State, 1688–1783* (New York: Alfred A. Knopf, 1989), 114.

63. Peter Mathias and Patrick K. O'Brien, "Taxation in Britain and France, 1715–1810: A Comparison of the Social and Economic Incidence of Taxes Collected for the Central Governments," *Journal of European Economic History 5,* no. 3 (1976): 601–650; Patrick K. O'Brien, "The Political Economy of British

Taxation, 1660–1815," *Economic History Review,* n.s., 41, no. 1 (February 1988): 1–32.

64. Peter Mathias, "Taxation and Industrialization in Britain," in *The Transformation of England: Essays in the Economic and Social History of England in the Eighteenth Century* (London: Methuen, 1979), 117.

65. Cited from Table 2 in J. V. Beckett, "Land Tax or Excise: The Levying of Taxation in Seventeenth- and Eighteenth-Century England," *English Historical Review* 100, no. 395 (April 1985): 306.

66. For example, the excises and stamp duties increased from £0.4 million in 1685 to £2.8 million in 1720 while the estimated national income (at current prices) increased only from £41.76 million in 1680 to £53.92 million in 1720. See O'Brien, "The Political Economy of British Taxation," 3 and 9.

67. For Weber's discussion of the contribution of rational bureaucracy to the development of capitalism, see Weber, *Economy and Society,* 2:974–975 and 1393–1394.

68. Brewer, *The Sinews of Power,* 68. The Excise Department as a bureaucracy is neglected by Bernard S. Silberman, who traces the beginning of a rationalized bureaucracy in England to around 1790. See Bernard S. Silberman, *Cages of Reason: The Rise of the Rational State in France, Japan, the United States, and Great Britain* (Chicago: University Press of Chicago, 1993), chapters 10–12.

69. Brewer, *The Sinews of Power,* 102–111.

70. W. R. Ward, *The English Land Tax in the Eighteenth Century* (Oxford: Oxford University Press, 1953), particularly section II. For the local gentry's retention of the collected revenue, see L. S. Pressnell, "Public Monies and the Development of English Banking," *Economic History Review,* n.s., 5, no. 3 (1953): 378–397; and Colin Brooks, "Public Finance and Political Stability: The Administration of the Land Tax, 1688–1720," *Historical Journal* 17, no. 2 (1974): 281–300.

71. Brewer, *The Sinews of Power,* chapter 3.

72. J. H. Plumb, *The Growth of Political Stability in England: 1675–1725* (London: Macmillan, 1967). For the severity of corruption in the eighteenth-century English government, see W. D. Rubinstein, "The End of 'Old Corruption' in Britain, 1780–1860," *Past and Present* 101 (November 1983): 55–56.

73. Brewer, *The Sinews of Power,* 129.

74. J. E. D. Binney, *British Public Finance and Administration, 1774–92* (Oxford: Clarendon, 1958), 140 and 151. Full centralization in the Treasury's management of government expenditures was not realized until the second half of the nineteenth century, when government departments uniformly adopted double-entry bookkeeping.

75. O'Brien and Hunt, "England, 1485–1815," 65.

76. For details about the extensive venality and corruption in the eighteenth-century British navy, see Daniel A. Baugh, *British Naval Administration in the Age of Walpole* (Princeton, NJ: Princeton University Press, 1965), particularly chapters 8 and 9. Systematic reforms to clear government corruption did not begin until the nineteenth century. On these, see Philip Harling and Peter Mandler, "From 'Fiscal-Military' State to Laissez-Faire State, 1760–1850," *Journal of British Studies,* 32, no. 1 (January 1993): 44–70; and Philip Harling, *The Waning of "Old Corruption": The Politics of Economical Reform in Britain, 1779–1846* (Oxford: Clarendon Press, 1996).

77. G. C. Allen, *A Short Economic History of Modern Japan,* 4th ed. (London: Macmillan, 1981). On the role of the state in late industrialization, see Alexander Gerschenkron, *Economic Backwardness in Historical Perspective* (Cambridge, MA: Belknap Press of Harvard University Press, 1962.

78. Michio Umegaki, *After the Restoration: The Beginning of Japan's Modern State* (New York: New York University Press, 1988). On the "corporate coherence" of the Meiji leaders, see Ellen K. Trimberger, *Revolution from Above: Military Bureaucrats and Development in Japan, Turkey, Egypt, and Peru* (New Brunswick, NJ: Transaction Books, 1978).

79. For the fiscal purpose of the industrial policies in early Meiji and their connection to the concept of a domain state *(kasan kokka),* see Yamamoto Hirofumi, "Shoki shokusan seisaku to sono shūsei" [The early industry-promotion policy and its revision], in *Nihon keizai seisaku shiron (jō)* [The history of economic policy in Japan (I)], ed. Andō Yoshio (Tokyo: Tōkyō Daigaku Shuppankai, 1973); Nagai Hideo, "Shokusan kōgyō seisaku no kichō: Kanei jigyō o chūshin tosite" [The basic tune in the industry-promotion policies], originally published in *Hokkaidō daigaku bungakubu kiyō* 10 (November 1969), reprinted in Nagai Hideo, *Meiji kokka keiseiki no gaisei to naisei* [External and domestic politics in the formative period of the Meiji state] (Sapporo: Hokkaidō Daigaku Tosho Kaikōkai, 1990).

80. See examples in Yamamura Kozo, "Entrepreneurship, Ownership, and Management in Japan," in *The Cambridge Economic History of Europe,* vol. 7, *The Industrial Economies Capital, Labour, and Enterprise, Part 2: The United States, Japan, and Russia,* ed. Peter Mathias and M. M. Postan (Cambridge: Cambridge University Press, 1978), 226–230; S. McCallion, "Trial and Error: The Model Filature at Tomioka," in *Managing Industrial Enterprise: Cases from Japan's Prewar Experience,* ed. W. Wray (Cambridge, MA: Council on East Asian Studies, Harvard University, 1989).

81. Thomas C. Smith, *Political Change and Industrial Development in Japan: Government Enterprise, 1868–1880* (Stanford, CA: Stanford University Press, 1955), chapter 8.

82. For the importance of public finance to Japan's economic modernization in the late nineteenth century, see Nakamura Takafusa, "Makuro keizai to sengo kei'ei" [The macroeconomy and post-war management], in *Nihon keizaishi* [The economic history of Japan], vol. 5, *Sangyōka no jidai (ge)* [The age of industrialization: part 2], ed. Nishikawa Shunsaku and Abe Takeshi (Tokyo: Iwanami Shoten, 1990); Henry Rosovsky, "Japan's Transition to Modern Economic Growth, 1868–1885," in *Industrialization in Two Systems: Essays in Honor of Alexander Gerschenkron*, ed. Henry Rosovsky (New York: John Wiley & Sons, 1966); and Richard Sylla, "Financial Systems and Economic Modernization," *Journal of Economic History* 62, no. 2 (June 2002): 277–292.

83. For the contribution of nonagricultural wealth to industrial investment in Meiji Japan, see Teranishi Jūrō, "Kin'yū no kindaika to sangyōka" [The modernization of finance and industrialization], in *Nihon keizaishi* [The economic history of Japan], vol. 5, *Sangyōka no jidai (ge)* [The age of industrialization: part 2], ed. Nishikawa Shunsaku and Abe Takeshi (Tokyo: Iwanami Shoten, 1990), 63.

84. This was quite low compared with 16.2 percent in France, 13.2 percent in Italy, and 12.5 percent in Sweden in the same period. Cited from Yasukichi Yasuba, "Did Japan Ever Suffer from a Shortage of Natural Resources before World War II?" *Journal of Economic History* 56, no. 3 (September 1996): 549.

85. Ishii Kanji, "Japan," in *International Banking: 1870–1914*, ed. Rondo Cameron, V. I. Bovykin, and B. V. Anan'ich (New York: Oxford University Press, 1991), 226; Steven J. Ericson, *The Sound of the Whistle: Railroads and the State in Meiji Japan* (Cambridge, MA: Council on East Asian Studies of the Harvard University Press, 1996), 174–189.

86. Cited from Fujiwara Takao, *Kindai Nihon shuzōgyōshi* [A history of sake brewing in modern Japan] (Kyoto: Mineruva Shobō, 1999), 2. For a discussion of the rising importance of indirect taxes in Japan after 1868, see Hayashi Takehisa, *Nihon ni okeru sozei kokka no seiritsu* [The formation of the tax state in Japan] (Tokyo: Tōkyō Daigaku Shuppankai, 1965).

87. Fujiwara Takao, *Kindai Nihon shuzōgyōshi*, 101–108.

88. Fukaya Tokujirō, *Meiji seifu zaisei kiban no kakuritsu* [Laying the foundation of Meiji public finance] (Tokyo: Ochanomizu Shobō, 1995), 110–111.

89. Muroyama Yoshimasa, *Kindai Nihon no gunji to zaisei: Kaigun kakuchō o meguru seisaku keisei katei* [Public finance and the military in modern Japan: The formation of policy regarding expansion of the navy] (Tokyo: Tōkyō Daigaku Shuppankai, 1984), 133–134.

90. Zhou Yumin, *Wan Qing caizheng yu shehui bianqian* [Public finance and social change in the late Qing] (Shanghai: Shanghai renmin chubanshe, 2000), 239.

91. Song Huizhong, "Piaoshang yu wan Qing caizheng" [Shanxi bankers and public finance in the late Qing], in *Caizheng yu jindaishi lunwenji* [Collected papers on public finance and early modern history], ed. Zhongyang yanjiuyuan. Jindaishi yanjiusuo. Shehui jingjishi zu (Taipei: Zhongyang yanjiuyuan jindaishi yanjiusuo, 1999), 1:402.

92. It is important to note that the Western officials in the Imperial Maritime Customs were only collecting agents and had no power or authority to decide the spending of the collected customs revenue. On this point, I benefited from discussions with Ren Zhiyong of Beijing University.

93. For the importance of salaried officials in the collection of lijin, see Susan Mann, *Local Merchants and the Chinese Bureaucracy, 1750–1950* (Stanford, CA: Stanford University Press, 1985), 104; Luo Yudong, *Zhongguo lijinshi* [A history of *lijin* in China] (Shanghai: Shangwu yinshuguan, 1936), 1:84–85. I will discuss the management of lijin collection in detail in Chapter 6.

94. Zhou Yumin, *Wan Qing caizheng yu shehui bianqian*, 282–283.

95. Takahashi Hidenao, *Nisshin sensō e no michi* [The road toward the Sino-Japanese War] (Tokyo: Tōkyō Sōgensha, 1995), 119–120.

96. Ma Linghe, *Wan Qing waizaishi yanjiu* [A study of the history of foreign loans in the late Qing] (Shanghai: Fudan daxue chubanshe, 2005), 43 and 53.

97. Banno Junji, "Meiji kokka no seiritsu" [The establishment of the Meiji state], in *Nihon keizaishi* [The economic history of Japan], vol. 3, *Kaikō to ishin* [The opening of Japan and the Restoration], ed. Umemura Mataji and Yamamoto Yūzō (Tokyo: Iwanami Shoten, 1989), 73–85.

98. Margaret Levi, *Of Rule and Revenue* (Berkeley: University of California Press, 1988), 97 and 118.

99. For examples of popular resentment of excises, see Peter Mathias, *The Brewing Industry in England: 1700–1830* (Cambridge: Cambridge University Press, 1959), 345; Edward Hughes, *Studies in Administration and Finance, 1558–1825* (Manchester: Manchester University Press, 1934), 327–328 and 332–333.

100. Jean-Laurent Rosenthal, "The Political Economy of Absolutism Reconsidered," in *Analytic Narratives*, ed. Robert H. Bates (Princeton, NJ: Princeton University Press, 1998).

101. Robert Bates and Da-Hsiang Donald Lien, "A Note on Taxation, Development, and Representative Government," *Politics and Society* 14, no. 1 (1985): 53–70.

102. Daron Acemoglu and James A. Robinson, "Economic Backwardness in Political Perspective," *American Political Science Review* 100, no. 1 (February 2006): 115–131.

103. For two prominent examples of political explanation of the English financial revolution, see Carruthers, *City of Capital*, chapter 6; David Stasavage,

Public Debt and the Birth of the Democratic State: France and Great Britain, 1688–1789 (Cambridge and New York: Cambridge University Press, 2003), chapter 5.

104. For such a definition of state capacity, see Joel S. Migdal, *Strong Societies and Weak States: State-Society Relations and State Capabilities in the Third World* (Princeton, NJ: Princeton University Press, 1988), chapter 2. For examples of using extraction of land taxes as the major criterion in measuring state capacities in late nineteenth-century Japan and China, see Thomas C. Smith, *The Agrarian Origins of Modern Japan* (Stanford, CA: Stanford University Press, 1959); Prasenjit Duara, *Culture, Power, and the State: Rural North China, 1900–1942* (Stanford, CA: Stanford University Press, 1988); and Philip A. Kuhn, *Origins of the Modern Chinese State* (Stanford, CA: Stanford University Press, 2002), chapter 3.

1. Credit Crises in the Rise of the Modern Fiscal State

1. Avner Greif and David D. Laitin, "A Theory of Endogenous Institutional Change," *American Political Science Review* 98, no. 4 (November 2004): 636; Kathleen Thelen, "How Institutions Evolve: Insights from Comparative Historical Analysis," in *Comparative Historical Analysis in the Social Sciences*, ed. James Mahoney and Dietrich Rueschemeyer (Cambridge and New York: Cambridge University Press, 2003).

2. Kathleen Thelen and James Mahoney, eds., *Explaining Institutional Change: Ambiguity, Agency, and Power* (Cambridge and New York: Cambridge University Press, 2010).

3. Stephen D. Krasner, "Approaches to the State: Alternative Conceptions and Historical Dynamics," *Comparative Politics* 16, no. 2 (January 1984): 223–246.

4. On the cognitive role of institutions as guides for actors, see Douglass C. North, *Institutions, Institutional Change and Economic Performance* (Cambridge and New York: Cambridge University Press, 1990), 96; Paul J. DiMaggio and Walter W. Powell, "Introduction," in *The New Institutionalism in Organizational Analysis*, ed. Paul J. DiMaggio and Walter W. Powell (Chicago: University of Chicago Press, 1991), 1–40.

5. For some representative studies, see Ruth Berins Collier and David Collier, *Shaping the Political Arena: Critical Junctures, the Labor Movement, and Regime Dynamics in Latin America* (Princeton, NJ: Princeton University Press, 1991); Gregory M. Luebbert, *Liberalism, Fascism, or Social Democracy: Social Classes and the Political Origins of Regimes in Interwar Europe* (New York and Oxford: Oxford University Press, 1991). For an effort to integrate pre-juncture structural features with critical junctures into one coherent causal narrative,

see Dan Slater and Erica Simmons, "Informative Regress: Critical Antecedents in Comparative Politics," *Comparative Political Studies* 43, no. 7 (2010): 886–917.

6. On the layering and conversion of existing institutions, see Kathleen Thelen, "How Institutions Evolve," 225–230.

7. In the trap of infinite regress, there are always some prior causal factors, going backward perpetually into the past. See James Fearon, "Causes and Counterfactuals in Social Science: Exploring an Analogy between Cellular Automata and Historical Processes," in *Counterfactual Thought Experiments in World Politics: Logical, Methodological, and Psychological Perspectives,* ed. Philip E. Tetlock and Aaron Belkin (Princeton, NJ: Princeton University Press, 1996), 39–67; and Gary King, Robert O. Keohane, and Sidney Verba, *Designing Social Inquiry: Scientific Inference in Qualitative Research* (Princeton, NJ: Princeton University Press, 1994), 86. See the discussion of episode analysis in historical institutionalism in Evan S. Lieberman, "Causal Inference in Historical Institutional Analysis: A Specification of Periodization," *Comparative Political Studies* 34, no. 9 (2001): 1011–1035.

8. See W. G. Hoskins, *The Age of Plunder: King Henry's England, 1500–1547* (London: Longman, 1976), 121.

9. Calculated from table 5.1 in Peter Cunich, "Revolution and Crisis in English State Finance, 1534–47," in *Crises, Revolutions, and Self-Sustained Growth: Essays in European Fiscal History, 1130–1830,* ed. W. M. Ormrod, Margaret Bonney, and Richard Bonney (Stamford, UK: Shaun Tyas, 1999), 123.

10. Penry Williams, *The Tudor Regime* (Oxford: Clarendon Press, 1979), 69.

11. Calculated from the figures in Richard W. Hoyle, "Crown, Parliament, and Taxation in Sixteenth-Century England," *English Historical Review* 109, no. 434 (November 1994): 1193.

12. Intensive use of gunpowder, heavy arms, new warships, and siege tactics rapidly increased the cost of fighting wars in early modern Europe. See Clifford J. Rogers, ed., *The Military Revolution Debate: Readings on the Military Transformation of Early Modern Europe* (Boulder, CO: Westview Press, 1995). For the impact of the military revolution on England in the early seventeenth century, see Conrad Russell, *Unrevolutionary England, 1603–1642* (London: Hambledon, 1990), 126.

13. C. G. A. Clay, *Economic Expansion and Social Change: England 1500–1700,* vol. 1, *People, Land, and Towns* (Cambridge: Cambridge University Press, 1984), 50.

14. For a general review of the price revolution in England between the mid-fifteenth and mid-seventeenth centuries, see R. B. Outhwaite, *Inflation in Tudor and Early Stuart England,* 2nd ed. (London: Macmillan Press, 1982). On the

contribution of urbanization, see Jack A. Goldstone, "Urbanization and Inflation: Lessons from the English Price Revolution of the Sixteenth and Seventeenth Centuries," *American Journal of Sociology* 89, no. 5 (1984): 1122–1160. On increasing monetary input as a cause of the price revolution, see Douglas Fisher, "The Price Revolution: A Monetary Interpretation," *Journal of Economic History* 49, no. 4 (December 1989): 883–902.

15. Penry Williams, *The Later Tudors: England, 1547–1603* (Oxford: Clarendon, 1995), 147; Conrad Russell, *The Addled Parliament of 1614: The Limits of Revision* (Reading, UK: University of Reading, 1992), 10.

16. By 1610, the royal government was facing a debt of £400,000 and an annual deficit of £140,000 in the ordinary account. See John Cramsie, *Kingship and Crown Finance under James VI and I, 1603–1625* (Woodbridge, UK, and Rochester, NY: Royal Historical Society/Boydell Press, 2002), 118.

17. This is one central thesis in the "revisionist school" of early Stuart history. See a succinct review of this literature in Thomas Cogswell, Richard Cust, and Peter Lake, "Revisionism and Its Legacies: The Work of Conrad Russell," in *Politics, Religion, and Popularity in Early Stuart Britain,* ed. Thomas Cogswell, Richard Cust, and Peter Lake (Cambridge and New York: Cambridge University Press, 2002).

18. Eric N. Lindquist, "The King, the People and the House of Commons: The Problem of Early Jacobean Purveyance," *Historical Journal* 31, no. 3 (1988): 550–556.

19. Cramsie, *Kingship and Crown Finance under James VI and I,* 68.

20. Russell, *The Addled Parliament of 1614;* Eric N. Lindquist, "The Failure of the Great Contract," *Journal of Modern History* 57, no. 4 (December 1985): 617–651.

21. Lindquist, "The King, the People and the House of Commons," 561 and 565; Lindquist, "The Failure of the Great Contract," 645, particularly footnote 108, and 648.

22. Roger Schofield, "Taxation and the Political Limits of the Tudor State," in *Law and Government under the Tudors: Essays Presented to Sir Geoffrey Elton,* ed. Claire Cross, David Loades, and J. J. Scarisbrick (Cambridge and New York: Cambridge University Press, 1988); Conrad Russell, *Parliaments and English Politics, 1621–1629* (Oxford: Clarendon, 1979), 49–51.

23. G. L. Harriss, "Medieval Doctrines in the Debates of Supply, 1610–1629," in *Faction and Parliament: Essays on Early Stuart History,* ed. Kevin Sharpe (Oxford: Clarendon Press, 1978); Cramsie, *Kingship and Crown Finance under James VI and I,* 190.

24. Joan Thirsk, "The Crown as Projector on Its Own Estates, from Elizabeth I to Charles I," and Richard W. Hoyle, "Disafforestation and Drainage:

The Crown as Entrepreneur?" Both in *The Estates of the English Crown, 1558–1640*, ed. Richard W. Hoyle (Cambridge and New York: Cambridge University Press, 1992).

25. Cramsie, *Kingship and Crown Finance under James VI and I*, 141 and 147.

26. John Cramsie, "Commercial Projects and the Fiscal Policy of James VI and I," *Historical Journal* 43, no. 2 (2000): 345–364; Kevin Sharpe, *The Personal Rule of Charles I* (New Haven, CT: Yale University Press, 1992), 122.

27. Russell, *The Addled Parliament of 1614*, 18.

28. David Harris Sacks, "The Countervailing of Benefits: Monopoly, Liberty, and Benevolence in Elizabethan England," in *Tudor Political Culture*, ed. Dale Hoak (Cambridge and New York: Cambridge University Press, 1995), particularly 280–281.

29. Cramsie, *Kingship and Crown Finance under James VI and I*, 177.

30. Michael J. Braddick, *The Nerves of State: Taxation and the Financing of the English State, 1558–1714* (Manchester: Manchester University Press, 1996), 53–54.

31. Andrew Thrush, "Naval Finance and the Origins and Development of Ship Money," in *War and Government in Britain, 1598–1650*, ed. Mark Charles Fissel (Manchester: Manchester University Press, 1991); Sharpe, *The Personal Rule of Charles I*, 594–595.

32. For details of these debates, see Sharpe, *The Personal Rule of Charles I*, 717–729; Glenn Burgess, *The Politics of the Ancient Constitution: An Introduction to English Political Thought, 1603–1642* (Basingstoke, UK: Macmillan, 1992), 202–211.

33. Cramsie, *Kingship and Crown Finance under James VI and I*, 160–162; and Kevin Sharpe, "The Personal Rule of Charles I," in *Before the English Civil War: Essays on Early Stuart Politics and Government*, ed. Howard Tomlinson (London: Macmillan Press, 1983), 60.

34. Russell, *Unrevolutionary England*, 135.

35. On the interdependence of the center and local governments in early Stuart England, see Steve Hindle, *The State and Social Change in Early Modern England, c. 1550–1640* (New York: Palgrave Macmillan, 2000), chapter 1.

36. Conrad Russell, *The Causes of the English Civil War: The Ford Lectures Delivered in the University of Oxford, 1987–1988* (Oxford: Clarendon Press, 1990), 175.

37. For assessments of the active role of the center in guiding local governance in early Stuart England, see Michael J. Braddick, "State Formation and Social Change in Early Modern England." *Social History* 16 (1991): 1–17; Paul Slack, *From Reformation to Improvement: Public Welfare in Early Modern England* (Oxford: Clarendon Press; New York: Oxford University Press, 1999);

and Michael J. Braddick and John Walter, eds., *Negotiating Power in Early Modern Society: Order, Hierarchy, and Subordination in Britain and Ireland* (Cambridge and New York: Cambridge University Press, 2001).

38. Michael J. Braddick, *State Formation in Early Modern England, c. 1550–1700* (Cambridge and New York: Cambridge University Press, 2000), 124–128.

39. Richard Cust, *The Forced Loan and English Politics, 1626–1628* (Oxford: Clarendon Press, 1987), 142–143; Russell, *Parliaments and English Politics, 1621–1629*, 64–65.

40. Ōno Mizuo, *Edo bakufu zaisei shiron* [A study of the fiscal history of the shogunate] (Tokyo: Yoshikawa Kōbunkan, 1996), 32–33. To prevent outflows of silver from Japan was one major consideration in the shogunate's "closure policy" *(sakoku)* between the 1630s and 1660s. See Tashiro Kazui, "Tokugawa jidai no bōeki" [Foreign trade in the Tokugawa period], in *Nihon keizaishi* [The economic history of Japan], vol. 1, *Keizai shakai no seiritsu: 17th–18th seiki* [The formation of an economic society: Seventeenth and eighteenth centuries], ed. Hayami Akira and Miyamoto Matao (Tokyo: Iwanami Shoten, 1988), 130–164.

41. Furushima Toshio, "The Village and Agriculture during the Edo Period," in *The Cambridge History of Japan*, vol. 4, *Early Modern Japan*, ed. John Whitney Hall (Cambridge and New York: Cambridge University Press, 1991), 495–498.

42. Ōguchi Yūjirō, "Bakufu no zaisei" [The public finance of the shogunate], in *Nihon keizaishi* [The economic history of Japan], vol. 2, *Kindai seichū no taidō* [Gathering momentum for modern growth], ed. Shinbo Hiroshi and Saitō Osamu (Tokyo: Iwanami Shoten, 1989), 152–155; Patricia Sippel, "Chisui: Creating a Sacred Domain in Early Modern and Modern Japan," in *Public Spheres, Private Lives in Modern Japan, 1600–1950*, ed. Gail Lee Bernstein, Andrew Gordon, and Kate Wildman Nakai (Cambridge, MA: Harvard University Asia Center, 2005), particularly 155–176.

43. Ōguchi Yūjirō, "Bakufu no zaisei," 141–144; John Whitney Hall, *Tanuma Okitsugu, 1719–1788: Forerunner of Modern Japan* (Cambridge, MA: Harvard University Press, 1955), chapter 4.

44. Nakai Nobuhiko, *Tenkanki bakuhansei no kenkyū: Hōreki, Tenmeiki no keizai seisaku to shōhin ryūtsū* [The shogunate-domain system in transition: Economic policy and the flow of goods in the period of Hōreki and Tenmei (1751–1788)] (Tokyo: Hanawa Shobō, 1971), 153–154.

45. See Conrad D. Totman, *Early Modern Japan* (Berkeley: University of California Press, 1995), 238–240.

46. Fujita Satoru, "Jūku seiki zenhan no Nihon" [Japan in the first half of the nineteenth century], in *Iwanami kōza Nihon tsūshi* [The Iwanami general

history of Japan], vol. 15, *Kinsei* (5) [The early modern period], ed. Asao Nao-hiro et al. (Tokyo: Iwanami Shoten, 1995), 8–12.

47. Ōguchi Yūjirō, "Kansei—Bunkaki no bakufu zaisei" [The public finance of the shogunate between 1789 and 1817], in vol. 1 of *Nihon kinseishi ronsō* [Works on the early modern history of Japan], ed. Bitō Masahide Sensei Kanreki-kinenkai (Tokyo: Yoshikawa Kōbunkan, 1984), 209–252.

48. For the increasing awareness of foreign threats in Japan between 1792 and 1818, see Totman, *Early Modern Japan,* 482–502.

49. Shinbo Hiroshi and Saitō Osamu, "Gaisetsu—19 seiki e" [An overview: Toward the nineteenth century], in *Nihon keizaishi* [An economic history of Japan], vol. 2, *Kindai seichō no taidō* [Gathering momentum for modern growth], ed. Shinbo Hiroshi and Saitō Osamu (Tokyo: Iwanami Shoten, 1989), 31. The estimate of the shogunate's annual income in the 1830s is cited from Ōyama Shikitarō, *Bakumatsu zaiseishi kenkyū* [A study of the fiscal history of the late Tokugawa] (Kyoto: Shibunkaku Shuppan, 1974), 46.

50. Shinbo Hiroshi and Saitō Osamu, "Gaisetsu—19 seiki e," 30–31.

51. Thomas C. Smith, "The Land Tax in the Tokugawa Period," reprinted in Thomas C. Smith, *Native Sources of Japanese Industrialization, 1750–1920* (Berkeley: University of California Press, 1988), 50–70.

52. Ōguchi Yūjirō, "Bakufu no zaisei," 138–140 and 150–151.

53. On the role of the shogunate as the central government in organizing national defense, see Fujita Satoru, *Bakuhansei kokka no seijishi teki kenkyū* [The political history of the shogunate-domain system] (Tokyo: Azekura Shobō, 1987), 213–214. For a discussion of the transfer of defense expenditures to domain governments, see Ōguchi Yūjirō, "Bakufu no zaisei," 166; Fujita Satoru, "Tenpō kaikakuki no kaibō seisaku ni tsuite" [A study of the policies of sea-borne defense in the Tenpō period], *Rekishigaku kenkyū* 469 (1979): especially 20–24.

54. Ōguchi Yūjirō, "Bunkyūki no bakufu zaisei" [Shogunal finance from 1861 to 1864], in *Bakumatsu Ishin no Nihon* [Japan in the late Tokugawa and Meiji Restoration], ed. Kindai Nihon Kenkyūkai (Tokyo: Yamakawa Shuppan-sha, 1981), 54–55.

55. For government encouragement of commercial development, see Gao Wangling, *Shiba shiji Zhongguo de jingji fazhan he zhengfu zhengce* [Economic development in eighteenth-century China and government policy] (Beijing: Zhongguo shehui kexue chubanshe, 1995); Zhang Xiaotang, "Qianlong nian-jian Qing zhengfu pingheng caizheng zhi yanjiu" [Fiscal adjustments during the Qianlong reign], *Qingshi yanjiuji* 7 (1990): 47–59; Xu Tan and Jing Junjian, "Qingdai qianqi shangshui wenti xintan" [A new study of commercial taxes during the Qing dynasty], *Zhongguo jingjishi yanjiu* 2 (1990): 87–100.

56. Zhang Xiaotang, "Qianlong nianjian Qing zhengfu pingheng caizheng zhi yanjiu," 27. For the contribution of commercial resources to the imperial wars and expansion in the eighteenth century, see Peter C. Perdue, *China Marches West: The Qing Conquest of Central Eurasia* (Cambridge, MA: Belknap Press of Harvard University Press, 2005); and Dai Yingcong, "The Qing State, Merchants, and the Military Labor Force in the Jinchuan Campaigns," *Late Imperial China* 22, no. 2 (December 2001): 35–90.

57. Xu Daling, "Qingdai juanna zhidu" [The sale of official rank during the Qing], in *Ming Qing shi lunji* [Collected papers on Ming-Qing history] (Beijing: Beijing daxue chubanshe, 2000).

58. On the supplementary roles these local surcharges played in the maintenance of the state, see Wang Yeh-chien, *Land Taxation in Imperial China,* 19; and Iwai Shigeki, *Chūgoku kinsei zaiseishi no kenkyū* [A study of the fiscal history of early modern China] (Kyoto: Kyōto Daigaku Gakujutsu Shuppankai, 2004), 43–62.

59. Ye Shichang, *Yapian zhanzheng qianhou woguo de huobi xueshuo* [Monetary theory in China before and after the Opium War] (Shanghai: Shanghai renmin chubanshe, 1963), 6.

60. For example, eighteenth-century England was on the gold standard, yet its small change still took the form of copper coins. Only after the 1820s did Western states possess the technology to mint small change as token money. See Thomas J. Sargent and François R. Velde, *The Big Problem of Small Change* (Princeton, NJ: Princeton University Press, 2002).

61. Calculated from table 1.2 in Wang Yeh-chien, "Secular Trends of Rice Prices in the Yangzi Delta, 1638–1935," in *Chinese History in Economic Perspective,* ed. Thomas G. Rawski and Lillian M. Li (Berkeley: University of California Press, 1992), 61. For silver inflow into China in the seventeenth and eighteenth centuries, see Andre Gunder Frank, *ReOrient: Global Economy in the Asian Age* (Berkeley: University of California Press, 1998), 143–149.

62. Lin Man-houng, *China Upside Down: Currency, Society, and Ideologies, 1801–1856* (Cambridge, MA: Harvard University Asia Center, 2006), chapter 2; Richard von Glahn, "Foreign Silver Coins in the Market Culture of Nineteenth Century China," *International Journal of Asian Studies* 4, no. 1 (2007): 51–78.

63. Wang Yeh-chien, *Zhongguo jindai huobi yu yinhang de yanjin (1644–1937)* [The evolution of currency and banking in early modern China (1644–1937)] (Taipei: Zhongyang yanjiuyuan jinji yanjiusuo, 1981), 27.

64. Lin Man-houng, "Yin yu yapian de liutong ji yinguiqianjian xianxiang de quyu fenbu: 1808–1854" [The circulation of silver and opium and a geographical distribution of the high value of silver in regard to copper coins:

1808–1854], *Zhongyang yanjiuyuan jindaishisuo jikan* 22, no. 1 (1993): 91–135.

65. Lin Man-houng, *China Upside Down,* chapter 3.

66. Lin Man-houng, "Jia Dao qianjian xianxiang chansheng yuanyin 'qian-duo qianlie lun' zhi shangque" [A study of the falling value of copper cash vis-à-vis silver in the period between 1808 and 1850], in *Zhongguo haiyang fazhan-shi lunwenji,* ed. Zhang Bingcun and Liu Shiji (Taipei: Zhongyang yanjiuyuan, 1993), 5:357–426.

67. Wei Jianyou, *Zhongguo jindai huobishi* [A history of currency in early modern China] (Hefei: Huangshang shushe, 1986), 116–118; von Glahn, "Foreign Silver Coins in the Market Culture of Nineteenth Century China," 64.

68. Ye Shichang, *Yapian zhanzheng qianhou woguo de huobi xueshuo,* 39.

69. William T. Rowe, "Money, Economy, and Polity in the Daoguang-Era Paper Currency Debates," *Late Imperial China* 31, no. 2 (2010): 69–96.

70. Lin Man-houng, "Two Social Theories Revealed: Statecraft Controversies over China's Monetary Crisis, 1808–1854," *Late Imperial China* 12, no. 2 (December 1991): 1–35.

71. Barry J. Eichengreen, *Golden Fetters: The Gold Standard and the Great Depression, 1919–1939* (Oxford and New York: Oxford University Press, 1992).

72. Zhou Yumin, *Wan Qing caizheng yu shehui bianqian* [Public finance and social change in the late Qing] (Shanghai: Shanghai renmin chubanshe, 2000), 71–74 and 96–102.

73. Okamoto Takashi, "Shinmatsu hyōhō no seiritsu" [The establishment of salt licenses in the late Qing], *Shigaku zasshi* 110, no. 12 (December 2001): 36–60.

74. Yamamoto Susumu, *Shindai zaiseishi kenkyū* [A study of the fiscal history of the Qing dynasty] (Tokyo: Kyūko Shoin, 2002), particularly chapters 2–6; Yamamoto Susumu, "Shindai kōki Shizen ni okeru chihō zaisei no keisei" [The formation of the provincial fiscal system in Sichuan Province in late Qing], *Shirin* 75, no. 6 (November 1992): 33–62.

75. Yamamoto Susumu, "Shindai kōki Kōse no zaisei kaikaku to zendō" [Fiscal reform and charitable halls in Jiangsu and Zhejiang during the late Qing], *Shigaku zasshi* 104, no. 12 (December 1995): 38–39; Yamamoto Susumu, "Shindai kōki Shizen ni okeru chihō zaisei no keisei," particularly 33–43.

76. For examples, see Daron Acemoglu, Simon Johnson, and James Robinson, "Institutions as the Fundamental Cause of Long-Run Growth," NBER Working Paper, Series 10481, 2004, 9; and Edgar Kiser and Michael Hechter, "The Role of General Theory in Comparative-Historical Sociology," *American Journal of Sociology* 97, no. 1 (July 1991): 19–20.

77. Paul Christianson, "Two Proposals for Raising Money by Extraordinary Means, c. 1627," *English Historical Review* 117, no. 471 (April 2002): 355–373.

78. *Jiaqing Daoguang liangchao shangyu dang* [Edicts during the reigns of Jiaqing and Daoguang], ed. Zhongguo diyi lishi dang'anguan (Guilin: Guangxi shifan daxue chubanshe, 2000), 48:331–334.

79. Sharpe, *The Personal Rule of Charles I,* 129 and 593.

80. In 1628, the City of London refused to provide fresh credit to the royal government until its previous debts had been satisfactorily cleared. See Robert Ashton, "Revenue Farming under the Early Stuarts," *Economic History Review,* n.s. 8, no. 3 (1956): 317.

81. The religious policy of Charles I in the context of "three kingdoms" is crucially important to account for the outbreak of the English Civil War. See Russell, *The Causes of the English Civil War,* chapter 5; Conrad Russell, *The Fall of the British Monarchies, 1637–1642* (Oxford: Clarendon Press, 1991).

82. For the explanation of the escalation and prolonging of the civil war from the perspective of religious and economic conflict in English society, see Ann Hughes, *The Causes of the English Civil War,* 2nd ed. (Basingstoke, UK: Macmillan, 1991); and David Wootton, "From Rebellion to Revolution: The Crisis of the Winter of 1642/3 and the Origins of Civil War Radicalism," *English Historical Review* 105, no. 416 (July 1990): 654–669.

83. The exchange rate between gold and silver was 1:5 in Japan as compared with 1:15 abroad. See the discussion of this phenomenon in Ohkura Takehiko and Shimbo Hiroshi, "The Tokugawa Monetary Policy in the Eighteenth and Nineteenth Centuries," *Explorations in Economic History* 15 (1978): 112–115.

84. Miyamoto Matao, "Bukka to makuro keizei no henka" [Changes in prices and macroeconomy], in *Nihon keizaishi* [The economic history of Japan], vol. 2, *Kindai seichō no taidō* [Gathering momentum for modern growth], ed. Shinbo Hiroshi and Saitō Osamu (Tokyo: Iwanami Shoten, 1989), 88.

85. The total amount of silver currency minted between 1860 and 1867 is estimated to be 81.68 million ryō. Ōkura Takehiko, "Yōgin ryūnyū to bakufu zaisei" [The inflow of Mexican silver and the shogunate's fiscal system], in *Kindai ikōki ni okeru keizai hatten* [Economic development in the transition to the modern period], ed. Kamiki Tetsuo and Matsuura Akira (Tokyo: Dōbunkan, 1987), 255.

86. Ibid., table 7–3, 250.

87. The net profit that Satsuma gained from counterfeiting is estimated to be as high as 2 million ryō between 1862 and 1865. See Ishii Kanji, Hara Akira, and Takeda Haruhito, eds., *Nihon keizaishi I: Bakumatsu-Ishinki* [An economic history of Japan (I): The late Tokugawa and early Meiji period] (Tokyo: Tōkyō

Daigaku Shuppankai, 2000), 16; Mōri Toshihiko, *Meiji Ishin no saihakken* [Rediscovering the Meiji Restoration] (Tokyo: Yoshikawa Kōbunkan, 1993), 70.

88. Of the total amount of currency in 1867, about 15 to 21 percent consisted of paper notes issued by domain governments. See Miyamoto Matao, "Bukka to makuro keizei no henka," 33 and 89.

89. Ishii Takashi, *Meiji Ishin to jiyū minken* [The Meiji Restoration and the Freedom and People's Rights Movement] (Yokohama: Yūrindō, 1993), 54–69.

90. Even officials who were in favor of legalizing the opium trade in the 1830s considered silver drainage a serious economic problem. They proposed that imported opium be exchanged only for Chinese goods rather than silver. Inoue Hiromasa, *Shindai ahen seisakushi no kenkyū* [Qing opium policy before the Opium War] (Kyoto: Kyōto Daigaku Gakujutsu Shuppankai, 2004), 193.

91. Eguchi Hisao, "Ahen sensōgo ni okeru ginka taisaku to sono zasetsu" [Post–Opium War measures to counter the silver problem and their failure], *Shakai keizai shigaku* 42, no. 3 (1976): 22–40.

92. Wang Yeh-chien, "Shiba shiji qianqi wujia xialuo yu Taiping Tianguo geming" [Deflation in the early nineteenth century and the Taiping Rebellion], reprinted in Wang Yeh-chien, *Qingdai jingjishi lunwenji* [Collected essays in the economic history of Qing China] (Banqiao: Daoxiang chubanshe, 2003), 2:251–287; Peng Zeyi, *Shijiu shiji houbanqi de Zhongguo caizheng yu jingji* [Economy and public finance in China in the second half of the nineteenth century] (Beijing: Renmin chubanshe, 1983), 24–71.

93. Edgar Kiser, "Markets and Hierarchies in Early Modern Tax Systems: A Principal-Agent Analysis," *Politics and Society* 22, no. 3 (September 1994): 284–315.

94. See Chapter 3 for more detail.

95. See Chapter 2 for more detail.

96. For a general discussion of spurious causality in comparative historical analysis, see Kiser and Hechter, "The Role of General Theory in Comparative-Historical Sociology," 7.

97. See Paul Pierson, *Politics in Time: History, Institutions, and Social Analysis* (Princeton, NJ: Princeton University Press, 2004), chapter 3; Paul Pierson and Theda Skocpol, "Historical Institutionalism," in *Political Science: The State of the Discipline,* ed. Ira Katznelson and Helen Milner (New York: W. W. Norton, 2002), 703–704.

98. For an excellent discussion of the uncertainty, multiplicity of possible outcomes, and contingency in critical junctures, see Giovanni Capoccia and R. Daniel Kelemen, "The Study of Critical Junctures: Theory, Narrative, and Counterfactuals in Historical Institutionalism," *World Politics* 59 (April 2007): 341–369.

99. On the enhanced role of agency in times of fundamental change, see Ira Katznelson, "Periodization and Preferences: Reflections on Purposive Action in

Comparative Historical Social Science," in *Comparative Historical Analysis in the Social Sciences,* ed. James Mahoney and Dietrich Rueschemeyer (Cambridge and New York: Cambridge University Press, 2003), 270–301. On the limits of rational design in the study of institutional dynamics, see Paul Pierson, "The Limits of Design: Explaining Institutional Origins and Change," *Governance* 13, no. 4 (October 2000), particularly 477–486.

100. For an example of the use of new political actors to explain institution change, see Daron Acemoglu, Simon Johnson, and James Robinson, "The Rise of Europe: Atlantic Trade, Institutional Change, and Economic Growth," *American Economic Review* 95, no. 3 (June 2005): 563–565.

101. For an example of using ideas to reduce uncertainties in institutional development, see Mark Blyth, *Great Transformations: Economic Ideas and Institutional Change in the Twentieth Century* (Cambridge and New York: Cambridge University Press, 2002), 34–45. For more on the importance of ideas in sociopolitical change, see Peter A. Hall, ed., *The Political Power of Economic Ideas: Keynesianism across Nations* (Princeton, NJ: Princeton University Press, 1989).

102. Kurt Weyland, "Toward a New Theory of Institutional Change," *World Politics* 60 (January 2008): 281–314.

103. For an emphasis on the interaction between the imported Western organizations and the Japanese environment, see D. Eleanor Westney, *Imitation and Innovation: The Transfer of Western Organizational Patterns to Meiji Japan* (Cambridge, MA: Harvard University Press, 1987).

104. Andrew Abbott, "Sequence Analysis: New Methods for Old Ideas," *Annual Review of Sociology* 21 (1995): 93–113.

105. For a discussion of feedback effects in institutional development, see Paul Pierson, "When Effect Becomes Cause: Policy Feedback and Political Change," *World Politics* 45, no. 4 (July 1993): 595–628.

106. For a review of the evolutionary theory of economic and technological change, see Richard R. Nelson, "Recent Evolutionary Theorizing about Economic Change," *Journal of Economic Literature* 33, no. 1 (March 1995): 48–90.

107. On the importance of path dependence to the study of social and political change, see Paul Pierson, "Increasing Returns, Path Dependence, and the Study of Politics," *American Political Science Review* 94, no. 2 (June 2000): 251–267; and James Mahoney, "Path Dependence in Historical Sociology," *Theory and Society* 29 (2000): 507–548.

108. See the discussion of path dependence as a nonlinear dynamic process in Scott Page, "Path Dependence," *Quarterly Journal of Political Science* 1, no. 1 (2006): 87–115; W. Brian Arthur, *Increasing Returns and Path Dependence in the Economy* (Ann Arbor: University of Michigan Press, 1994); and Paul

A. David, "Clio and the Economics of QWERTY," *American Economic Review* 75, no. 2 (May 1985): 332–337.

109. For a discussion of the counterfactual nature of a path-dependent explanation, see R. Cowan and P. Gunby, "Sprayed to Death: Path Dependence, Lock-in, and Pest Control Strategies," *Economic Journal* 106, no. 436 (1996): 521. The counterfactual argument in path dependence is similar to what the historian John L. Gaddis calls the "plausible counterfactual arguments," which "would have seemed feasible to decision-makers at the time." See John L. Gaddis, *The Landscape of History: How Historians Map the Past* (Oxford and New York: Oxford University Press, 2002), 102.

110. Paul A. David, "Path Dependence, Its Critics and the Quest for 'Historical Economics,'" in *Evolution and Path Dependence in Economic Ideas: Past and Present,* ed. Pierre Garrouste and Stavros Ioannides (Northampton, MA: Edward Elgar, 2001), 20–21 and 31; Jack A. Goldstone, "Initial Conditions, General Laws, Path Dependence, and Explanation in Historical Sociology," *American Journal of Sociology* 104, no. 3 (November 1998): 829–845; and Page, "Path Dependence," 91 and 102.

111. Douglass C. North and Barry R. Weingast, "Constitutions and Commitment: The Evolution of Institutions Governing Public Choice in Seventeenth-Century England," *Journal of Economic History* 49, no. 4 (December 1989): 803–832.

112. Calculated from B. R. Mitchell, *Abstract of British Historical Statistics* (Cambridge: Cambridge University Press, 1962), 401.

113. J. Lawrence Broz and Richard S. Grossman, "Paying for Privilege: The Political Economy of Bank of England Charters, 1694–1844," *Explorations in Economic History* 41 (2004): 48–72.

114. David Stasavage, *Public Debt and the Birth of the Democratic State: France and Great Britain, 1688–1789* (Cambridge and New York: Cambridge University Press, 2003), 5.

115. North and Weingast, "Constitutions and Commitment," 823–824.

116. John Brewer, *The Sinews of Power: War, Money, and the English State, 1688–1783* (New York: Alfred A. Knopf, 1989), 138.

117. Larry Neal, "The Monetary, Financial, and Political Architecture of Europe, 1648–1815," in *Exceptionalism and Industrialization: Britain and Its European Rivals, 1688–1815,* ed. Leandro Prados de la Escosura and Patrick K. O'Brien (Cambridge and New York: Cambridge University Press, 2004), 180–181.

118. Edgar Kiser and Joshua Kane, "Revolution and State Structure: The Bureaucratization of Tax Administration in Early Modern England and France," *American Journal of Sociology* 107, no. 1 (July 2001): 187 and 195.

119. Thomas Ertman, *Birth of the Leviathan: Building States and Regimes in Medieval and Early Modern Europe* (Cambridge and New York: Cambridge University Press, 1997), 28.

120. Ibid., 171–178 and 187–207.

121. Henry Roseveare, *The Treasury 1660–1870: The Foundations of Control* (London: Allen and Unwin, 1973), 52–54.

122. Jeffrey Haydu, "Making Use of the Past: Time Periods as Cases to Compare and as Sequences of Problem Solving," *American Journal of Sociology* 104, no. 2 (September 1998): particularly 353–359.

123. Gerard Alexander, "Institutions, Path Dependence, and Democratic Consolidation," *Journal of Theoretical Politics* 13, no. 3 (2001): 257–260.

124. On the asynchronical nature of institutional development and its implications for historical causation, see Giovanni Capoccia and Daniel Ziblatt, "The Historical Turn in Democratization Studies: A New Research Agenda for Europe and Beyond," *Comparative Political Studies* 43, no. 8/9 (2010): 940.

125. For the eventful approach in social science, see William H. Sewell Jr., "Three Temporalities: Toward an Eventful Sociology," in *The Historic Turn in the Human Sciences,* ed. Terrence J. McDonald (Ann Arbor: University of Michigan Press, 1996), 245–280; Sewell, *Logics of History: Social Theory and Social Transformation* (Chicago: University of Chicago Press, 2005), chapter 5; Tim Büthe, "Taking Temporality Seriously: Modeling History and the Use of Narrative and Counterfactuals in Historical Institutionalism," *American Political Science Review* 96, no. 3 (2002): 481–493.

126. On the lack of a "hard" selection mechanism in the political world, see Pierson, "Increasing Returns, Path Dependence, and the Study of Politics," 261.

127. See the emphasis on this point in Page, "Path Dependence," 89; and Douglass C. North, "Five Propositions about Institutional Change," in *Explaining Social Institutions* (Ann Arbor: University of Michigan Press, 1995), 25.

128. These boundary conditions are often implicitly assumed in the theoretical discussion of path dependence. See Paul A. David, "Why Are Institutions the 'Carriers of History'?: Path Dependence and the Evolution of Conventions, Organizations, and Institutions," *Structural Change and Economic Dynamics* 5, no. 2 (1994): 208; Pierson, "Increasing Returns, Path Dependence, and the Study of Politics," 265; and S. J. Liebowitz and S. E. Margolis, "The Fable of the Keys," *Journal of Law and Economics* 32, no. 1 (1990): 1–26.

2. England's Path, 1642–1752

1. Larry Neal, "The Finance of Business during the Industrial Revolution," in *The Economic History of Britain Since 1700,* ed. Roderick Floud and D. N.

McCloskey, 2nd ed. (Cambridge and New York: Cambridge University Press, 1992), 1:165 and 172–173.

2. M. P. Ashley, *Financial and Commercial Policy under the Cromwellian Protectorate* (Oxford: Oxford University Press, H. Milford, 1934), 66.

3. James S. Wheeler, *The Making of a World Power: War and the Military Revolution in Seventeenth-Century England* (Stroud, UK: Sutton, 1999), 118–119.

4. Ashley, *Financial and Commercial Policy under the Cromwellian Protectorate,* 40–41.

5. Wheeler, *The Making of a World Power,* 141.

6. James S. Wheeler, "Navy Finance, 1649–1660," *Historical Journal* 39, no. 2 (June 1996): 459–460.

7. Ian Gentles, *The New Model Army in England, Ireland, and Scotland, 1645–1653* (Oxford and Cambridge, MA: B. Blackwell, 1992), 28.

8. Wheeler, *The Making of a World Power,* 157. This percentage went as high as 60 percent in the period from March 1658 to August 1660. Ibid., 166.

9. In this period, even taxation in kind was not infrequent, as only half of taxes were required to be paid in cash. See Michael J. Braddick, *Parliamentary Taxation in Seventeenth-Century England: Local Administration and Response* (Woodbridge, UK, and Rochester, NY: Royal Historical Society/Boydell Press, 1994), 153, particularly footnote 155.

10. Gentles, *The New Model Army in England, Ireland, and Scotland,* 48.

11. Wheeler, *The Making of a World Power,* 158.

12. Ashley, *Financial and Commercial Policy under the Cromwellian Protectorate,* 82. For details of the decentralized system of assignments in tax revenue in Hampshire, see Andrew M. Coleby, *Central Government and the Localities: Hampshire, 1649–1689* (Cambridge and New York: Cambridge University Press, 1987), 47–48.

13. Calculated from Wheeler, *The Making of a World Power,* 213.

14. Patrick K. O'Brien and Philip A. Hunt, "Excises and the Rise of a Fiscal State in England, 1586–1688," in *Crises, Revolutions, and Self-Sustained Growth: Essays in European Fiscal History, 1130–1830,* ed. W. M. Ormrod, Margaret Bonney, and Richard Bonney (Stamford, UK: Shaun Tyas, 1999), 209–214; Michael J. Braddick, "Popular Politics and Public Policy: The Excise Riots at Smithfield in February 1647 and Its Aftermath," *Historical Journal* 34, no. 3 (September 1991): 597–626.

15. Braddick, *Parliamentary Taxation in Seventeenth-Century England,* 191–193.

16. Ibid., 135–136.

17. Peter Clark, *The English Alehouse: A Social History, 1200–1830* (London: Longman, 1983), 177; and Peter Haydon, *The English Pub: A History* (London: Robert Hale, 1994), 71.

18. Ashley, *Financial and Commercial Policy under the Cromwellian Protectorate*, 96.

19. For Cromwell's abortive efforts to build centralized governance, see David Underdown, "Settlement in the Counties, 1653–1658," in *The Interregnum: The Quest for Settlement, 1646–1660*, ed. G. E. Aylmer (London: Macmillan, 1972).

20. Wheeler, *The Making of a World Power*, 193.

21. Ashley, *Financial and Commercial Policy under the Cromwellian Protectorate*, 98–99.

22. Ibid., 107.

23. The percentage varied between 60.5 percent and 82.2 percent in the period between 1651 and 1660. Cited from Wheeler, "Navy Finance, 1649–1660," 463.

24. Bernard Capp, *Cromwell's Navy: The Fleet and the English Revolution, 1648–1660* (Oxford: Clarendon Press, 1989), 364; Wheeler, "Navy Finance, 1649–1660," 465.

25. Wheeler, "Navy Finance, 1649–1660," 460.

26. C. D. Chandaman, *The English Public Revenue, 1660–1688* (Oxford: Clarendon Press, 1975), 206.

27. Glenn O. Nichols, "English Government Borrowing, 1660–1688," *Journal of British Studies* 10, no. 2 (May 1971): 89; and Chandaman, *The English Public Revenue*, 196.

28. Robert Ashton, "Revenue Farming under the Early Stuarts," *Economic History Review*, n.s., 8, no. 3 (1956): 311–313.

29. Nichols, "English Government Borrowing," 89.

30. In the case of Backwell, more than 90 percent of his investment in 1666 was lent to the government. See Henry Roseveare, *The Financial Revolution, 1660–1760* (London: Longman, 1991), 20.

31. On the use of tallies for deficit financing under the early Stuarts, see Robert Ashton, *The Crown and the Money Market, 1603–1640* (Oxford: Clarendon Press, 1960), 48–50. For their use in the Restoration period, see Chandaman, *The English Public Revenue*, 287–294.

32. For example, Sir Stephen Fox, the paymaster of the guard in 1661 and later the paymaster of the forces and garrison and of the royal household, was able to have his tallies cashed at the Exchequer on time, and he thus profited handsomely in the process of handling government expenditures. See C. G. A. Clay, *Public Finance and Private Wealth: The Career of Sir Stephen Fox, 1626–1716* (Oxford: Clarendon Press, 1978), particularly chapters 3 and 4.

33. Paul Seaward, "The House of Commons Committee of Trade and the Origins of the Second Anglo-Dutch War, 1664," *Historical Journal* 30, no. 2 (June 1987): 437–452.

34. Paul Seaward, *The Cavalier Parliament and the Reconstruction of the Old Regime, 1660–1667* (Cambridge and New York: Cambridge University Press, 1989), 239–240 and 303.

35. Downing had some practical experience in public finance under the Protectorate. He had observed firsthand how the Dutch government established its creditworthiness by efficiently managing its tax revenue and thus could borrow easily from the financial markets. For the early background of Sir George Downing and its relevance to his invention of the Order system, see Jonathan Scott, "'Good Night Amsterdam.' Sir George Downing and Anglo-Dutch State-building," *English Historical Review* 118, no. 476 (April 2003): 334–356.

36. Henry Roseveare, *The Treasury, 1660–1870: The Foundations of Control* (London: Allen & Unwin, 1973), 18 and 24–26.

37. Ibid., 52–53.

38. J. R. Jones, *The Anglo-Dutch Wars of the Seventeenth Century* (London: Longman, 1996), 96.

39. Chandaman, *The English Public Revenue*, 211–212; Seaward, *The Cavalier Parliament and the Reconstruction of the Old Regime*, 317.

40. The contract for the excise expired in 1668, that for the customs in 1671, and that for the hearth tax in 1673. See Chandaman, *The English Public Revenue*, 215–216.

41. Howard Tomlinson, "Financial and Administrative Developments in England, 1660–88," in *The Restored Monarchy, 1660–1688*, ed. J. R. Jones (Totowa, NJ: Rowman and Littlefield, 1979), 96–97.

42. Chandaman, *The English Public Revenue*, 216 and 219.

43. Ibid., 297; Nichols, "English Government Borrowing," 99.

44. Roseveare, *The Treasury*, 22–36; Chandaman, *The English Public Revenue*, 213–214; Stephen B. Baxter, *The Development of the Treasury, 1660–1702* (Cambridge, MA: Harvard University Press, 1957), 180–184.

45. Tomlinson, "Financial and Administrative Developments in England," 98–99.

46. Roseveare, *The Treasury*, 27–28.

47. Chandaman, *The English Public Revenue*, 220.

48. Ibid., 226.

49. Nichols, "English Government Borrowing," 100–101.

50. After 1674, the royal government managed to make interest payments on this debt out of its ordinary revenue. See J. Keith Horsefield, "The 'Stop of the Exchequer' Revisited," *Economic History Review*, n.s., 35, no. 4 (November 1982): 511–528.

51. Roseveare, *The Financial Revolution*, 22.

52. Chandaman, *The English Public Revenue*, 47–49; Roseveare, *The Treasury*, 54–56; J. R. Jones, *Country and Court: England, 1658–1714* (Cambridge, MA: Harvard University Press, 1978), 192–196.

53. Roseveare, *The Treasury,* 54.

54. Ibid., 34.

55. Chandaman, *The English Public Revenue,* 54.

56. Ibid., 59–61; and Edward Hughes, *Studies in Administration and Finance, 1558–1825, with Special Reference to the History of Salt Taxation in England* (Manchester: Manchester University Press, 1934), 148–152.

57. Chandaman, *The English Public Revenue,* 62–64.

58. On the competition between the groups of financiers associated with Danby and with Clifford in 1673, see Clay, *Public Finance and Private Wealth,* 98–100.

59. Edgar Kiser, "Markets and Hierarchies in Early Modern Tax Systems: A Principal-Agent Analysis," *Politics and Society* 22, no. 3 (September 1994): 294.

60. For similar reasons, the General Tax Farm in France also developed centralized organizational methods to monitor and discipline collecting agents. See Eugene N. White, "From Privatized to Government-Administered Tax Collection: Tax Farming in Eighteenth-Century France," *Economic History Review* 57, no. 4 (2004): 636–663.

61. Chandaman, *The English Public Revenue,* 64.

62. Ibid., 72–73.

63. Miles Ogborn, "The Capacities of the State: Charles Davenant and the Management of the Excise, 1683–1698," *Journal of Historical Geography* 24, no. 3 (1998): especially 295–306.

64. Chandaman, *The English Public Revenue,* 35.

65. Clark, *The English Alehouse,* 184.

66. Peter Mathias, *The Brewing Industry in England, 1700–1830* (Cambridge: Cambridge University Press, 1959), 363–364.

67. Chandaman, *The English Public Revenue,* 75.

68. Seaward, *The Cavalier Parliament and the Reconstruction of the Old Regime,* 111

69. Chandaman, *The English Public Revenue,* 88–106.

70. C. D. Chandaman, "The Financial Settlement in the Parliament of 1685," in *British Government and Administration: Studies Presented to S. B. Chrimes,* ed. H. Hearder and H. R. Loyn (Cardiff: University of Wales Press, 1974), 151–152.

71. John Childs, *The Army, James II, and the Glorious Revolution* (Manchester: Manchester University Press, 1980), 2 and 5; and Geoffrey S. Holmes, *The Making of A Great Power: Late Stuart and Early Georgian Britain, 1660–1722* (London and New York: Longman, 1993), 177.

72. In Chandaman's estimate, James II spent nearly £1 million prior to 1688 to clear previous government debts. Chandaman, "The Financial Settlement in the Parliament of 1685," 152.

73. Jonathan I. Israel, "The Dutch Role in the Glorious Revolution," in *The Anglo-Dutch Moment: Essays on the Glorious Revolution and Its World Impact,* ed. Jonathan I. Israel (Cambridge and New York: Cambridge University Press, 1991).

74. The crown's ordinary revenue was set at less than £700,000 a year, which would lead to an annual deficit of between £200,000 and £300,000 even in peacetime. Clayton Roberts, "The Constitutional Significance of the Financial Settlement of 1690," *Historical Journal* 20, no. 1 (1977): 59–76.

75. E. A. Reitan, "From Revenue to Civil List, 1689–1702: The Revolution Settlement and the 'Mixed and Balanced' Constitution," *Historical Journal* 13, no. 4 (1970): 571–588.

76. John Childs, *The British Army of William III, 1689–1702* (Manchester: Manchester University Press, 1987), 142 and 144.

77. For details, see Daniel A. Baugh, *British Naval Administration in the Age of Walpole* (Princeton, NJ: Princeton University Press, 1965), 452–480.

78. John Brewer, *The Sinews of Power: War, Money, and the English State, 1688–1783* (New York: Alfred A. Knopf, 1989), 149–153.

79. Marjolein 't Hart, "'The Devil or the Dutch': Holland's Impact on the Financial Revolution in England, 1643–1694," *Parliament, Estates and Representation* 11, no. 1 (June 1991): 50–52.

80. P. G. M. Dickson, *The Financial Revolution in England: A Study in the Development of Public Credit, 1688–1756* (London: Macmillan, 1967), 351.

81. The amount of short-term borrowing is calculated from ibid., 344, table 53.

82. Among these methods, the English preferred annuities rather than tontines. See David R. Weir, "Tontines, Public Finance, and Revolution in France and England, 1688–1789," *Journal of Economic History* 49, no. 1 (March 1989): 95–124.

83. Calculated from table 2 (No. 1, No. 2, No. 3, No. 4, No. 6, and No. 7) in Dickson, *The Financial Revolution in England,* 48–49.

84. Ibid., 49.

85. J. Keith Horsefield, *British Monetary Experiments, 1650–1710* (Cambridge, MA: Harvard University Press, 1960), 126.

86. Roseveare, *The Financial Revolution,* 37.

87. In 1696, it fell to 12.8 percent in the spring and even 2.7 percent by the autumn. See Horsefield, *British Monetary Experiments,* 264.

88. Dennis Bubini, "Politics and the Battle for the Banks, 1688–1697," *English Historical Review* 85, no. 337 (October 1970): 693–714.

89. For the initial issues of the Exchequer bills, see Dickson, *The Financial Revolution in England,* 368–372.

90. J. V. Beckett, "Land Tax or Excise: The Levying of Taxation in Seventeenth- and Eighteenth-Century England," *English Historical Review* 100, no. 395 (April 1985): 298.

91. D. W. Jones, *War and Economy in the Age of William III and Marlborough* (New York: Basil Blackwell, 1988), chapter 2; and William J. Ashworth, *Customs and Excise: Trade, Production, and Consumption in England, 1640–1845* (Oxford and New York: Oxford University Press, 2003), 113–114.

92. Brewer, *The Sinews of Power,* 74 and 94; Hughes, *Studies in Administration and Finance,* 192–194.

93. B. R. Mitchell, *Abstract of British Historical Statistics* (Cambridge: Cambridge University Press, 1962), 401.

94. Anne L. Murphy, *The Origins of English Financial Markets: Investment and Speculation before the South Sea Bubble* (Cambridge and New York: Cambridge University Press, 2009).

95. Larry Neal, *The Rise of Financial Capitalism: International Capital Markets in the Age of Reason* (Cambridge and New York: Cambridge University Press, 1990), 10–12.

96. Bruce G. Carruthers, *City of Capital: Politics and Markets in the English Financial Revolution* (Princeton, NJ: Princeton University Press, 1996), 139.

97. John Brewer, "The English State and Fiscal Appropriation, 1688–1789," *Politics and Society* 16, no. 2–3 (September 1988): 367.

98. Hughes, *Studies in Administration and Finance,* 214; D. M. Joslin, "London Private Bankers, 1720–1785," *Economic History Review,* n.s., 7, no. 2 (1954): 169.

99. J. H. Clapham, *The Bank of England: A History* (Cambridge: Cambridge University Press; New York: Macmillan, 1945), 1:22–23; A. Andréadès, *History of the Bank of England, 1640–1903,* 4th ed. (London: Frank Cass, 1966), 111–112.

100. Horsefield, *British Monetary Experiments,* 140.

101. Henry Horwitz, *Parliament, Policy, and Politics in the Reign of William III* (Newark: University of Delaware Press, 1977), 187–188.

102. For example, cashiers of the government departments often made handsome profits by using the heavily discounted Exchequer bills at their par value to pay taxes. See David Ogg, *England in the Reigns of James II and William III* (Oxford: Clarendon Press; New York: Oxford University Press, 1955), 88–89; Dickson, *The Financial Revolution in England,* 416.

103. Julian Hoppit, "Attitudes to Credit in Britain," *Historical Journal* 33, no. 2 (1990): 308–311.

104. Horwitz, *Parliament, Policy, and Politics in the Reign of William III,* chapters 10 and 11.

105. Mitchell, *Abstract of British Historical Statistics,* 401.

106. Ibid., 401.

107. This contingent event was vital to the swift resumption of conflict as France, the United Provinces, and England were all too financially exhausted to have fought another major war so soon.

108. The long-term borrowings included £12.5 million in "irredeemable" annuities (the longer annuities ended in 1792–1807 at 9 percent, the shorter ones in the 1740s at 7 percent); £27.5 million in "redeemable" loans owned to both the public and the three government-chartered corporations, the Bank of England (£3.37 million), the East India Company (£3.2 million), and the South Sea Company (£9.2 million); and a total of £7.5 million of unfunded short-term debts, such as the Exchequer bills and the bills issued by the Navy, Ordnance, and Victualling Board to meet their spending. See Roseveare, *The Financial Revolution,* 52–53.

109. The Whig ministry put candles on the excise list in 1710. The new Tory ministry added hops, hides, and waterborne coal in 1711 and soap, paper, starch, printed calicoes, hackney chairs, cards, and dice in 1712. See T. S. Ashton, *Economic Fluctuations in England, 1700–1800* (Oxford: Clarendon, 1959), 28.

110. Brewer, *The Sinews of Power,* 75; Hughes, *Studies in Administration and Finance,* 272–273.

111. Dickson, *The Financial Revolution in England,* 416.

112. Andréadès, *History of the Bank of England,* 120.

113. Dickson, *The Financial Revolution in England,* 373–376.

114. In regard to government finance, the Tory ministry in 1710 continued to work with big financiers who were closely connected with the Whigs. See B. W. Hill, "The Change of Government and the 'Loss of the City', 1710–1711," *Economic History Review,* n.s., 21, no. 3 (August 1971): 395–413.

115. Neal, *The Rise of Financial Capitalism,* 91.

116. For the details of the bank's proposal to gradually convert government debt, see William R. Scott, *The Constitution and Finance of English, Scottish and Irish Joint-Stock Companies to 1720* (1912; Bristol: Thoemmes Press, 1993), 1:305–306.

117. Ibid., 1:306.

118. Forrest Capie, "Money and Economic Development in Eighteenth-Century England," in *Exceptionalism and Industrialization: Britain and Its European Rivals, 1688–1815,* ed. Leandro Prados de la Escosura (Cambridge and New York: Cambridge University Press, 2004), table 10.2, 224.

119. Dickson, *The Financial Revolution in England,* 390.

120. It was only in the 1780s that the Bank of England began to manage these funds. See J. E. D. Binney, *British Public Finance and Administration, 1774–92* (Oxford: Clarendon Press, 1958), 147.

121. W. R. Ward, *The English Land Tax in the Eighteenth Century* (London: Oxford University Press, 1953), 48.

122. Neal, *The Rise of Financial Capitalism,* 93–94.

123. In 1720, their prices kept rising from £128 in January to the peak of £950 (recorded price) in June and then fell to £155 in December. On the background and impact of this financial fraud, see Julian Hoppit, "The Myths of the South Sea Bubble," *Transactions of the Royal Historical Society,* 6th ser., 12 (2002): 141–165.

124. Dickson, *The Financial Revolution in England,* 134.

125. Neal, "The Finance of Business during the Industrial Revolution," 165 and 172–173.

126. Beckett, "Land Tax or Excise," 305.

127. Ward, *The English Land Tax in the Eighteenth Century,* chapter 7.

128. Big antiexcise protests occurred in 1733 when Sir Robert Walpole tried to use extra excise rates on imported tobacco and wine to replace the tariff duties on these goods. These protests were instigated mainly by wealthy tobacco merchants who had benefited from smuggled tobacco, rather than by ordinary consumers. On the role of big tobacco merchants in this "excise crisis," see Paul Langford, *The Excise Crisis: Society and Politics in the Age of Walpole* (Oxford: Clarendon Press, 1975); on the role of American tobacco planters in these protests, see Jacob M. Price, "The Excise Affair Revisited: The Administrative and Colonial Dimensions of a Parliamentary Crisis," in *England's Rise to Greatness, 1660–1763,* ed. Stephen B. Baxter (Berkeley: University of California Press, 1983).

129. Binney, *British Public Finance and Administration,* 31–32; Brewer, *The Sinews of Power,* 101–102.

130. By 1748, more than 40 percent of beer in London was produced by the twelve biggest common brewers. See Mathias, *The Brewing Industry in England,* 26.

131. For the development of big brewers' control of retailing channels, see Clark, *The English Alehouse,* 184;

132. Mathias, *The Brewing Industry in England,* 342.

133. Ibid., 342.

134. Haydon, *The English Pub,* 89 and 95–96.

135. Integration of the financial markets in England did not appear until the second half of the eighteenth century. See Moshe Buchinsky and Ben Polak, "The Emergence of a National Capital Market in England, 1710–1880," *Journal of Economic History* 53, no. 1 (March 1993): 1–24; Julian Hoppit, "Financial Crises in Eighteenth-Century England," *Economic History Review,* n.s., 39, no. 1 (February 1986): 52–56.

136. Roseveare, *The Financial Revolution,* 68.

137. Neal, *The Rise of Financial Capitalism,* chapter 3; and Larry Neal and Stephen Quinn, "Networks of Information, Markets, and Institutions in the Rise of London as a Financial Centre, 1660–1720," *Financial History Review* 8, no. 1 (April 2001): 7–26.

138. Roseveare, *The Financial Revolution,* 74.

139. Of the 80 percent, London itself accounted for one-third. Ashton, *Economic Fluctuations in England,* 29.

140. Miles Ogborn, *Spaces of Modernity: London's Geographies, 1680–1780* (New York: Guilford Press, 1998), 194.

3. The Rapid Centralization of Public Finance in Japan, 1868–1880

1. Banno Junji, "Meiji kokka no seiritsu" [The establishment of the Meiji state], in *Nihon keizaishi* [The economic history of Japan], vol. 3, *Kaikō to Ishin* [The opening of Japan and the Restoration], ed. Umemura Mataji and Yamamoto Yūzō (Tokyo: Iwanami Shoten, 1989), 57.

2. Richard J. Samuels, *"Rich Nation, Strong Army": National Security and the Technological Transformation of Japan* (Ithaca, NY: Cornell University Press, 1994), chapter 2.

3. Marius B. Jansen, "The Meiji Restoration," in *The Cambridge History of Japan,* ed. Marius B. Jansen, vol. 5, *The Nineteenth Century* (Cambridge and New York: Cambridge University Press, 1989), 345–353.

4. This view is often seen in recent characterizations of the Meiji Restoration. For such examples, see Philip D. Curtin, *The World and the West: The European Challenge and the Overseas Response in the Age of Empire* (Cambridge: Cambridge University Press, 2000), 163; and Peter Duus, *Modern Japan,* 2nd ed. (Boston: Houghton Mifflin, 1998), 85.

5. On the importance of historical experience in Meiji institution building, see Richard J. Samuels, *Machiavelli's Children: Leaders and Their Legacies in Italy and Japan* (Ithaca, NY: Cornell University Press, 2003).

6. Luke S. Roberts, *Mercantilism in a Japanese Domain: The Merchant Origins of Economic Nationalism in 18th-Century Tosa* (Cambridge and New York: Cambridge University Press, 1998); Nishikawa Shunsaku and Amano Masatoshi, "Shohan no sangyō to keizai seisaku" [The industrial and economic policies of domains], in *Nihon keizaishi* [The economic history of Japan], vol. 2, *Kindai seichō no taidō* [Gathering momentum for modern growth], ed. Shinbo Hiroshi and Saitō Osamu (Tokyo: Iwanami Shoten, 1989), 206–210.

7. Hirakawa Arata, "Chiiki keizai no tenkai" [The development of a regional economy], in *Iwanami kōza Nihon tsūshi* [The Iwanami general history

of Japan], vol. 15, *Kinsei* (5) [The early modern period], ed. Asao Naohiro et al. (Tokyo: Iwanami Shoten, 1995), 139–143.

8. Takano Toshihiko, "18 seiki zenhan no Nihon—Taihei no naka no ten-kan" [Japan in the first half of the eighteenth century: A transformation in the great peace], in *Iwanami kōza Nihon tsūshi* [The Iwanami general history of Japan], vol. 13, *Kinsei* (3) [The early modern period], ed. Asao Naohiro et al. (Tokyo: Iwanami Shoten, 1994.

9. Ōguchi Yūjirō, "Kokka ishiki to Tennō" [State consciousness and the Emperor], in *Iwanami kōza Nihon tsūshi* [The Iwanami general history of Japan], vol. 15, *Kinsei* (5) [The early modern period], ed. Asao Naohiro et al. (Tokyo: Iwanami Shoten, 1995), 207–208.

10. Bitō Masahide, "Sonnō jōi shisō" [The ideology of revering the Emperor and expelling the barbarians], in *Iwanami kōza Nihon rekishi* [The Iwanami history of Japan], vol. 13, *Kinsei* (5) [The early modern period], ed. Asao Naohiro et al. (Tokyo: Iwanami Shoten, 1977), 78–80.

11. Ono Masao, "Daimyō no ahen sensō ninshiki" [Knowledge of the Opium War among domain lords], in *Iwanami kōza Nihon tsūshi* [The Iwanami general history of Japan], vol. 15, *Kinsei* (5) [The early modern period], ed. Asao Naohiro et al. (Tokyo: Iwanami Shoten, 1995), 299–310.

12. Although both treaties implemented a fixed 5 percent tariff rate on exports and created consular courts, the shogunate did not grant American businessmen or missionaries the right to travel freely in Japan, nor did it grant the United States most-favored-nation status. See Jansen, "The Meiji Restoration," 316.

13. Duus, *Modern Japan,* 72–74; Yasumaru Yoshio, "1850–70 nendai no Nihon: Ishin henkaku" [Japan between the 1850s and 1870s: Restoration and change], in *Iwanami kōza Nihon tsūshi* [The Iwanami general history of Japan], vol. 16, *Kindai* (1) [The modern period], ed. Asao Naohiro et al. (Tokyo: Iwanami Shoten, 1994), 20–21.

14. For the leadership of Satsuma and its collaboration with the shogunate to purge anti-Western radicals so as to stop the "immediate expulsion of Westerners," see Sasaki Suguru, *Bakumatsu seiji to Satsuma han* [Satsuma and late Tokugawa politics] (Tokyo: Yoshikawa Kōbunkan, 2004), chapter 3.

15. Ibid., 286–288.

16. For the opinions of domain lords in Chūgoku and Kyūshū, see Aoyama Tadamasa, *Meiji Ishin to kokka keisei* [The Meiji Restoration and state formation] (Tokyo: Yoshikawa Kōbunkan, 2000), 211–221. For Echizen, see Mikami Kazuo, *Kōbu gattairon no kenkyū: Echizen han Bakumatsu Ishinshi bunseki* [A study of the efforts to unify the court and Shogun: An analysis of the history of Echizen in late Tokugawa and early Meiji], rev. ed. (Tokyo: Ochanomizu Shobō, 1990), 212–214.

17. See Conrad D. Totman, *The Collapse of the Tokugawa Bakufu, 1862–1868* (Honolulu: University of Hawaii Press, 1980), chapter 8.

18. Aoyama Tadamasa, *Meiji Ishin to kokka keisei,* 233–234.

19. Ibid., 240–242.

20. W. G. Beasley, *The Meiji Restoration* (Stanford, CA: Stanford University Press, 1972), 269.

21. M. William Steele, *Mō hitotsu no kindai: Sokumen kara mita Bakumatsu Meiji* [Localism and nationalism in modern Japanese history] (Tokyo: Perikansha, 1998), 175.

22. Ishii Takashi, *Boshin sensō ron* [On the Boshin Civil War] (Tokyo: Yoshikawa Kōbunkan, 1984), 22; Takahashi Hirobumi, "Buryoku tōbaku hōshin o meguru Satsuma hannai hantaiha no dōkō" [The trend of opposition in Satsuma in regard to the armed overthrow of the shogunate], in *Mō hitotsu no Meiji Ishin: Bakumatsushi no saikentō* [Another Meiji Restoration: A reexamination of the history of late Tokugawa], ed. Iechika Yoshiki (Tokyo: Yūshisha, 2006), 230–260.

23. Sasaki Suguru, *Bakumatsu seiji to Satsuma han,* 382.

24. Ibid., 409.

25. Tanaka Akira, "Bakufu no tōkai" [The fall of the shogunate], in *Iwanami kōza Nihon rekishi* [The Iwanami history of Japan], vol. 13, *Kinsei (5)* [The early modern period], ed. Asao Naohiro et al. (Tokyo: Iwanami Shoten, 1977), 338–342.

26. Miyachi Masato, "Ishin seiken ron" [On the restored government], in *Iwanami kōza Nihon tsūshi* [The Iwanami general history of Japan], vol. 16, *Kindai (1)* [The modern period], ed. Asao Naohiro et al. (Tokyo: Iwanami Shoten, 1994), 113. Yokoi Shōnan also proposed that Japan revise the inappropriate terms in the signed treaties and replace them with fair terms. Yokoi Shōnan, "Shinsei ni tsuite Shungaku ni kengen" [Proposal to Shungaku in regard to the new regime], 28 November 1867, in Satō Shōsuke, Uete Michiari, and Yamaguchi Muneyuki, eds., *Watanabe Kazan, Takano Chōei, Sakuma Shōzan, Yokoi Shōnan, Hashimoto Sanai* [Watanabe Kazan, Takano Chōei, Sakuma Shōzan, Yokoi Shōnan, Hashimoto Sanai], vol. 55 of *Nihon shisō taikei* (Tokyo: Iwanami Shoten, 1971), 467.

27. On the key difference between Tosa and Satsuma, see Sasaki Suguru, "Taiseihōkan to tōbaku mitchoku" [Returning power to the emperor and the secret imperial order to overthrow the shogunate], *Jinmon gakuhō* 80 (1997): 14.

28. Takahashi Hidenao, *Bakumatsu Ishin no seiji to Tennō* [Late Tokugawa and Restoration politics and the emperor] (Tokyo: Yoshikawa Kōbunkan, 2007), chapters 10 and 11.

29. Fujimura Tōru, *Meiji zaisei kakuritsu katei no kenkyū* [Building the public finance of the Meiji regime] (Tokyo: Chūō Daigaku Shuppansha, 1968), 14.

30. More than 60 percent was used to dispense the Meiji government's expenditures, 20 percent was lent to various domain governments, and 14 percent was used to "encourage businesses" *(kangyō)*. Calculated from Sawada Akira, *Meiji zaisei no kisoteki kenkyū: Ishin tōsho no zaisei* [The foundation of the public finance of the early Meiji regime] (Tokyo: Hōbunkan, 1934), 121.

31. Fujimura Tōru, *Meiji zaisei kakuritsu katei no kenkyū*, 27–28 and 38.

32. Yamazaki Yūkō, "Kōgi chūshutsu kikō no keisei to hōkai" [The formation and collapse of the institutions of public discussion], in *Nihon kindaishi no saikōchiku* [A reconstruction of the modern history of Japan], ed. Itō Takashi (Tokyo: Yamakawa Shuppansha, 1993), 60–61.

33. Kasahara Hidehiko, *Meiji kokka to kanryōsei* [The Meiji state and bureaucracy] (Tokyo: Ashi Shobō, 1991), 41; Mikami Kazuo, *Kōbu gattairon no kenkyū*, 244–245.

34. The Office of Reform formulated plans on a wide range of issues, including monetary consolidation, fiscal centralization, the postal system, the metrological system, household registration and management, and corporation laws. Niwa Kunio, *Chiso kaiseihō no kigen: Kaimei kanryō no keisei* [The origin of the land tax reform: The formation of the enlightened bureaucrats] (Kyoto: Mineruva Shobō, 1995), chapter 3.

35. Sekiguchi Eiichi, "Min-Zō bunri mondai to Kido Takayoshi" [The separation of the Ministry of Civil Affairs from the Ministry of Finance and Kido Takayoshi], *Hōgaku* 39, no. 1 (March 1975): 42.

36. Matsuo Masahito, "Ishin kanryōsei no keisei to Dajōkansei" [The formation of the bureaucrats of the Restoration regime and the Council of State], in *Kanryōsei no keisei to tenkai* [The formation and development of bureaucracy], ed. Kindai Nihon Kenkyūkai (Tokyo: Yamakawa Shuppansha, 1986), 18.

37. Sekiguchi Eiichi, "Min-Zō bunri mondai to Kido Takayoshi," 43–47; Matsuo Masahito, "Meiji shonen no seijō to chihō shihai" [The political situation and local rule in the early Meiji: Before and after "Minzobunri"], *Tochi seido shigaku* 123, no. 3 (April 1981): 48.

38. Yamamoto Hirofumi, "Shoki shokusan seisaku to sono shūsei" [The early industry-promotion policy and its revision], in *Nihon keizai seisaku shiron (jō)* [The history of economic policy in Japan], ed. Andō Yoshio (Tokyo: Tōkyō Daigaku Shuppankai, 1973), 1:23; and Nagai Hideo, "Shokusan kōgyō seisaku no kichō: Kanei jigyō o chūshin tosite" [The basic tune in the industry-promotion policies]. Originally published in *Hokkaidō daigaku bungakubu kiyō* 10 (November 1969); reprinted in Nagai Hideo, *Meiji kokka keiseiki no gaisei to naisei* [External and domestic politics in the formative period of the Meiji state] (Sapporo: Hokkaidō Daigaku Tosho Kankōkai, 1990), 220–222.

39. Kamiyama Tsuneo, "Inoue zaisei kara Ōkuma zaisei he no tankan: Junbikin o chūshin ni" [The policy change in public finance from Inoue to Ōkuma:

The use of government reserve funds], in *Meiji zenki no Nihon keizai: Shihon shugi e no michi* [The Japanese economy in the early Meiji: The way toward capitalism], ed. Takamura Naosuke (Tokyo: Nihon Keizai Hyōronsha, 2004), 25.

40. Nagai Hideo, "Shokusan kōgyō seisaku no kichō," 225. For criticism of the government-sponsored railway building in the early 1870s, see Nakamura Naofumi, *Nihon tetsudōgyō no keisei, 1869–1894 nen* [The formation of the railway industry in Japan, 1869–1894] (Tokyo: Nihon Keizai Hyōronsha, 1998), 49–50.

41. This loan was first arranged secretly so as to avoid the opposition of conservatives. See the details in Tatewaki Kazuo, *Meiji seifu to Orientaru Banku* [The Meiji government and the British Oriental Bank] (Tokyo: Chūō Kōronsha, 1992), 74–96.

42. Senda Minoru, *Ishin seiken no chokuzoku guntai* [The central army of the Meiji regime] (Tokyo: Kaimei Shoin, 1978), 56.

43. Matsuo Masahito, "Hantaisei kaitai to Iwakura Tomomi" [The collapse of the domain system and Iwakura Tomomi], in *Bakumatsu Ishin no shakai to shisō* [Society and thought in the late Tokugawa and Meiji Restoration], ed. Tanaka Akira (Tokyo: Yoshikawa Kōbunkan, 1999), 217–218.

44. Senda Minoru, *Ishin seiken no chokuzoku guntai*, 162.

45. Ibid., 116.

46. Ibid., 180–188.

47. Senda Minoru, *Ishin seiken no chitsuroku shobun: Tennōsei to haihan chiken* [The Restoration regime's commutation of the stipends of lords and samurai: The emperor system and the abolishing of the domains] (Tokyo: Kaimei Shoin, 1979), 421.

48. For attempts to imitate the American federal system in the late Tokugawa and early Meiji, see Inoue Katsuo, *Bakumatsu Ishin seijishi no kenkyū: Nihon kindai kokka no seisei ni tsuite* [Studies in the political history of late Tokugawa and early Meiji] (Tokyo: Hanawa Shobō, 1994), 304–305 and 409–411.

49. Matsuo Masahito, *Haihan chiken no kenkyū* [A study of the abolishing of the domains] (Tokyo: Yoshikawa Kōbunkan, 2001), 81–84.

50. At that time, in addition to the nonconvertible paper notes *(dajōkansatsu)* that the Meiji government had introduced, there were coins minted by the former shogunate; shogunate currencies counterfeited by some domain governments, particularly those of Satsuma, Tosa, and Saga; paper notes issued by domain governments *(hansatsu)*; and foreign currencies, such as the Mexican silver dollar, circulating in the opened ports.

51. *Meiji zenki zaisei keizai shiryō shūsei* [Collected materials on the finance and economy of early Meiji], ed. Ōuchi Hyōe, Tsuchiya Takao, and Ōkurashō (Tokyo: Meiji Bunken Shiryō Kankōkai, 1962), 2:211 and 352.

52. Fumoto Shin'ichi, "Ishin seifu no hoppo seisaku" [The northern policy of the Restoration regime], *Rekishigaku kenkyū* 725 (July 1999): 25, particularly footnote 86.

53. Ōkuma Shigenobu, "Ōkuma sangi zenkoku itchi no giron" [Ōkuma on the conformity of the whole country], in *Ōkuma monjo* [Documents on Ōkuma Shigenobu], ed. Waseda Daigaku Shakai Kagaku Kenkyūjo (Tokyo: Waseda Daigaku Shakai Kagaku Kenkyūjo, 1958), 1:A1, 1–3.

54. Haraguchi Kiyoshi, "Haihan chiken seiji katei no hitotsu kōsatsu" [An investigation of the political process of abolishing the domain system], *Meijō shōgaku* 29, special issue (January 1980): 47–94; Takahashi Hidenao, "Haihan chiken ni okeru kenryoku to shakai" [Power and society in the abolishing of the domains], in *Kindai Nihon no seitō to kanryō* [Political parties and bureaucrats in modern Japan], ed. Yamamoto Shirō (Tokyo: Tōkyō Sōgensha, 1991), 23.

55. Shimoyama Saburō, *Kindai Tennōsei kenkyū josetsu* [A study of the emperor system] (Tokyo: Iwanami Shoten, 1976), 329.

56. Yamamuro Shin'ichi, "Meiji kokka no seido to rinen" [The institutions and principles of the Meiji state], in *Iwanami kōza Nihon tsūshi* [The Iwanami general history of Japan], vol. 17, *Kindai* (2) [The modern period], ed. Asao Naohiro et al. (Tokyo: Iwanami Shoten, 1994), 117.

57. Miyachi Masato, "Haihan chiken no seiji katei" [The political process of abolishing the domains], in *Nihon kindaishi ni okeru tenkanki no kenkyū* [Studies of the transition period in the modern history of Japan], ed. Banno Junji and Miyachi Masato (Tokyo: Yamakawa Shuppansha, 1985), 70.

58. Satō Shigerō, *Kindai Tennosei keiseiki no kenkyū: Hitotsu no haihan shikenron* [The emperor system in its formative period: Another perspective on the abolishing of the domains] (Tokyo: San'ichi Shobō, 1987), 118–119.

59. Miyachi Masato, "Haihan chiken no seiji katei," 104–107. For the details of the political crisis in 1870, see also Shimoyama Saburō, *Kindai Tennōsei kenkyū josetsu*, 315–316.

60. Ishii Takashi, "Haihan no katei ni okeru seikyoku no dōkō" [Political trends in the process of abolishing the domains], originally published in *Tōhoku Daigaku bungakubu kenkyū nenpō* 19 (July 1969); reprinted in *Ishin seiken no seiritsu* [The establishment of the Restoration government], ed. Matsuo Masahito (Tokyo: Yoshikawa Kōbunkan, 2001), 268; Fukuchi Atsushi, *Meiji shinseiken no kenryoku kōzō* [The power structure of the new Meiji government] (Tokyo: Yoshikawa Kōbunkan, 1996), 6.

61. Fukuchi Atsushi, *Meiji shinseiken no kenryoku kōzō*, 8.

62. Niwa Kunio, *Chiso kaiseihō no kigen*, 235 and 239–240.

63. Matsuo Masahito, *Haihan chiken no kenkyū*, 297–299; Takahashi Hidenao, "Haihan chiken ni okeru kenryoku to shakai," 59–64.

64. A letter from Ōkuma Shigenobu and Inoue Kaoru to Itō Hirobumi, 19 May 1871. Cited in *Shibusawa Eiichi denki shiryō* [Biographical materials of Shibusawa Eiichi], ed. Shibusawa Seien Kinen Zaidan Ryūmonsha (Tokyo: Shibusawa Eiichi Denki Shiryō Kankōkai, 1955–1971), 3:548.

65. The Meiji government paid 4 million yen in cash to clear loans from foreign sources. For the debt of 12.82 million yen that had accrued between 1868 and 1872, it issued bonds bearing an interest rate of 4 percent and planned to repay them over twenty-five years. As to the 11.23 million yen debt that had accrued before 1842, it decided to return it without interest over fifty years. Yamamoto Yūzō, "Meiji Ishinki no zaisei to tsūka" [Finance and currency in the Meiji Restoration], in *Nihon keizaishi* [The economic history of Japan], vol. 3, *Kaikō to Ishin* [The opening of Japan and the Restoration], ed. Umemura Mataji and Yamamoto Yūzō (Tokyo: Iwanami Shoten, 1989), 147 and 150.

66. Before the end in September 1869 of the counterfeiting of shogunate coins, the annual profit that the domain government in Satsuma received from this practice was 1.5 million ryō; this was its largest item of revenue. Cited from Niwa Kunio, *Chiso kaiseihō no kigen*, 10.

67. Sekiguchi Eiichi, "Haihan chiken to Min-Zō gappei: Rususeifu to Ōkurasho—1" [The abolishing of the domains and the merging of the Ministries of Civil Affairs and Finance, part 1], *Hōgaku* 43, no. 3 (December 1979): 308.

68. Shibusawa Eiichi recalled many years later that "Ōkubo was not only unfamiliar with financial affairs but also found their principles difficult to understand." Cited in Niwa Kunio, *Chiso kaiseihō no kigen*, 251.

69. Fujimura Tōru, *Meiji zaisei kakuritsu katei no kenkyū*, 154–155.

70. Sawada Akira, *Meiji zaisei no kisoteki kenkyū*, 115.

71. Mamiya Kunio, "Shōhōshi no soshiki to kinō" [Organization and function of the Bureau of Commerce], *Shakai keizai shigaku* 29, no. 2 (1963): 138–158.

72. Yunoki Manabu, "Hyogo shōsha to Ishin seifu no keizai seisaku" [The commercial house of Hyogo and the economic policy of the Restoration government], *Shakai keizai shigaku* 35, no. 2 (1969): 17.

73. Shinbo Hiroshi, *Nihon kindai shin'yō seido seiritsu shiron* [The establishment of the credit system in modern Japan] (Tokyo: Yūhikaku, 1968), 16. Nakamura Naomi also emphasizes that the semiofficial, semiprivate nature of Tsūhōshi and the concentration of its lending to lords were the main reasons for its failure. See Nakamura Naomi, *Ōkuma zaisei no kenkyū* [The public finance policies of Ōkuma] (Tokyo: Azekura Shobō, 1968), 29–30.

74. Yamamoto Yūzō, "Meiji Ishinki no zaisei to tsūka," 3:129.

75. In 1864, Ōkuma and other samurai officials had opened trading houses in Osaka and Nagasaki to promote the sales of commodities made in Saga and

used the monies earned thereby to back up the paper notes issued by the Saga government. Nakamura Naomi, *Ōkuma Shigenobu* (Tokyo: Yoshikawa Kō-bunkan, 1961), 27–28.

76. Shinbo Hiroshi, *Nihon kindai shin'yō seido seiritsu shiron*, 32.

77. Ibid., 33.

78. Umemura Mataji, "Meiji Ishinki no keizai seisaku" [Meiji Restoration economic policies], *Keizai kenkyū* 30, no. 1 (January 1979): 36.

79. Niwa Kunio, *Chiso kaiseihō no kigen*, 62–63 and 75.

80. Okada Shunpei, "Meiji shoki no tsūka kyōkyū seisaku" [Monetary supply policy in the early Meiji], in *Meiji shoki no zaisei kin'yū seisaku* [Early Meiji fiscal and financial policies], ed. Okada Shunpei (Tokyo: Seimeikai Sōsho, 1964); Niwa Kunio, *Chiso kaiseihō no kigen*, 67.

81. The Ministry of Finance, "Shihei kaitei no gi" [A note on the reformation of paper notes], 1872, in *Ōkuma monjo*, microfilm A 1748.

82. Yamamoto Yūzō, "Meiji Ishinki no zaisei to tsūka," 133.

83. Harada Mikio, *Nihon no kindaika to keizai seisaku: Meiji kōgyōka seisaku kenkyū* [Economic policies and the modernization of Japan] (Tokyo: Tōyō Keizai Shinpōsha, 1972), 174.

84. Senda Minoru, "Meiji rokunen shichibu ritsuki gaisai no boshū katei" [On the 7 percent sterling foreign loan floated in 1873], *Shakai keizai shigaku* 49, no. 5 (December 1983): 445–470.

85. Suzuki Eiki, "Iwakura shisetsudan hensei katei e no ashitana shiten" [A new perspective on organizing the Iwakura Mission], *Jinmon gakuhō* 78 (March 1996): 43.

86. As early as December 1871, Inoue Kaoru and Yoshida Kiyonari had pointed out the importance of the customs not only to raise government revenue but also to reduce the burden of land taxes. Inoue Kaoru and Yoshida Kiyonari, "Shokusan kōgyō seisaku to zeisei kaikaku ni tsuite no kengi" [On reforming the domestic taxation (November 1871)], in *Nihon kindai shisō taikei* [Compendium of modern thought in Japan], vol. 8, *Keizai kōsō* [Economic schemes], ed. Nakamura Masanori et al. (Tokyo: Iwanami Shoten, 1988), 145.

87. See Banno Junji, *Kindai Nihon no kokka kōsō, 1871–1936* [Visions of the state in modern Japan, 1871–1936] (Tokyo: Iwanami Shoten, 1996), chapter 1.

88. For the proposals from ordinary samurai and commoners in 1874 to establish a parliamentary system to supervise public finance, see Makihara Norio, *Meiji shichinen no daironsō: Kenpakusho kara mite kindai kokka to minshū* [The great debates of 1874: The modern state and the people as viewed from the "Proposals from the People"] (Tokyo: Nihon Keizai Hyōronsha, 1990), 32–36.

89. Banno Junji, "Meiji kokka no seiritsu," 78.

90. Ibid., 72.

91. Cited in Fukushima Masao, *Chiso kaisei no kenkyū* [Land tax reform] (Tokyo: Yūhikaku, 1970), 99, footnote 2.

92. Matsukata Masayoshi, "Kokka fukyō no konpon o shōreishi hukyū no hi o habukubeki no ikensho" [A proposal on encouraging the basic enterprises of the country and cutting nonurgent expenditures], (to Ōkuma, 1873), in *Ōkuma monjo,* 2:A968, 2.

93. Calculated from table 19 in Fujimura Tōru, *Meiji zenki kōsai seisakushi kenkyū* [Bond policy in early Meiji] (Tokyo: Daitō Bunka Daigaku Tōyō Kenkyū-sho, 1977), 85.

94. Ibid., 86.

95. Yoshiwara Shigetoshi and Wakayama Norikazu, "Dairokuka nenpō" [No. 6 annual report], December 1875, in *Ōkuma monjo,* microfilm, A1899.

96. Fukuchi Atsushi, *Meiji shinseiken no kenryoku kōzō,* 122–123.

97. Yamazaki Yūkō, "Nihon kindaika Shuhō o meguru sōkoku: Naimushō to Kōbushō" [Conflicts in the modernization policies in Japan: The Ministry of Civil Affairs and the Ministry of Industry], in *Kōbushō to sono jidai* [The Ministry of Industry and its time], ed. Suzuki Jun (Tokyo: Yamakawa Shuppansha, 2002), 125–126 and 134–135.

98. *Meiji zaiseishi* [A fiscal history of the Meiji], ed. Meiji zaiseishi hensankai (Tokyo: Yoshikawa Kōbunkan, 1972), 11:338.

99. Mikami Ryūzō, *En no tanjō: Kindai kahei seido no seiritsu* [The birth of the yen: The establishment of the modern monetary system], rev. and enlarged ed. (Tokyo: Tōyō Keizai Shinpōsha, 1989), 211.

100. On the establishment of the gold standard in the international markets in the 1870s, see Barry J. Eichengreen, *Globalizing Capital: A History of the International Monetary System* (Princeton, NJ: Princeton University Press, 1996), 17–18.

101. Yamamoto Yūzō, "Nai ni shihei ari gai ni bokugin ari" [Paper money for domestic transactions and Mexican dollars for foreign trade], *Jinmon gakuhō* 55 (September 1983): 40–44.

102. Ōkurashō [The Ministry of Finance], "Kahei chūzo no ji" [On the coinage of currency, 1875], in *Ōkuma monjo,* microfilm, A. 1748.

103. In Ōkuma's words, "the use of paper notes depended solely on the guarantee of specie in gold. . . . [Therefore] the outflow of gold will ultimately ruin the credibility of paper notes and put the country in danger." Ōkuma Shigenobu, "Zeikan shūnyūkin ni kansuru jōshinsho" [A memorial in regard to the customs], (20 July 1875), in *Ōkuma monjo,* 3:A2341, 117.

104. In August 1874, the Meiji government's total debt was 138.44 million yen, of which the total amount of paper notes was 97.64 million yen. Cited from *Ōkuma monjo,* microfilm, A 2399.

105. For example, Shimazu Hisamitsu, former lord of Satsuma and a prominent political figure in the Meiji Restoration, urged the government to implement "fiscal retrenchment" to overcome the fiscal difficulties. See Banno Junji, "Meiji kokka no seiritsu," 74–75.

106. Seki Yoshiomi, "Meiji hachi-nendō Ōkurashō nenpō sakusei iken" [A note on the making of the 1875 annual report of the Ministry of Finance], in Ōkuma monjo, microfilm, A 2205.

107. The Ministry of Finance, "Kahei chūzō no ji" [On the mintage of coins], in Ōkuma monjo, microfilm, A 1748.

108. Kawaji Hirodō, "Genka ranshutsu ron [On the outflow of specie: A report to Ōkuma, October 1875)," in Ōkuma monjo, 4:A3415, 112–113, 114.

109. Matsukata Masayoshi, "Tsūka ryūshutsu o bōshi suru no kengi" [Proposal on preventing the outflow of specie] (September 1875), in Matsukata Masayoshi kankei monjo [Documents related to Matsukata Masayoshi], ed. Ōkubo Tatsumasa (Tokyo: Daitō Bunka Daigaku Tōyō Kenkyūjo, 2001), 20:36.

110. Ōkuma Shigenobu, "Shūnyū shishutsu no genryū o sumashi rizai kaikei no konpon o tatsru no gi" [On rectifying the sources of state revenues and building the foundation of public finance (January 1875)], in Ōkuma monjo, 3:A7, 104.

111. In fact, "chōrei bokai" (that a decree issued in the morning is changed in the evening) was one of the most frequent criticisms of the Meiji government's policy making.

112. Ōkuma Shigenobu, "Shūnyū shishutsu no genryū o sumashi rizai kaikei no konpon o tatsuru no gi" [On rectifying the sources of state revenues and building the foundation of public finance (January 1875)], in Ōkuma monjo, 3:A7, 104–105.

113. See the proposal in Ōkuma Shigenobu and Ōkubo Toshimichi, "Gaisai shōkyaku o mokuteki to suru Naimu-Ōkura ryōshō kiyaku hei kankei shorui" [On the cooperation of the Ministries of Finance and Civil Affairs in regard to the returning of foreign debt (November 1875)], Ōkuma monjo, 3:A2410, especially 147–149.

114. Nagai Hideo, "Shokusan kōgyō seisaku no kichō," 241.

115. The books and brochures published by the Government Printing Office of America, as well as the U.S. National Currency Act (3 June 1864), were translated into Japanese. Knowledge of the Bank of England mostly came from Arthur Latham Perry's Elements of Political Economy (1866), which had also been translated. Senda Minoru, "Kinsatsu shobun to kokuritsu ginkō" [The redemption of kinsatsu and the national banks], Shakai keizai shigaku 48, no. 1 (1982): 32.

116. Nakamura Naomi, Ōkuma zaisei no kenkyū, 38.

117. Senda Minoru, "Kinsatsu shobun to kokuritsu ginkō," 41–42.

118. The national bank *(kokuritsu ginkō)* was a direct translation of the term "national bank" as used in the United States. A national bank in Meiji Japan was thus not a state-owned bank but a private bank that received from the government the privilege to issue banknotes.

119. Nakamura Naomi, *Ōkuma zaisei no kenkyū*, 45.

120. *Shibusawa Eiichi denki shiryō*, 3:376–377.

121. Imuta Yoshimitsu, "Nihon ginkō no hakken seido to seifu kin'yū" [The Bank of Japan: Note issue and public finance], *Shakai keizai shigaku* 38, no. 2 (1972): 125–126.

122. Yamamoto Yūzō, "Meiji Ishinki no zaisei to tsūka," 155.

123. For the wasteful investment and inefficiency of the import-substitution projects in agriculture, animal husbandry, and woolen and cotton weaving, see Ishizuka Hiromichi, "Shokusan kōgyō seisaku no tenkai" [The unfolding of the shokusan kōgyō policies], in *Nihon keizeishi taikei* [Compendium of materials on the economic history of Japan], vol. 5, *Kindai* [The modern period], ed. Kajinishi Mitsuhaya (Tokyo: Tōkyō Daigaku Shuppankai, 1965), 55–56.

124. Ōkuma Shigenobu, "Ōkurashō dainikai nenpōsho" [The second annual report of the Ministry of Finance (12 July 1877)], in *Ōkuma monjo*, 3:A1567, 278.

125. Cited from Harada Mikio, *Nihon no kindaika to keizai seisaku*, 146.

126. Kawase Hideji, "Zaisei no gi ni tsuke kengen" [Proposals on public finance (5 July 1879)], in *Ōkuma monjo*, 2:A980, 103.

127. Yamamoto Yūzō, "Meiji Ishinki no zaisei to tsūka," 158.

128. Ochiai Hiroki, *Meiji kokka to shizoku* [The Meiji state and the samurai] (Tokyo: Yoshikawa Kōbunkan, 2001), 218.

129. Iwakura Tomomi, "Proposal on helping the enterprises of peers and samurai" (July 1878), cited in ibid., 216.

4. The Emergence of the Modern Fiscal State in Japan, 1880–1895

1. On Matsukata Masayoshi and his financial policies after 1882, see Jackson H. Bailey, "The Meiji Leadership: Matsukata Masayoshi," in *Japan Examined: Perspectives on Modern Japanese History,* ed. Harry Wray and Hilary Conroy (Honolulu: University of Hawaii Press, 1983); Steven J. Ericson, "'Poor Peasant, Poor Country!' The Matsukata Deflation and Rural Distress in Mid-Meiji Japan," in *New Directions in the Study of Meiji Japan,* ed. Helen Hardacre and Adam L. Kern (Leiden and New York: Brill, 1997); and Muroyama Yoshimasa, *Matsukata zaisei kenkyū* [Matsukata's public finance policies] (Kyoto: Mineruva Shobō, 2004).

2. In April 1872, the total number of prefectures where the Ono house had offices and branches (or planned to do so) was thirty-five; Mitsui, thirteen; and Shimada, eight. See Iwasaki Hiroshi, "Kokuritsu ginkō seido no seiritsu to fuken kawasekata" [The establishment of the national banking system and the money transmitters of cities and prefectures], *Mitsui bunko ronso* 2 (March 1968): 215.

3. Ibid., 212.

4. When the Ono house declared bankruptcy, it had only 20,000 yen in cash and 110,000 yen in bonds and land deeds, while its total liabilities were 7.5 million yen, including 4.5 million yen in government deposits. Katō Kōzaburō, "Seishō shihon no keisei" [The formation of the capital of political merchants], in *Nihon keizaishi taikei*, vol. 5, *Kindai* [The modern period], ed. Kajinishi Mitsuhaya (Tokyo: Tōkyō Daigaku Shuppankai, 1965), 143.

5. Tatewaki Kazuo, *Meiji seifu to Orientaru Banku* [The Meiji government and the British Oriental bank] (Tokyo: Chūō Kōronsha, 1992), 156–157.

6. Fukaya Tokujirō, *Meiji seifu zaisei kiban no kakuritsu* [Laying the foundation of Meiji public finance] (Tokyo: Ochanomizu Shobō, 1995.), 69 and 70.

7. Sugiyama Kazuo, "Kin'yū seido no sōsetsu" [The establishment of the financial system], in *Nihon keizaishi taikei* [Compendium of materials on the economic history of Japan], vol. 5, *Kindai* [The modern period], ed. Kajinishi Mitsuhaya (Tokyo: Tōkyō Daigaku Shuppankai, 1965), 210.

8. Ikeda Kōtarō, "Kankin toriatsuka seisaku to shihonshūgi no seiritsu" [The handling of government funds and the establishment of capitalism], in *Meiji shoki no zaisei kin'yū seisaku* [Early Meiji fiscal and financial policies], ed. Okada Shunpei (Tokyo: Seimeikai Sōsho, 1964), 161.

9. Fukaya Tokujirō, *Meiji seifu zaisei kiban no kakuritsu*, 97–98.

10. Ikeda Kōtarō, "Kankin toriatsuka seisaku to shihonshūgi no seiritsu," 164.

11. Ōkuma Shigenobu, "Kensatsuka hashutsu no gi tsuke jōshin" [A proposal to send out inspecting financial officials], 30 October 1877, in *Ōkuma monjo*, microfilm, A2242.

12. Fukaya Tokujirō, *Meiji seifu zaisei kiban no kakuritsu*, 74.

13. Yamamura Kozo, "The Meiji Land Tax Reform and Its Effects," in *Japan in Transition: From Tokugawa to Meiji*, ed. Marius B. Jansen and Gilbert Rozman (Princeton, NJ: Princeton University Press, 1986), 387–388. For more on the collection of land taxes, see Fukushima Masao, *Chiso kaisei no kenkyū* [Land tax reform] (Tokyo: Yūhikaku, 1970).

14. Senda Minoru and Matsuo Masahito, *Meiji Ishin kenkyū josetsu: Ishin seiken no chokkatsuchi* [An introduction to the study of the Meiji Restoration: The territories under the direct administration of the Restoration government] (Tokyo: Kaimei Shoin, 1977), 253–254.

15. Niwa Kunio, "Chiso kaisei to nōgyō kōzō no henka" [Land tax reform and changes in the structure of agriculture], in *Nihon keizaishi taikei*, vol. 5, *Kindai* [The modern period], ed. Kajinishi Mitsuhaya (Tokyo: Tōkyō Daigaku Shuppankai, 1965), 236.

16. Yoshiwara Shigetoshi, "Sozei chōshūhō no kengi" [Proposals on the methods to collect taxes], September 1876, in *Ōkuma monjo,* microfilm, A1907.

17. Komatsu Kazuo, "Meiji zenki no shuzei seisaku to toshi shuzōgyō no dōkō" [The tax policy on sake production in the early Meiji and the trend of urban sake production], *Ōsaka daigaku keizaigaku* 17, no. 1 (June 1967): 39–40.

18. *Meiji zenki zaisei keizai shiryō shūsei* [Collected primary materials on the finance and economy of early Meiji], ed. Ōuchi Hyōe, Tsuchiya Takao, and Ōkurashō (Tokyo: Meiji Bunken Shiryō Kankōkai, 1962), 2:239 and 329.

19. Ōkurashō Honyakuka, "Gasshū ōkoku naikokuzei nenpō hensansho" [The annual report of the domestic taxation in the United Kingdom], in *Ōkuma monjo,* microfilm, A1842.

20. Yoshiwara Shigetoshi and Wakayama Norikazu, "Dairokuka nenpō" [No. 6 annual report], December 1875, in *Ōkuma monjo,* microfilm, A1899.

21. Fukaya Tokujirō, *Meiji seifu zaisei kiban no kakuritsu,* 186.

22. Ibid., 169–172.

23. This was the Japanese version of "political arithmetic," and former shogunate officials who had studied statistics in Holland, such as Tsuda Mamichi and Mitsukuri Rinshō, made important contributions to these efforts. See Haga Shōji, "Meiji Ishin to 'seihyō' no hensei" [The Meiji Restoration and the making of statistical data], *Nihonshi kenkyū* 388 (December 1994): 49–74.

24. Ōkurasho, "Sozei kōhai kōsei no gi tsuke jōshin" [A proposal on reforming taxation], in *Ōkuma monjo,* 3:A 1889, 52–53.

25. Fukaya Tokujirō, *Meiji seifu zaisei kiban no kakuritsu,* 171–176.

26. Ibid., 172.

27. Fujiwara Takao, *Kindai Nihon shuzōgyōshi* [A history of sake brewing in modern Japan] (Kyoto: Mineruva Shobō, 1999), 94–103.

28. Ibid., 109.

29. Tsuchiya Takao and Okazaki Saburō, *Nihon shihon shugi hattatsushi gaisetsu* [An outline of the development of capitalism in Japan] (Tokyo: Yūhikaku, 1948), 371.

30. Fukaya Tokujirō, *Meiji seifu zaisei kiban no kakuritsu,* 193.

31. Yoshikawa Akimasa's letter to Inoue Kaoru, 7 May 1873, in *Ōkuma monjo,* microfilm, A2174.

32. *Hundred-Year Statistics of the Japanese Economy,* ed. Nihon Ginkō Tōkeikyoku (Tokyo: Nihon Ginkō, 1966), 166.

33. Godai Tomoatsu, "Reply to the Inquiry about the Protection Tariffs" (5 October 1879), in *Godai Tomoatsu denki shiryō* [Biographical materials on

Godai Tomoatsu], ed. Nihon Keieishi Kenkyūjo (Tokyo: Tōyō Keizai Shinpō Sha, 1972), 2:254–263.

34. Miwa Ryōichi, *Nihon kindai no keizai seisakushiteki kenkyū* [A historical study of economic policy in modern Japan] (Tokyo: Nihon Keizai Hyōronsha, 2002), 47.

35. Tsurumi Masayoshi, *Nihon shin'yō kikō no kakuritsu: Nihon Ginkō to kin'yū shijō* [The establishment of a credit system in Japan: The Bank of Japan and the financial markets] (Tokyo: Yūhikaku, 1991), 104.

36. Ibid., 110–112.

37. Norio Tamaki, *Japanese Banking: A History, 1859–1959* (Cambridge and New York: Cambridge University Press, 1995), 45.

38. Emura Eiichi, *Jiyū minken kakumei no kenkyū* [The revolution of the People's Rights Movement] (Tokyo: Hōsei Daigaku Shuppankyoku, 1984), 92.

39. Masumi Junnosuke, *Nihon seijishi* [A political history of Japan] (Tokyo: Tōkyō Daigaku Shuppankai, 1988), 1:185.

40. Cited in Harada Mikio, *Nihon no kindaika to keizai seisaku: Meiji kōgyōka seisaku kenkyū* [Economic policies and the modernization of Japan] (Tokyo: Tōyō Keizai Shinpōsha, 1972), 162.

41. Ibid., 149.

42. Harada Mikio, *Nihon no kindaika to keizai seisaku*, 229.

43. Muroyama Yoshimasa, *Matsukata zaisei kenkyū*, 70.

44. Ōkuma Shigenobu, "Zaisei shiken o kyokō sen koto o kou no gi" [On four measures in public finance], 29 June 1879, in *Ōkuma monjo*, 3:A15, 348.

45. Kokaze Hidemasa, "Ōkuma zaisei matsuki ni okeru zaisei rongi no tenkai" [The development of the discussions on public finance in the later period of Ōkuma's public finance], in *Kindai Nihon no keizai to seiji* [Politics and economy in modern Japan], ed. Hara Akira (Tokyo: Yamakawa Shuppansha, 1986), 14–21.

46. Yoshihara Tatsuyuki, "Meiji zenki chūki no Yokohama Shōkin Ginkō" [The Yokohama Specie Bank in the early and middle Meiji], in *Nihon ni okeru kindai shakai no keisei* [The formation of a modern society in Japan], ed. Shōda Kenichirō (Tokyo: Sanrei Shoten, 1995), 262.

47. For private merchants' critiques of the direct export program, see *Yokohama shishi* [A history of Yokohama City] (Yokohama: Yokohamashi; distributed by Yūrindō, 1958–1982), vol. 3, part 1, 635–636.

48. Asukai Masamichi, "Kindai Tennōzō no tenkai" [The unfolding of the image of the emperor in modern Japan], in *Iwanami koza Nihon tsushi* [The Iwanami general history of Japan], vol. 17, *Kindai* (2) [The modern period], ed. Asao Naohiro et al. (Tokyo: Iwanami Shoten, 1994), 236–244.

49. Ōkuma Shigenobu, "Tsūka no seido o aramen ji o koto o kou no gi" [On changing the currency system], May 1880, in *Ōkuma monjo,* 3:A18, 447–450.

50. Muroyama Yoshimasa, *Kindai Nihon no gunji to zaisei: Kaigun kakuchō o meguru seisaku keisei katei* [Public finance and the military in modern Japan: The formation of policy regarding expansion of the navy] (Tokyo: Tōkyō Daigaku Shuppankai, 1984), 28–29.

51. Matsukata Masayoshi, "Zaisei kanki gairyaku" [My humble views on public finance], June 1880, in *Matsukata Masayoshi kankei monjo,* 20:529–535.

52. Ōkuma called this a "natural way of recovery" *(tennen kaifuku)* in international trade, which he considered an "eternal principle" *(jōhō)* of the economy. Ōkuma Shigenobu, "Tsūka no seido o aramen ji o koto o kou no gi" [On changing the currency system], May 1880, *Ōkuma monjo,* 3:A18, 453.

53. Ibid., 454.

54. Godai Tomoatsu, "Zaisei kyūji ikensho" [Views on rescuing public finance], in *Godai Tomoatsu denki shiryō,* 2:333.

55. Inoki Takenori, "Chiso beinōron to zaisei seiri" [The proposal of land taxation in rice and the adjustment of public finance], in *Matsukata zaisei to shokusan kōgyō seisaku* [Matsukata public finance and the policy of fostering production and encouraging enterprises], ed. Umemura Mataji and Nakamura Takafusa (Tokyo: Kokusai Rengō Daigaku, 1983), 108.

56. Ikegami Kazuo, "Meijiki no shuzei seisaku" [Sake tax policy in the Meiji era], *Shakai keizai shigaku* 55, no. 2 (June 1989): 74.

57. Ōkuma Shigenobu and Itō Hirobumi, "Zaisei kōkaku no gi" [On fundamentally reforming public finance], September 1880, in *Ōkuma monjo,* 3:A16.

58. Kokaze Hidemasa, "Ōkuma zaisei matsuki ni okeru zaisei rongi no tenkai," 15–19.

59. Ōkuma Shigenobu and Itō Hirobumi, "Kōsai o shinboshi oyobi ginkō o setsuritsu sen koto o kou no gi" [A proposal to issue new government bonds and to establish a bank], in *Ōkuma monjo,* 3:A21, 472–474.

60. Matsukata Masayoshi, "Zaisei gi" [On public finance], September 1881, in *Matsukata Masayoshi kankei monjo,* 20:340.

61. Muroyama Yoshimasa, *Matsukata zaisei kenkyū,* 127.

62. Muroyama Yoshimasa, "Matsukata defureishon no mekanizumu" [The mechanism of the Matsukata deflation], in *Matsukata zaisei to shokusan kōgyō seisaku* [Matsukata public finance and the policy of fostering production and encouraging enterprise], ed. Umemura Mataji and Nakamura Takafusa (Tokyo: Kokusai Rengō Daigaku, 1983), 149–151.

63. Ōishi Kaichirō, *Jiyū minken to Ōkuma, Matsukata zaisei* [The Freedom and People's Rights Movement and the public finance of Ōkuma and Matsukata] (Tokyo: Tōkyō Daigaku Shuppansha, 1989), 246.

64. Masumi Junnosuke, *Nihon seijishi*, 1:199. For an example of local elites' participation in the making of a prefectural government budget in the Kanagawa prefectural assembly in 1880, see M. William Steele, *Alternative Narratives in Modern Japanese History* (London: RoutledgeCurzon, 2003), 142–148.

65. Ōishi Kaichirō, *Nihon chihōzai gyōseishi josetsu: Jiyū Minken Undō to chihō jichisei* [A history of local public finance in Japan: The Freedom and People's Rights Movement and local self-governance], rev. ed. (Tokyo: Ochanomizu Shobō, 1978), 355–361.

66. Yokoyama Kōichirō, "Keibatsu chian kikō no seibi" [The arrangement of the institutions of punishment and security], in *Nihon kindai hōtaisei no keisei* [The formation of legal institutions in modern Japan], ed. Fukushima Masao (Tokyo: Nihon Hyōronsha, 1981), 1:328.

67. A copy of Ōkuma Shigenobu's proposal of March 1881 can be found in *Itō Hirobumi kankei monjo, shorui no bu*, no. 502, Modern Japanese Political History Materials Room, National Diet Library.

68. Inoue Kowashi, "Letter to Itō" (June 1881), cited in Ōkubo Toshiaki, *Meiji kokka no keisei* [The formation of the Meiji state] (Tokyo: Yoshikawa Kōbunkan, 1986), 330.

69. Ōkubo Toshiaki, *Meiji kokka no keisei*, 296.

70. Matsukata Masayoshi, "Zaisei gi" [On public finance], (September 1881), in *Matsukata Masayoshi kankei monjo*, 20:337–338.

71. Ibid., 332–335.

72. For the influence of the Belgian banking model in Japan, see Michael Schiltz, "An 'Ideal Bank of Issue': The Banque Nationale de Belgique as a Model for the Bank of Japan," *Financial History Review* 13, no. 2 (2006): 179–196.

73. The Postal Savings System in Japan was not important to public finance until the early twentieth century. See Katalin Ferber, "'Run the State Like a Business': The Origin of the Deposit Fund in Meiji Japan," *Japanese Studies* 22, no. 2 (2002): 131–151.

74. Muroyama Yoshimasa, *Kindai Nihon no gunji to zaisei*, 68.

75. In his proposal on issuing state bonds in December 1883, Matsukata argued that the level of 100 million yen in 1876 was appropriate for government paper notes, as these nonconvertible notes were used according to their face value at the time. Matsukata Masayoshi, "Kōsai shōsho hakkō ikensho" [A proposal on issuing state bonds], December 1883, in *Matsukata Masayoshi kankei monjo*, 20:99. Some government officials had expressed this view in the discussion of how to recover the value of paper notes in 1880. For example, an official from Aichi County, Kurokawa Haruyoshi, proposed to the central government that an efficient way to curb inflation was to quickly return the level of paper notes to that of 1877 and contended that the elimination of excessive and

unnecessary paper notes would not cause deflation. See Kurokawa Haruyoshi, "Kengi" [Proposal], October 1880, in *Inoue Kaoru kankei monjo*, no. 677-4, Modern Japanese Political History Materials Room, National Diet Library.

76. Fukaya Tokujirō, *Meiji seifu zaisei kiban no kakuritsu*, 144; Muroyama Yoshimasa, "Matsukata defureishon no mekanizumu," 146.

77. Fukaya Tokujirō, *Meiji seifu zaisei kiban no kakuritsu*, 144–145.

78. Godai Tomoatsu, "Ōsakafu kangyōka" [Reply to the Office of Encouraging Enterprises in the Ōsaka municipal government], 23 February 1883, in *Godai Tomoatsu denki shiryō*, 2:381.

79. "Dai-Ichi kokuritsu ginkō hanki jissai kōkajō, No. 18" [The No. 18 half-year performance reports of the Dai-Ichi National Bank], in *Shibusawa Eiichi denki shiryō* [Biographical materials of Shibusawa Eiichi], ed. Shibusawa Seien Kinen Zaidan Ryūmonsha (Tokyo: Shibusawa Eiichi Denki Shiryō Kankō-kai, 1955–1971), 4:425–426.

80. Masumi Junnosuke, *Nihon seijishi*, 204–205.

81. "Dai-Ichi Kokuritsu Ginkō hanki jissai kōkajō, No. 19 and No. 20" [The No. 19 and No. 20 half-year performance reports of the Dai-Ichi National Bank], in *Shibusawa Eiichi denki shiryō*, 4:427 and 428.

82. "Dai-Ichi Kokuritsu Ginkō hanki jissai kōkajō, No. 21" [The No. 21 half-year performance reports of the Dai-Ichi National Bank], in *Shibusawa Eiichi denki shiryō*, 4:430.

83. Matsukata Masayoshi, "Shurui zōkokuzei zōka no gi" [The proposal to raise the duties on alcohol production], month unknown, 1882, in *Matsukata Masayoshi kankei monjo*, 20:250.

84. Godai Tomoatsu, "Reply to the Osaka municipal government's inquiry," 19 January 1884, in *Godai Tomoatsu denki shiryō*, 2:484.

85. Takahashi Hidenao, "Matsukata zaiseiki no gunbi kakuchō mondai" [The issue of military expansion in the public finance of Matsukata], *Shakai keizai shigaku* 56, no. 1 (April 1990): 7, table 3.

86. Matsukata Masayoshi, "Ōkurashō ni kakuchihōkan shūkai no sekijō ni oite" [A talk to magistrates convened by the Ministry of Finance], 10 December 1883, in *Matsukata Masayoshi kankei monjo*, 20:619.

87. Ibid., 622.

88. Matsukata Masayoshi, "Nihon Ginkō sōritu no gi" [On the establishment of the Bank of Japan], 1 March 1883, in *Matsukata Masayoshi kankei monjo*, 20:351.

89. Hugh T. Patrick, "Japan, 1868–1914," in *Banking in the Early Stages of Industrialization: A Study in Comparative Economic History*, ed. Rondo Cameron, Olga Crisp, and Hugh T. Patrick (Oxford and New York: Oxford University Press, 1967), 248.

90. Yagi Yoshikazu, "'Meiji 14 nen seihen' to Nihon Ginkō: Kyōdō Un'yu Kaisha o megutte" [The "1881 coup d'état" and the loan of the Bank of Japan to the Kyodo Un'yu Kaisha], *Shakai keizai shigaku* 53, no. 5 (December 1987): 643.

91. Ibid., 637.

92. Ibid., 636.

93. Kamiyama Tsuneo, *Meiji keizai seisakushi no kenkyū* [A history of Meiji economic policies] (Tokyo: Hanawa Shobō, 1995), 56–57.

94. Ibid., 28–29.

95. *Yokohama shishi,* vol. 3, part 1, 625.

96. The Dai-Ichi National Bank noted this at the time. "Dai-Ichi Kokuritsu Ginkō hanki jissai kōkajō, No. 25" [The No. 25 half-year performance reports of the Dai-Ichi National Bank], in *Shibusawa Eiichi denki shiryō,* 4:437.

97. Kamiyama Tsuneo, *Meiji keizai seisakushi no kenkyū,* 24–26.

98. Muroyama Yoshimasa, *Matsukata zaisei kenkyū,* 210.

99. Tsurumi Masayoshi, *Nihon shin'yō kikō no kakuritsu,* 157–177.

100. Ishii Kanji, ed., *Nihon Ginkō kin'yū seisakushi* [Historical studies of the financial policy of the Bank of Japan] (Tokyo: Tōkyō Daigaku Shuppankai, 2001), 27.

101. Nakamura Takafusa, "Makuro keizei to sengo kei'ei" [The macroeconomy and postwar management], in *Nihon keizaishi* [The economic history of Japan], vol. 5, *Sangyōka no jidai (ge)* [The age of industrialization, part 2], ed. Nishikawa Shunsaku and Abe Takeshi (Tokyo: Iwanami Shoten, 1990), 11.

102. Nagaoka Shinkichi, *Meiji kyōkōshi josetsu* [Financial panic in Meiji Japan] (Tokyo: Tōkyō Daigaku Shuppankai, 1971), 19–21; Steven J. Ericson, *The Sound of the Whistle: Railroads and the State in Meiji Japan* (Cambridge, MA: Council on East Asian Studies of Harvard University Press, 1996), 123–126.

103. Henry Rosovsky, "Japan's Transition to Modern Economic Growth, 1868–1885," in *Industrialization in Two Systems: Essays in Honor of Alexander Gerschenkron by a Group of His Students,* ed. Henry Rosovsky (New York: John Wiley & Sons, 1966); Richard Sylla, "Financial Systems and Economic Modernization," *Journal of Economic History* 62, no. 2 (June 2002): 277–292.

104. Komatsu Kazuo, "Meiji zenki no shuzei seisaku to toshi shuzōgyō no dōkō," 48.

105. Yunoki Manabu, *Sakazukuri no rekishi* [A history of sake manufacturing] (Tokyo: Yūzankaku, 1987), 345–346.

106. Nakamura Takafusa, "Shuzōgyō no sūryōshi—Meiji-Shōwa shoki" [A quantitative history of sake brewing—Meiji to early Shōwa], *Shakai keizai shigaku* 55, no. 2 (June 1989): 217.

107. Fukaya Tokujirō, *Meiji seifu zaisei kiban no kakuritsu,* 110–111.

108. Banno Junji, *The Establishment of the Japanese Constitutional System*, trans. J. A. A. Stockwin (London and New York: Routledge, 1992), chapter 2.
109. Nakamura Takafusa, "Makuro keizai to sengo kei'ei," 13–16.

5. Economic Disruption and the Failure of
Paper Money in China, 1851–1864

1. Peng Zeyi, *Shijiu shiji houbanqi de Zhongguo caizheng yu jingji* [Economy and public finance in China in the second half of the nineteenth century] (Beijing: Renmin chubanshe, 1983), 136.

2. The Qing government issued a limited amount of paper notes in 1651 and 1661 to cover deficits but stopped this practice in 1661 when the government had adequate revenue. Peng Xinwei, *Zhongguo huobishi* [A history of currency in China], 2nd ed. (Shanghai: Shanghai renmin chubanshe, 1965), 808.

3. Ibid., 834; Yang Duanliu, *Qingdai huobi jinrong shigao* [A financial and monetary history of the Qing dynasty] (Beijing: Sanlian shudian, 1962), 105–108; Peng Zeyi, *Shijiu shiji houbanqi de Zhongguo caizheng yu jingji*, 91–96. Zhou Yumin, *Wan Qing caizheng yu shehui bianqian* [Public finance and social change in the late Qing] (Shanghai: Shanghai renmin chubanshe, 2000), 198; Katō Shigeshi, "On the Currency during the Reign of Xianfeng," in Katō Shigeshi, *Shina keizaishi kōshō* [Studies in Chinese economic history] (Tokyo: Tōyō Bunko, 1953), 2:438; and Jerome Ch'en, "The Hsien-Feng Inflation," *Bulletin of the School of Oriental and African Studies* 21 (1958): 578–586.

4. The memorial of Shen Zhaolin, 10 September 1857, in *Zhongguo jindai huobishi ziliao* (henceforth *ZJHZ*) [Historical materials on the monetary history of early modern China], ed. Zhongguo renmin yinhang canshishi jinrongshiliaozu (Beijing: Zhonghua shuju, 1964), 1:209.

5. For an emphasis on the state's political authority in creating a monopoly of currency, see Eric Helleiner, *The Making of National Money: Territorial Currencies in Historical Perspective* (Ithaca, NY: Cornell University Press 2003).

6. Peng Zeyi, *Shijiu shiji houbanqi de Zhongguo caizheng yu jingji*, 96; Wei Jianyou, *Zhongguo jindai huobishi* [A history of currency in early modern China] (Hefei: Huangshan shushe, 1986), 89–90.

7. Chiu Peng-sheng, "Shiba shiji Diantong shichang zhong de guanshang guanxi yu liyi guannian" ["Interests" in economic organization: The shaping of the Yunnan copper market in eighteenth-century China], *Zhongyang yanjiuyuan lishiyuyan yanjiusuo jikan* 72, no. 1 (2001): particularly 91–104; on the grain market, see Kishimoto Mio, "Shinchō chūki keizei seisaku no kichō" [The basic tune in the making of mid-Qing economic policies], in *Shindai Chūgoku no*

bukka to keizai hendō [Price and economic changes in Qing China] (Tokyo: Kenbun shuppan, 1997), 289–325; and Helen Dunstan, *State or Merchant? Political Economy and Political Process in 1740s China* (Cambridge, MA: Harvard University Asia Center, 2006), chapter 3.

8. Frank H. H. King, *Money and Monetary Policy in China, 1845–1895* (Cambridge, MA: Harvard University Press, 1965), 154.

9. See Chen Chau-nan, *Yongzheng Qianlong nianjian de yinqian bijia biandong* [A study of the fluctuations of the exchange rates between silver and copper coins during the reigns of Yongzheng and Qianlong] (Taipei: Zhongguo xueshu zhuzuo jiangzhu weiyuanhui, 1966), 42; Adachi Keiji, "Shindai zenki ni okeru kokka to zeni" [The state and cash in the early Qing period], *Tōyōshi kenkyū* 49, no. 4 (March 1991): 47–73; and Kuroda Akinobu, "Kenryū no senki" [The appreciation of copper cash in the Qianlong era], *Tōyōshi kenkyū* 45, no. 4 (March 1987): 692–723.

10. For a discussion of these policies and the underlying reasoning of supply and demand, see Hans Ulrich Vogel, "Chinese Central Monetary Policy, 1644–1800," *Late Imperial China* 8, no. 2 (December 1987): 13–14.

11. These two measures, along with four others, were recommended to provincial governments as "effective means" to reduce the value of copper coins in Beijing in an imperial decree dated 9 February 1745. Replies from Hunan, Hubei, Sichuan, Fujian, and Jiangxi Provinces and Suzhou Prefecture all considered them either impractical (e.g., to limit the stocks of copper coins in pawnshops) or unnecessary (e.g., to require the use of silver in large transactions). The Qianlong emperor admitted that these measures were temporary rectifications rather than efficacious solutions in the long run. *PM*, Box 60, No. 1610–1616, No. 1622–1625, No. 1637–1643, No. 1657–1661, No. 1662–1667, No. 1746–1750. See Qianlong's comment in No. 1610–1616.

12. Counterfeiting was more frequent when the Qing government began to mint light copper coins (1 *qian*, approximately 3.7 g) in 1684, and the melting of copper coins was widespread when the government minted heavy copper coins (1.4 qian) in 1702. Kuroda Akinobu, "Kenryū no senki," 694.

13. Kuroda Akinobu, "Kenryū no senki," 694; Richard von Glahn, *Fountain of Fortune: Money and Monetary Policy in China, 1000–1700* (Berkeley: University of California Press, 1996), 211; and the memorial of Haiwang, 18 March 1736, PM, Box 60, No. 119–124.

14. The memorial of Haiwang, 18 March 1736, *PM*, Box 60, No. 119–124. This famous memorial was later compiled into *Huangchao jingshi wenbian*, the canon of the statecraft school in the nineteenth century.

15. The emperor commented: "I am happy to read this discussion . . . which is clear, comprehensive, and well-reasoned." In the memorial of Shi Yizhi, 7 May 1736, *PM*, Box 60, No. 142–145.

16. Although the official copper content for copper coin was set at 1.2 mace (1.2 qian, approximately 4.44 g), the center allowed the provincial mints in Jiangsu and Hubei to cast copper coins with a copper content of 1 mace (1 qian) and 0.8 mace per wen (8 *fen*), respectively, in order to meet the increasing demand for cash in these two provinces. Kuroda Akinobu, "Kenryū no senki," 698.

17. Vogel, "Chinese Central Monetary Policy, 1644–1800," 45 and 48–49.

18. Imperial decree of 30 July 1769, *PM,* Box 61, No. 2482–2484. A decree of 27 May 1791 stated unambiguously that the use of private copper coins was against the law. *PM,* Box 63, No. 75–77.

19. Wang Yeh-chien, *Zhongguo jindai huobi yu yinhang de yanjin (1644–1937)* [The evolution of currency and banking in early modern China (1644–1937)] (Taipei: Zhongyang yanjiuyuan jingji yanjiusuo, 1981), 16–18.

20. If the money was deposited by wage laborers or ordinary soldiers, the period was limited to two months; in the case of commercial transactions, the period could be two years. The memorial of Mohe et al., 22 April 1825, *Grand Council Memorial Copies* (henceforth GCMC), Box 678, No. 147–150.

21. Ye Shichang, *Yapian zhanzheng qianhou woguo de huobi xueshuo* [Monetary theory in China before and after the Opium War] (Shanghai: Shanghai renmin chubanshe, 1963), 39.

22. Lin Man-houng, "Two Social Theories Revealed: Statecraft Controversies over China's Monetary Crisis, 1808–1854," *Late Imperial China* 12, no. 2 (December 1991): 1–35."

23. The memorial of the Board of Revenue, 10 January 1843, *ZJHZ,* 1:150.

24. Cited from the memorial of the Board of Revenue, 20 December 1850, *ZJHZ,* 1:171.

25. The memorial of Baoji, 25 February 1854, *GCMC,* Box 678, No. 2557–2560.

26. See the memorial of Lü Quansun and the reply from the Board of Revenue in *ZJHZ,* 1:191–194.

27. The memorial of Jia Shixing, 2 January 1854, *ZJHZ,* 1:379.

28. The memorial of the Board of Revenue, 25 August 1853, *ZJHZ,* 1:361.

29. The Qing government seemed to consider that it was repressing domestic rebellions for the benefit of the wealthy, and therefore merchants should not charge high interest in lending to the government. See this attitude in the memorial of Prince Ruihua and the Board of Revenue, 4 August 1860, *GCMC,* Box 679, No. 2920–2923.

30. See the memorial of the Fujian governor Wang Yide, 6 July 1852, in the Board of Revenue's reply to his proposal in *ZJHZ,* 1:322.

31. See the memorial of the Jiangsu governor Yang Wending, 23 December 1852, in the Board of Revenue's reply to his memorial in *ZJHZ,* 1:324–327.

32. Ibid., 1:327.

33. The memorial of Board of Revenue, *ZJHZ*, 1:203–205.

34. Ibid., 1:206–207.

35. The memorial of the Board of Revenue, 26 February 1853, *GCMC*, Box 310, Vol. 4463, No. 24.

36. The memorial of the Board of Revenue, 23 December 1852, *ZJHZ*, 1:327.

37. The memorial of Wang Yide, 14 April 1853, *ZJHZ*, 1:338.

38. The memorial of the Board of Revenue on the issue of silver notes, 26 March 1853, *ZJHZ*, 1:349–351.

39. The memorial of the Board of Revenue, 7 August 1853, *ZJHZ*, 1:352–355.

40. The memorial of the Board of Revenue, 17 December 1853, *ZJHZ*, 1:372–377.

41. The memorial of Board of Revenue, *GCMC*, Box 679, No. 2985–2986.

42. The Board of Revenue regulations on paper notes, in *ZJHZ*, 1:359.

43. The imperial decree of issuing paper notes, 5 April 1853, *ZJHZ*, 1:352.

44. The imperial decree on issuing paper notes, 5 April 1853, *ZJHZ*, 1:352.

45. The memorial of the Board of Revenue, 5 April 1853, *GCMC*, Box 678, No. 1993–2001.

46. The memorial of the Board of Revenue, 7 August 1853, *ZJHZ*, 1:354.

47. The memorial of Board of Revenue, 17 December 1853, *ZJHZ*, 1:373.

48. The memorial of the censor Zhang Siheng, 24 September 1853, *ZJHZ*, 1:364–365.

49. The memorial of Yang Yizeng, 19 December 1853, *ZJHZ*, 1:378.

50. Huang Jianhui, *Shanxi piaohaoshi* [A history of Shanxi bankers], rev. ed. (Taiyuan: Shanxi jingji chubanshe, 2002), 114–121.

51. The memorial of the governor-general of Jiangnan and Jiangxi Yiliang and Jiangsu governor Jierhanga, 11 July 1854, *GCMC*, Box 678, No. 2876–2877.

52. The memorial of Zhejiang governor Huang Zonghan, 26 January 1855, *GCMC*, Box 678, No. 3499–3501.

53. The local government in Jiangsu first reported the collection of lijin as an effective way to raise revenue to the center, and the center immediately approved this method and requested that other provincial governments adopt the same measure. See Susan Mann, *Local Merchants and the Chinese Bureaucracy, 1750–1950* (Stanford, CA: Stanford University Press, 1987), 95–96.

54. The memorial of the Board of Revenue, 26 September 1853, *ZJHZ*, 1:260–261.

55. Ni Yuping, *Qingdai caoliang haiyun yu shehui bianqian* [The seaborne transport of tribute grain and social change in the Qing dynasty] (Shanghai: Shanghai shudian chubanshe, 2005), 101–102.

56. Along the Grand Canal in peaceful years, manufactured goods from Jiangsu, Zhejiang, Anhui, Jiangxi, and Hubei, including cotton cloth, tea, and paper, were sent to the north, and grains and soy beans from Shandong, Henan, and Zhili were sent to the south. See Li Wenzhi and Jiang Taixin, *Qingdai caoyun* [The transportation of tribute grain in the Qing] (Beijing: Zhonghua shuju, 1993), 482–513.

57. Huang Jianhui, *Shanxi piaohaoshi,* 174.

58. The memorial of the censor Zhang Siheng, 24 September 1853; and the memorial of Wang Maoyin, 2 April 1854; both in *ZJHZ,* 1:364 and 392, respectively.

59. The memorial of the Board of Revenue on the issue of paper notes, 7 August 1853, *ZJHZ,* 1:354.

60. The memorial of Wang Maoyin, 2 April 1854, *ZJHZ,* 1:392.

61. A reply to the memorial of Wang Maoyin from the Grand Councilors and Board of Revenue, 5 April 1854, *ZJHZ,* 1:395.

62. As the censor Wu Aisheng pointed out, businessmen in Beijing had ready access to the *Capital Gazette,* which freely copied the memorials on the financial situation of the government. The memorial of the censor Wu Aisheng, 20 May 1854, *ZJHZ,* 1:402.

63. For example, the funds from Guangdong that the center allocated to Jiangxi Province were directly sent to the Jiangnan military supply station, without going through the provincial treasury of Jiangxi Province. See the memorial of the governor-general of Liangguang Ye Mingchen and Guangdong governor Baigui, in *Qing zhengfu zhenya Taiping Tianguo dang'an shiliao* (henceforth *QZZTTDS*) [Archival materials on the Qing government's suppression of the Taiping Heavenly Kingdom], ed. Zhongguo diyi lishi dang'anguan (Beijing: Shehui kexue wenxian chubanshe, 1994), 11:442.

64. The view of Wang Yide was representative. "The available silver stocks were inadequate to meet military spending, and therefore there was little surplus fund [for the Yongfeng Money Exchange Office]." The memorial of acting governor-general of Fujian and Zhejiang Wang Yide, 28 August 1853, *ZJHZ,* 1:431.

65. The memorial of the Jiangnan Director-General of the Grand Canal Yang Yizeng, 6 June 1854, GCMC, Box 678, No. 2839–2841.

66. The memorial of the censor Zhang Siheng, 24 September 1853; and the memorial of Wang Maoyin, 2 April 1854; both in *ZJHZ,* 1:364 and 392, respectively.

67. Cui Zhiqing et al., *Taiping Tianguo zhanzheng quanshi* [A comprehensive military history of the Taiping Rebellion] (Nanjing: Nanjing daxue chubanshe, 2002), 2:851–852, 864–866, and 890–894.

68. The memorial of Wang Maoyin, *QZZTTDS,* 10:234.

69. The memorial of Shanxi governor, *QZZTTDS*, 10:103 and 232.

70. Ni Yuping, *Boyi yu junheng: Qingdai Lianghuai yanzheng gaige* [Games and equilibria: Reforms in the salt administration of Lianghuai in the Qing dynasty] (Fuzhou: Fujian renmin chubanshe, 2006), 157.

71. The memorial of Changlu Salt Supervisor Wenqian, 20 November 1853, *QZZTTDS*, 10:602.

72. In Southern Song, merchants were willing to hold government nonconvertible paper notes because the government granted them a monopoly on the sale of salt. See Gao Congming, *Songdai huobi yu huobi liutong yanjiu* [Money and monetary circulation in the Song dynasty] (Baoding: Heibei daxue chubanshe, 2000), 290–293.

73. The memorial of the Board of Revenue, 28 October 1858, *GCMC*, Box 679, No. 1773–1782.

74. The memorial of Yinggui, 19 June 1854, *GCMC*, Box 678, No. 2852–2856.

75. The memorial of Zhang Liangji, 6 January 1854, *GCMC*, Box 310, Vol. 4462, No. 56–57.

76. The memorial of the Board of Revenue, 10 March 1854, *QZZTTDS*, 12:493–494.

77. The memorial of the Jiangnan Director-General of the Grand Canal Yang Yizeng et al., 24 October 1854, *GCMC*, Box 678, No. 3314–3315.

78. The memorial of Gengchang, 25 July 1856, *GCMC*, Box 679, No. 709–711.

79. The memorial of Guizhou governor Jiang Weiyuan, 13 July 1855, *GCMC*, Box 679, No. 281–283.

80. The memorial of Yang Yizeng et al., 21 August 1854, *GCMC*, Box 678, No. 2876–2877.

81. The memorial of the governor-general of Fujian and Zhejiang and Fujian governor Wang Yide, 7 April 1854, *GCMC*, Box 678, No. 2687–2691.

82. The memorial of Wang Maoyin, 1853, in *Dao Xian Tong Guang sichao zouyi* [Memorials from the four reign periods of Dao[guang], Xian[feng], Tong[zhi], and Guang[xu]], ed. Wang Yunwu (Taipei: Taiwan shangwu yinshuguan, 1970), 3:1098.

83. The memorial of the Jiangnan Director-General of the Grand Canal Yang Yizeng et al., 21 August 1854, *GCMC*, Box 678, No. 3054–3056.

84. The censor Chen Qingyong observed that the value of copper coins relative to silver in early 1853 was almost double; sometimes people could not even exchange their silver for copper coins. The memorial of Chen Qingyong, 25 March 1853, *ZJHZ*, 1:342.

85. The censor Jia Shixing proposed that the government lend official notes to money exchangers *(zhangju)* and pawnshops to resume their normal

operation. In his view, "the dearth of private notes provides an opportunity for the circulation of official notes." The memorial of censor Jia Shixing, 8 June 1853, *GCMC*, Box 678, No. 2095–2096.

86. These offices were named Tianyuan, Tianheng, Tianli, Tianzhen, and Xitianyuan. The Imperial Household allocated them 500,000 tael silver as capital. See the memorial of Jingzheng, 16 January 1842, *ZJHZ*, 1:467.

87. The memorial of the Board of Revenue, 28 March 1855, *ZJHZ*, 1:409.

88. The memorial of the Board of Revenue, 28 October 1858, *GCMC*, Box 679, No. 1773–1782.

89. The imperial edict to urge the establishment of money exchange offices, 22 November 1855, *ZJHZ*, 1:450.

90. The memorial of the Board of Revenue, 22 November 1855, *ZJHZ*, 1:448.

91. The memorial of Shandong governor Wenyi, 15 December 1860, *GCMC*, Box 679, No. 2964–2966.

92. See an example in the memorial of Qiao Songnnian, in *Wu Xu dang'an xuanbian* [Selected materials from the Wu Xu archives], ed. Taiping Tianguo lishi bowuguan (Nanjing: Jiangsu renmin chubanshe, 1983), 6:97.

93. Yang Duanliu, *Qingdai huobi jinrong shigao*, 35.

94. The memorial of Prince Mianyu et al., 25 February 1857; and the memorials of Chengzhi and Woren, 24 April 1857; both in *GCMC*, Box 679, No. 1008–1011 and No. 1090–1091, respectively.

95. See the big variations of copper contents in mintage in *ZJHZ*, 1:252–259.

96. The memorial of the Board of Revenue, 24 September 1854, *GCMC*, Box 678, No. 3192–3194.

97. King, *Money and Monetary Policy in China*, 149–150.

98. The memorial of Prince Zaiyuan and the Board of Revenue, 1 April 1860, *GCMC*, Box 679, No. 2554–2557.

99. The memorial of the Board of Revenue, 10 January 1858, *GCMC*, Box 679, No. 1448–1450.

100. The memorial of the Jiangnan Director-General of the Grand Canal Gengchang, 26 January 1858; and the memorial of the Shandong-Henan Director-General of the Grand Canal Li Jun, 25 April 1858; both in *GCMC*, Box 679, No. 1512–1516 and No. 1643–1645, respectively.

101. The reply of the Board of Revenue noted on the memorial of Li Jun, 11 May 1858, *GCMC*, Box 679, No. 1646–1649.

102. The memorial of the Shandong-Henan Director-General of the Grand Canal Li Jun, 1 April 1858; and the memorial of the Jiangnan Director-General of the Grand Canal Gengchang, 22 June 1859; both in *GCMC*, Box 679, No. 1623–1625 and No. 1953–1955, respectively.

103. The memorial of Prince Mianyu et al., 1 March 1860, *ZJHZ*, 1:412.

104. The memorial of the Board of Revenue, 25 October 1860, *GCMC*, Box 679, No. 2949–2950.

105. Peng Zeyi, *Shijiu shiji houbanqi de Zhongguo caizheng yu jingji*, 95–96.

106. The memorial of Zhang Zhiwan, 26 February 1855, *ZJHZ*, 1:441.

107. The memorials of the governor-general of Fujian and Zhejiang Wang Yide, 24 April 1854, *ZJHZ*, 1:399; and 22 July 1854, *GCMC*, Box 678, No. 3059–3061.

108. The memorial of Wu Tang, 12 April 1862, *GCMC*, Box 679, No. 3199.

109. The memorial of Shaanxi governor Yingqi, 17 April 1862, *GCMC*, Box 679, No. 3224–3225.

110. Peng Xinwei, *Zhongguo huobishi*, 832; Wang Hongbin, "Lun Guangxu shiqi yinjia xialuo yu bizhi gaige" [On the falling value of silver and monetary reform during the reign of Guangxu], *Shixue yuekan* 5 (1988): 47–53.

111. The memorial of the governor-general of Fujian and Zhejiang Wang Yide et al., 6 March 1859, *GCMC*, Box 679, No. 1873–1877.

112. The memorial of Shandong governor Chongen, 21 January 1858, *GCMC*, Box 679, No. 1498–1500.

113. The memorial of the Grand Council, 1 June 1857, *GCMC*, Box 679, No. 1161–1170.

114. C. John Stanley, *Late Ch'ing Finance: Hu Kuang-yung as an Innovator* (Cambridge, MA: East Asian Research Center of Harvard University, 1961), 9–12.

115. The memorial of the governor-general of Fujian and Zhejiang Qingduan and Fujian governor Ruibing, 8 March 1860, *GCMC*, Box 679, No. 2734–2737.

116. *Shanxi piaohao shiliao* [Historical materials on the Shanxi banks], ed. Huang Jianhui et al., rev. ed. (Taiyuan: Shanxi jingji chubanshe, 2002), 75–80.

117. When the Jiangxi governor Shen Baozhen was concerned about entrusting 50,000 tael to the Xintaihou Bank for remittance to Beijing, his subordinates told him that this bank had a good reputation in the province for remitting both official and commercial funds. The memorial of Shen Baozhen, 12 April 1863, cited in ibid., 80.

6. The Persistence of Fiscal Decentralization in China, 1864–1911

1. For a classic description of this era, see Mary C. Wright, *The Last Stand of Chinese Conservatism: The T'ung-Chih Restoration, 1862–1874* (Stanford, CA: Stanford University Press, 1957).

2. The amount of silver that flowed into China between 1871 and 1913 is estimated to have been around 241 million in Haikwan tael. Calculated from

table IV in Charles F. Remer, *The Foreign Trade of China* (Shanghai: Commercial Press, 1926), 215.

3. Xu Daling, *Qingdai juanna zhidu* [The sale of official rank during the Qing] (Beijing: Yanjing daxue Hafo Yanjing xueshe, 1950); reprinted in *Ming Qing shi lunji* [Collected papers on Ming-Qing history] (Beijing: Beijing daxue chubanshe, 2000), 158. For the discussion of officials titles sold to raise income in the 1860s and 1870s, see Elisabeth Kaske, "Fund-Raising Wars: Office Selling and Interprovincial Finance in Nineteenth-Century China," *Harvard Journal of Asiatic Studies* 71, no. 1 (June 2010): 69–141.

4. On informal provincial finance in the early nineteenth century, see Iwai Shigeki, "Shindai kokka zaisei ni okeru chūō to chihō" [The center-local relationship in the fiscal system of the Qing dynasty], *Tōyōshi kenkyū* 42, no. 2 (September 1983): 338–340.

5. Zhou Yumin, *Wan Qing caizheng yu shehui bianqian* [Public finance and social change in the late Qing] (Shanghai: Shanghai renmin chubanshe, 2000), 242; and Ho Hon-wai, "Qingji zhongyang yu gesheng caizheng guanxi de fansi" [A reflection upon the fiscal relationship between the center and provinces in the late Qing], *Zhongyang yanjiuyuan lishiyuyansuo jikan* 72, no. 3 (September 2001): 608.

6. Ho Hon-wai, "Qingji zhongyang yu gesheng caizheng guanxi de fansi," 633; and Marianne Bastid, "The Structure of Financial Institutions of the State in the Late Qing," in *The Scope of State Power in China,* ed. S. R. Schram (New York: St. Martin's Press, 1985), 66–67.

7. For example, in a memorial to the center in 2 July 1881, the governor-general of Sichuan Ding Baozhen highly praised the performance of Tang Jiong, the official in charge of the management of the official transportation of Sichuan salt in Sichuan and Guizhou. Although Ding expressed a strong desire to retain him in this post, the center appointed Tang as the treasurer of Yunnan Province a few months later. See *Guangxu chao Donghua lu* [The Guangxu period *Donghua lu*], ed. Zhu Shoupeng, (Beijing: Zhonghua shuju, 1958), 1:1108 and 2:1298.

8. Wei Guangqi, "Qingdai houqi zhongyang jiquan caizheng tizhi de wajie" [The collapse of the centralized fiscal system in the late Qing], *Jindaishi yanjiu* 31, no. 1 (1986): 207–230; Chen Feng, "Qingdai zhongyang caizheng yu difang caizheng de tiaozheng" [The adjustment of the relationship between the center and local governments in public finance], *Lishi yanjiu* 5 (1997): 111–114; and He Lie, *Lijin zhidu xintan* [A new exploration of the institution of *lijin*] (Taipei: Shangwu yinshuguan, 1972), 157–160.

9. Liu Kwang-ching, "Wan Qing dufu quanli wenti shangque" [A reexamination of the power of provincial governors during the late Qing], reprinted in

Jingshi sixiang yu xinxing qiye [The statecraft approach and the new enterprises] (Taipei: Lianjing chuban shiye gongsi, 1990), 243–297. For an emphasis on central authority over governors in the late Qing, see Liu Wei, "Jiawu qian sishi nianjian dufu quanli de yanbian" [Changes to the power of provincial governors between 1855 and 1895], *Jindaishi yanjiu* 2 (1998): 59–81. As to the modern navy established in 1885, Hosomi Kazuhiro notes that the Board of Revenue could assert the central authority by controlling the allocation of naval expenditures. See Hosomi Kazuhiro, "Ri Kōshō to kobu" [Li Hongzhang and the Board of Revenue], *Tōyōshi kenkyū* 56, no. 4 (March 1998): 811–838.

10. Ho Hon-wai, "Qingji zhongyang yu gesheng caizheng guanxi de fansi," 611.

11. Ma Linghe, *Wan Qing waizaishi yanjiu* [A study of the history of foreign loans in the late Qing] (Shanghai: Fudan daxue chubanshe, 2005), 43 and 53.

12. Stanley F. Wright, *Hart and the Chinese Customs* (Belfast: W. Mullan, 1950), chapters 10 and 11.

13. Luo Yudong, *Zhongguo lijinshi* [A history of *lijin* in China] (Shanghai: Shangwu yinshuguan, 1936), 1:224.

14. As the Shanxi governor Zhang Zhidong pointed out in a memorial, because provincial governments needed to report to the Board of Revenue the total amount of lijin revenue collected, the 10 percent retained within provinces was thus different in nature from other kinds of provincial revenues independent of central supervision. The memorial of Zhang Zhidong, 14 January 1884, *Guangxu chao Donghua lu*, 2:1643.

15. Huang Jianhui, *Shanxi piaohaoshi* [A history of Shanxi bankers], rev. ed. (Taiyuan: Shanxi jingji chubanshe, 2002), 203 and 208.

16. Song Huizhong, "Piaoshang yu wan Qing caizheng," 424–425.

17. Huang Jianhui, *Shanxi piaohaoshi*, 240.

18. The memorial of the Board of Revenue, 24 October 1885, GCMC, Box 680, No. 409–410.

19. The memorial of Li Hongzhang, 1885 (month unknown), in *Guangxu chao zhupi zouzhe* [Imperially rescripted palace memorials of the Guangxu reign], ed. Zhongguo diyi lishi dang'anguan (Beijing: Zhonghua shuju, 1995–1996), 91:675.

20. Li Hu, *Zhongguo jingjishi conggao* [Collected essays in the economic history of China] (Changsha: Hunan renmin chubanshe, 1986), 242–244; Wang Jingyu, "Luelun Zhongguo tongshang yinhang chengli de lishi tiaojian jiqi zai duiwai guanxi fangmian de tezheng" [On the historical conditions of the establishment of the Imperial Bank of China and its characteristics in foreign relations], *Zhongguo jingjishi yanjiu* 3 (1988): 95–97.

21. Yan Jingming was promoted to be in charge of the Board of Revenue because of his outstanding performance in financial management and tax collection in Hubei and Shandong Provinces. See Wei Xiumei, "Yan Jingming zai Shandong—Tongzhi yuannian shiyue–liunian eryue" [Yan Jingming in Shandong—1862–1867], *Gugong xueshu jikan* 24, no. 1 (Fall 2006): 117–153.

22. The memorial of Board of Revenue, 24 October 1885, *GCMC*, Box 680, No. 389–394, No. 414, and No. 420.

23. The memorial of Li Hongzhang, 18 September 1887, *GCMC*, Box 680, No. 670–673.

24. Wang Erh-min, "Sheng Xuanhuai yu Zhongguo shiye liquan zhi weihu" [Sheng Xuanhuai and the protection of the interests of Chinese enterprises], *Zhongyang yanjiuyuan jindaishisuo jikan* 27 (June 1997): 26.

25. Huang Jianhui, *Shanxi piaohaoshi*, 266–272.

26. For Shaanxi, see the memorial of Shaanxi governor Lu Chuanlin, 17 November 1894, *GGCZ*, 8:560. For Jiangxi, see the memorial of Jiangxi governor Dexin, 12 June 1895, *GCMC*, Box 680, No. 1156.

27. The memorial of Bian Baoquan, 10 February 1885, *PM*, Box 32, No. 695–699.

28. The approval of the Board of Revenue is quoted in the memorial of Bian Baoquan, 12 August 1885, *PM*, Box 32, No. 722–724.

29. Marianne Bastid, "The Structure of Financial Institutions of the State in the Late Qing," 75.

30. Liu Zenghe, "Guangxu qianqi Hubu zhengdun caizheng zhong de guifu jiuzhi jiqi xiandu" [The Ministry of Revenue's financial rectification measures in the early years of Emperor Guangxu's reign: Between restoration and innovation], *Zhongyang yanjiuyuan lishiyuyansuo jikan* 79, no. 2 (June 2008): 273–274.

31. For an example of assigning different incomes from the salt tax to meet different spending needs in 1900, see S. A. M. Adshead, *The Modernization of the Chinese Salt Administration, 1900–1920* (Cambridge, MA: Harvard University Press, 1970), 26–27.

32. The other two major means of "informal financing" in provinces were to remove money from funds allocated by the center or to collect surcharges from the local population. See Madeleine Zelin, *The Magistrate's Tael: Rationalizing Fiscal Reform in Eighteenth-Century Ch'ing China* (Berkeley: University of California Press, 1992), 47.

33. The imperial edict of 30 September 1822, *Jiaqing Daoguang liangchao shangyudang* [Edicts during the reigns of Jiaqing and Daoguang], ed. Zhongguo diyi lishi dang'anguan (Guilin: Guangxi shifan daxue chubanshe, 2000), 27:448–449.

34. On 20 October 1839, the censor Zhang Hao memorialized that he noticed that the actual amounts of silver stored in provincial treasuries often came

to less than half of what was recorded in account books due to accumulated arrears and previous unreported withdrawals to meet public spending in provinces. *GCMC*, Box 678, No. 974–978.

35. The memorial of Zeng Guoquan, 14 July 1883, *Guangxu chao Donghua lu*, 2:1557.

36. The memorial of Ma Piyao, 7 January 1891, *Gongzhongdang Guangxu chao zouzhe* (henceforth *GGCZ*) [Palace memorials of the Guangxu reign], ed. Guoli gugong bowuyuan Gugong wenxian bianji weiyuanhui (Taipei: Guoli gugong bowuyuan, 1973), 5:802.

37. For this practice in the customs office of Guangzhou, see the memorial of the Guangdong Customs Superintendent Chongguang, 6 February 1882, *GGCZ*, 2:348–350.

38. The memorial of Zeng Guoquan, 11 August 1886, *Guangxu chao Donghua lu*, 2:2133–2144.

39. These numbers are from Zhou Yumin, *Wan Qing caizheng yu shehui bianqian*, 267, 271, and 282–283.

40. For example, in order to make the annual interest payment of 680,000 tael of silver to the Hong Kong and Shanghai Co., the Guangdong provincial government had to remove money from sources such as provincial military expenditures, revenue preassigned for Beijing, and even revenue preassigned for the Naval Admiralty. The memorial of the governor-general of Liangguang Zhang Zhidong and Guangdong governor Wu Dacheng, 25 August 1887, *PM*, Box 32, No. 879–882.

41. For example, the Board of Revenue in 1887 requested that provincial governors collect funds for famine relief in Jiangsu and Anhui Provinces by selling official titles. The Shanxi governor Gangyi reported that he had sent to Jiangsu 40,000 tael out of the "funds saved from reconstruction," an item of revenue undesignated by the center. The memorial of Gangyi, 18 December 1887, *GGCZ*, 7:501. In 1888, the Board of Revenue assigned 50,000 tael out of the land taxes in Anhui Province for famine relief in Henan Province. As there was no surplus in this designated item, the Anhui governor Chen Yi had to take the same amount out of the tribute grain, an item undesignated by the board, to meet this order. The memorial of Chen Yi, 14 January 1888, *GGCZ*, 7:540.

42. Huang Jianhui, *Shanxi piaohaoshi*, 244.

43. Zhou Yumin, *Wan Qing caizheng yu shehui bianqian*, 269–270.

44. As the censor Zhang Daoyuan pointed out in 1875, "memorials from provinces always claim that they either had inadequate funds to meet the assignment orders or they could not clear the revenue in arrears and asked the Board of Revenue to seek sources in other provinces." The memorial of Zhang Daoyuan, 16 January 1876, *Guangxu chao Donghua lu*, 1:171. For a historian's description of a similar phenomenon, see He Lie, *Qing Xian Tong shiqi de*

caizheng [The public finance of the Qing government in the reigns of Xianfeng and Tongzhi] (Taipei: Guoli bianyiguan, 1981), 402–404; Liu Zenghe, "Guangxu qianqi Hubu zhengdun caizheng zhong de guifu jiuzhi jiqi xiandu," 278–283.

45. Liu Kwang-ching, "Wan Qing dufu quanli wenti shangque," 251–252.

46. When the central government allocated the huge Boxer indemnity to the provinces after 1900, it essentially lost control of the collection of lijin, and tax farming in collection became more frequent. For details, see Susan Mann, *Local Merchants and the Chinese Bureaucracy, 1750–1950* (Stanford, CA: Stanford University Press, 1987), chapters 8 and 9.

47. The memorial of the governor-general of Guangdong and Guangxi Yan Ruanshu, 4 August 1862, *GCMC*, Box 361, No. 1652–1660.

48. See both memorials in *Dao Xian Tong Guang sichao zouyi* [Memorials from the four reign periods of Dao[guang], Xian[feng], Tong[zhi], and Guang[xu]], ed. Wang Yunwu (Taipei: Taiwan shangwu yinshuguan, 1970), 4:1437–1439.

49. The memorial of the governor-general of Guangdong and Guangxi Yan Ruanshu, 4 August 1862, *GCMC*, Box 361, No. 1652–1660.

50. The memorial of the governor-general of Liangguang Zhang Zhidong and Guangdong governor Wu Dacheng, 6 August 1886, *PM*, Box 32, No. 879–882.

51. The memorial of the governor-general of Hubei and Hunan Zhang Zhidong, 4 December 1887, *Guangxu chao Donghua lu*, 2:2371–2372.

52. For a hierarchical organization chart of lijin collection, see Luo Yudong, *Zhongguo lijinshi*, 1:69–70.

53. Ibid., 1:87.

54. The memorial of Encheng and Xue Yunsheng, *GGCZ*, 3:306.

55. The memorial of Bian Baodi, 14 July 1887, *PM*, Box 32, No. 854–856.

56. The memorial of Li Hongzhang, 21 May 1880, *GCMC*, Box 488, No. 954–956.

57. Luo Yudong, *Zhongguo lijinshi*, 1:38.

58. The memorial of the governor-general of Shaanxi and Gansu Lebin, 9 June 1858, *PM*, Box 31, No. 2800–2803.

59. Zhang Xiaoye, *Qingdai siyan wenti yanjiu* [Nonofficial salt in the Qing] (Beijing: Shehui kexue wenxian chubanshe, 2001), 39.

60. The memorial of Zhuo Bingtian, 22 November 1831, *GCMC*, Box 6, No. 2866–2869.

61. Luo Yudong, *Zhongguo lijinshi*, 1:117–118.

62. Ibid., 1:119–121.

63. The memorial of Shandong governor Huiling, 17 August 1800. *PM*, Box 2, No. 2262.

64. The memorial of the governor-general of Huguang Ma Huiyu and Hubei governor Zhang Yinghan, 29 March 1813, *PM*, Box 3, No. 44–24.

65. Memorial of an unknown official (very likely the Jiangxi governor), 1864 (month unknown), *PM*, Box 32, No. 206–207.

66. The memorial of Shaanxi governor Ye Boying, 12 October 1888, *GCMC*, Box 489, No. 391–392.

67. The memorial of the governor-general of Guangdong and Guangxi Zhang Zhidong, 3 August 1887, *PM*, Box 32, No. 868.

68. The memorial of the governor-general of Yunnan and Guizhou, Cen Yuying, 26 June 1883, *GCMC*, Box 488, No. 1849–1850.

69. Luo Yudong, *Zhongguo lijinshi*, 1:97–99.

70. The memorial of Yu Lu and Kui Bin, 26 October 1889, *GCMC*, Box 489, No. 733–736.

71. Luo Yudong, *Zhongguo lijinshi*, 1:188.

72. The memorial of Shaanxi governor Ye Boying, 23 March 1887, *PM*, Box 32, No. 814–816; the memorial of the governor-general of Hubei and Hunan Yulu and Hubei governor Kuibin, 12 April 1887, *PM*, Box 32, No. 823–825.

73. Dai Yifeng, *Jindai Zhongguo haiguan yu Zhongguo caizheng* [The customs and public finance in early modern China] (Xiamen: Xiamen daxue chubanshe, 1993), 136–139.

74. In the collection of lijin duties on opium in Hunan Province, the Hunan governor Zhang Xu told the Board of Revenue that high duties in Hunan simply made merchants go through neighboring Guizhou or Guangxi, where duties were low, to reach Jiangxi. The memorial of Hunan governor Zhang Xu, 30 October 1891, *PM*, Box 32, No. 1544–1547.

75. For such examples in Hubei, Anhui, and Jiangxi, see the memorial of the acting governor-general of Hubei and Hunan Bian Baodi and Hubei governor Peng Zuxian, 13 April 1885, *PM*, Box 32, No. 700–704; the memorial of the governor-general of Jiangnan and Jiangxi Zeng Guoquan, 11 June 1888, *GCMC*, Box 489, No. 245–246; and the memorial of Jiangxi provincial treasurer Fang Ruyi, 12 May 1893, *GCMC*, Box 489, No. 2276–2278.

76. When famine struck Shanxi, Shaanxi, and Henan in 1877, the Board of Revenue repealed the lijin duties on grain for one year. Cited from the memorial of the Anhui governor Yulu, 13 April 1878, *GCMC*, Box 488, No. 475–476. When a poor harvest drove up grain prices in Hubei in 1885, the Hubei provincial government temporarily suspended the lijin on the grain trade to attract merchants to ship grain in from other provinces. See the memorial of the Hubei governor Tan Junpei, 1885 (month unknown), *PM*, Box 32, No. 732. The provincial government of Jiangsu adopted a similar measure in 1888. See the memorial of the governor-general of Jiangsu and Jiangxi Zeng Guoquan, 1888 (month unknown), *PM*, Box 32, No. 1078–1079.

77. For the details of this official transportation system, see Madeleine Zelin, *The Merchants of Zigong: Industrial Entrepreneurship in Early Modern China* (New York: Columbia University Press, 2005), chapter 6.

78. Sir Richard Dane, who established the centralized institutions to collect salt taxes in China after 1911, considered the salt administration of Sichuan "perhaps the best in China." Cited from Adshead, *The Modernization of the Chinese Salt Administration*, 123.

79. The memorial of the Board of Revenue, 23 January 1885, *Guangxu chao Donghua lu*, 2:1873.

80. The memorial of Li Hongzhang, 13 July 1881, *GCMC*, Box 488, No. 1327–1329.

81. The memorial of the Office of Foreign Affairs, 3 January 1887, *GCMC*, Box 488, No. 2843–2847; the memorial of the governor-general of Fujian and Zhejiang Yang Changjun, 28 March 1887, *GCMC*, Box 488, No. 3005–3007.

82. Dai Yifeng, "Wan Qing zhongyang yu difang caizheng guanxi," [The fiscal relationship between the center and provinces in the late Qing], *Zhongguo jingjishi yanjiu* 4 (2000): 53–54.

83. This casts doubt on Luo Yudong's claim that the reason that governors did not report lijin revenue from opium in separate accounts was to prevent the board from having access to this information. See Luo Yudong, *Zhongguo lijinshi*, 1:156. For the provinces that used separate accounts to report lijin from domestic opium to the board, see the memorials from the governor-general of Liangguang Li Hanzhang, 5 October 1890, No. 1327–1331; and the memorial of the governor-general of Hubei and Hunan Zhang Zhidong and Hubei governor Tan Jixun, 7 October 1890, No. 1335–1341, all in *PM*, Box 32.

84. Lin Man-houng, "Wan Qing de yapianshui, 1858–1909" [Opium taxes in the late Qing, 1858–1909], *Si yu yan* 16, no. 5 (1979): 11–59.

85. The memorial of the governor-general of Hubei and Hunan Zhang Zhidong and Hubei governor Tan Jixun, 7 October 1890, *PM*, Box 32, No. 1335–1341.

86. The memorial of the governor-general of Sichuan Liu Bingzhang, 15 November 1890, *PM*, Box 32, No. 1407–1408.

87. The memorial of the Office of Foreign Affairs and the Board of Revenue, 1 May 1891, *PM*, Box 32, No. 1454–1460.

88. See the unwillingness of the Jiangsu governor Gangyi in his memorial in 27 August 1890, *GCMC*, Box 489, No. 1018–1026.

89. The 450 million tael Boxer Indemnity, imposed only five years later in 1900, did bankrupt the Qing state.

90. For the natural experiment as a methodology in historical studies, see Jared Diamond and James Robinson, eds., *Natural Experiments of History* (Cambridge, MA.: The Belknap Press of Harvard University Press, 2010).

91. The memorial of the Office of Foreign Affairs, 6 February 1895, *GCMC*, Box 680, No. 1067–1088.

92. The memorial of the Board of Revenue, 8 August 1895, *GCMC*, Box 680, No. 1170–1177.

93. The imperial decree of reform and self-strengthening, 19 July 1895, *ZJHZ*, 2:636.

94. Nakamura Tetsuo, "Kindai Chūgoku no tsūka taisei no kaikaku" [The reform of the monetary system in modern China: The opening of the Chinese Imperial Bank], *Shakai keizai shigaku* 62, no. 3 (August/September 1996): 318.

95. Qian Jiaju, ed., *Jiu Zhongguo gongzhaishi ziliao, 1894–1949 nian* [Historical materials on state borrowing in China, 1894–1949] (Beijing: Zhonghua shuju, 1984), 1–31.

96. The memorial of Zhang Zhidong, 2 February 1896, *GCMC*, Box 489, No. 2970–2973.

97. The memorial of Tie Liang, 4 December 1904, *GCMC*, Box 490, No. 2285–2288.

98. For this process toward centralization after 1897, see Ho Hon-wai, "Qingji guochan yapian de tongjuan yu tongshui" [Centralization in opium tax collection in the late Qing], in *Xinhuoji: Chuangtong yu jindai bianqianzhong de Zhongguo jingji; Quan Hansheng jiaoshou jiuzhi rongqing zhushou lunwenji* [The traditional and early modern Chinese economy: Essays in honor of Professor Quan Hansheng's ninetieth birthday], ed. Quan Hansheng jiaoshou jiuzhi rongqing zhushuo lunwenji bianji weiyuanhui (Banqiao: Daoxiang chubanshe, 2001), 560–570. For the disputes between governors and the center over how to divide the yields, see Liu Zenghe, *Yapian shuishou yu Qingmo Xinzheng* [The tax revenues from Opium and the New Policies in the last decade of the Qing] (Beijing: Sanlian shudian, 2005), 43–85.

99. Adshead, *The Modernization of the Chinese Salt Administration, 1900–1920, 52–59.*

100. The annual receipts of liquor taxes were 630,000 tael in Sichuan in 1906, 800,000 tael in Zhili in 1902, and 500,000 tael in Fengtian in 1906. See Ho Hon-wai, "Qingmo fushui jizhun de kuoda jiqi juxian" [The expansion of and limits to tax collection in the late Qing], *Zhongyang yanjiuyuan jindaishi yanjiusuo jikan* 17, no. 2 (December 1988): 69–98.

101. The memorial of the Princes and Grand Ministers and the Board of Revenue, 23 February 1896, *GCMC*, Box 680, No. 1285–1294.

102. For the early history of the Imperial Bank of China, see Albert Feuerwerker, *China's Early Industrialization: Sheng Hsuan-Huai (1844–1916) and Mandarin Enterprise* (Cambridge, MA: Harvard University Press, 1958), 225–241.

103. Huang Zunxian, *Riben guo zhi* [A history of Japan] (Shanghai: Tushu jicheng yinshuju, 1898; reprint, Taipei: Wenhai chubanshe, 1968), 524.

104. The memorial of the Board of Revenue, 23 March 1898, *GCMC*, Box 680, No. 1735–1739.

105. Sheng Xuanhuai, "Memorial note on the establishment of an official bank," 31 October 1896. Cited from Xia Dongyuan, ed., *Sheng Xuanhuai nianpu changbian* [A chronology of the life of Sheng Xuanhuai] (Shanghai: Shanghai jiao-tong daxue chubanshe, 2004), 2:541.

106. The memorial of the Board of Revenue, 27 January 1899. *GCMC*, Box 680, No. 2012–2020.

107. For the circulation of HSBC banknotes in Chinese cities in the late nineteenth and early twentieth centuries, see Niv Horesh, *Shanghai's Bund and Beyond: British Banks, Banknote Issuance, and Monetary Policy in China, 1842–1937* (New Haven and London: Yale University Press, 2009).

108. Hamashita Takeshi, "Shinmatsu Chūgoku ni okeru 'ginkōron' to Chūgoku Tsūshō Ginkō no setsuritsu" [Discussions on the state bank in late nineteenth-century China and the establishment of the Imperial Bank of China], *Hitotsubashi ronsō* 85, no. 6 (June 1981): 747–766.

109. The memorial of the Board of Revenue, 28 March 1896, *ZJHZ*, 2:684–685.

110. Ho Hon-wai, "Cong yinjian qianhuang dao tongyuan fanlang: Qingmo xinhuobi de faxing jiqi yingxiang" [From scarcity of copper cash to excessive mintage of copper currency: The impact of minting new currencies in the last years of the Qing], *Zhongyang yanjiuyuan lishiyuyansuo jikan* 62, no. 3 (1993): 432–447.

111. Sheng Xuanhuai, "Reply to the inquiry of the Office of Foreign Affairs *(Zongli yamen)*," 12 April 1897. Cited from Xia Dongyuan, ed., *Sheng Xuanhuai nianpu changbian*, 2:572.

112. Calculated from Luo Yudong, "Guangxu chao bujiu caizheng zhi fang'an" [Methods to cover public finance in the reign of the Guangxu emperor], in *Zhongguo jindai shehui jingjishi lunji* [Collected essays in the socioeconomic history of early modern China], ed. Zhou Kangxie (Hong Kong: Chongwen shu-dian, 1971), 2:205.

113. The memorial of the Board of Revenue, 23 September 1896, *GCMC*, Box 507, No. 2428–2430.

114. The memorials of the governor-general of Jiangnan and Jiangxi Liu Kunyi, 8 June 1899, *GCMC*, Box 507, No. 2796–2798; and 21 September 1900, *GCMC*, Box 507, No. 3087–3089, respectively.

115. Tian Yongxiu, "1862–1883 nian Zhongguo de gupiao shichang" [The stock market in China: 1862–1883], *Zhongguo jingjishi yanjiu* 2 (1995): 58–59.

116. Ibid., 64.

117. Xu Dixin and Wu Chengming, eds., *Zhongguo zibenzhuyi fazhanshi* [A history of the development of capitalism in China] (Beijing: Renmin chubanshe, 1990), 2:175.

118. The memorial of the governor-general of Fujian and Zhejiang Tan Zhonglin, 11 October 1894, *GCMC*, Box 680, No. 1029–1030; the memorial of the governor-general of Zhili Li Hongzhang, 18 January 1895, *GCMC*, Box 680, No. 1050–1054; and the memorial of Jiangxi governor Dexin, 17 March 1895, *GCMC*, Box 680, No. 1124–1127.

119. The memorial of Hubei governor Tan Jixun, 23 March 1895, *GCMC*, Box 680, No. 1133–1135.

BIBLIOGRAPHY

Archival Sources

Chinese

Grand Council Memorial Copies (军机处录副奏折) *[GCMC]*
Palace Memorials (宫中硃批奏折) *[PM]*

Japanese

Inoue Kaoru kankei monjo 井上馨関係文書 [Inoue Kaoru archive], No. 677-4, Modern Japanese Political History Materials Room, National Diet Library, Tokyo.

Itō Hirobumi kankei monjo, shorui no bu 伊藤博文関係文書、書類の部 [Itō Room, National Diet Library, Tokyo.

Ōkuma monjo 大隈文書 [Collected works of Ōkuma Shigenobu], microfilm of unpublished materials held at Waseda University.

Articles and Books

Abbott, Andrew. "Sequence Analysis: New Methods for Old Ideas." *Annual Review of Sociology* 21 (1995): 93–113.

———. *Time Matters: On Theory and Method.* Chicago: University of Chicago Press, 2001.

Acemoglu, Daron, Simon Johnson, and James Robinson. "Institutions as the Fundamental Cause of Long-Run Growth." NBER Working Paper, Series 10481, 2004.

———. "The Rise of Europe: Atlantic Trade, Institutional Change, and Economic Growth." *American Economic Review* 95, no. 3 (June 2005): 546–579.

Acemoglu, Daron, and James A. Robinson. "Economic Backwardness in Political Perspective." *American Political Science Review* 100, no. 1 (2006): 115–131.

Adachi Keiji 足立啓二. "Shindai zenki ni okeru kokka to zeni" 清代前期にお け る 国家と銭 [The state and cash in the early Qing period]. *Tōyōshi kenkyū* 東洋史研究 49, no. 4 (1991): 47–73.

Adshead, S. A. M. *The Modernization of the Chinese Salt Administration, 1900–1920.* Cambridge, MA: Harvard University Press, 1970.

Alexander, Gerard. "Institutions, Path Dependence, and Democratic Consolidation." *Journal of Theoretical Politics* 13, no. 3 (2001): 249–270.

Allen, G. C. *A Short Economic History of Modern Japan.* 4th ed. London: Macmillan, 1981.

Andréadès, A. *History of the Bank of England, 1640–1903.* 4th ed. London: Frank Cass, 1966.

Aoyama Tadamasa 青山忠正. *Meiji Ishin to kokka keisei* 明治維新と国家形成 [The Meiji Restoration and state formation]. Tokyo: Yoshikawa Kōbunkan, 2000.

Ardant, Gabriel. "Financial Policy and Economic Infrastructure of Modern States and Nations." In *The Formation of National States in Western Europe,* edited by Charles Tilly. Princeton, NJ: Princeton University Press, 1975.

Arthur, W. Brian. *Increasing Returns and Path Dependence in the Economy.* Ann Arbor: University of Michigan Press, 1994.

Ashley, M. P. *Financial and Commercial Policy under the Cromwellian Protectorate.* London: Oxford University Press, H. Milford, 1934.

Ashton, Robert. *The Crown and the Money Market, 1603–1640.* Oxford: Clarendon Press, 1960.

———. "Revenue Farming under the Early Stuarts." *Economic History Review,* n.s., 8, no. 3 (1956): 310–322.

Ashton, T. S. *Economic Fluctuations in England, 1700–1800.* Oxford: Clarendon Press, 1959.

Ashworth, William J. *Customs and Excise: Trade, Production, and Consumption in England, 1640–1845.* Oxford and New York: Oxford University Press, 2003.

Asukai Masamichi 飛鳥井雅道. "Kindai Tennōzō no tenkai" 近代天皇像の 展開 [The unfolding of the image of the emperor in modern Japan]. In

Iwanami Koza Nihon tsushi 岩波講座日本通史 [The Iwanami general history of Japan]. Vol. 17, *Kindai* (2) 近代 (2) [The modern period], edited by Asao Naohiro 朝尾直弘 et al. Tokyo: Iwanami Shoten, 1994.

Bailey, Jackson H. "The Meiji Leadership: Matsukata Masayoshi." In *Japan Examined: Perspectives on Modern Japanese History,* edited by Harry Wray and Hilary Conroy. Honolulu: University of Hawaii Press, 1983.

Banno Junji 坂野潤治. *The Establishment of the Japanese Constitutional System.* Translated by J. A. A. Stockwin. London and New York: Routledge, 1992.

————. *Kindai Nihon no kokka kōsō, 1871–1936* 近代日本の国家構想, 1871–1936 [Visions of the state in modern Japan, 1871–1936]. Tokyo: Iwanami Shoten, 1996.

————. "Meiji kokka no seiritsu" 明治国家の成立 [The establishment of the Meiji state]. In *Nihon keizaishi* 日本経済史 [The economic history of Japan]. Vol. 3, *Kaikō to Ishin* 開港と維新 [The opening of Japan and the Restoration], edited by Umemura Mataji 梅村又次 and Yamamoto Yūzō 山本有造. Tokyo: Iwanami Shoten, 1989.

Bartlett, Beatrice S. *Monarchs and Ministers: The Grand Council in Mid-Ch'ing China, 1723–1820.* Berkeley: University of California Press, 1991.

Bastid, Marianne. "The Structure of Financial Institutions of the State in the Late Qing." In *The Scope of State Power in China,* edited by S. R. Schram. New York: St. Martin's Press, 1985.

Bates, Robert H., and Da-Hsiang Donald Lien. "A Note on Taxation, Development, and Representative Government." *Politics and Society* 14, no. 1 (1985): 53–70.

Baugh, Daniel A. *British Naval Administration in the Age of Walpole.* Princeton, NJ: Princeton University Press, 1965.

Baxter, Stephen B. *The Development of the Treasury, 1660–1702.* Cambridge, MA: Harvard University Press, 1957.

Beasley, W. G. *The Meiji Restoration.* Stanford, CA: Stanford University Press, 1972.

Beckett, J. V. "Land Tax or Excise: The Levying of Taxation in Seventeenth- and Eighteenth-Century England." *English Historical Review* 100, no. 395 (April 1985): 285–308.

Berger, Suzanne, and Ronald Philip Dore, eds. *National Diversity and Global Capitalism.* Ithaca, NY: Cornell University Press, 1996.

Berry, Mary Elizabeth. "Public Peace and Private Attachment: The Goals and Conduct of Power in Early Modern Japan." *Journal of Japanese Studies* 12, no. 2 (Summer 1986): 237–271.

Binney, J. E. D. *British Public Finance and Administration, 1774–92.* Oxford: Clarendon Press, 1958.

Bitō Masahide 尾藤正英. "Sonnō jōi shisō" 尊皇攘夷思想 [The ideology of revering the emperor and expelling the barbarians]. In *Iwanami kōza Nihon rekishi* 岩波講座日本暦史 [The Iwanami history of Japan]. Vol. 13, *Kinsei (5)* 近世 (5) [The early modern period], edited by Asao Naohiro 朝尾直弘 et al. Tokyo: Iwanami Shoten, 1977.

Blyth, Mark. *Great Transformations: Economic Ideas and Institutional Change in the Twentieth Century.* Cambridge and New York: Cambridge University Press, 2002.

Bonney, Richard. "Revenues." In *Economic Systems and State Finance,* edited by Richard Bonney (London: Oxford University Press, 1995).

———, ed. *The Rise of the Fiscal State in Europe, c. 1200–1815.* Oxford and New York: Oxford University Press, 1999.

Braddick, Michael J. "The Early Modern English State and the Question of Differentiation, from 1550 to 1700." *Comparative Studies in Society and History* 38, no. 1 (1996): 92–111.

———. *The Nerves of State: Taxation and the Financing of the English State, 1558–1714.* Manchester: Manchester University Press, 1996.

———. *Parliamentary Taxation in Seventeenth-Century England: Local Administration and Response.* Woodbridge, UK, and Rochester, NY: Royal Historical Society/Boydell Press, 1994.

———. "Popular Politics and Public Policy: The Excise Riot at Smithfield in February 1647 and Its Aftermath." *Historical Journal* 34, no. 3 (1991): 597–626.

———. "State Formation and Social Change in Early Modern England." *Social History* 16 (1991): 1–17.

———. *State Formation in Early Modern England, c. 1550–1700.* Cambridge and New York: Cambridge University Press, 2000.

Braddick, Michael J., and John Walter, eds. *Negotiating Power in Early Modern Society: Order, Hierarchy, and Subordination in Britain and Ireland.* Cambridge and New York: Cambridge University Press, 2001.

Brewer, John. "The English State and Fiscal Appropriation, 1688–1789." *Politics and Society* 16, no. 2–3 (September 1988): 335–385.

———. *The Sinews of Power: War, Money, and the English State, 1688–1783.* New York: Alfred A. Knopf, 1989.

Brooks, Colin. "Public Finance and Political Stability: The Administration of the Land Tax, 1688–1720." *Historical Journal* 17, no. 2 (1974): 281–300.

Broz, J. Lawrence, and Richard S. Grossman. "Paying for Privilege: The Political Economy of Bank of England Charters, 1694–1844." *Explorations in Economic History* 41, no. 1 (2004): 48–72.

Bubini, Dennis. "Politics and the Battle for the Banks, 1688–1697." *English Historical Review* 85, no. 337 (October 1970): 693–714.

Buchinsky, Moshe, and Ben Polak. "The Emergence of a National Capital Market in England, 1710–1880." *Journal of Economic History* 53, no. 1 (March 1993): 1–24.

Burgess, Glenn. *The Politics of the Ancient Constitution: An Introduction to English Political Thought, 1603–1642.* Basingstoke, UK: Macmillan, 1992.

Büthe, Tim. "Taking Temporality Seriously: Modeling History and the Use of Narrative and Counterfactuals in Historical Institutionalism," *American Political Science Review* 96, no. 3 (2002): 481–493.

Campbell, John L. "An Institutional Analysis of Fiscal Reform in Postcommunist Europe." *Theory and Society* 25, no. 1 (1996): 45–84.

Capie, Forrest. "Money and Economic Development in Eighteenth-Century England." In *Exceptionalism and Industrialization: Britain and Its European Rivals,* edited by Leandro Prados de la Escosura. Cambridge and New York: Cambridge University Press, 2004.

Capoccia, Giovanni, and R. Daniel Kelemen. "The Study of Critical Junctures: Theory, Narrative, and Counterfactuals in Historical Institutionalism." *World Politics* 59 (April 2007): 341–369.

Capoccia, Giovanni, and Daniel Ziblatt. "The Historical Turn in Democratization Studies: A New Research Agenda for Europe and Beyond." *Comparative Political Studies* 43, no. 8/9 (2010): 931–968.

Capp, Bernard S. *Cromwell's Navy: The Fleet and the English Revolution, 1648–1660.* Oxford: Clarendon Press, 1989.

Carruthers, Bruce G. *City of Capital: Politics and Markets in the English Financial Revolution.* Princeton, NJ: Princeton University Press, 1996.

Chandaman, C. D. *The English Public Revenue, 1660–1688.* Oxford: Clarendon Press, 1975.

———. "The Financial Settlement in the Parliament of 1685." In *British Government and Administration: Studies Presented to S. B. Chrimes,* edited by H. Hearder and H. R. Loyn. Cardiff: University of Wales Press, 1974.

Chaudhry, Kiren Aziz. "The Myths of the Market and the Common History of Late Developers." *Politics and Society* 21, no. 3 (1993): 245–274.

Chen Chau-nan 陳昭南. *Yongzheng Qianlong nianjian de yinqian bijia biandong (1723–95)* 雍正乾隆年間的銀錢比價變動 (1723–95) [A study of the fluctuations of the exchange rates between silver and copper coins during the reigns of Yongzheng and Qianlong (1723–95)]. Taipei: Zhongguo xueshu zhuzuo jiangzhu weiyuanhui, 1966.

Chen Feng 陈锋. "Qingdai qianqi zouxiao zhidu yu zhengce yanbian" 清代前期奏销制度的政策演变 [The early Qing central auditing system and policy change]. *Lishi yanjiu* 历史研究 2 (2000): 63–74.

———. "Qingdai zhongyang caizheng yu difang caizheng de tiaozheng" 清代中央财政与地方财政的调整 [The adjustment of the relationship between the center and local governments in public finance]. *Lishi yanjiu* 历史研究 5 (1997): 100–114.

Ch'en, Jerome. "The Hs'ien-Feng Inflation." *Bulletin of the School of Oriental and African Studies* 21 (1958): 578–586.

Childs, John. *The Army, James II, and the Glorious Revolution.* Manchester: Manchester University Press, 1980.

———. *The British Army of William III, 1689–1702.* Manchester: Manchester University Press, 1987.

Chiu Peng-sheng 邱澎生. "Shiba shiji Diantong shichang zhong de guanshang guanxi yu liyi guannian" 十八世紀滇銅市場中的官商關係與利益觀念 ["Interests" in economic organization: The shaping of the Yunnan copper market in eighteenth-century China]. *Zhongguo yanjiuyuan lishi yuyan yanjiusuo jikan* 中央研究院歷史語言研究所集刊 72, no. 1 (2001): 49–119.

Christianson, Paul. "Two Proposals for Raising Money by Extraordinary Means, c. 1627." *English Historical Review* 117, no. 471 (April 2002): 355–373.

Chubb, Basil. *The Control of Public Expenditures: Financial Committees of the House of Commons.* Oxford: Clarendon Press, 1952.

Clapham, J. H. *The Bank of England: A History.* 2 vols. Cambridge: Cambridge University Press; New York: Macmillan, 1945.

Clark, Peter. *The English Alehouse: A Social History, 1200–1830.* London: Longman, 1983.

Clay, C. G. A. *Economic Expansion and Social Change: England 1500–1700.* Vol. 1, *People, Land, and Towns.* Cambridge and New York: Cambridge University Press, 1984.

———. *Public Finance and Private Wealth: The Career of Sir Stephen Fox, 1627–1716.* Oxford: Clarendon Press, 1978.

Cogswell, Thomas, Richard Cust, and Peter Lake. "Revisionism and Its Legacies: The Work of Conrad Russell." In *Politics, Religion, and Popularity in Early Stuart Britain: Essays in Honour of Conrad Russell,* edited by Thomas Cogswell, Richard Cust, and Peter Lake. Cambridge and New York: Cambridge University Press, 2002.

Coleby, Andrew M. *Central Government and the Localities: Hampshire, 1649–1689.* Cambridge and New York: Cambridge University Press, 1987.

Collier, David, and James Mahoney. "Insights and Pitfalls: Selection Bias in Qualitative Research." *World Politics* 49, no. 1 (1996): 56–91.

Collier, Ruth Berins, and David Collier. *Shaping the Political Arena: Critical Junctures, the Labor Movement, and Regime Dynamics in Latin America.* Princeton, NJ: Princeton University Press, 1991.

Cowan, R., and P. Gunby. "Sprayed to Death: Path Dependence, Lock-in and Pest Control Strategies." *Economic Journal* 106, no. 436 (1996): 521–542.

Cramsie, John. "Commercial Projects and the Fiscal Policy of James VI and I." *Historical Journal* 43, no. 2 (2000): 345–364.

———. *Kingship and Crown Finance under James VI and I, 1603–1625*. Woodbridge, UK, and Rochester, NY: Royal Historical Society/Boydell Press, 2002.

Cui Zhiqing 崔之清 et al., *Taiping Tianguo zhanzheng quanshi* 太平天国战争全史 [A comprehensive military history of the Taiping Rebellion]. 4 vols. Nanjing: Nanjing daxue chubanshe, 2002.

Cunich, Peter. "Revolution and Crisis in English State Finance, 1534–47." In *Crises, Revolutions and Self-Sustained Growth: Essays in European Fiscal History, 1130–1830,* edited by W. M. Ormrod, Margaret Bonney, and Richard Bonney. Stamford, UK: Shaun Tyas, 1999.

Curtin, Philip D. *The World and the West: The European Challenge and the Overseas Response in the Age of Empire.* Cambridge and New York: Cambridge University Press, 2000.

Cust, Richard. *The Forced Loan and English Politics, 1626–1628.* Oxford: Clarendon Press, 1987.

Dai Yifeng 戴一峰. *Jindai Zhongguo haiguan yu Zhongguo caizheng* 近代中国海关与中国财政 [The customs and public finance in early modern China]. Xiamen: Xiamen daxue chubanshe, 1993.

———. "Wan Qing zhongyang yu difang caizheng guanxi" 晚清中央与地方财政关系 [The fiscal relationship between the center and provinces in the late Qing]. *Zhongguo jingjishi yanjiu* 中国经济史研究 4 (2000): 59–73.

Dai Yingcong. "The Qing State, Merchants, and the Military Labor Force in the Jinchuan Campaigns." *Late Imperial China* 22, no. 2 (December 2001): 35–90.

Dao Xian Tong Guang sichao zouyi 道咸同光4朝奏議 [Memorials from the four reign periods of Dao[guang], Xian[feng], Tong[zhi], and Guang[xu]], edited by Wang Yunwu 王雲五. 12 vols. Taipei: Taiwan shangwu yinshu-guan, 1970.

David, Paul A. "Clio and the Economics of QWERTY." *American Economic Review* 75, no. 2 (May 1985): 332–337.

———. "Path Dependence, Its Critics and the Quest for 'Historical Economics.'" In *Evolution and Path Dependence in Economic Ideas: Past and Present,* edited by Pierre Garrouste and Stavros Ioannides. Northampton, MA: Edward Elgar, 2001.

———. "Why Are Institutions the 'Carriers of History'? Path Dependence and the Evolution of Conventions, Organizations, and Institutions." *Structural Change and Economic Dynamics* 5, no. 2 (1994): 205–220.

Diamond, Jared, and James Robinson, eds. *Natural Experiments of History.* Cambridge, MA: Belknap Press of Harvard University Press, 2010.

Dickson, P. G. M. *The Financial Revolution in England: A Study in the Development of Public Credit, 1688–1756.* London: Macmillan, 1967.

DiMaggio, Paul J., and Walter W. Powell. "Introduction." In *The New Institutionalism in Organizational Analysis,* edited by Paul J. DiMaggio and Walter W. Powell. Chicago: University of Chicago Press, 1991.

Downing, Brian M. *The Military Revolution and Political Change: Origins of Democracy and Autocracy in Early Modern Europe.* Princeton, NJ: Princeton University Press, 1992.

Duara, Prasenjit. *Culture, Power, and the State: Rural North China, 1900–1942.* Stanford, CA: Stanford University Press, 1988.

Dunstan, Helen. *State or Merchant? Political Economy and Political Process in 1740s China.* Cambridge, MA: Harvard University Asia Center, 2006.

Duus, Peter. *Modern Japan.* 2nd ed. Boston: Houghton Mifflin, 1998.

Eguchi Hisao 江口久雄. "Ahen sensōgo ni okeru ginka taisaku to sono zasetsu" 阿片戦争後における銀価対策とその挫折 [Post-Opium War measures to counter the silver problem and their failure]. *Shakai keizai shigaku* 社會經濟史學 42, no. 3 (1976): 22–40.

Eichengreen, Barry J. *Globalizing Capital: A History of the International Monetary System.* Princeton, NJ: Princeton University Press, 1996.

———. *Golden Fetters: The Gold Standard and the Great Depression, 1919–1939.* Oxford and New York: Oxford University Press, 1992.

Elton, G. R. *England under the Tudors.* 3rd ed. London: Routledge, 1991.

Emura Eiichi 江村栄一. *Jiyū minken kakumei no kenkyū* 自由民権革命の研究 [The revolution of the People's Rights Movement]. Tokyo: Hōsei Daigaku Shuppankyoku, 1984.

Epstein, Stephan R. "The Rise of the West." In *An Anatomy of Power: The Social Theory of Michael Mann,* edited by John A. Hall and Ralph Schroeder. Cambridge and New York: Cambridge University Press, 2006.

Ericson, Steven J. "'Poor Peasant, Poor Country!': The Matsukata Deflation and Rural Distress in Mid-Meiji Japan." In *New Directions in the Study of Meiji Japan,* edited by Helen Hardacre and Adam L. Kern. Leiden and New York: Brill, 1997.

———. *The Sound of the Whistle: Railroads and the State in Meiji Japan.* Cambridge, MA: Council on East Asian Studies of Harvard University Press, 1996.

Ertman, Thomas. *Birth of the Leviathan: Building States and Regimes in Medieval and Early Modern Europe.* Cambridge and New York: Cambridge University Press, 1997.

Fearon, James. "Causes and Counterfactuals in Social Science: Exploring an Analogy between Cellular Automata and Historical Processes." In *Counterfactual Thought Experiments in World Politics: Logical, Methodological,*

and *Psychological Perspectives,* edited by Philip E. Tetlock and Aaron
Belkin. Princeton, NJ: Princeton University Press, 1996.

Ferber, Katalin. "'Run the State Like a Business': The Origin of the Deposit
Fund in Meiji Japan." *Journal of Japanese Studies* 22, no. 2 (2002):
131–151.

Ferguson, Niall. *The Cash Nexus: Money and Power in the Modern World,
1700–2000* (New York: Basic Books, 2001).

Feuerwerker, Albert. *China's Early Industrialization: Sheng Hsuan-Huai
(1844–1916) and Mandarin Enterprise.* Cambridge, MA: Harvard
University Press, 1958.

Fisher, Douglas. "The Price Revolution: A Monetary Interpretation." *Journal
of Economic History* 49, no. 4 (1989): 883–902.

Frank, Andre Gunder. *ReOrient: Global Economy in the Asian Age.* Berkeley:
University of California Press, 1998.

Fujii Jōji 藤井讓治. "Jūshichi seiki no Nihon—Buke no kokka no keisei"
十七世紀の日本－武家の国家の形成 [Japan in the seventeenth century:
The formation of a military state]. In *Iwanami kōza Nihon tsūshi* 岩波講座
日本通史 [The Iwanami general history of Japan]. Vol. 12, *Kinsei* (2) 近世
(2) [The early modern period], edited by Asao Naohiro 朝尾直弘 et al.
Tokyo: Iwanami Shoten, 1994.

Fujimura Tōru 藤村通. *Meiji zaisei kakuritsu katei no kenkyū* 明治財政確立過
程の研究 [Building the public finance of the Meiji regime]. Tokyo: Chūō
Daigaku Shuppanbu, 1968.

———. *Meiji zenki kōsai seisakushi kenkyū* 明治前期公債政策史研究 [Bond
policy in early Meiji]. Tokyo: Daitō Bunka Daigaku Tōyō Kenkyūjo, 1977.

Fujita Satoru 藤田覚. *Bakuhansei kokka no seijishi teki kenkyū* 幕藩制国家の
政治史的研究 [The political history of the shogunate-domain system].
Tokyo: Azekura Shobō, 1987.

———. "Jūku seiki zenhan no Nihon" 十九世紀前半の日本 [Japan in the first
half of the nineteenth century]. In *Iwanami kōza Nihon tsūshi* 岩波講座日
本通史 [The Iwanami general history of Japan]. Vol. 15, *Kinsei* (5) 近世 (5)
[The early modern period], edited by Asao Naohiro 朝尾直弘 et al. Tokyo:
Iwanami Shoten, 1995.

———. "Tenpō kaikakuki no kaibō seisaku ni tsuite" 天保改革期の海防政策
について [A study of the policies of seaborne defense in the Tenpō period].
Rekishigaku kenkyū 歴史学研究 469 (1979): 19–33.

Fujiwara Takao 藤原隆男. *Kindai Nihon shuzōgyōshi* 近代日本酒造業史 [A
history of sake brewing in modern Japan]. Kyoto: Mineruva Shobō, 1999.

Fukaya Tokujirō 深谷徳次郎. *Meiji seifu zaisei kiban no kakuritsu* 明治政府財
政基盤の確立 [Laying the foundation of Meiji public finance]. Tokyo:
Ochanomizu Shobō, 1995.

Fukuchi Atsushi 福地惇. *Meiji shinseiken no kenryoku kōzō* 明治新政権の権力構造 [The power structure of the new Meiji government]. Tokyo: Yoshikawa Kōbunkan, 1996.

Fukushima Masao 福島正夫. *Chiso kaisei no kenkyū* 地租改正の研究 [Land tax reform]. Rev. ed. Tokyo: Yūhikaku, 1970.

Fumoto Shin'ichi 麓慎一. "Ishin seihu no hoppo seisaku" 維新政府の北方政策 [The northern policy of the Restoration regime]. *Rekishigaku kenkyū* 歴史学研究 725 (July 1999): 14–31.

Furushima Toshio. "The Village and Agriculture during the Edo Period." In *The Cambridge History of Japan.* Vol. 4, *Early Modern Japan,* edited by John Whitney Hall. Cambridge and New York: Cambridge University Press, 1991.

Gaddis, John L. *The Landscape of History: How Historians Map the Past.* Oxford and New York: Oxford University Press, 2002.

Gao Congming 高聡明. *Songdai huobi yu huobi liutong yanjiu* 宋代貨幣與貨幣流通研究 [Money and monetary circulation in the Song dynasty]. Baoding: Hebei daxue chubanshe, 2000.

Gao Wangling 高王陵. *Shiba shiji Zhongguo de jingji fazhan he zhengfu zhengce* 十八世纪中国的经济发展和政府政策 [Economic development in eighteenth-century China and government policy]. Beijing: Zhongguo shehui kexue chubanshe, 1995.

Gentles, Ian. *The New Model Army in England, Ireland, and Scotland, 1645–1653.* Oxford and Cambridge, MA: B. Blackwell, 1992.

Gerschenkron, Alexander. *Economic Backwardness in Historical Perspective.* Cambridge, MA: Belknap Press of Harvard University Press, 1962.

Godai Tomoatsu denki shiryō 五代友厚伝記資料 [Biographical materials on Godai Tomoatsu]. Vol. 2, edited by Nihon Keieishi Kenkyūjo 日本経営史研究所. Tokyo: Tōyō Keizai Shinpō Sha, 1972.

Goldstone, Jack A. "Efflorescences and Economic Growth in World History: Rethinking the 'Rise of the West' and the British Industrial Revolution." *Journal of World History* 13 (2002): 323–389.

———. "Initial Conditions, General Laws, Path Dependence, and Explanation in Historical Sociology." *American Journal of Sociology* 104, no. 3 (November 1998): 829–845.

———. *Revolution and Rebellion in the Early Modern World.* Berkeley: University of California Press, 1991.

———. "Urbanization and Inflation: Lessons from the English Price Revolution of the Sixteenth and Seventeenth Centuries." *American Journal of Sociology* 89, no. 5 (1984): 1122–1160.

Gongzhongdang Guangxu chao zouzhe [GGCZ] 宮中檔光緒朝奏摺 [Palace memorials of the Guangxu reign], edited by Guoli gugong bowuyuan

Gugong wenxian bianji weiyuanhui 國立故宮博物院故宮文獻編輯委員會.
24 vols. Taipei: Guoli gugong bowuyuan, 1973–1975.

Greif, Avner. *Institutions and the Path to the Modern Economy: Lessons from
Medieval Trade.* Cambridge and New York: Cambridge University Press,
2006.

Greif, Avner, and David D. Laitin. "A Theory of Endogenous Institutional
Change." *American Political Science Review* 98, no. 4 (November 2004):
633–652.

Guangxu chao Donghua lu 光緒朝東華錄 [The Guangxu period *Donghua lu*],
edited by Zhu Shoupeng 朱壽朋. 5 vols. Beijing: Zhonghua shuju, 1958.

Guangxu chao zhupi zouzhe 光緒朝硃批奏摺 [Imperially rescripted palace
memorials of the Guangxu reign], edited by Zhongguo diyi lishi
dang'anguan 中國第一歷史檔案館. 120 vols. Beijing: Zhonghua shuju,
1995–1996.

Haga Shōji 羽賀祥二. "Meiji Ishin to 'seihyō' no hensei" 明治維新と「政表」
の編製 [The Meiji Restoration and the making of statistical data]. *Nihonshi kenkyū* 日本史研究 388 (December 1994): 49–74.

Hall, John Whitney. *Tanuma Okitsugu, 1719–1788: Forerunner of Modern
Japan.* Cambridge, MA: Harvard University Press, 1955.

Hall, Peter A. "Aligning Ontology and Methodology in Comparative Re-
search." In *Comparative Historical Analysis in the Social Sciences,* edited by
James Mahoney and Dietrich Rueschemeyer. Cambridge and New York:
Cambridge University Press, 2003.

———, ed. *The Political Power of Economic Ideas: Keynesianism across
Nations.* Princeton, NJ: Princeton University Press, 1989.

Hall, Peter A., and David W. Soskice. *Varieties of Capitalism: The Institutional
Foundations of Comparative Advantage.* Oxford and New York: Oxford
University Press, 2001.

Hamashita Takeshi 浜下武志. "Shinmatsu Chūgoku ni okeru 'ginkōron' to
Chūgoku Tsūshō Ginkō no setsuritsu" 清末中国における「銀行論」と中
国通商銀行の設立 [Discussions on the state bank in late nineteenth-century
China and the establishment of the Imperial Bank of China]. *Hitotsubashi
ronsō* 一橋論叢 85, no. 6 (June 1981): 747–766.

Harada Mikio 原田三喜雄. *Nihon no kindaika to keizai seisaku: Meiji
kōgyōka seisaku kenkyū* 日本の近代化と經濟政策：明治工業化政策研究
[Economic policy and Japan's modernization: Research into Meiji industrialization policy]. Tokyo: Tōyō Keizai Shinpōsha, 1972.

Haraguchi Kiyoshi 原口清. "Haihan chiken seiji katei no hitotsu kōsatsu" 廃藩
置県政治過程の一考察 [An investigation of the political process of
abolishing the domain system]. *Meijō shōgaku* 名城商学 29 (special issue)
(1980): 47–94.

Harling, Philip. *The Waning of "Old Corruption": The Politics of Economical Reform in Britain, 1779–1846.* Oxford: Clarendon Press, 1996.

Harling, Philip, and Peter Mandler. "From 'Fiscal-Military' State to Laissez-Faire State, 1760–1850." *Journal of British Studies* 32, no. 1 (January 1993): 44–70.

Harriss, G. L. "Medieval Doctrines in the Debates of Supply, 1610–1629." In *Faction and Parliament: Essays on Early Stuart History,* edited by Kevin Sharpe. Oxford: Clarendon Press, 1978.

———. "Political Society and the Growth of Government in Late Medieval England." *Past and Present* 138 (February 1993): 28–57.

Hayami Akira 速水融 and Miyamoto Matao 宮本又郎, eds. *Keizai shakai no seiritsu: 17–18-seiki* 経済社会の成立: 17–18世紀 [The formation of an economic society: Seventeenth and eighteenth centuries]. Vol. 1 of *Nihon keizaishi* 日本経済史 [The economic history of Japan]. Tokyo: Iwanami Shoten, 1988.

Hayashi Takehisa 林健久. *Nihon ni okeru sozei kokka no seiritsu* 日本における租税国家の成立 [The formation of the tax state in Japan]. Tokyo: Tōkyō Daigaku Shuppankai, 1965.

Haydon, Peter. *The English Pub: A History.* London: Robert Hale, 1994.

Haydu, Jeffrey. "Making Use of the Past: Time Periods as Cases to Compare and as Sequences of Problem Solving." *American Journal of Sociology* 104, no. 2 (September 1998): 339–371.

He Lie 何烈. *Lijin zhidu xintan* 厘金制度新探 [A new exploration of the institution of *lijin*]. Taipei: Taiwan shangwu yinshuguan, 1972.

———. *Qing Xian Tong shiqi di caizheng (1851–1874)* 清咸同時期的財政 (1851–1874) [The public finance of the Qing government in the reigns of Xianfeng and Tongzhi (1851–1874)]. Taipei: Guoli bianyiguan, 1981.

Helleiner, Eric. *The Making of National Money: Territorial Currencies in Historical Perspective.* Ithaca, NY: Cornell University Press, 2003.

Hicks, John. *A Theory of Economic History.* Oxford: Oxford University Press, 1969.

Hill, B. W. "The Change of Government and the 'Loss of the City,' 1710–1711." *Economic History Review,* n.s. 21, no. 3 (August 1971): 395–413.

Hindle, Steve. *The State and Social Change in Early Modern England, c. 1550–1640.* New York: Palgrave Macmillan, 2000.

Hirakawa Arata 平川新. "Chiiki keizai no tenkai" 地域経済の展開 [The development of a regional economy]. In *Iwanami kōza Nihon tsūshi* 岩波講座日本通史 [The Iwanami general history of Japan]. Vol. 15, *Kinsei (5)* 近世 (5) [The early modern period], edited by Asao Naohiro et al. Tokyo: Iwanami Shoten, 1995.

Ho Hon-wai 何漢威. "Cong yinjian qianhuang dao tongyuan fanlan: Qingmo xinhuobi de faxing jiqi yingxiang" 從銀賤錢荒到銅元氾濫: 清末新貨幣的

發行及其影響 [From scarcity of copper cash to excessive minting of copper currency: The impact of minting new currencies in the last years of the Qing]. *Zhongyang yanjiuyuan lishiyuyansuo jikan* 中央研究院歷史言語所集刊 62, no. 3 (1993): 389–494.

———. "Qingji guochan yapian de tongjuan yu tongshui" 清季國產鴉片的統捐與統稅 [Centralization in opium tax collection in the late Qing]. In *Xinhuoji: chuantong yu jindai bianqianzhong de Zhongguo jingji; Quan Hansheng jiaoshou jiuzhi rongqing zhushou lunwenji* 薪火集：传统与近代变迁中的中国经济；全漢升教授九秩榮慶祝壽論文集 [The traditional and early modern Chinese economy: Essays in honor of Professor Quan Hansheng's ninetieth birthday], edited by Quan Hansheng jiaoshou jiuzhi rongqing zhushuo lunwenji bianji weiyuanhui. Banqiao: Daoxiang chubanshe, 2001.

———. "Qingji zhongyang yu gesheng caizheng guanxi de fansi" 清季中央與各省財政關係的反思 [A reflection on the fiscal relationship between the center and the provinces in the late Qing]. *Zhongyang yanjiuyuan lishiyuyansuo jikan* 中央研究院歷史言語所集刊 72, no. 3 (September 2001): 597–698.

———. "Qingmo fushui jizhun de kuoda jiqi juxian" 清末賦稅基準的擴大及其局限 [The expansion of and limits to tax collection in the late Qing]. *Zhongyang yanjiuyuan jindaishi yanjiusuo jikan* 中央研究院近代史研究所集刊 17, no. 2 (December 1988): 69–98.

Holmes, Geoffrey S. *The Making of a Great Power: Late Stuart and Early Georgian Britain, 1660–1722*. London and New York: Longman, 1993.

Hoppit, Julian. "Attitudes to Credit in Britain." *Historical Journal* 33, no. 2 (1990): 308–311.

———. "Financial Crises in Eighteenth-Century England." *Economic History Review*, n.s., 39, no. 1 (February 1986): 39–58.

———. "The Myths of the South Sea Bubble." *Transactions of the Royal Historical Society*, 6th s., 12 (2002): 141–165.

Horesh, Niv. *Shanghai's Bund and Beyond: British Banks, Banknote Issuance, and Monetary Policy in China, 1842–1937*. New Haven and London: Yale University Press, 2009.

Horsefield, J. Keith. *British Monetary Experiments, 1650–1710*. Cambridge, MA: Harvard University Press, 1960.

———. "The 'Stop of the Exchequer' Revisited." *Economic History Review*, n.s., 35, no. 4 (November 1982): 511–528.

Horwitz, Henry. *Parliament, Policy, and Politics in the Reign of William III*. Newark: University of Delaware Press, 1977.

Hoskins, W. G. *The Age of Plunder: King Henry's England, 1500–1547*. London: Longman, 1976.

Hosomi Kazuhiro 細見和弘. "Ri Kōshō to kobu" 李鴻章と戸部 [Li Hong-zhang and the Board of Revenue]. *Tōyōshi kenkyū* 東洋史研究 56, no. 4 (March 1998): 811–838.

Howell, David L. *Capitalism from Within: Economy, Society, and the State in a Japanese Fishery.* Berkeley: University of California Press, 1995.

Hoyle, Richard W. "Crown, Parliament, and Taxation in Sixteenth-Century England." *English Historical Review* 109, no. 434 (November 1994): 1174–1196.

———. "Disafforestation and Drainage: The Crown as Entrepreneur?" In *The Estates of the English Crown, 1558–1640,* edited by Richard W. Hoyle. Cambridge and New York: Cambridge University Press, 1992.

Huang Jianhui 黄鉴晖. *Shanxi piaohaoshi* 山西票号史 [A history of Shanxi bankers]. Rev. ed. Taiyuan: Shanxi jingji chubanshe, 2002.

Huang, Ray. *Taxation and Governmental Finance in Sixteenth-Century Ming China.* London and New York: Cambridge University Press, 1974.

Huang Zunxian 黄遵憲. *Riben guo zhi* 日本國志 [A history of Japan]. Shang-hai: Tushu jicheng yinshuju, 1898; reprint, Taipei: Wenhai chubanshe, 1968.

Hughes, Ann. *The Causes of the English Civil War.* 2nd ed. Basingstoke, UK: Macmillan, 1991.

Hughes, Edward. *Studies in Administration and Finance, 1558–1825, with Special Reference to the History of Salt Taxation in England.* Manchester: Manchester University Press, 1934.

Hundred-Year Statistics of the Japanese Economy / Meiji ikō honpō shuyō keizai tōkei 明治以降本邦主要経済統計, edited by Nihon Ginkō Tōkei-kyoku 日本銀行統計局. Tokyo: Nihon Ginkō Tōkeikyoku, 1966.

Ikeda Kōtarō 池田浩太郎. "Kankin toriatsuka seisaku to shihonshūgi no seiritsu" 官金取扱政策と資本主義の成立 [The handling of government funds and the establishment of capitalism]. In *Meiji shoki no zaisei kin'yū seisaku* 明治初期の財政金融政策 [Early Meiji fiscal and financial policies], edited by Okada Shunpei 岡田俊平. Tokyo: Seimeikai Sōsho, 1964.

Ikegami, Eiko. *The Taming of the Samurai: Honorific Individualism and the Making of Modern Japan.* Cambridge, MA: Harvard University Press, 1995.

Ikegami Kazuo 池上和夫. "Meijiki no shuzei seisaku" 明治期の酒税政策 [Sake tax policy in the Meiji era]. *Shakai keizai shigaku* 社会経済史学 55, no. 2 (June 1989): 189–212.

Imuta Yoshimitsu 伊牟田敏充. "Nihon Ginkō no hakken seido to seifu kin'yū" 日本銀行の発券制度と政府金融 [The Bank of Japan: Note issue and public finance]. *Shakai keizai shigaku* 社會經濟史學 38, no. 2 (1972): 116–154, 249–250.

Inoki Takenori 猪木武徳. "Chiso beinōron to zaisei seiri" 地租米納論と財政整理 [The proposal of land taxation in rice and the adjustment of public finance]. In *Matsukata zaisei to shokusan kōgyō seisaku* 松方財政と殖産興業政策 [Matsukata public finance and the policy of fostering production and encouraging enterprises], edited by Umemura Mataji 梅村又次 and Nakamura Takafusa 中村隆英. Tokyo: Kokusai Rengō Daigaku, 1983.

Inoue Hiromasa 井上裕正. *Shindai ahen seisakushi no kenkyū* 清代アヘン政策史の研究 [Qing opium policy before the Opium War]. Kyoto: Kyōto Daigaku Gakujutsu Shuppankai, 2004.

Inoue Katsuo 井上勝生. *Bakumatsu Ishin seijishi no kenkyū: Nihon kindai kokka no seisei ni tsuite* 幕末維新政治史の研究：日本近代国家の生成について [Studies in the political history of late Tokugawa and early Meiji]. Tokyo: Hanawa Shobō, 1994.

Ishii Kanji 石井寛治. "Japan." In *International Banking, 1870–1914,* edited by Rondo Cameron, V. I. Bovykin, and B. V. Anan'ich. New York: Oxford University Press, 1991.

———. *Nihon Ginkō kin'yū seisakushi* 日本銀行金融政策史 [Historical studies of the financial policy of the Bank of Japan]. Tokyo: Tōkyō Daigaku Shuppankai, 2001.

Ishii Kanji 石井寛治, Hara Akira 原朗, and Takeda Haruhito 武田晴人, eds., *Nihon keizaishi I: Bakumatsu-Ishinki* 日本経済史（1）：幕末維新期 [An economic history of Japan (I): The late Tokugawa and early Meiji period]. Tokyo: Tōkyō Daigaku Shuppankai, 2000.

Ishii Takashi 石井孝. *Boshin Sensō ron* 戊辰戦争論 [On the Boshin Civil War]. Tokyo: Yoshikawa Kōbunkan, 1984.

———. "Haihan no katei ni okeru seikyoku no dōkō" 廃藩の過程における政局の動向 [Political trends in the process of abolishing the domains]. Originally published in *Tōhoku Daigaku bungakubu kenkyū nenpō* 東北大学文学部研究年報 19 (July 1969); reprinted in *Ishin seiken no seiritsu* 維新政権の成立 [The establishment of the Restoration government], edited by Matsuo Masahito 松尾正仁. Tokyo: Yoshikawa Kōbunkan, 2001.

———. *Meiji Ishin to jiyū minken* 明治維新と自由民権 [The Meiji Restoration and the Freedom and People's Rights Movement]. Yokohama: Yūrindō, 1993.

Ishizuka Hiromichi 石塚裕道. "Shokusan kōgyō seisaku no tenkai" 殖産興業政策の展開 [The unfolding of the shokusan kōgyō policies]. In *Nihon keizaishi taikei* 日本経済史大系 [Compendium of materials on the economic history of Japan]. Vol. 5, *Kindai* 近代 [The modern period], edited by Kajinishi Mitsuhaya 楫西光速. Tokyo: Tōkyō daigaku Shuppankai, 1965.

Israel, Jonathan I. "The Dutch Role in the Glorious Revolution." In *The Anglo-Dutch Moment: Essays on the Glorious Revolution and Its World*

Impact, edited by Jonathan I. Israel. Cambridge and New York: Cambridge University Press, 1991.

Iwai Shigeki 岩井茂樹. *Chūgoku kinsei zaiseishi no kenkyū* 中国近世財政史の研究 [A study of the fiscal history of early modern China]. Kyoto: Kyōto Daigaku Gakujutsu Shuppankai, 2004.

———. "Shindai kokka zaisei ni okeru chūō to chihō" 清代国家財政における中央と地方 [The center-local relationship in the fiscal system of the Qing dynasty]. *Tōyōshi kenkyū* 東洋史研究 42, no. 2 (September 1983): 318–346.

Iwasaki Hiroshi 岩崎宏之. "Kokuritsu ginkō seido no seiritsu to fuken kawasekata" 国立銀行制度の成立と府県為替方 [The establishment of the national banking system and the money transmitters of cities and prefectures]. *Mitsui bunko ronso* 三井文庫論叢 2 (1968): 167–231.

Jansen, Marius B. "The Meiji Restoration." In *The Cambridge History of Japan.* Vol. 5, *The Nineteenth Century,* edited by Marius B. Jansen. Cambridge and New York: Cambridge University Press, 1989.

Jiaqing Daoguang liangchao shangyu dang 嘉慶道光兩朝上諭檔 [Edicts during the reigns of Jiaqing and Daoguang], edited by Zhongguo diyi lishi dang'anguan 中國第一歷史檔案館. 55 vols. Guilin: Guangxi shifan daxue chubanshe, 2000.

Jones, D. W. *War and Economy in the Age of William III and Marlborough.* Oxford: Basil Blackwell, 1988.

Jones, J. R. *The Anglo-Dutch Wars of the Seventeenth Century.* London: Longman, 1996.

———. *Country and Court: England, 1658–1714.* Cambridge, MA: Harvard University Press, 1978.

Jones, Susan M. "Finance in Ning-Po: The Ch'ien-chuang." In *Economic Organization in Chinese Society,* edited by W. E. Willmott. Stanford, CA: Stanford University Press, 1972.

Joslin, D. M. "London Private Bankers, 1720–1785." *Economic History Review,* n.s., 7, no. 2 (1954): 167–186.

Kamiyama Tsuneo 神山恒雄. "Inoue zaisei kara Ōkuma zaisei e no tankan: Junbikin o chūshin ni" 井上財政から大隈財政への転換 ： 準備金を中心に [The policy change in public finance from Inoue to Ōkuma: The use of government reserve funds]. In *Meiji zenki no Nihon keizai: Shihon shugi he no michi* 明治前期の日本経済 ： 資本主義への道 [The Japanese economy in the early Meiji: The way toward capitalism], edited by Takamura Naosuke 高村直助. Tokyo: Nihon Keizai Hyōronsha, 2004.

———. *Meiji keizai seisakushi no kenkyū* 明治経済政策史の研究 [A history of Meiji economic policies]. Tokyo: Hanawa Shobō, 1995.

Karl, Terry Lynn. *The Paradox of Plenty: Oil Booms and Petro-States.* Berkeley: University of California Press, 1997.

Kasahara Hidehiko 笠原英彦. *Meiji kōkka to kanryōsei* 明治国家と官僚制 [The Meiji state and bureaucracy]. Tokyo: Ashi Shobō, 1991.

Kaske, Elisabeth. "Fund-Raising Wars: Office Selling and Interprovincial Finance in Nineteenth-Century China." *Harvard Journal of Asiatic Studies* 71, no. 1 (June 2010): 69–141.

Katō Kōzaburō 加藤幸三郎. "Seishō shihon no keisei" 政商資本の形成 [The formation of the capital of political merchants]. In *Nihon keizaishi taikei* 日本経済史大系 [Compendium of materials on the economic history of Japan]. Vol. 5, *Kindai* 近代, edited by Kajinishi Mitsuhaya 楫西光速. Tokyo: Tōkyō Daigaku Shuppankai, 1965.

Katō Shigeshi 加藤繁. *Shina keizaishi kōshō* 支那經濟史考證 [Studies in Chinese economic history]. Vol. 2. Tokyo: Tōyō Bunko, 1953.

Katznelson, Ira. "Periodization and Preferences: Reflections on Purposive Action in Comparative Historical Social Science." In *Comparative Historical Analysis in the Social Sciences,* edited by James Mahoney and Dietrich Rueschemeyer. Cambridge and New York: Cambridge University Press, 2003.

———. "Structure and Configuration in Comparative Politics." In *Comparative Politics: Rationality, Culture, and Structure,* edited by Mark Irving Lichbach and Alan S. Zuckerman. Cambridge and New York: Cambridge University Press, 1997.

Kerridge, Eric. *Trade and Banking in Early Modern England.* Manchester: Manchester University Press, 1988.

King, Frank H. H. *Money and Monetary Policy in China, 1845–1895.* Cambridge, MA: Harvard University Press, 1965.

King, Gary, Robert O. Keohane, and Sidney Verba. *Designing Social Inquiry: Scientific Inference in Qualitative Research.* Princeton, NJ: Princeton University Press, 1994.

Kiser, Edgar. "Markets and Hierarchies in Early Modern Tax Systems: A Principal-Agent Analysis." *Politics and Society* 22, no. 3 (September 1994): 284–315.

Kiser, Edgar, and Michael Hechter. "The Role of General Theory in Comparative-Historical Sociology." *American Journal of Sociology* 97, no. 1 (July 1991): 1–30.

Kiser, Edgar, and Joshua Kane. "Revolution and State Structure: The Bureaucratization of Tax Administration in Early Modern England and France." *American Journal of Sociology* 107, no. 1 (July 2001): 183–223.

Kishimoto Mio 岸本美緒. *Shindai Chūgoku no bukka to keizai hendō* 清代中国の物価と経済変動 [Price and economic changes in Qing China]. Tokyo: Kenbun Shuppan, 1997.

Knight, Jack. *Institutions and Social Conflict.* Cambridge and New York: Cambridge University Press, 1992.

Kokaze Hidemasa 小風秀雅. "Ōkuma zaisei matsugi ni okeru zaisei rongi no tenkai" 大隈財政末期における財政論議の展開 [The development of the discussions on public finance in the later period of Ōkuma's public finance]. In *Kindai Nihon no keizai to seiji* 近代日本の経済と政治 [Politics and economy in modern Japan], edited by Hara Akira 原朗. Tokyo: Yamakawa Shuppansha, 1986.

Komatsu Kazuo 小松和生. "Meiji zenki no shuzei seisaku to toshi shuzōgyō no dōkō" 明治前期の酒税政策と都市酒造業の動向 [The tax policy on sake production in the early Meiji and the trend of urban sake production]. *Ōsaka daigaku keizaigaku* 大阪大学経済学 17, no. 1 (June 1967): 37–57.

Krasner, Stephen D. "Approaches to the State: Alternative Conceptions and Historical Dynamics." *Comparative Politics* 16, no. 2 (January 1984): 223–246.

Kuhn, Philip A. *Origins of the Modern Chinese State*. Stanford, CA: Stanford University Press, 2002.

Kuroda Akinobu 黒田明伸. "Kenryū no senki" 乾隆の銭貴 [The appreciation of copper cash in the Qianlong era]. *Tōyōshi kenkyū* 東洋史研究 45, no. 4 (March 1987): 692–723.

Langford, Paul. *The Excise Crisis: Society and Politics in the Age of Walpole*. Oxford: Clarendon Press, 1975.

Levi, Margaret. *Of Rule and Revenue*. Berkeley: University of California Press, 1988.

Li Bozhong 李伯重. *Jiangnan de zaoqi gongyehua: 1550–1850 nian* [Early industrialization in the Lower Yangzi Delta, 1550–1850]. Beijing: Shehui kexue wenxian chubanshe, 2000.

Li Hu 李瑚. *Zhongguo jingjishi conggao* 中國經濟史叢稿 [Collected essays in the economic history of China]. Changsha: Hunan renmin chubanshe, 1986.

Li Wenzhi 李文治 and Jiang Taixin 江太新. *Qingdai caoyun* 清代漕运 [The transportation of tribute grain in the Qing dynasty]. Beijing: Zhonghua shuju, 1995.

Lieberman, Evan S. "Causal Inference in Historical Institutional Analysis: A Specification of Periodization." *Comparative Political Studies* 34, no. 9 (2001): 1011–1035.

Liebowitz, S. J., and S. E. Margolis. "The Fable of the Keys." *Journal of Law and Economics* 32, no. 1 (1990): 1–26.

Lin Man-houng 林滿紅. *China Upside Down: Currency, Society, and Ideologies, 1808–1856*. Cambridge, MA: Harvard University Asia Center, 2006.

———. "Jia Dao qianjian xianxiang chansheng yuanyin 'qianduo qianlie lun' zhi shangque" 嘉道錢賤現象產生原因「錢多錢劣論」之商榷 [A study of the falling value of copper cash vis-à-vis silver in the period between 1808 and 1850]. In *Zhongguo haiyang fazhanshi lunwenji* 中國海洋發展史論文集 [Collected essays on the history of the development of maritime China], vol. 5, edited by Zhang Bincun 張彬村 and Liu Shiji 劉石吉. Taipei: Zhongyang yanjiuyuan, 1993.

———. "Two Social Theories Revealed: Statecraft Controversies over China's Monetary Crisis, 1808–1854." *Late Imperial China* 12, no. 2 (December 1991): 1–35.

———. "Wan Qing de yapianshui, 1858–1909" 晚清的鴉片稅, 1858–1909 [Opium taxes in the late Qing, 1858–1909]. *Si yu yan* 思與言 16, no. 5 (1979): 11–59.

———. "Yin yu yapian de liutong ji yinguiqianjian xianxiang de quyu fenbu: 1808–1854 銀與鴉片的流通及銀貴錢賤現象的區域分部: 1808–1854" [The circulation of silver and opium and the geographical distribution of the high value of silver in regard to copper coins]. *Zhongyang yanjiuyuan jindaishisuo jikan* 中央研究院近代史所集刊 22, no. 1 (1993): 91–135.

Lindquist, Eric N. "The Failure of the Great Contract." *Journal of Modern History* 57, no. 4 (1985): 617–651.

———. "The King, the People and the House of Commons: The Problem of Early Jacobean Purveyance." *Historical Journal* 31, no. 3 (1988): 549–570.

Liu Kwang-ching 劉廣京. *Jingshi sixiang yu xinxing qiye* 經世思想與新興企業 [The statecraft approach and the new enterprises]. Taipei: Lianjing chuban shiye gongsi, 1990.

Liu Wei 刘伟. "Jiawu qian sishi nianjian dufu quanli de yanbian" 甲午前四十年間督撫权力的演变 [Changes to the power of provincial governors between 1855 and 1895]. *Jindaishi yanjiu* 近代史研究, no. 2 (1998): 59–81.

Liu Zenghe 刘增合. "Guangxu qianqi Hubu zhengdun caizheng zhong de guifu jiuzhi jiqi xiandu" 光緒前期戶部整頓財政中的歸附舊制及其限度 [The Ministry of Revenue's financial rectification measures in the early years of Emperor Guangxu's reign: Between restoration and innovation], *Zhongyang yanjiuyuan lishiyuyansuo jikan* 中央研究院歷史言語所集刊 79, no. 2 (June 2008): 235–297.

———. *Yapian shuishou yu Qingmo Xinzheng* 鴉片稅收与清末新政 [The tax revenues from opium and the New Policies in the last decade of the Qing]. Beijing: Sanlian shudian, 2005.

Luebbert, Gregory M. *Liberalism, Fascism, or Social Democracy: Social Classes and the Political Origins of Regimes in Interwar Europe*. Oxford and New York: Oxford University Press, 1991.

Luo Yudong 羅玉東. "Guangxu chao bujiu caizheng zhi fang'an" 光緒朝補救財政之方案 [Methods to cover public finance in the reign of the Guangxu emperor]. In *Zhongguo jindai shehui jingjishi lunji* 中國近代社會經濟史論集

[Collected essays in the socioeconomic history of early modern China], edited by Zhou Kangxie 周康燮. 2 vols. Hong Kong: Chongwen shudian, 1971.

———. *Zhongguo lijinshi* 中國釐金史 [A history of *lijin* in China]. Shanghai: Shangwu yinshuguan, 1936.

Lustick, Ian S. "History, Historiography, and Political Science: Multiple Historical Records and the Problem of Selection Bias." *American Political Science Review* 90, no. 3 (1996): 605–618.

Ma Linghe 马陵合. *Wan Qing waizhaishi yanjiu* 晚清外债史研究 [A study of the history of foreign loans in the late Qing]. Shanghai: Fudan daxue chubanshe, 2005.

Mahoney, James. "Path Dependence in Historical Sociology." *Theory and Society* 29, no. 4 (2000): 507–548.

Mahoney, James, and Gary Goertz. "The Possibility Principle: Choosing Negative Cases in Comparative Research." *American Political Science Review* 98, no. 4 (November 2004): 653–669.

Makihara Norio 牧原憲夫. *Meiji shichinen no daironsō: Kenpakusho kara mita kindai kokka to minshū* 明治七年の大論争：建白書から見た近代国家と民衆 [The great debates of 1874: The modern state and the people as viewed from the "Proposals from the People"]. Tokyo: Nihon Keizai Hyōronsha, 1990.

Mamiya Kuniyo 間宮国夫. "Shōhōshi no soshiki to kinō" 商法司の組織と機能 [Organization and function of the Bureau of Commerce]. *Shakai keizai shigaku* 社會經濟史學 29, no. 2 (1963): 138–158.

Mann, Michael. *The Sources of Social Power.* 2 vols. Cambridge and New York: Cambridge University Press, 1986–1993.

Mann, Susan. *Local Merchants and the Chinese Bureaucracy, 1750–1950.* Stanford, CA: Stanford University Press, 1987.

Masumi Junnosuke 升味準之輔. *Nihon seijishi* 日本政治史 [A political history of Japan]. 4 vols. Tokyo: Tōkyō Daigaku Shuppankai, 1988.

Mathias, Peter. *The Brewing Industry in England, 1700–1830.* Cambridge: Cambridge University Press, 1959.

———. *The Transformation of England: Essays in the Economic and Social History of England in the Eighteenth Century.* London: Methuen, 1979.

Mathias, Peter, and Patrick K. O'Brien. "Taxation in Britain and France, 1715–1810: A Comparison of the Social and Economic Incidence of Taxes Collected for the Central Governments." *Journal of European Economic History* 5, no. 3 (1976): 601–650.

Matsukata Masayoshi kankei monjo 松方正義関係文書 [Documents related to Matsukata Masayoshi], edited by Ōkubo Tatsumasa 大久保達正. 20 vols. Tokyo: Daitō Bunka Daigaku Tōyō Kenkyūjo, 1979–2001.

Matsuo Masahito 松尾正人. *Haihan chiken no kenkyū* 廃藩置県の研究 [A study of the abolishing of the domains]. Tokyo: Yoshikawa Kōbunkan, 2001.

———. "Hantaisei kaitai to Iwakura Tomomi" 藩体制解体と岩倉具視 [The collapse of the domain system and Iwakura Tomomi]. In *Bakumatsu Ishin no shakai to shisō* 幕末維新の社会と思想 [Society and thought in the late Tokugawa and Meiji Restoration], edited by Tanaka Akira 田中彰. Tokyo: Yoshikawa Kōbunkan, 1999.

———. "Ishin kanryōsei no keisei to Dajōkansei" 維新官僚制の形成と太政官製 [The formation of the bureaucrats of the Restoration regime and the Council of State]. In *Kanryōsei no keisei to tenkai* 官僚制の形成と展開 [The formation and development of bureaucracy], edited by Kindai Nihon Kenkyūkai 近代日本研究会. Tokyo: Yamagawa Shuppansha, 1986.

———. "Meiji shonen no seijō to chihō shihai" 明治初年の政情と地方支配 : 「民蔵分離」問題前後 [The political situation and local rule in the early Meiji: Before and after "Minzobunri"]. *Tochi seido shigaku* 土地制度史学 23, no. 3 (1981): 42–57.

McCallion, S. "Trial and Error: The Model Filiature at Tomioka." In *Managing Industrial Enterprise: Cases from Japan's Prewar Experience*, edited by William D. Wray. Cambridge, MA: Council on East Asian Studies, Harvard University, 1989.

Meiji zaiseishi 明治財政史 [A fiscal history of the Meiji], edited by Meiji zaiseishi hensankai 明治財政史編纂会. 15 vols. Tokyo: Yoshikawa Kōbunkan, 1972.

Meiji zenki zaisei keizai shiryō shūsei 明治前期財政経済史料集成 [Collected primary materials on the finance and economy of early Meiji], edited by Ōuchi Hyōe 大内兵衛, Tsuchiya Takao 土屋喬雄, and Ōkurashō 大蔵省. 21 vols. Tokyo: Meiji Bunken Shiryō Kankōkai, 1962.

Migdal, Joel S. *Strong Societies and Weak States: State-Society Relations and State Capabilities in the Third World*. Princeton, NJ: Princeton University Press, 1988.

Mikami Kazuo 三上一夫. *Kōbu gattairon no kenkyū: Echizen-han Bakumatsu Ishinshi bunseki* 公武合体論の研究 : 越前藩幕末維新史分析 [A study of the efforts to unify the court and the shogun: An analysis of the history of Echizen in late Tokugawa and early Meiji]. Rev. ed. Tokyo: Ochanomizu Shobō, 1990.

Mikami Ryūzō 三上隆三. *En no tanjō: Kindai kahei seido no seiritsu* 円の誕生 : 近代貨幣制度の成立 [The birth of the yen: The establishment of the modern monetary system]. Rev. and enlarged ed. Tokyo: Tōyō Keizai Shinpōsha, 1989.

Mitchell, B. R. *Abstract of British Historical Statistics*. Cambridge: Cambridge University Press, 1962.

Miwa Ryōichi 三和良一. *Nihon kindai no keizai seisakushiteki kenkyū* 日本近代の経済政策史的研究 [A historical study of economic policy in modern Japan]. Tokyo: Nihon Keizai Hyōronsha, 2002.

Miyachi Masato 宮地正人. "Haihan chiken no seiji katei" 廃藩置県の政治過程 [The political process of abolishing the domains]. In *Nihon kindaishi ni okeru tentanki no kenkyū* 日本近代史における転換期の研究 [Studies of the transition period in the modern history of Japan], edited by Banno Junji 坂野潤治 and Miyachi Masato 宮地正人. Tokyo: Yamakawa Shuppansha, 1985.

———. "Ishin seiken ron" 維新政権論 [On the restored government]. In *Iwanami kōza Nihon tsūshi* 岩波講座日本通史 [The Iwanami general history of Japan]. Vol. 16, *Kindai* (1) 近代 (1) [The modern period], edited by Asao Naohiro 朝尾直弘 et al. Tokyo: Iwanami Shoten, 1994.

Miyamoto Matao 宮本又郎. "Bukka to makuro keizai no henka" 物価とマクロ経済の変化 [Changes in prices and macroeconomy]. In *Nihon keizaishi* 日本経済史 [The economic history of Japan]. Vol. 2, *Kindai seichō no taidō* 近代成長の胎動 [Gathering momentum for modern growth], edited by Shinbo Hiroshi 新保博 and Saitō Osamu 斎藤修. Tokyo: Iwanami Shoten, 1989.

Mōri Toshihiko 毛利敏彦. *Meiji Ishin no saihakken* 明治維新の再発見 [Rediscovering the Meiji Restoration]. Tokyo: Yoshikawa Kōbunkan, 1993.

Muroyama Yoshimasa 室山義正. *Kindai Nihon no gunji to zaisei: Kaigun kakuchō o meguru seisaku keisei katei* 近代日本の軍事と財政：海軍拡張をめぐる政策形成過程 [Public finance and the military in modern Japan: The formation of policy regarding expansion of the navy]. Tokyo: Tōkyō Daigaku Shuppankai, 1984.

———. "Matsukata defureishon no mekanizumu" 松方デフレーションのメカニズム [The mechanism of the Matsukata deflation]. In *Matsukata zaisei to shokusan kōgyō seisaku* 松方財政と殖産興業政策 [Matsukata public finance and the policy of fostering production and encouraging enterprise], edited by Umemura Mataji 梅村又次 and Nakamura Takafusa 中村隆英. Tokyo: Kokusai Rengō Daigaku, 1983.

———. *Matsukata zaisei kenkyū* 松方財政研究 [Matsukata's public finance policies]. Kyoto: Mineruva Shobō, 2004.

Murphy, Anne L. *The Origins of English Financial Markets: Investment and Speculation before the South Sea Bubble.* Cambridge and New York: Cambridge University Press, 2009.

Nagai Hideo 永井秀夫. "Shokusan kōgyō seisaku no kichō: Kanei jigyō o chūshin tosite" 殖産興業政策の基調—官営事業を中心として [The basic tune in the industry-promotion policies]. Originally published in *Hokkaidō daigaku bungakubu kiyō* 10 (November 1969); reprinted in Nagai Hideo,

Meiji kokka keiseiki no gaisei to naisei 明治国家形成期の外政と内政
[External and domestic politics in the formative period of the Meiji state].
Sapporo: Hokkaidō Daigaku Tosho Kankōkai, 1990.

Nagaoka Shinkichi 長岡新吉. *Meiji kyōkōshi josetsu* 明治恐慌史序説 [A study
of the history of financial panic in Meiji Japan]. Tokyo: Tōkyō Daigaku
Shuppankai, 1971.

Nakai Nobuhiko 中井信彦. *Tenkanki bakuhansei no kenkyū: Hōreki, Tenmeiki no keizai seisaku to shōhin ryūtsū* 転換期幕藩制の研究: 宝暦. 天明期
の経済政策と商品流通 [A study of the shogunate-domain system in
transition: Economic policy and the flow of goods in the period of Hōreki
and Tenmei (1751–1788)]. Tokyo: Hanawa Shobō, 1971.

Nakamura Masanori 中村政則, Ishii Kanji 石井寛治, and Kasuga Yutaka
春日豊, eds. *Keizai kōsō* 経済構想 [Economic schemes]. Vol. 8 of *Nihon
kindai shisō taikei* 日本近代思想大系 [Compendium of modern thought in
Japan]. Tokyo: Iwanami Shoten, 1988.

Nakamura Naofumi 中村尚史. *Nihon tetsudōgyō no keisei: 1869–1894-nen*
日本鉄道業の形成: 1869–1894年 [The formation of the railway industry
in Japan, 1869–1894]. Tokyo: Nihon Keizai Hyōronsha, 1998.

Nakamura Naomi 中村尚美. *Ōkuma Shigenobu* 大隈重信. Tokyo: Yoshikawa
Kōbunkan, 1961.

———. *Ōkuma zaisei no kenkyū* 大隈財政の研究 [The public finance policies
of Ōkuma]. Tokyo: Azekura Shobō, 1968.

Nakamura Takafusa 中村隆英. "Makuro keizai to sengo kei'ei" マクロ経済と
戦後経営 [The macroeconomy and postwar management]. In *Nihon
keizaishi* 日本経済史 [The economic history of Japan]. Vol. 5, *Sangyōka no
jidai (ge)* 産業化の時代（下） [The age of industrialization, part 2], edited
by Nishikawa Shunsaku 西川俊作 and Abe Takeshi 阿部武司. Tokyo:
Iwanami Shoten, 1990.

———. "Shuzōgyō no sūryōshi—Meiji-Shōwa shoki" 酒造業の数量史—明
治-昭和初期 [A quantitative history of sake brewing—Meiji to early
Shōwa]. *Shakai keizai shigaku* 社會經濟史學 55, no. 2 (June 1989):
213–241.

Nakamura Tetsuo 中村哲夫. "Kindai Chūgoku no tsūka taisei no kaikaku"
近代中国の通貨体制の改革：中国通商銀行の創業 [The reform of the
monetary system in modern China: The opening of the Chinese Imperial
Bank]. *Shakai keizai shigaku* 社會經濟史學 62, no. 3 (August/September
1996): 313–341.

Neal, Larry. "The Finance of Business during the Industrial Revolution." In
The Economic History of Britain since 1700, Vol. 1, edited by Roderick
Floud and Deirdre N. McCloskey. 2nd ed. Cambridge and New York:
Cambridge University Press, 1994.

———. "The Monetary, Financial, and Political Architecture of Europe, 1648–1815." In *Exceptionalism and Industrialization: Britain and Its European Rivals, 1688–1815,* edited by Leandro Prados de la Escosura and Patrick K. O'Brien. Cambridge and New York: Cambridge University Press, 2004.

———. *The Rise of Financial Capitalism: International Capital Markets in the Age of Reason.* Cambridge and New York: Cambridge University Press, 1990.

Neal, Larry, and Stephen Quinn. "Networks of Information, Markets, and Institutions in the Rise of London as a Financial Centre, 1660–1720." *Financial History Review* 8, no. 1 (April 2001): 7–26.

Nelson, Richard R. "Recent Evolutionary Theorizing about Economic Change." *Journal of Economic Literature* 33, no. 1 (March 1995): 48–90.

Ni Yuping 倪玉平. *Boyi yu junheng: Qingdai Lianghuai yanzheng gaige* 博弈与均衡 : 清代两淮盐政改革 [Games and equilibria: Reforms in the salt administration of Lianghuai in the Qing dynasty]. Fuzhou: Fujian renmin chubanshe, 2006.

———. *Qingdai caoliang haiyun yu shehui bianqian* 清代漕粮海运与社会变迁 [The seaborne transport of tribute grain and social change in the Qing dynasty]. Shanghai: Shanghai shudian chubanshe, 2005.

Nichols, Glenn O. "English Government Borrowing, 1660–1688." *Journal of British Studies* 10, no. 2 (May 1971): 83–104.

Nishikawa Shunsaku 西川俊作 and Amano Masatoshi 天野雅敏. "Shohan no sangyō to keizai seisaku" 諸藩の産業と経済政策 [The industrial and economic policies of domains]. In *Nihon keizaishi* 日本経済史 [The economic history of Japan]. Vol. 2, *Kindai seichō no taidō* 近代成長の胎動 [Gathering momentum for modern growth], edited by Shinbo Hiroshi 新保博 and Saitō Osamu 斎藤修. Tokyo: Iwanami Shoten, 1989.

Niwa Kunio 丹羽邦男. "Chiso kaisei to nōgyō kōzō no henka" 地租改正と農業構造の変化 [Land tax reform and changes in the structure of agriculture]. In *Nihon keizaishi taikei* 日本経済史大系 [Compendium of materials on the economic history of Japan]. Vol. 5, *Kindai* 近代 [The modern period], edited by Kajinishi Mitsuhaya 楫西光速. Tokyo: Tōkyō Daigaku Shuppankai, 1965.

———. *Chiso kaiseihō no kigen: Kaimei kanryō no keisei* 地租改正法の起源 : 開明官僚の形成 [The origin of land tax reform: The formation of the enlightened bureaucrats]. Kyoto: Mineruva Shobō, 1995.

North, Douglass C. "Five Propositions about Institutional Change." In *Explaining Social Institutions,* edited by Jack Knight and Itai Sened. Ann Arbor: University of Michigan Press, 1995.

———. *Institutions, Institutional Change, and Economic Performance.* Cambridge and New York: Cambridge University Press, 1990.

North, Douglass C., and Barry R. Weingast. "Constitutions and Commitment: The Evolution of Institutions Governing Public Choice in Seventeenth-Century England." *Journal of Economic History* 49, no. 4 (1989): 803–832.

O'Brien, Patrick K. "Fiscal Exceptionalism: Great Britain and Its European Rivals from Civil War to Triumph at Trafalgar and Waterloo." In *The Political Economy of British Historical Experience, 1688–1914,* edited by Donald Winch and Patrick K. O'Brien. Oxford: Published for the British Academy by Oxford University Press, 2002.

———. "The Political Economy of British Taxation, 1660–1815." *Economic History Review,* n.s., 41, no. 1 (February 1988): 1–32.

O'Brien, Patrick K., and Philip A. Hunt. "England, 1485–1815." In *The Rise of the Fiscal State in Europe, 1200–1815,* edited by Richard Bonney. Oxford and New York: Oxford University Press, 1999.

———. "Excises and the Rise of a Fiscal State in England, 1586–1688." In *Crises, Revolutions, and Self-Sustained Growth: Essays in European Fiscal History, 1130–1830,* edited by W. M. Ormrod, Margaret Bonney, and Richard Bonney. Stamford, UK: Shaun Tyas, 1999.

———. "The Rise of a Fiscal State in England, 1485–1815." *Historical Research* 66, no. 160 (1993): 129–176.

Ochiai Hiroki 落合弘樹. *Meiji kokka to shizoku* 明治国家と士族 [The Meiji state and the samurai]. Tokyo: Yoshikawa Kōbunkan, 2001.

Ogborn, Miles. "The Capacities of the State: Charles Davenant and the Management of the Excise, 1683–1698." *Journal of Historical Geography* 24, no. 3 (1998): 289–312.

———. *Spaces of Modernity: London's Geographies, 1680–1780.* New York: Guilford Press, 1998.

Ogg, David. *England in the Reigns of James II and William III.* Oxford: Clarendon Press; New York: Oxford University Press, 1955.

Ōguchi Yūjirō 大口勇次郎. "Bakufu no zaisei" 幕府の財政 [The public finance of the shogunate]. In *Nihon keizaishi* 日本経済史 [The economic history of Japan]. Vol. 2, *Kindai seichū no taidō* 近代成長の胎動 [Gathering momentum for modern growth], edited by Shinbo Hiroshi 新保博 and Saitō Osamu 斎藤修. Tokyo: Iwanami Shoten, 1989.

———. "Bunkyūki no bakufu zaisei" 文久期の幕府財政 [Shogunal finance from 1861 to 1864]. In *Bakumatsu Ishin no Nihon* 幕末維新の日本 [Late Tokugawa and early Meiji Japan], edited by Kindai Nihon Kenkyūkai 近代日本研究会. Tokyo: Yamagawa Shuppansha, 1981.

———. "Kansei—Bunkaki no bakufu zaisei" 寛政—文化期の幕府財政 [The public finance of the shogunate between 1789 and 1817]. In *Nihon kinseishi ronsō* 日本近世史論叢 [Works on the early modern history of

Japan]. Vol. 1, edited by Bitō Masahide Sensei Kanreki-Kinenkai 尾藤正英
先生還暦記念会. Tokyo: Yoshikawa Kōbunkan, 1984.

———. "Kokka ishiki to Tennō" 国家意識と天皇 [State consciousness and the
Emperor]. In *Iwanami kōza Nihon tsūshi* 岩波講座日本通史 [The Iwanami
general history of Japan]. Vol. 15, *Kinsei* (5) 近世 (5) [The early modern
period], edited by Asao Naohiro 朝尾直弘 et al. Tokyo: Iwanami Shoten,
1995.

Ohkura Takehiko [大倉健彦], and Shinbo Hiroshi [新保博]. "The Tokugawa
Monetary Policy in the Eighteenth and Nineteenth Centuries." *Explorations
in Economic History* 15 (1978): 101–124.

Ōishi Kaichirō 大石嘉一郎. *Jiyū minken to Ōkuma, Matsukata zaisei* 自由民
権と大隈. 松方財政 [The Freedom and People's Rights Movement and the
public finance of Ōkuma and Matsukata]. Tokyo: Tōkyō Daigaku Shuppankai, 1989.

———. *Nihon chihōzai gyōseishi josetsu: Jiyū Minken Undō to chihō jichisei*
日本地方財行政史序説：自由民権運動と地方自治制 [A history of local
public finance in Japan: The Freedom and People's Rights Movement and
local self-governance]. Rev. ed. Tokyo: Ochanomizu Shobō, 1978.

Ōishi Manabu 大石学. "Kyōhō kaikaku no rekishiteki ichi" 享保改革の歴史的
位置 [The historical place of the Kyōhō Reform]. In *Bakuhansei kaikaku
no tenkai* [The development of the reforms in the shogunate-domain
system], edited by Fujita Satoru 藤田覚. Tokyo: Yamakawa Shuppansha,
2001.

Okada Shunpei 岡田俊平. "Meiji shoki no tsūka kyōkyū seisaku" 明治初期の
通貨供給政策 [Monetary supply policy in the early Meiji]. In *Meiji shoki
no zaisei kin'yū seisaku* 明治初期の財政金融政策 [Early Meiji fiscal and
financial policies], edited by Okada Shunpei. Tokyo: Seimeikai Sōsho, 1964.

Okamoto Takashi 岡本隆司. "Shinmatsu hyōhō no seiritsu" 清末票法の成
立—道光期両淮塩政改革再論 [The establishment of salt licenses in the late
Qing]. *Shigaku zasshi* 史学雑誌 110, no. 12 (December 2001): 36–60.

Ōkubo Toshiaki 大久保利謙. *Meiji kokka no keisei* 明治国家の形成 [The
formation of the Meiji state]. Tokyo: Yoshikawa Kōbunkan, 1986.

Ōkuma monjo 大隈文書 [Documents on Ōkuma Shigenobu], edited by
Waseda Daigaku Shakai Kagaku Kenkyūjo 稲田大學社會科學研究所.
6 vols. Tokyo: Waseda Daigaku Shakai Kagaku Kenkyūjo, 1958.

Ōkura Takehiko 大倉健彦. "Yōgin ryūnyū to bakufu zaisei" 洋銀流入と幕府
財政 [The inflow of Mexican silver and the shogunate's fiscal system]. In
Kindai ikōki ni okeru keizai hatten 近代移行期における経済発展
[Economic development in the transition to the modern period], edited by
Kamiki Tetsuo 神木哲男 and Matsuura Akira 松浦昭. Tokyo: Dōbunkan,
1987.

Olson, Mancur. *The Logic of Collective Action: Public Goods and the Theory of Groups.* Cambridge, MA: Harvard University Press, 1965.

Ono Masao 小野正雄. "Daimyō no ahen sensō ninshiki" 大名の鴉片戦争認識 [Knowledge of the Opium War among domain lords]. In *Iwanami kōza Nihon tsūshi* 岩波講座日本通史 [The Iwanami general history of Japan]. Vol. 15, *Kinsei* (5) 近世 (5) [The early modern period], edited by Asao Naohiro 朝尾直弘 et al. Tokyo: Iwanami Shoten, 1995.

Ōno Mizuo 大野瑞男. *Edo bakufu zaisei shiron* 江戸幕府財政史論 [A study of the fiscal history of the shogunate]. Tokyo: Yoshikawa Kōbunkan, 1996.

Ormrod, W. M. "England in the Middle Ages." In *The Rise of the Fiscal State in Europe, 1200–1815,* edited by Richard Bonney. Oxford and New York: Oxford University Press, 1999.

Outhwaite, R. B. *Inflation in Tudor and Early Stuart England.* 2nd ed. London: Macmillan Press, 1982.

Ōyama Shikitarō 大山敷太郎. *Bakumatsu zaiseishi kenkyū* 幕末財政史研究 [A study of the fiscal history of the late Tokugawa]. Kyoto: Shibunkaku Shuppan, 1974.

Page, Scott. "Path Dependence." *Quarterly Journal of Political Science* 1, no. 1 (2006): 87–115.

Patrick, Hugh T. "Japan, 1868–1914." In *Banking in the Early Stages of Industrialization: A Study in Comparative Economic History,* edited by Rondo E. Cameron, Olga Crisp, Hugh T. Patrick, and Richard Tilly. Oxford and New York: Oxford University Press, 1967.

Peng Xinwei 彭信威. *Zhongguo huobishi* 中國貨幣史 [A history of currency in China]. 2nd ed. Shanghai: Shanghai renmin chubanshe, 1965.

Peng Yuxin 彭雨新. "Qingdai tianfu qiyun cunliu zhidu de yanjin" 清代田賦起运存留制度的演进 [The development of the system of land tax retention and transportation in the Qing dynasty]. *Zhongguo jingjishi yanjiu* 中国经济史研究 4 (1992): 124–133.

Peng Zeyi 彭泽益. *Shijiu shiji houbanqi de Zhongguo caizheng yu jingji* 十九世纪后半期的中国财政与经济 [Economy and public finance in China in the second half of the nineteenth century]. Beijing: Renmin chubanshe, 1983.

Perdue, Peter C. *China Marches West: The Qing Conquest of Central Eurasia.* Cambridge, MA: Belknap Press of Harvard University Press, 2005.

Pierson, Paul. "Increasing Returns, Path Dependence, and the Study of Politics." *American Political Science Review* 94, no. 2 (June 2000): 251–267.

———. "The Limits of Design: Explaining Institutional Origins and Change." *Governance* 13, no. 4 (October 2000): 475–499.

———. *Politics in Time: History, Institutions, and Social Analysis.* Princeton, NJ: Princeton University Press, 2004.

———. "When Effect Becomes Cause: Policy Feedback and Political Change," *World Politics* 45, no. 4 (July 1993): 595–628.

Pierson, Paul, and Theda Skocpol. "Historical Institutionalism." In *Political Science: The State of the Discipline,* edited by Ira Katznelson and Helen V. Milner. New York: W. W. Norton, 2002.

Plumb, J. H. *The Growth of Political Stability in England: 1675–1725.* London: Macmillan, 1967.

Pomeranz, Kenneth. *The Great Divergence: China, Europe, and the Making of the Modern World Economy.* Princeton, NJ: Princeton University Press, 2000.

Pratt, Edward E. *Japan's Protoindustrial Elite: The Economic Foundations of the Gōnō.* Cambridge, MA: Harvard University Asia Center, 1999.

Pressnell, L. S. "Public Monies and the Development of English Banking." *Economic History Review,* n.s., 5, no. 3 (1953): 378–397.

Price, Jacob M. "The Excise Affair Revisited: The Administrative and Colonial Dimensions of a Parliamentary Crisis." In *England's Rise to Greatness, 1660–1763,* edited by Stephen B. Baxter. Berkeley: University of California Press, 1983.

Qian Jiaju 千家駒, ed. *Jiu Zhongguo gongzhaishi ziliao, 1894–1949 nian* 舊中國公債史資料, 1894–1949年 [Historical materials on state borrowing in China, 1894–1949]. Beijing: Zhonghua shuju, 1984.

Qianlong chao shangyu dang 乾隆朝上諭檔 [Edicts from the Qianlong reign], edited by Zhongguo diyi lishi dang'anguan 中國第一歷史檔案館. 18 vols. 2nd ed. Beijing: Dang'an chubanshe, 1998.

Qing zhengfu zhenya Taiping Tianguo dang'an shiliao [QZZTTDS] 清政府鎮壓太平天国檔案史料 [Archival materials on the Qing government's suppression of the Taiping Heavenly Kingdom], edited by Zhongguo diyi lishi dang'anguan 中國第一歷史檔案館. 26 vols. Beijing: Shehui kexue wenxian chubanshe, 1992–.

Ravina, Mark. *Land and Lordship in Early Modern Japan.* Stanford, CA: Stanford University Press, 1999.

Reitan, E. A. "From Revenue to Civil List, 1689–1702: The Revolution Settlement and the 'Mixed and Balanced' Constitution." *Historical Journal* 13, no. 4 (1970): 571–588.

Remer, Charles F. *The Foreign Trade of China.* Shanghai: Commercial Press, 1926.

Roberts, Clayton. "The Constitutional Significance of the Financial Settlement of 1690." *Historical Journal* 20, no. 1 (1977): 59–76.

Roberts, Luke S. *Mercantilism in a Japanese Domain: The Merchant Origins of Economic Nationalism in 18th-Century Tosa.* Cambridge and New York: Cambridge University Press, 1998.

Rogers, Clifford J., ed. *The Military Revolution Debate: Readings on the Military Transformation of Early Modern Europe.* Boulder, CO: Westview Press, 1995.

Rosenthal, Jean-Laurent. "The Political Economy of Absolutism Reconsidered." In *Analytic Narratives,* edited by Robert H. Bates, Avner Greif, Margaret Levi, Jean-Laurent Rosenthal, and Barry R. Weingast. Princeton, NJ: Princeton University Press, 1998.

Rosenthal, Jean-Laurent, and R. Bin Wong. *Before and Beyond Divergence: The Politics of Economic Change in China and Europe.* Cambridge, MA: Harvard University Press, 2011.

Roseveare, Henry. *The Financial Revolution, 1660–1760.* London: Longman, 1991.

———. *The Treasury, 1660–1870: The Foundations of Control.* London: Allen and Unwin, 1973.

Rosovsky, Henry. "Japan's Transition to Modern Economic Growth, 1868–1885." In *Industrialization in Two Systems: Essays in Honor of Alexander Gerschenkron by a Group of His Students,* edited by Henry Rosovsky. New York: John Wiley & Sons, 1966.

Rowe, William T. "Money, Economy, and Polity in the Daoguang-Era Paper Currency Debates." *Late Imperial China* 31, no. 2 (2010): 69–96.

Rubinstein, W. D. "The End of 'Old Corruption' in Britain, 1780–1860." *Past and Present* 101 (1983): 55–85.

Russell, Conrad. *The Addled Parliament of 1614: The Limits of Revision.* [Reading, UK]: University of Reading, 1992.

———. *The Causes of the English Civil War: The Ford Lectures Delivered in the University of Oxford, 1987–1988.* Oxford: Clarendon Press, 1990.

———. *The Fall of the British Monarchies, 1637–1642.* Oxford: Clarendon Press, 1991.

———. *Parliaments and English Politics, 1621–1629.* Oxford: Clarendon Press, 1979.

———. *Unrevolutionary England, 1603–1642.* London: Hambledon Press, 1990.

Sacks, David Harris. "The Countervailing of Benefits: Monopoly, Liberty, and Benevolence in Elizabethan England." In *Tudor Political Culture,* edited by Dale Hoak. Cambridge and New York: Cambridge University Press, 1995.

Saitō Osamu 斎藤修. "Bakumatsu-Ishin no seiji sanjutsu" 幕末維新の政治算術 [Political arithmetic and Japan in late Tokugawa and early Meiji Restoration]. In *Nenpō kindai Nihon kenkyū* 年報．近代日本研究 [Annual report: Research on modern Japan]. Vol. 14, *Meiji Ishin no kakushin to renzoku* 明治維新の革新と連続 [Innovation and continuity in the Meiji Restoration], edited by Kindai Nihon Kenkyūkai 近代日本研究会. Tokyo: Yamakawa Shuppansha, 1992.

Samuels, Richard J. *Machiavelli's Children: Leaders and Their Legacies in Italy and Japan.* Ithaca, NY: Cornell University Press, 2003.

———. *"Rich Nation, Strong Army": National Security and the Technological Transformation of Japan.* Ithaca, NY: Cornell University Press, 1994.

Sargent, Thomas J., and François R. Velde. *The Big Problem of Small Change.* Princeton, NJ: Princeton University Press, 2002.

Sasaki Suguru 佐々木克. *Bakumatsu seiji to Satsuma han* 幕末政治と薩摩藩 [Satsuma and late Tokugawa politics]. Tokyo: Yoshikawa Kōbunkan, 2004.

———. "Taiseihōkan to tōbaku mitchoku" 大政奉還と討幕密勅 [Returning power to the emperor and the secret imperial order to overthrow the shogunate]. *Jinmon gakuhō* 人文學報 80 (1997): 1–32.

Satō Shigerō 佐藤誠朗. *Kindai Tennōsei keiseiki no kenkyū: Hitotsu no haihan chikenron* 近代天皇制形成期の研究: ひとつの廃藩置県論 [The emperor system in its formative period: Another perspective on the abolishing of the domains]. Tokyo: San'ichi Shobō, 1987.

Satō Shōsuke 佐藤昌介, Uete Michiari 植手通有, and Yamaguchi Muneyuki 山口宗之, eds. *Watanabe Kazan, Takano Chōei, Sakuma Shōzan, Yokoi Shōnan, Hashimoto Sanai* 渡辺華山. 高野長英. 佐久間象山. 横井小楠. 橋本左内 [Watanabe Kazan, Takano Chōei, Sakuma Shōzan, Yokoi Shōan, Hashimoto Sanai]. Vol. 55 of *Nihon shisō taikei* 日本思想大系 [Compendium of thought in Japan]. Tokyo: Iwanami Shoten, 1971.

Sawada Akira 澤田章. *Meiji zaisei no kisoteki kenkyū: Ishin tōsho no zaisei* 明治財政の基礎的研究: 維新當初の財政 [The foundation of the public finance of the early Meiji regime]. Tokyo: Hōbunkan, 1934.

Schiltz, Michael. "An 'Ideal Bank of Issue': The Banque Nationale de Belgique as a Model for the Bank of Japan." *Financial History Review* 13, no. 2 (2006): 179–196.

Schofield, Roger. "Taxation and the Political Limits of the Tudor State." In *Law and Government under the Tudors: Essays Presented to Sir Geoffrey Elton,* edited by Claire Cross, David Loades, and J. J. Scarisbrick. Cambridge and New York: Cambridge University Press, 1988.

Schremmer, D. E. "Taxation and Public Finance: Britain, France, and Germany." In *The Cambridge Economic History of Europe.* Vol. 8, *The Industrial Economies,* edited by Peter Mathias and Sidney Pollard. Cambridge: Cambridge University Press, 1989.

Scott, Jonathan. "'Good Night Amsterdam.' Sir George Downing and Anglo-Dutch Statebuilding." *English Historical Review* 118, no. 476 (April 2003): 334–356.

Scott, William R. *The Constitution and Finance of English, Scottish and Irish Joint-Stock Companies to 1720.* 3 vols. 1912; repr., Bristol, UK: Thoemmes Press, 1993.

Seaward, Paul. *The Cavalier Parliament and the Reconstruction of the Old Regime, 1661–1667.* Cambridge and New York: Cambridge University Press, 1989.

———. "The House of Commons Committee of Trade and the Origins of the Second Anglo-Dutch War, 1664." *Historical Journal* 30, no. 2 (June 1987): 437–452.

Sekiguchi Eiichi 関口栄一. "Haihan chiken to Min-Zō gappei—Rususeihu to Ōkurasho—1" 廃藩置県と民蔵合併—留守政府と大蔵省—1 [The abolishing of the domains and the merging of the Ministries of Civil Affairs and Finance, part 1]. *Hōgaku* 法学 43, no. 3 (December 1979): 295–335.

———. "Min-Zō bunri mondai to Kido Takayoshi" 民蔵分離問題と木戸孝允 [The separation of the [Ministry of] Civil Affairs from the [Ministry of] Finance and Kido Takayoshi]. *Hōgaku* 法学 39, no. 1 (March 1975): 1–60.

Senda Minoru 千田稔. *Ishin seiken no chitsuroku shobun: Tennōsei to haihan chiken* 維新政権の秩禄処分 ： 天皇制と廃藩置県 [The Restoration regime's commutation of the stipends of lords and samurai: The emperor system and the abolishing of the domains]. Tokyo: Kaimei Shoin, 1979.

———. *Ishin seiken no chokuzoku guntai* 維新政権の直属軍隊 [The central army of the Meiji regime]. Tokyo: Kaimei Shoin, 1978.

———. "Kinsatsu shobun to kokuritsu ginkō" 金札処分と国立銀行 ： 金札引換公債と国立銀行の提起. 導入 [The redemption of *kinsatsu* and the national banks: The bonds issued in exchange for *kinsatsu* and the introduction of the national banks]. *Shakai keizai shigaku* 社会経済史學 48, no. 1 (1982): 29–50, 128–129.

———. "Meiji rokunen shichibu ritsuki gaisai no boshū katei" 明治六年七分利付外債の募集過程 [On the 7 percent sterling foreign loan floated in 1873]. *Shakai keizai shigaku* 社會經濟史學 49, no. 5 (December 1984): 445–470, 555–556.

Senda Minoru 千田稔 and Matsuo Masahito 松尾正人. *Meiji Ishin kenkyū josetsu: Ishin seiken no chokkatsuchi* 明治維新研究序説: 維新政権の直轄地 [An introduction to the study of the Meiji Restoration: The territories under the direct administration of the Restoration government]. Tokyo: Kaimei Shoin, 1977.

Sewell, William H., Jr. *Logics of History: Social Theory and Social Transformation.* Chicago: University of Chicago Press, 2005.

———. "Three Temporalities: Toward an Eventful Sociology." In *The Historic Turn in the Human Sciences,* edited by Terrence J. McDonald. Ann Arbor: University of Michigan Press, 1996.

Shanxi piaohao shiliao 山西票号史料 [Historical materials on the Shanxi banks], edited by Huang Jianhui 黄鉴晖 et al. Rev. ed. Taiyuan: Shanxi jingji chubanshe, 2002.

Sharpe, Kevin. *The Personal Rule of Charles I.* New Haven, CT: Yale University Press, 1992.

———. "The Personal Rule of Charles I." In *Before the English Civil War: Essays on Early Stuart Politics and Government,* edited by Howard Tomlinson. London: Macmillan, 1983.

Shibusawa Eiichi denki shiryō 渋沢栄一伝記資料 [Biographical materials of Shibusawa Eiichi], edited by Shibusawa Seien Kinen Zaidan Ryūmonsha 渋沢青淵記念財団竜門社. 68 vols. Tokyo: Shibusawa Eiichi Denki Shiryō Kankōkai, 1955–1971.

Shikano Yoshiaki 鹿野嘉昭. "Edo-ki Osaka ni okeru ryōgaeshō no kin'yū kinō o megutte" 江戸期大坂における両替商の金融機能をめぐって [The economic organization of Osaka's *ryogaesho* moneychangers in the early modern era of Japan]. *Keizaigaku ronsō* 經濟學論叢 52, no. 2 (2000): 205–264.

Shils, Edward. *Political Development in the New States.* Paris: Mouton, 1968.

Shimoyama Saburō 下山三郎. *Kindai Tennōsei kenkyū josetsu* 近天皇研究序説 [A study of the emperor system]. Tokyo: Iwanami Shoten, 1976.

Shinbo Hiroshi 新保博. *Kinsei no bukka to keizai hatten: Zenkōgyōka shakai e no sūryōteki sekkin* 近世の物価と経済発展：前工業化社会への数量的接近 [Prices in the early modern period and economic development: A quantitative approach toward a preindustrial society]. Tokyo: Tōyō Keizai Shinpō-sha, 1978.

———. *Nihon kindai shin'yō seido seiritsu shiron* 日本近代信用制度成立史論 [The establishment of the credit system in modern Japan]. Tokyo: Yūhikaku, 1968.

Shinbo Hiroshi 新保博 and Saitō Osamu 斎藤修. "Gaisetsu—19 seiki-e" 概説—１９世紀へ [An overview: Toward the nineteenth century]. In *Nihon keizaishi* 日本経済史 [The economic history of Japan], vol. 2, *Kindai seichō no taidō* 近代成長の胎動 [Gathering momentum for modern growth], edited by Shinbo Hiroshi 新保博 and Saitō Osamu 斉藤修. Tokyo: Iwanami Shoten, 1989.

Silberman, Bernard S. *Cages of Reason: The Rise of the Rational State in France, Japan, the United States, and Great Britain.* Chicago: University of Chicago Press, 1993.

Sippel, Patricia. "Chisui: Creating a Sacred Domain in Early Modern and Modern Japan." In *Public Spheres, Private Lives in Modern Japan, 1600–1950,* edited by Gail Lee Bernstein, Andrew Gordon, and Kate Wildman Nakai. Cambridge, MA: Harvard University Press Asia Center, 2005.

Skinner, Quentin. "The State." In *Political Innovation and Conceptual Change,* edited by Terence Ball, James Farr, and Russell L. Hanson. Cambridge and New York: Cambridge University Press, 1989.

Skocpol, Theda. "Bringing the State Back In: Strategies of Analysis in Current Research." In *Bringing the State Back In,* edited by Peter B. Evans, Dietrich Rueschemeyer, and Theda Skocpol. Cambridge and New York: Cambridge University Press, 1985.

———. *States and Social Revolutions: A Comparative Analysis of France, Russia, and China.* Cambridge and New York: Cambridge University Press, 1979.

Slack, Paul. *From Reformation to Improvement: Public Welfare in Early Modern England.* Oxford: Clarendon Press; New York: Oxford University Press, 1998.

Slater, Dan, and Erica Simmons. "Informative Regress: Critical Antecedents in Comparative Politics." *Comparative Political Studies* 43, no. 7 (2010): 886–917.

Smith, Thomas C. *The Agrarian Origins of Modern Japan.* Stanford, CA: Stanford University Press, 1959.

———. *Native Sources of Japanese Industrialization, 1750–1920.* Berkeley: University of California Press, 1988.

———. *Political Change and Industrial Development in Japan: Government Enterprise, 1868–1880.* Stanford, CA: Stanford University Press, 1955.

Song Huizhong 宋惠中. "Piaoshang yu wan Qing caizheng" 票商與晚清財政 [Shanxi bankers and public finance in the late Qing]. In *Caizheng yu jindai lishi: Lunwenji* 財政與近代歷史: 論文集 [Collected papers on public finance and early modern history], edited by Zhongyang yanjiuyuan. Jindaishi yanjiusuo. Shehui jingjishi zu 中央研究院.近代史研究所.社會經濟史組. Taipei: Zhongyang yanjiuyuan jindaishi yanjiusuo, 1999.

Stanley, C. Johnson. *Late Ch'ing Finance: Hu Kuang-yung as an Innovator.* Cambridge, MA: East Asian Research Center of Harvard University, 1961.

Stasavage, David. *Public Debt and the Birth of the Democratic State: France and Great Britain, 1688–1789.* Cambridge and New York: Cambridge University Press, 2003.

Steele, M. William. *Alternative Narratives in Modern Japanese History.* London: RoutledgeCurzon, 2003.

———. *Mō hitotsu no kindai: Sokumen kara mita Bakumatsu Meiji* もう一つの近代: 側面から見た幕末明治 [Localism and nationalism in modern Japanese history]. Tokyo: Perikansha, 1998.

Sugiyama Kazuo 杉山和雄. "Kin'yū seido no sōsetsu" 金融制度の創設 [The establishment of the financial system]. In *Nihon keizaishi taikei* 日本経済史大系 [Compendium of materials on the economic history of Japan]. Vol. 5,

Kindai 近代 [The modern period], edited by Kajinishi Mitsuhaya 楫西光速 朝尾直弘. Tokyo: Tōkyō Daigaku Shuppankai, 1965.

Suzuki Eiki 鈴木栄樹. "Iwakura shisetsudan hensei katei e no ashitana shiten" 岩倉使節団編成過程への新たな視点 [A new perspective on organizing the Iwakura Mission]. *Jinmon gakuhō* 人文學報 78 (March 1996): 27–49.

Sylla, Richard. "Financial Systems and Economic Modernization." *Journal of Economic History* 62, no. 2 (June 2002): 277–292.

'T Hart, Marjolein. "'The Devil or the Dutch': Holland's Impact on the Financial Revolution in England, 1643–1694." *Parliament, Estates and Representation* 11, no. 1 (June 1991): 39–52.

Takahashi Hidenao 高橋秀直. *Bakumatsu Ishin no seiji to Tennō* 幕末維新の政治と天皇 [Late Tokugawa and Restoration politics and the emperor]. Tokyo: Yoshikawa Kōbunkan, 2007.

———. "Haihan chiken ni okeru kenryoku to shakai" 廃藩置県における権力と社会 [Power and society in the abolishing of the domains]. In *Kindai Nihon no seitō to kanryō* 近代日本の政党と官僚 [Political parties and bureaucrats in modern Japan], edited by Yamamoto Shirō 山本四郎. Tokyo: Tōkyō Sōgensha, 1991.

———. "Matsukata zaiseiki no gunbi kakuchō mondai" 松方財政期の軍備拡張問題 [The issue of military expansion in the public finance of Matsukata]. *Shakai keizai shigaku* 社會經濟史學 56, no. 1 (April 1990): 1–30.

———. *Nisshin sensō e no michi* 日清戦争への道 [The road toward the Sino-Japanese war]. Tokyo: Tōkyō Sōgensha, 1995.

Takahashi Hirobumi 高橋裕文. "Buryoku tōbaku hōshin o meguru Satsuma hannai hantaiha no dōkō" 武力倒幕方針をめぐる薩摩藩内反対派の動向 [The trend of opposition in Satsuma in regard to the armed overthrow of the shogunate]. In *Mō hitotsu no Meiji Ishin: Bakumatsushi no saikentō* もうひとつの明治維新 [Another Meiji Restoration: A reexamination of the history of late Tokugawa], edited by Iechika Yoshiki 家近良樹. Tokyo: Yūshisha, 2006.

Takano Toshihiko 高埜利彦. "18 seiki zenhan no Nihon—Taihei no naka no tenkan" 18世紀前半の日本―泰平のなかの転換 [Japan in the first half of the eighteenth century: A transformation in the great peace]. In *Iwanami kōza Nihon tsūshi* 岩波講座日本通史 [The Iwanami general history of Japan]. Vol. 13, *Kinsei* (3) 近世 (3) [The early modern period], edited by Asao Naohiro 朝尾直弘 et al. Tokyo: Iwanami Shoten, 1994.

Tamaki, Norio. *Japanese Banking: A History, 1859–1959*. Cambridge and New York: Cambridge University Press, 1995.

Tanaka Akira 田中彰. "Bakufu no tōkai" 幕府の倒壊 [The fall of the shogunate]. In *Iwanami kōza Nihon rekishi* 岩波講座日本暦史 [The Iwanami history of Japan]. Vol. 13, *Kinsei* (5) 近世 (5) [The early modern period], edited by Asao Naohiro 朝尾直弘 et al. Tokyo: Iwanami Shoten, 1977.

Tashiro Kazui 田代和生. "Tokugawa jidai no bōeki" 徳川時代の貿易 [Foreign trade in the Tokugawa period]. In *Nihon keizaishi* 日本経済史 [The economic history of Japan]. Vol. 1, *Keizai shakai no seiritsu: 17th–18th seiki* 経済社会の成立: 17–18 世紀 [The formation of an economic society: Seventeenth and eighteenth centuries], edited by Hayami Akira 速水融 and Miyamoto Matao 宮本又郎. Tokyo: Iwanami Shoten, 1988.

Tatewaki Kazuo 立脇和夫. *Meiji seifu to Orientaru Banku* 明治政府と英国東洋銀行 [The Meiji government and the British Oriental bank]. Tokyo: Chūō Kōronsha, 1992.

Tatsuya, Tsuji. "Politics in the Eighteenth Century." In *Cambridge History of Japan*. Vol. 4, *Early Modern Japan,* edited by John Whitney Hall. Cambridge: Cambridge University Press, 1991.

Teranishi Jūrō 寺西重郎. "Kin'yū no kindaika to sangyōka" 金融の近代化と産業化 [The modernization of finance and industrialization]. In *Nihon keizaishi* 日本経済史 [The economic history of Japan]. Vol. 5, *Sangyōka no jidai (ge)* 産業化の時代（下） [The age of industrialization: Part 2], edited by Nishikawa Shunsaku 西川俊作 and Abe Takeshi 阿部武司. Tokyo: Iwanami Shoten, 1990.

Thelen, Kathleen. "Historical Institutionalism in Comparative Politics," *Annual Review of Political Science* 2, no. 1 (1999): 369–404.

———. "How Institutions Evolve." In *Comparative Historical Analysis in the Social Sciences,* edited by James Mahoney and Dietrich Rueschemeyer. Cambridge and New York: Cambridge University Press, 2003.

———. *How Institutions Evolve: The Political Economy of Skills in Germany, Britain, the United States, and Japan.* Cambridge: Cambridge University Press, 2004.

Thelen, Kathleen, and James Mahoney, eds. *Explaining Institutional Change: Ambiguity, Agency, and Power.* Cambridge and New York: Cambridge University Press, 2010.

Thelen, Kathleen, and Sven Steinmo. "Historical Institutionalism in Comparative Politics." In *Structuring Politics: Historical Institutionalism in Comparative Politics,* edited by Sven Steinmo, Kathleen Thelen, and Frank Longstreth. Cambridge and New York: Cambridge University Press, 1992.

Thirsk, Joan. "The Crown as Projector on Its Own Estates, from Elizabeth I to Charles I." In *The Estates of the English Crown, 1558–1650,* edited by Richard W. Hoyle. Cambridge and New York: Cambridge University Press, 1992.

Thrush, Andrew. "Naval Finance and the Origins and Development of Ship Money." In *War and Government in Britain, 1598–1650,* edited by Mark Charles Fissel. Manchester: Manchester University Press, 1991.

Tian Yongxiu 田永秀. "1862–1883 nian Zhongguo de gupiao shichang: 1862–1883" 年中国的股票市场 [The stock market in China: 1862–1883]. *Zhongguo jingjishi yanjiu* 中国经济史研究 2 (1995): 55–68.

Tilly, Charles. *Coercion, Capital, and European States, A.D. 990–1992.* Rev. ed. Cambridge, MA: Blackwell, 1992.

———, ed. *The Formation of National States in Western Europe.* Princeton, NJ: Princeton University Press, 1975.

———. "Mechanisms in Political Processes." *Annual Review of Political Science* 4, no. 1 (2001): 21–41.

Tomlinson, Howard. "Financial and Administrative Developments in England, 1660–88." In *The Restored Monarchy, 1660–1688,* edited by J. R. Jones. Totowa, NJ: Rowman and Littlefield, 1979.

Totman, Conrad D. *The Collapse of the Tokugawa Bakufu, 1862–1868.* Honolulu: University Press of Hawaii, 1980.

———. *Early Modern Japan.* Berkeley: University of California Press, 1995.

Trimberger, Ellen K. *Revolution from Above: Military Bureaucrats and Development in Japan, Turkey, Egypt, and Peru.* New Brunswick, NJ: Transaction Books, 1978.

Tsuchiya Takao 土屋喬雄 and Okazaki Saburō 岡崎三郎. *Nihon shihon shugi hattatsushi gaisetsu* 日本資本主義發達史概說 [An outline of the development of capitalism in Japan]. Tokyo: Yūhikaku, 1948.

Tsurumi Masayoshi 靍見誠良. *Nihon shin'yō kikō no kakuritsu: Nihon Ginkō to kin'yū shijō* 日本信用機構の確立: 日本銀行と金融市場 [The establishment of a credit system in Japan: The Bank of Japan and the financial markets]. Tokyo: Yūhikaku, 1991.

Umegaki, Michio. *After the Restoration: The Beginning of Japan's Modern State.* New York: New York University Press, 1988.

Umemura Mataji 梅村又次. "Meiji Ishinki no keizai seisaku" 明治維新期の経済政策 [Meiji Restoration economic policies]. *Keizai kenkyū* 経済研究 30, no. 1 (January 1979): 30–38.

Underdown, David. "Settlement in the Counties, 1653–1658." In *The Interregnum: The Quest for Settlement, 1646–1660,* edited by G. E. Aylmer. London: Macmillan, 1972.

Vogel, Hans Ulrich. "Chinese Central Monetary Policy, 1644–1800." *Late Imperial China* 8, no. 2 (1987): 1–51.

Von Glahn, Richard. "Foreign Silver Coins in the Market Culture of Nineteenth Century China." *International Journal of Asian Studies* 4, no. 1 (2007): 51–78.

———. *Fountain of Fortune: Money and Monetary Policy in China, 1000–1700.* Berkeley: University of California Press, 1996.

Wang Erh-min 王爾敏. "Sheng Xuanhuai yu Zhongguo shiye liquan zhi weihu" 盛宣懷與中國實業利權之維護 [Sheng Xuanhuai and the protection of the interests of Chinese enterprises]. *Zhongyang yanjiuyuan jindaishi yanjiusuo jikan* 中央研究院近代史研究所集刊 27 (1997): 5–43.

Wang Hongbin 王宏斌. "Lun Guangxu shiqi yinjia xialuo yu bizhi gaige" 论光绪时期银价下落与币制改革 [On the falling value of silver and monetary reform during the reign of Guangxu]. *Shixue yuekan* 史学月刊 5 (1988): 47–53.

Wang Jingyu 汪敬虞. "Luelun Zhongguo tongshang yinhang chengli de lishi tiaojian jiqi zai duiwai guanxi fangmian de tezheng" 略论中国通商银行成立的历史条件极其在对外关系方面的特征 [On the historical conditions of the establishment of the Imperial Bank of China and its characteristics in foreign relations]. *Zhongguo jingjishi yanjiu* 中国经济史研究 3 (1988): 90–102.

Wang Yeh-chien 王業鍵. *Land Taxation in Imperial China, 1750–1911.* Cambridge, MA: Harvard University Press, 1973.

———. *Qingdai jingjishi lunwenji* 清代經濟史論文集 [Collected essays in the economic history of Qing China]. 3 vols. Banqiao: Daoxiang chubanshe, 2003.

———. "Secular Trends of Rice Prices in the Yangzi Delta, 1638–1935." In *Chinese History in Economic Perspective,* edited by Thomas G. Rawski and Lillian M. Li. Berkeley: University of California Press, 1992.

———. *Zhongguo jindai huobi yu yinhang de yanjin (1644–1937)* 中國近代貨幣與銀行的演進 (1644–1937) [The evolution of currency and banking in early modern China (1644–1937)]. Taipei: Zhongyang yanjiuyuan jingji yanjiusuo, 1981.

Ward, W. R. *The English Land Tax in the Eighteenth Century.* London: Oxford University Press, 1953.

Weber, Max. *Economy and Society: An Outline of Interpretative Sociology.* 2 vols. Berkeley: University of California Press, 1978.

———. "Politics as a Vocation." In *From Max Weber: Essays in Sociology,* edited by H. H. Gerth and C. Wright Mills. New York: Oxford University Press, 1958.

Wei Guangqi 魏光奇. "Qingdai houqi zhongyang jiquan caizheng tizhi de wajie" 清代后期中央集权财政体制的瓦解 [The collapse of the centralized fiscal system in the late Qing]. *Jindaishi yanjiu* 近代史研究 31, no. 1 (1986): 207–230.

Wei Jianyou 魏建猷. *Zhongguo jindai huobishi* 中国近代货币史 [A history of currency in early modern China]. Hefei: Huangshan shushe, 1986.

Wei Xiumei 魏秀梅. "Yan Jingming zai Shandong—Tongzhi yuannian shiyue–liunian eryue" 閻敬銘在山東—同治元年十月－六年二月 [Yan Jingming in Shandong—1862–1867]. *Gugong xueshu jikan* 故宮學術季刊 24, no. 1 (Fall 2006): 117–153.

Weingast, Barry R. "Rational Choice Institutionalism." In *Political Science: The State of the Discipline,* edited by Ira Katznelson and Helen V. Milner. New York: W. W. Norton, 2002.

Weir, David R. "Tontines, Public Finance, and Revolution in France and England, 1688–1789." *Journal of Economic History* 49, no. 1 (March 1989): 95–124.

Westney, D. Eleanor. *Imitation and Innovation: The Transfer of Western Organizational Patterns to Meiji Japan.* Cambridge, MA: Harvard University Press, 1987.

Weyland, Kurt. "Toward a New Theory of Institutional Change," *World Politics* 60 (January 2008): 281–314.

Wheeler, James S. *The Making of a World Power: War and the Military Revolution in Seventeenth-Century England.* Stroud, UK: Sutton, 1999.

———. "Navy Finance, 1649–1660." *Historical Journal* 39, no. 2 (July 1996): 457–466.

White, Eugene N. "From Privatized to Government-Administered Tax Collection: Tax Farming in Eighteenth-Century France." *Economic History Review* 57, no. 4 (2004): 636–663.

White, James W. "State Growth and Popular Protest in Tokugawa Japan." *Journal of Japanese Studies* 14, no. 1 (Winter 1988): 1–25.

Will, Pierre-Étienne. *Bureaucracy and Famine in Eighteenth-Century China.* Translated by Elborg Foster. Stanford, CA: Stanford University Press, 1990.

Will, Pierre-Étienne, and R. Bin Wong. *Nourish the People: The State Civilian Granary System in China, 1650–1850.* Ann Arbor: Center for Chinese Studies, University of Michigan, 1991.

Williams, Penry. *The Later Tudors: England, 1547–1603.* Oxford: Clarendon Press, 1995.

———. *The Tudor Regime.* Oxford: Clarendon Press, 1979.

Wolffe, B. P. *The Crown Lands, 1461 to 1536: An Aspect of Yorkist and Early Tudor Government.* London: Allen and Unwin, 1970.

———. *The Royal Demesne in English History: The Crown Estate in the Governance of the Realm from the Conquest to 1509.* London: Allen and Unwin, 1971.

Wong, R. Bin. *China Transformed: Historical Change and the Limits of European Experience.* Ithaca, NY: Cornell University Press, 1997.

Woodruff, David. *Money Unmade: Barter and the Fate of Russian Capitalism.* Ithaca, NY: Cornell University Press, 1999.

Wootton, David. "From Rebellion to Revolution: The Crisis of the Winter of 1642/3 and the Origins of Civil War Radicalism." *English Historical Review* 105, no. 416 (July 1990): 654–669.

Wright, Mary C. *The Last Stand of Chinese Conservatism: The T'ung-Chih Restoration, 1862–1874*. Stanford, CA: Stanford University Press, 1957.

Wright, Stanley F. *Hart and the Chinese Customs*. Belfast: W. Mullan, 1950.

Wu Chengming 吴承明. *Zhongguo zibenzhuyi yu guonei shichang* 中国资本主义与国内市场 [Capitalism and the domestic market in China]. Beijing: Zhongguo shehui kexue chubanshe, 1985.

Wu Xu dang'an xuanbian 吴煦档案选编 [Selected materials from the Wu Xu archives]. Vol. 6, edited by Taiping Tianguo lishi bowuguan 太平天国历史博物馆. Nanjing: Jiangsu renmin chubanshe, 1983.

Xia Dongyuan, 夏东元, ed. *Sheng Xuanhuai nianpu changbian* 盛宣怀年谱长编 [A chronology of the life of Sheng Xuanhuai]. 2 vols. Shanghai: Shanghai jiaotong daxue chubanshe, 2004.

Xu Daling 許大齡. *Qingdai juanna zhidu* 清代捐納制度 [The sale of official rank during the Qing]. Beijing: Yanjing daxue Hafo Yanjing xueshe, 1950; reprinted in *Ming Qing shi lunji* 明清史论集 [Collected papers on Ming-Qing history]. Beijing: Beijing daxue chubanshe, 2000.

Xu Dixin 许涤新 and Wu Chengming 吴承明. *Zhongguo zibenzhuyi fazhanshi* 中国资本主义发展史 [A history of the development of capitalism in China]. 2 vols. Beijing: Renmin chubanshe, 1990.

Xu Tan 许壇 and Jing Junjian 经君健. "Qingdai qianqi shangshui wenti xintan" 清代前期商税问题新探 [A new study of commercial taxes during the Qing dynasty]. *Zhongguo jingjishi yanjiu* 中国经济史研究 2 (1990): 87–100.

Yagi Yoshikazu 八木慶和. "'Meiji 14 nen seihen' to Nihon Ginkō" 「明治一四年政変」と日本銀行: 共同運輸会社貸出をめぐって [The "1881 coup d'état" and the loan of the Bank of Japan to the Kyodo Un'yu Kaisha]. *Shakai keizai shigaku* 社會經濟史學 53, no. 5 (December 1987): 636–660.

Yamamoto Hirofumi 山本弘文. "Shoki shokusan seisaku to sono shūsei" 初期殖産政策とその修正 [The early industry-promotion policy and its revision]. In *Nihon keizai seisaku shiron (jō)* 日本経済政策史論（上）[The history of economic policy in Japan]. Vol. 1, edited by Andō Yoshio 安藤良雄. Tokyo: Tōkyō Daigaku Shuppankai, 1973.

Yamamoto Susumu 山本進. "Shindai kōki Kōse no zaisei kaikaku to zendō" 清代後期江浙の財政改革と善堂 [Fiscal reform and charitable halls in Jiangsu and Zhejiang during the late Qing]. *Shigaku zasshi* 史学雑誌 104, no. 12 (December 1995): 38–60.

———. "Shindai kōki Shizen ni okeru chihō zaisei no keisei" 清代後期四川における地方財政の形成—会館と釐金 [The formation of the provincial fiscal system in Sichuan Province in late Qing]. *Shirin* 史林 75, no. 6 (November 1992): 33–62.

———. *Shindai zaiseishi kenkyū* 清代財政史研究 [A study of the fiscal history of the Qing dynasty]. Tokyo: Kyūko Shoin, 2002.

Yamamoto Yūzō 山本有造. "Meiji Ishinki no zaisei to tsūka" 明治維新期の財政と通貨 [Finance and currency in the Meiji Restoration]. In *Nihon keizaishi* 日本経済史 [The economic history of Japan]. Vol. 3, *Kaikō to Ishin* 開港と維新 [The opening of Japan and the Restoration], edited by Umemura Mataji 梅村又次 and Yamamoto Yūzō 山本有造. Tokyo: Iwanami Shoten, 1989.

———. "Nai ni shihei ari gai ni bokugin ari" 内ニ紙幣アリ外ニ墨銀アリ [Paper money for domestic transactions and Mexican dollars for foreign trade]. *Jinmon gakuhō* 人文学報 55 (1983): 37–55.

Yamamura Kozo. "Entrepreneurship, Ownership, and Management in Japan." In *The Cambridge Economic History of Europe*. Vol. 7, *The Industrial Economies: Capital, Labour, and Enterprise, Part 2: The United States, Japan, and Russia*, edited by Peter Mathias and M. M. Postan. Cambridge: Cambridge University Press, 1978.

———. "The Meiji Land Tax Reform and Its Effect." In *Japan in Transition: From Tokugawa to Meiji*, edited by Marius B. Jansen and Gilbert Rozman. Princeton, NJ: Princeton University Press, 1986.

Yamamuro Shin'ichi 山室信一. "Meiji kokka no seido to rinen" 明治国家の制度と理念 [The institutions and principles of the Meiji state]. In *Iwanami kōza Nihon tsūshi* 岩波講座日本通史 [The Iwanami general history of Japan]. Vol. 17, *Kindai* (2) 近代 (2) [The modern period], edited by Asao Naohiro 朝尾直弘 et al. Tokyo: Iwanami Shoten, 1994.

Yamazaki Yūkō 山崎祐子. "Kōgi chūshutsu kikō no keisei to hōkai" 公議抽出機構の形成と崩壊 [The formation and collapse of the institutions of public discussion]. In *Nihon kindaishi no saikōchiku* 日本近代史の再構築 [A reconstruction of the modern history of Japan], edited by Itō Takashi 伊藤隆. Tokyo: Yamakawa Shuppansha, 1993.

———. "Nihon kindaika shuhō o meguru sōkoku: Naimushō to Kōbushō" 日本近代化手法をめぐる相克――内務省と工部省 [Conflicts in the modernization policies in Japan: The Ministry of Civil Affairs and the Ministry of Industry]. In *Kōbushō to sono jidai* 工部省とその時代 [The Ministry of Industry and its time], edited by Suzuki Jun 鈴木淳. Tokyo: Yamakawa Shuppansha, 2002.

Yang Duanliu 楊端六. *Qingdai huobi jinrong shigao* 清代貨幣金融史稿 [A financial and monetary history of the Qing dynasty]. Beijing: Sanlian shudian, 1962.

Yasuba, Yasukichi. "Did Japan Ever Suffer from a Shortage of Natural Resources before World War II?" *Journal of Economic History* 56, no. 3 (September 1996): 543–560.

Yasukuni Ryōichi 安国良知. "Kahei no kinō" 貨幣の機能 [Functions of currency]. In *Iwanami kōza Nihon tsūshi* 岩波講座日本通史 [The Iwanami general history of Japan]. Vol. 12, *Kinsei* (2) 近世 (2) [The early modern period], edited by Asao Naohiro 朝尾直弘 et al. Tokyo: Iwanami Shoten, 1994.

Yasumaru Yoshio 安丸良夫. "1850–70 nendai no Nihon: Ishin henkaku" 1850–70 年代の日本: 維新変革 [Japan between the 1850s and 1870s: Restoration and change]. In *Iwanami kōza Nihon tsūshi* 岩波講座日本通史 [The Iwanami general history of Japan]. Vol. 16, *Kindai* (1) 近代 (1) [The modern period], edited by Asao Naohiro 朝尾直弘 et al. Tokyo: Iwanami Shoten, 1994.

Ye Shichang 叶世昌. *Yapian zhanzheng qianhou woguo de huobi xueshuo* 鸦片战争前后我国的货币学說 [Monetary theory in China before and after the Opium War]. Shanghai: Shanghai renmin chubanshe, 1963.

Yokohama shishi 横浜市史 [A history of Yokohama City]. 7 vols. Yokohama: Yokohamashi, distributed by Yūrindō, 1958–1982.

Yokoyama Kōichirō 横山晃一郎. "Keibatsu chian kikō no seibi" 刑罰・治安機構の整備 [The arrangement of the institutions of punishment and security]. In *Nihon kindai hōtaisei no keisei* 日本近代法体制の形成 [The formation of legal institutions in modern Japan], edited by Fukushima Masao 福島正夫. 2 vols. Tokyo: Nihon Hyōronsha, 1981.

Yoshihara Tatsuyuki 莨原達之. "Meiji zenki chūki no Yokohama Shōkin Ginkō" 明治前. 中期の横浜正金銀行 [The Yokohama Specie Bank in the early and middle Meiji]. In *Nihon ni okeru kindai shakai no keisei* 日本における近代社会の形成 [The formation of a modern society in Japan], edited by Shōda Kenichirō 正田健一郎. Tokyo: Sanrei Shoten, 1995.

Yunoki Manabu 柚木学. "Hyogo shōsha to Ishin seifu no keizai seisaku" 兵庫商社と維新政府の経済政策 [The commercial house of Hyogo and the economic policy of the Restoration government]. *Shakai keizai shigaku* 社會經濟史學 35, no. 2 (1969): 114–136.

———. *Sakazukuri no rekishi* 酒造りの歴史 [A history of sake manufacturing]. Tokyo: Yūzankaku Shuppan, 1987.

Zelin, Madeleine. *The Magistrate's Tael: Rationalizing Fiscal Reform in Eighteenth-Century Ch'ing China*. Berkeley: University of California Press, 1992.

———. *The Merchants of Zigong: Industrial Entrepreneurship in Early Modern China*. New York: Columbia University Press, 2005.

Zhang Xiaotang 张晓棠. "Qianlong nianjian Qing zhengfu pingheng caizheng zhi yanjiu" 乾隆年间清政府平衡财政之研究 [Fiscal adjustments during the Qianlong reign]. *Qingshi yanjiuji* 清史研究集 7 (1990): 26–60.

Zhang Xiaoye 张小也. *Qingdai siyan wenti yanjiu* 清代私盐问题研究 [Nonofficial salt in the Qing]. Beijing: Shehui kexue wenxian chubanshe, 2001.

Zhongguo jindai huobishi ziliao [ZJHZ] 中國近代貨幣史資料 [Historical materials on the monetary history of early modern China], edited by Zhongguo renmin yinhang canshishi jinrongshiliaozu 中國人民銀行參事室金融史料組. 2 vols. Beijing: Zhonghua shuju, 1964.

Zhou Yumin 周育民. *Wan Qing caizheng yu shehui bianqian* 晚清财政与社会变迁 [Public finance and social change in the late Qing]. Shanghai: Shanghai renmin chubanshe, 2000.

INDEX

Acemoglu, Daron, 20–21

Agency, 23, 40, 180–183

Akizuki Tanetatsu, 87; expelled from shūgiin, 88

Alcohol taxes, 54; in Japan, 16, 49, 105, 110–112; in England, 37, 54, 59–60, 62, 75; direct collection of, 59–60; large-scale brewing encouraged through, 62; as barrier to entry, 75; smuggling and, 75; centralized, 105, 185; self-reporting, 110–111; investigations, 111; supervision of, 111; elasticity in yields of, 112; deflation and, 124; Matsukata and, 124, 127–128; protesting, 127; small-scale brewers driven out of business from, 127; in China, 175, 255n100

Annual central auditing system (zouxiao), 155

Annuities: perpetual, 2, 12, 14, 43, 49, 51, 52, 73–74, 185; redeemable, 12, 71, 73–74; single-life, 65; irredeemable, 71, 73

Assignment orders (zhibo), 154, 155, 156; information asymmetry in matching, 160–161; fictitious account numbers and, 162

Association of Patriots, 114

Backwell, Edward, 56, 215n30

Bank of Amsterdam, 64

Bank of England, 67, 101, 185; as a model in Japan, 41, 80, 101, 119; founding of, 42–43; initial capital stock of, 65; note-issuing charter, 65–66, 68, 71, 72; as private investment trust, 68; Exchequer bills underwritten by, 71; War of the Spanish Succession and, 71; as a model in China, 158, 177, 179

Bank of Japan, 16, 185; fiscal surplus forming, 119; initial capital of, 125; as political weapon, 125; regulatory ability of, 125; discounting bills, 126; lending of, 126, 129; as central bank, 128

Banno Junji, 78; on Meiji Restoration, 96

Baochao. *See* Copper notes